CHRISTIANITY AMONG THE RELIGIONS OF THE WORLD

Carlos G. Martin

University Press of America,® Inc.
Lanham · Boulder · New York · Toronto · Plymouth, UK

CONTENTS

PART II: RELIGIONS OF SOUTH ASIA

PART III: BUDDHISM

PART IV: RELIGIONS OF EAST ASIA

PART V: RELIGIONS OF THE MIDDLE EAST

PART VI: CHRISTIANITY

PART VII: TRADITIONAL AND ALTERNATIVE RELIGIONS

PREFACE

The study of the religions of the world is a must for Christians who take the Great Commission seriously. The evangelization of the peoples of the world require understanding of their beliefs and sensitivity to their cultures. It is not just Christians who are exploring new ways to penetrate the world. We are witnessing the renewal of ancient religions and a demographic explosion among other faiths. Along with missionary activities of the ancient passive religions, there is religious dispersion due to refugee migration. Sooner or later, most of us will meet someone with a different belief system. Since the economic center of gravity is moving toward countries where other religions predominate, and as a result of the process of globalization, Christians have new opportunities to interact with people of other religions. Learning about other religions is simply a matter of common sense for Christians. This is one of the first steps toward the fulfillment of the church's missionary task in the twenty-first century.

As the title indicates, this text considers the living religions of the world from a Christian perspective. This study of religions has the purpose of enabling students not only to expand their understanding of other belief systems, but also to prepare the student to offer a sensitive and intelligent Christian witness. This book intends to serve as an introduction to world religions. It t is designed as a textbook for Christian colleges, seminaries, and universities and it is written from an interdenominational Protestant/Evangelical perspective. It deals with the evangelization of the religions of the world. Each chapter contains a historical background, a summary of beliefs, and suggestions for witnessing.

The book is divided into seven parts. Part I offers a general introduction to the concept of religion, discusses major categories of religions, and explores key theological issues related to the evangelization of the religions of the world. Part II considers the religions of South Asia: Hinduism, Jainism, and Sikhism. Part III studies Buddhism as manifested in four major groups. Part IV surveys the religions of East Asia: Confucianism, Taoism, and Shintoism. Part V focuses on the religions of the Middle East: Judaism, Zoroastrianism, Islam, and Baha'ism. Part VI deals with Christianity in four major groups: Catholicism, Protestantism, Cults and Sects, and secularized people in their midst. Part VII concludes the book with a review of Traditional Folk Religions and selected forms of Occultism.

During eight years of missionary work in Asia, I visited many temples, shrines, and mosques. Interviews with worshipers, monks, priests, and rabbis helped me to gain valuable insights. I read extensively about other religions and researched their sources. However, students have also shaped this book throughout the years by sharing their discoveries and insights.

When I went to college, I discovered that in only a few days after the class began, I was not able to read my own handwriting. I solved the problem by typing my notes immediately after class. Since then, I have typed my notes as a student, my sermons as a pastor, and my class notes as a professor. As a student, I did not keep my handwritten notes, but I still have many valuable typed materials from my college years. I also kept class notes that my professors shared with their students. Once in a while, I still review some of the class notes a professor shared with me almost forty years ago. I thought that my classes would be more useful if the students could take my class notes with them. Those notes were eventually updated and arranged in the form of a book.

I hope that this book will motivate some readers to a life of missionary service among the religions of the world. To others, may it be motivation to participate in the proclamation of the Good News wherever they are, as they develop awareness of the remaining task and an appreciation for their own faith.

This textbook was designed in the form of an outline in order to help both readers and instructors to be "on the same page." A study guide, available online at http://erc.southern.edu/, may help professors and students pinpoint terms, definitions, concepts, listings, paragraphs, quotations, and Bible texts that have a special relevance for a class on world religions. Unless otherwise stated, all biblical references are from the New King James Version.

I must express my gratitude to Southern Adventist University for allowing me to spend many months focused on the writing of this book. I am thankful to those who helped me with suggestions and editorial work, especially to Star Stevens and Stephanie Sheehan. I have a special debt of gratitude to Nolly, my spouse, for her patience and support during the months of research and writing.

PART I

INTRODUCTION TO WORLD RELIGIONS

CHAPTER 1

Religion

1. *Introduction*

a. The exploration of world religions is an exciting adventure. There is much to see, sort through, and comprehend. However, since this study deals with the deepest hopes and dreams, the most careful thoughts and views, and the most cherished rituals and practices of sincere people, the student of world religions must enter into the holy ground of others with a humble and respectful attitude.

b. As the world becomes a "global village," the need to identify and have a basic understanding of world religions becomes vitally important. People from all around the world can be found in any of our cities. More than ever, they are becoming our neighbors, and we have explicit instructions about our responsibilities towards them. Muslims, Hindus, Buddhists, Confucians, and Jews regularly enter our homes via television and Internet.

c. Religious traditions, beliefs, and practices are intertwined with the cultural, political, and economic activities that make up the human enterprise. Since religion plays a significant role in the lives of people and the cultures they live, the study of religions is essential to understanding the world. The student of religious beliefs will become sensitive to other cultures, capable of having an intelligent conversation with people of diverse backgrounds, and better prepared to serve as a citizen of the world.

d. In a certain sense, it would be ideal to see world religions from a neutral perspective, without our own filters of understanding and personal beliefs. However, this book is written from a Christian perspective. We are setting out on an adventure of understanding. We want to become acquainted with different belief systems in order for us to be better equipped to dialogue, share our convictions and, ideally, persuade others to accept Jesus Christ and His message.

2. *Definition of "Religion"*

a. The word religion comes from Latin, *religio*. The word evolved from two possible origins: 1) From *relegare*, to "re-read," to treat with care, to consider, to review. Religion is passed on along chains of tradition. 2) From *religare*, to "bind fast," to bind again, to tie, to unite. In this case, religion means a "bond" linking worshipers of a god together.[1] Others go beyond these etymological distinctions. What for some is "religion," for others is "fanaticism," "ignorance," "idolatry," or "superstition." Karl Marx stated that "religion is the opiate of the people."[2] In the name of religion some would kill, while others would give their own lives.

b. One set of definitions emphasizes the human response to the supernatural. Religion is a belief in divine beings and the practices (rituals) and moral codes (ethics) that result from that belief. "Beliefs are the ideas that make any religion what it is. Of the three elements that make something a religion (beliefs, rituals, and ethics), beliefs are the most important because they give rise to and shape the ethics and the rituals of a faith."[3] A shorter definition along the same line: "The service and worship of God or the supernatural."[4] One problem with these definitions is that not all religious traditions make the supernatural dimension central (e.g., in certain forms of Buddhism, Jainism, and Confucianism). The concept of God is not central to all religions.

c. Another approach to a definition of religion focuses on the answer to the deepest questions of humankind. Religion is "a system of symbols, myths, doctrines, ethics, and rituals for the expression of ultimate relevance."[5] In this line, religion is a set of beliefs that answer the questions such as, What is the ultimate reality? What is the nature of the world? What is the nature of humanity? What happens after death? Buddhism, Secularism, and Marxism do not teach the existence of a supernatural realm, nor say anything about God; however, these belief systems answer these ultimate questions within their own framework of beliefs.

d. Religion is inherently grounded in the supernatural. Human response to the supernatural is as varied as most human experiences. Some reject the supernatural, while others deal with it through magic or religion. Both magic and religion begin with a belief in the supernatural, but they differ in their orientation to the supernatural. In religion, man recognizes the superiority of the supernatural. His attitude is one of submission, worship, reverence, and adoration. In magic, man seeks to control the supernatural. He believes by using the proper formulas he can get the supernatural to obey his command. Magic is the manipulation of the supernatural.[6]

e. For Christians, religion also focuses on the practical applications of religion: "Pure and undefiled religion before God and the Father is this: to visit orphans and widows in their trouble, and to keep oneself unspotted from the world" (Jas 1:27). "Religion is not merely an emotion, a feeling. It is a principle which is interwoven with all the daily duties and transactions of life."[7]

3. *Religions and Their Understanding of God*

a. Qualitative concepts about the divine:

1) Monism: One being who is the infinite sum of all natural forces (Brahaman in Hinduism).

2) Pantheism: Everything is divine, yet God does not have personality. God is nature (Upanishadic Hinduism).

3) Theism: There is just one personal, intelligent God; He created and sustains creation. He reveals Himself and answers prayer (most Christians).

4) Deism: A rationalistic view of God that admits His existence and yet rejects His revelation (Thomas Jefferson, Benjamin Franklin, James Madison, John Adams[8]).

5) Animism: Spirits are in everything. The attribution of anthropomorphic will, passions, and powers to material objects (tribal cultures).

6) Fetishism: The representation of God, demons, etc. in the form of idols. From Latin *fectitius*, made by hand, artificial (Voodoo).

7) Evemerism: The exaltation of heroes (Greeks, Romans, Scandinavians).

b. Quantitative concepts about the divine:

1) Monotheism: One exclusive, all-powerful, absolute, creator God (Judaism, Islam, Christianity).

2) Dualism: Two independent, eternal divinities who created and maintain the universe: good and evil (Zoroastrianism).

3) Polytheism: The belief in many gods (Chinese Folk Religion).

4) Henotheism: The worship of one god without denying the existence of other gods.[9] It is also called "monolatry" (Worship of Isis in Egypt).

5) Atheism: Negation of the existence of God (Marxism).

6) Pantheon: Several gods, arranged in a hierarchy (Aztecs, Teutons).

4. *The Origin of Religion: A Christian Perspective*

a. God created man as a biological, psychological, and spiritual being with needs in all three areas. Because all men have common needs, the cultural systems men develop to meet these needs most likely includes some form of religion. The missionary anthropologist knows that even the elementary tendencies toward religion are evidences of the remaining "image of God" in humankind.

b. Religion is as old as man. A strong case against evolutionary theories, historians say that "at the dawn of recorded history, the first written records (ca. 3500 B.C.) of the Sumerians demonstrate religion as occupying a very important place in the lives of people, if not actually providing the focal point of existence. Comparable data exist for other early civilizations."[10]

c. "The sacrificial system committed to Adam, was also perverted by his descendants. Superstition, idolatry, cruelty, and licentiousness corrupted the simple and significant service that God had appointed.[11] Eventually, God decided to destroy the human race through the Flood and give it an opportunity to enter into a new covenant with Him.

d. As the nations dispersed after the Flood and after the events at the Tower of Babel, they carried with them the notions of true worship. Some maintained aspects of the original forms, such as sacrifices and the belief in one true God. In time, their beliefs and practices became more and more distorted. One of the few notions that survived almost universally was the story of the Flood, which is found in all continents and in virtually all cultures.[12]

   e. Evolutionary ideas insist on animism, totemism, or fetishism as being the primal religion of humankind; monotheism, they say, emerged only alongside the relatively advanced civilizations of the Mediterranean in historic times. Christian revelation and social science indicate that monotheism was the earliest form of religion,[13] but it was later corrupted by animism and degenerated into polytheism.[14] "Men put God out of their knowledge and worshiped the creatures of their own imagination; and as a result, they became more and more debased. . . . The worshipers of false gods clothed their deities with human attributes and passions, and thus their standard of character was degraded to the likeness of sinful humanity. They were defiled in consequence."[15]

```
650 640 630 620 610 600 590 580 570 560 550 540 530 520 510 500 490 480 470
 .   .   .   .   .   .   .   .   .   .   .   .   .   .   .   .   .   .   .


Tenno, first Japanese emperor, early Shintoism
660-------------------585


Zarathushtra, founder of Zoroastrism, Iran
       630------------583


Mahavira, founder of Jainism, India
              599--------------------527


Siddhartha Gautama (Buddha), founder of Buddhism, India
                    563----------------------483


Lao-tzu, founder of Taoism, China
              604----------------------517


Confucius, founder of Confucianism, China
                    551--------------------479


              Ministry of prophet Daniel
       605----------------539
```

Table 1.1

f. It is significant that at least five major world religions (Zoroastrianism, Jainism, Buddhism, Taoism, and Confucianism) emerged during the prophet Daniel's ministry (Table 1.1). It is this writer's opinion that when God revealed through Daniel the date of the coming of the Messiah to this earth (Daniel 7:25-26), Satan decided to launch a major strategy of confusion and falsification. He realized that if the Messiah had come without competitors, His religion would have become universal too soon. Satan's plan was that the religion in Israel should not be the universal religion but, rather, one more religion in the world.

g. The descendants of Abraham preserved the sacrificial system given to the fallen race. Through prophets, God prepared a people to be ready for the coming of the promised One. At the same time, Satan was also active, trying to lead the elected nation into apostasy. When the Messiah came, only a remnant was waiting for Him. The Lamb of God died as the true sacrifice for the sins of the world. When Israel rejected Jesus as the Messiah, the responsibilities of the kingdom were given to the Church. Today, His faithful followers are spreading the good news of salvation "to every nation, tribe, tongue and people" (Rev 14:6).

Notes

1   Elizabeth Ramsey and Shannon Ledbetter, "Studying Religion: Issues in Definition and Method," in *Encountering Religion*, ed. Ian S. Markham and Tinu Ruparell (Oxford: Blackwell, 2001), 2.

2   Karl Marx, "Towards a Critique of Hegel's Philosophy of Right," in *Karl Marx: Selected Writings*, ed. David McLellan (Oxford: Oxford University Press, 1977), 64.

3   Marc Gellman and Thomas Hartman, *Religion for Dummies* (New York: Wiley, 2002), 10.

4   "Religion," *Merriam-Webster Online Dictionary*, 2005; retrieved on January 27, 2006, from http://www.m-w.com/cgi-bin/dictionary?book=Dictionary&va=religion.

5   Denise L. Carmody and T. L. Brink, *Ways to the Center: An Introduction to World Religions* (Belmont, CA: Wadsworth, 2006), 1.

6   Merwyn S. Garbarino, *Sociocultural Theory in Anthropology: A Short Story* (Prospect Heights, IL: Waveland, 1993), 35.

7   Ellen G. White, *Testimonies for the Church* (Mountain View, CA: Pacific Press, 1948), 2:506.

8   Rick Deshpande, "America's Most Famous Deists," *Deism*, 2005 [article online]; retrieved on January 10, 2006, from http://www.deism.org/foundingfathers.htm.

9   Roger Schmidt, Gene C. Sager, Gerald T. Carney, Albert C. Muller, Kenneth J. Zanca, Julius J. Jackson Jr., C. Wayne Mayhall, and Jeffrey C. Burke, *Patterns of Religion*, 2nd edition (Belmont, CA: Wadsworth, 2005), 37.

10   John J. Collins, *Primitive Religion* (Totowa, NJ: Littlefield Adams, 1978), 7.

11   Ellen G. White, *Patriarchs and Prophets* (Mountain View, CA: Pacific Press, 1948), 364.

12   While in college, this researcher wrote a paper on "Flood Stories Among Tribal People in South America." He found amazing parallelisms with the Bible story in all modern countries except Uruguay, simply because its native population was exterminated. See Alan Dundes, ed., *The Flood Myth* (Berkeley, CA: University of California Press, 1988).

13   Ethnologist Wilhelm Schmidt (1868-1954) affirmed that all humankind once believed in a single God and that to this simple monotheism, later beliefs in lesser gods and spirits were added. William Wedenoja, "Diffusionism as an Anthropological Paradigm," 2002 [article online]; retrieved on November 30, 2006, from http://courses.missouristate.edu/waw105f/ diffusionism.htm.

14   David Rooney, "The First Religion of Mankind," *EWTN Global Catholic Network* [article online]; retrieved on January 15, 2006, from http://www.ewtn.com/library/humanity/ fr93206.txt.

15   White, *Patriarchs and Prophets*, 91.

CHAPTER 2

World Religions

1. *A Global Picture*

a. About one-third of the world is Christian. This includes all denominations, cults, and sects. It even includes nominal Christians.

b. Another one-third of the world is comprised of non-Christians living among Christians. These non-Christians have Christian neighbors. They can be reached through home missions.

Figure 2.1

c. The last one-third of the world is culturally isolated from Christianity. These non-Christians have no contact with any Christians. They can be reached only through cross-cultural evangelism. These non-Christians' only hope is that committed Christians will move to the non-evangelized areas where they live.

2. *Two Major Sacred Paths*

Sacred Path of the East	Sacred Path of the West
Springs from an Indian root.	Springs from a Semitic root.
Includes Hinduism, Buddhism, and their offshoots.	Includes Judaism, Christianity, Islam, and their offshoots.
Searching religions.	Revealed religions.
Mystical. Emphasizes the finding of God by men from within the human spirit.	Prophetic. Emphasizes the revelation of God to men from outside the human spirit.
Pantheism/Monism/Polytheism	Personal God/Monotheism
Problem = Ignorance	Problem = Sin
Matter is evil or an illusion.	Matter is good.
Time is cyclical.	Time is linear.

Table 2.1

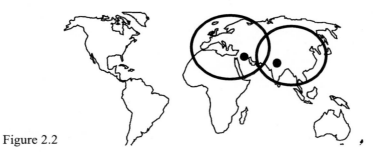

Figure 2.2

3. *Classification of World Religions*

a. World religions by their location:

Near East	Middle East	Far East
Judaism	Zoroastrianism	Hinduism
Christianity	Islam	Jainism
	Baha'i'sm	Buddhism
		Shintoism
		Taoism
		Confucianism
		Sikhism

Table 2.2

Notice that all living world religions originated in Asia. This continent also had many religions that are no longer practiced. Both Judaism and Christianity are also Asian religions by birth, but their strategic location–in the confluence of Asia, Europe, and Africa–gave them world exposure, enabling them to spread their message.

b. World religions by their permanence:

1) Dead

Africa	America	Europe	Asia
Old Egypt	Inca	Greek	Babylonian
	Aztec	Roman	Phoenician
	Mayan	Teutonic	Hittite
		Scandinavian	Maniqueism

Table 2.3

2) Alive

In process of extinction	In process of stagnation	In continued growth
Jainism	Buddhism	Islam
Shintoism	Judaism	Christianity
Zoroastrianism	Taoism	Confucianism
	Sikhism	Hinduism
		Baha'i'sm

Table 2.4

c. World religions by their chronological origin:

Parent religions	Religions born within a period of 150 years	Religions born during the Christian era
By 2300 B.C. Hinduism	By 660 B.C Shintoism	By A.D. 33 Christianity
By 1500 B.C. Judaism	By 600 B.C. Zoroastrianism	By A.D. 622 Islam
	By 580 B.C Taoism	By A.D. 1469 Sikhism
	By 570 B.C. Jainism	By A.D. 1844 Baha'i'sm
	By 540 B.C. Buddhism	
	By 530 B.C. Confucianism	

Table 2.5

d. World religions by their concept of a Supreme Being:

Monotheists	Polytheists	Dualists	Atheists
Judaism	Hinduism	Zoroastrianism	Jainism
Christianity	Confucianism		Buddhism
Islam	Shintoism		
Sikhism	Taoism		
Baha'i'sm			

Table 2.6

e. World religions by the origin of their names:

From the name of their founder	From the title of their founder	From a fundamental teaching	From the people who practice it
Confucianism from Confucius	**Buddhism** from Buddha, "the illuminated one"	**Taoism** from Tao, "divine path"	**Hinduism** from Hindus, India
Zoroastrianism from Zarathushtra	**Jainism** from Jina, "the conqueror"	**Shintoism** from Shinto, "the way of the gods"	**Judaism** from Jews, Judah
	Christianity from Christ, "the anointed one"	**Islam** from Islam, "submission"	
	Baha'i'sm from Baha'u'llah, the "glory of God"	**Sikhism** from Sikhs, "disciples"	

Table 2.7

f. World religions by their range:

Four aspire to be universal	The rest are national or hereditary	
Christianity	Confucianism	Hinduism
Islam	Jainism	Judaism
Buddhism	Shintoism	Sikhism
Baha'i'sm	Taoism	Zoroastrianism

Table 2.8

4. *The Importance of the Study of World Religions*

a. Growing interest in the supernatural in the modern world.

b. Proliferation of new sects and cults in all religions.

c. Renewal of ancient religions.

d. Relationship of ancient religions and nationalism.

e. Demographic explosion among other faiths.

f. Common threat of religious extremists.

g. Religious dispersion due to refugee migration.

h. Revolution in technology, transportation, and communication.

i. Missionary activities of the ancient, passive religions.

j. The change of the economic center of gravity toward countries where other religions predominate.

CHAPTER 3

Is There Salvation Outside Christianity?

1. *Introduction*

a. What will happen with non-Christians who have never heard the gospel and therefore cannot be charged with having rejected it? Is every person given, through conscience, sufficient light for his salvation? Are people lost because they failed to follow the light they had, or are they lost because the light of the gospel never reached them? Many sincere Christians may hold different opinions on this matter.

b. Before we attempt to answer these difficult questions, it may be useful to review some definitions related to this topic.

1) The term "pagan" is from the Latin word *paganus*, originally meaning "rural," "rustic" or "of the country," "country dweller," "villager." After Emperor Constantine recognized Christianity as a state religion, Christianity spread slower in rural areas than it did in the cities. In time, the word for "country dweller" became synonymous with someone who was "not

Christian," giving rise to the modern meaning of "pagan."[1] Today, Paganism is a religion in its own right, with most of its adherents concentrated in Britain, North America, Australia, and New Zealand.[2]

2) The term "heathen" originally meant someone who lived in the wild, uncultivated heath that was outside the parish boundary. Like the word "pagan," it came to mean a person holding onto non-Christian customs and beliefs, often used in a pejorative sense of an unbaptized savage. A heathen has been described as a polytheist who adheres to the religion of a people or nation that does not acknowledge the God of Judaism, Christianity, or Islam.[3] In short, a heathen is an idol worshiper and idolater.

3) The term "infidel" comes from the Latin term for "unfaithful." It refers to anyone who lacks faith in a particular religion, especially Christianity or Islam. Thus, an adherent of one religion would be an infidel to another religion.[4] A wider application is for one who has no religious beliefs.

4) The label "Gentile" comes from the Latin word *gens*, which is a translation of the Hebrew word *goy*. It means "nation" or "people." "Gentile" is roughly equivalent to the Greek *ethnos*, though in Hebrew usage it occurs exclusively in reference to non-Jewish nations and people. It was often used as a synonym of "pagan" and "heathen." In this chapter the terms are used interchangeably.

c. Before we enter into the core of this chapter, it is also important to state that, according to the Bible, salvation is available only through Jesus. Jesus is the only mediator between God and men. A mediator is a person who stands between two parties in a dispute and helps them to resolve their differences. A mediator must understand and respect the positions of each party in the dispute. He must be able to communicate the meaning of each party's position to the other party. He must be trusted by both parties. It is Jesus Christ who performs this task between God and men. Only He possesses the attributes necessary to stand between God and His children to resolve their differences.

John 14:6	"No one comes to the Father except through Me."
Acts 4:12	"There is no other name . . . by which we must be saved."
Acts 16:31	"Believe on the Lord Jesus Christ and you will be saved."
Rom 10:13	"Whoever calls on the name of the Lord shall be saved."
1 Cor 3:11	"No other foundation . . . , which is Jesus Christ."
1 Tim 2:5	"One Mediator between God and men, . . . Christ Jesus."

2. *The Bible and Other Religions*

a. The Bible recognizes the existence of non-biblical religions and considers them operating forces in the history of mankind.

b. It accepts the fact that man is innately a religious being.

c. It is mostly silent about the origin of religion as an organized institution with its officialdom and practices.

d. The Bible does not ascribe intrinsic spiritual values to any non-biblical religion.

e. It most definitely commands the worship of God as the only true God, in contrast with all other "gods."

f. The Bible breathes a spirit of intolerance, exclusiveness, hostility, and condemnation for all forms of idolatry.

g. It condemns all attempts of religious syncretism (the fusion of two beliefs) as "spiritual adultery" and godless apostasy.

h. It considers the present forms and practices of non-biblical religions as the perversion of an original revelation.

i. The Bible predicts the eventual and complete annihilation of all other systems of religious thought.

3. *How God Deals with Fallen Humans*

a. To begin with, the nations were not idolaters. They became heathen when they deliberately gave up their knowledge of God. "They changed the glory of . . . God into an image" (Rom 1:21-23). In their progressive apostasy, the heathen did not lose all knowledge of God. God did not abandon sinners. They were not left in complete darkness. God revealed Himself to the fallen race in different ways.

b. Nature reveals the handiwork of a Creator (Ps 19:1). "His invisible attributes are clearly seen, being understood by the things that are made, even His eternal power and Godhead, so they are without excuse" (Rom 1:20). God "did not leave Himself without witness," for He gave us rain, food, and many blessings (Acts 14:17).

c. The revelation of God through creation is supplemented by providential acts such as dreams and miracles. The angels of heaven are "sent forth to minister for those who will inherit salvation" (Heb 1:14).

d. There is still another form of revelation given to the heathen: "Their conscience also bears witness" (Rom 2:14-15).

e. God revealed Himself in explicit ways through the Scriptures. "The word that came to Jeremiah from God, saying . . ." (Jer 7:1) is an example of how the prophets transmitted messages from God.

f. God's most complete revelation of Himself was through Jesus Christ. "God, who at various times and in various ways spoke in time past to the fathers by the prophets, has in these last days spoken to us by His Son" (Heb 1:1,2).

g. In some way God reveals Himself to all humans (John 1:9). The following is a summary and a few samples of biblical references related to this issue:

1) Nature	Ps 8:3; 19:1; Rom 1:20
2) Conscience	Rom 2:14-15; John 8:9
3) Providence	Acts 10:3; Jonah 1:10-16
4) Scriptures	John 5:39; 17:17; 2 Tim 3:16; Rev 1:1
5) His Son	Heb 1:1-2; John 14:6-11; John 1:14-18

4. *How Will God Save the Nations?*

a. The popular argument: There is only one way to be saved, and that is through faith in Christ. The heathen, having never heard of Christ, cannot exercise faith; consequently, he is doomed to eternal condemnation for something quite beyond his control. The false assumption is that all men will be judged on the same basis—namely, they will be condemned for failing to believe the gospel. The Bible makes it plain that all men will be judged according to the light they have: "For everyone to whom much is given, from him much will be required" (Luke 12:48).

b. All humans receive some form of light, and they will be judged by that light and no other. Jesus is "the true Light [that] gives light to every man who comes into the world" (John 1:9). The greater the light, the heavier is the responsibility. Some will be condemned because they openly rejected the gospel (2 Cor 4:4); they rejected the gospel while having access to the Scriptures, which were able to make them wise unto salvation (1 Tim 3:16). Others will be condemned because they failed to live according to the light they received.

c. In all nations there are men and women who are praying for light and knowledge. They are honest in heart and desire to learn a better way. However, sincerity is not enough. Honesty of heart is not salvation. A person may be perfectly sincere in following a wrong road, but that will not make it the right road, or bring him to the place he wishes to reach.

d. In Romans 2:11-16 (NIV), the apostle lists three groups of people who will be judged according to the light they received: 1) The Jew, with the light of the law; 2) the Gentile, with the light of the gospel; and 3) all men, with the light of conscience:

> For God does not show favoritism. All who sin apart from the law will also perish apart from the law, and all who sin under the law will be judged by the law. For it is not those who hear the law who are righteous in God's sight, but it is those who obey the law who will be declared righteous. (Indeed, when Gentiles, who do not have the law, do by nature things required by the law, they are a law for themselves, even though they do not have the law, since they show that the requirements of the law are written on their hearts, their consciences also bearing witness, and their thoughts now accusing, now even defending them). This will take place on the day when God will judge men's secrets through Jesus Christ, as my gospel declares (NIV).

e. Many non-Christians have never received the light of the gospel but "have done the things that the law required. Their works are evidence that the Holy Spirit has touched their hearts, and they are recognized as the children of God."[5]

f. Zechariah 13:6 gives the idea that some will go to heaven without knowing Jesus. The context of Zechariah 13 has messianic ideas in expressions such as the "Pierced One" (12:10) and the "Shepherd" (13:7). One day, people will look unto Jesus and will ask Him: "What are these scars in your hands?" (it is assumed that they will go to heaven without knowing about Jesus), and then Jesus will tell them, "These scars are from wounds I received from my friends when I stayed at their house" (13:6, *Clear Word*; see John 1:11).

g. We are not called on to pass judgment in the case of the Gentiles who did not receive the full light of the gospel. If God saves them, it is because He is sovereign in the exercise of His grace. He is "a righteous Judge" (2 Tim 4:8), and "shall not the Judge of all the earth do right?" (Gen 18:25).

5. *What Is Our Responsibility?*

a. Even if God decides to save some who did not receive all the light, we still have an important part to act in His plan of salvation. We have a responsibility for those who do not know the gospel.

b. Although there may be some who will be in heaven without having been exposed to the full light of the gospel, the fact is that if we don't go, many will be condemned. Many ruined lives will be restored and many more will be saved if they know the gospel. An illustration: Let us assume that in a village just one person in one thousand is sincere before God to the point that he genuinely practices what he knows about God. The other 999 are slaves of passions and give up exercising what they know about God. One day, a missionary goes to that village and preaches the gospel. Many drunkards, drug addicts, thieves, homosexuals, and prostitutes accept the plan of salvation. They are transformed by the gospel, and a congregation of two hundred members is established in that village. Instead of having only one person in heaven from that village, many more are ready because they learned about Jesus and accepted His salvation. It is not for us to speculate who will be saved, even if they do not know the plan of salvation. Our responsibility is to go in obedience and to "preach the gospel to every creature" (Mark 16:15). God wants to save as many as possible (2 Pet 3:9; 1 Tim 2:4).

Notes

1   "Pagan," *Wikipedia: The Free Encyclopedia*, 2005 [encyclopedia online] retrieved on January 6, 2006, from http://en.wikipedia.org/wiki/Paganism.

2   Barbara Jane Davy, *Introduction to Pagan Studies* (Lanham, MD: Altamira Press, 2007), 2-4.

3   "Pagan," *Wikipedia.*

4   "Infidel," *About*, 2005 [encyclopedia online]; retrieved on January 1, 2006, from http://atheism.about.com/library/glossary/general/bldef_infidel.htm.

5   Ellen G. White, *The Desire of Ages* (Mountain View, CA: Pacific Press, 1958), 638.

CHAPTER 4

Evangelism

1. *Introduction*

a. This chapter provides a biblical and theological background for the evangelization of non-Christians. Christians understand that their mission is to "make disciples of all nations" (Matt 28:19) by teaching them "the everlasting gospel" (Rev 14:6). The English word "gospel" is equivalent to the Greek *euanggelion,* meaning "good news." It refers to the message of Christianity, the message of salvation through Jesus Christ. Evangelism is the proclamation of the good news. While witnessing is the sharing of our experience with Jesus, evangelism is the sharing of the message of Jesus.

b. Evangelism is the presentation of biblical doctrines, in the power of the Holy Spirit, in such a way that people will be persuaded to accept Jesus as Savior, be baptized, and serve Him in the fellowship of the church.

1) Most Christians agree that the *sine qua non* (the absolute essential) for salvation is the personal knowledge and acceptance of Jesus Christ. However, they also understand that they must teach "all things" (Matt 28:20), "the whole counsel of God" (Acts 20:27), in order to help converts become responsible members of the body of Christ.

2) Conversion is not a human act, but the work of the Holy Spirit. Conversion is a change of the basic assumptions that form a worldview. A Christian witness who shares his faith with non-Christians will soon discover that

arguing about doctrines is virtually useless. The change of a worldview is a miracle that only the Holy Spirit can produce. Prayer is an indispensable tool of evangelism, especially in the evangelization of non-Christians.

3) The goal of the Great Commission is more than just leading people to baptism. The imperative of the Great Commission is to "make disciples" (Matt 28:19). Disciples are mature Christians and responsible members of the body of Christ who will serve Him according to their spiritual gifts. This takes on additional nuances when global issues are present. Cross-cultural witnessing and evangelism leading to church planting is a process that may take much longer than it might in one's own culture.

2. *Three Basic Approaches to Evangelism*

The following paradigm (Figure 4.1) suggests that evangelism is not an event but a process. The following stages of evangelism are not mutually exclusive but complementary.[1]

a. Presence Evangelism (P-1):

1) "Presence evangelism" deals with the impact of the Christian way of life. The Christian does evangelism by living the gospel in the presence of the lost, which involves being a positive influence. Examples: Medical missionary work, English schools, and community services.

2) This approach is strongly advocated in ecumenical circles. In the World Council of Churches, it is considered by many as "the basic form of witness."[2]

3) The emphasis of presence evangelism is on testimony.

4) The purpose is to meet the needs of the people, to meet them where they are. As the Christian witness models the Christian life and helps people, he earns a hearing.

5) This approach is compared to a door that allows access to people's hearts.

b. Proclamation Evangelism (P-2):

1) "Proclamation evangelism" deals with the proclamation of the Word. Example: Church preaching, radio/TV programs. Many preachers limit their "evangelism" to their weekly sermons. Many will never even offer invitations or altar calls.

2) This approach is widely practiced in Protestant churches. Typical evangelists will offer a financial report, statistics of how many people attended, and how many indicated their desire to receive Christ. They may speak of "decisions." The evangelist is not responsible for the outcome. "Share Christ and leave the results to God."

3) The emphasis is on the Scripture.

4) The purpose is to expose people to the Bible. They hear and understand the message of the Bible throughout an extended period of time.

5) This approach is compared to the windows of a building that allow the light to illuminate the interior.

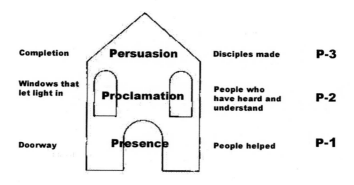

Figure 4.1

c. Persuasion Evangelism (P-3):

1) "Persuasion evangelism" is not only proclaiming the gospel, but it also involves persuading or motivating the unsaved to respond (Acts 18:4; 2 Cor 5:11). It is intentional preaching with a view to bringing men to Christ and into responsible church membership. Examples: Personal Bible studies on doctrines, public evangelism, small groups evangelism, baptismal classes.

2) This is the approach of some evangelical churches.[3]

3) The emphasis is on the doctrine.

4) The purpose is to help people to decide for Jesus and His truth. Believers express their commitment through baptism. Only committed and baptized believers are counted.

5) This approach is compared to the finishing touches of the construction of a building. The work is not completed until the believer is a mature disciple.

d. Summary of the three approaches to evangelism:

	Building	**Goal**	**Emphasis**	**Preferred by**
Persuasion	Completion	Disciples	Doctrines	Evangelicals
Proclamation	Windows	People heard	Scripture	Protestants
Presence	Entrance door	People helped	Testimony	Ecumenicals

Table 4.1

e. These three approaches are not mutually exclusive.

1) Evangelists must begin with **presence** evangelism (1-P), by "winning a hearing." They must have a good testimony and be interested in meeting the needs of the lost. Matthew 5:16 admonishes, "See your good works and glorify God."

2) Next, the evangelist must **proclaim** (2-P) the gospel to the unsaved. They must hear and understand the message. Make sure that "Christ is preached" (Phil 1:18).

3) Finally, ministers must **persuade** (3-P) people to receive Christ and make them disciples. It may done both "with great emotion" (Rom 9:2; 10:1) and "with rational arguments" (Acts 13:43).

4) This approach is criticized by those who want to limit evangelism at the point of proclamation (P-2) without moving to persuasion (P-3). They do not believe that the essence of evangelizing is producing converts. They argue, "The way to tell whether in fact you are evangelizing is . . . to ask whether you are faithfully making known the gospel message."[4]

3. *Cross-cultural Evangelism*

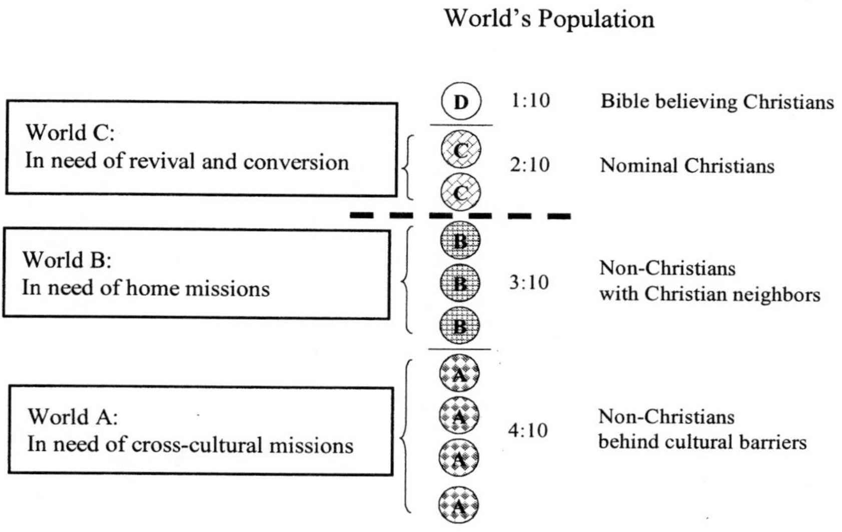

World's Population

Figure 4.2

a. In the graphic shown in Figure 4.2, each circle represents a segment of about 10% of the world's population. Obviously, the evangelization of World A and World B cannot depend on World C. World D (about 7% of the world's population) is responsible for the evangelization of the rest of the world.

b. About 97% of the non-evangelized peoples of the world live in the so-called "10/40 Window," a geographic region that stretches from West Africa to East Asia, between the 10th and the 40th latitudes north of the equator.   Most of the people living in the 10/40 Window are Muslims, Hindus, Buddhists, Shintoists, Confucianists, Taoists, Zoroastrians, and Jains (Figure 4.3).

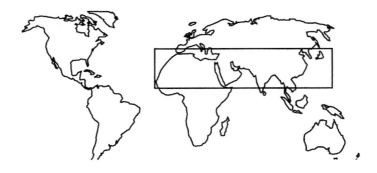

Figure 4.3

c. Missiologist Ralph D. Winter developed a model of cross-cultural evangelism that is used below with some modifications (Figure 4.4). He spoke

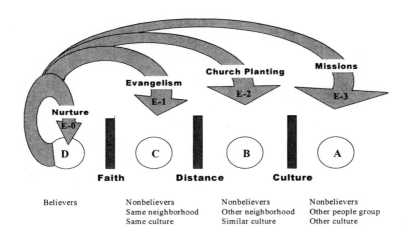

Figure 4.4

of evangelism across three different barriers and cultural distances.[5] According to the following model, when a preacher addresses the spiritual needs of a congregation, he is doing nurture. When we reach out to those who are not believers, we are doing evangelism. If we do evangelism across distance, we are doing church planting. When we do evangelism across cultures, we are doing missions. Unfortunately, most Christians have only a very vague idea of just how many peoples there are in the world among whom there is no E-1 witness.

e. "Until every tribe and tongue has a strong E-1, powerful evangelizing church in it, and thus, an E-1 witness within it, E-2 and E-3 efforts coming from outside are still essential and highly urgent."[6] About one-third of the world is comprised of non-Christians living without a viable chance of hearing the gospel because of their isolation. The finishing of God's work demands that committed Christians set aside the conveniences of their culture and go as missionaries "where people have not yet heard about Christ" (Rom 15:20, *Clear Word*).

d. According to Acts 1:8, Jesus went beyond the command, "Go into all the world," given in Mark 16:15. He distinguished between different parts of that world and did so according to the relative distance of those people from his hearers. Jesus divided the task into four significant components:

Acts 1:8	Evangelism	Barriers	Strategy	Growth	Result
Jerusalem	E-0 No evangelism	No barrier	Pastoral care	Internal Growth	Nurture
Judea	E-1 Across 1 barrier	Faith	Evangelism in the neighborhood	Expansion Growth	Evangelism
Samaria	E-2 Across 2 barriers	Faith Distance	Evangelism across distance	Extension Growth	Church Planting
The Ends	E-3 Across 3 barriers	Faith Distance Culture	Evangelism in another culture	Cross-cultural Growth	Missions

Table 4.2

4. *Why Do Missions?*

a. First, God said so.[7] The gospel commission given by Jesus commands His followers to go, preach, baptize, and teach. No reasons given, no questions asked. "We engage in evangelism today not because we want to or because we choose to or because we like to, but because we have been told to. The Church is under orders."[8]

b. Second, if we do missions, the nonbelievers have a better chance at salvation. If we can get them to hear, if they have the knowledge, the probability of their being saved is increased (Rom 10:13-15).

c. Third, missions should come naturally to a Christian. One who is full of Christ will naturally bubble over with love to God and man. He will naturally share what he has learned. Witnessing is a natural outcome of one's Christian experience.

d. Fourth, missionary work–at home or abroad, personal or public–is necessary to the believer. Believers will keep in much better spiritual health if actively engaged in some form of outreach. This is the exercise of the soul. Probably humans need to be involved in missions more than God needs human involvement.

e. Fifth, there is a reward for doing mission. We not only sing about "stars in my crown," we read the words of Jesus: "Well done, good and faithful servant. . . . Enter into the joy of your lord" (Matt 25:21, 23). There is satisfaction here and now in doing God's work–in fulfilling His commission. There is also an "eternal weight of glory" (2 Cor 4:17) promised to those who do their part here on earth.

f. Sixth, the mission of the remnant serves to vindicate God. Salvation has a cosmic dimension that includes more than personal redemption. Not only before humans but before the expectant universe God's way is to be shown as the best and only way. The faithful remnant has the privilege of participating in this vindication of God's character.

g. Seventh, although God can grant ultimate salvation to those who never heard of His love and power, He cannot provide them with benefits of being a Christian this side of His coming. Salvation consists of two parts: life eternal in the "sweet by and by" and life eternal here and now Jesus came that we might have life abundant now–joy, peace, health, security, and spiritual well-being, as well as the everlasting hope. The purpose of missions is to provide life more abundantly (John 10:10), both here and there.

h. Eight, to fail to make the present life more meaningful–as well as to ensure eternal life–is cheating human beings out of what God meant for us to give them. In keeping the good news of salvation to ourselves, we also cheat those we fail to tell. They miss out on the blessings and challenges of belonging to the remnant. Furthermore, we cheat ourselves out of participating in the grandest enterprise.

i. Ninth, it is effective. God recognized that supernatural means might be overpowering and thus chose to use human agents who could present the good news of the gospel in terms their fellows could more easily understand. God understood human psychology very well and knew that the "one-beggar-telling-another-where-to-find-bread" approach would be the most effective.

Notes

1   The concept and the illustration are from Elmer L. Towns, "Evangelism: The Why and How," in *Church Growth: State of the Art*, ed. C. Peter Wagner, with Win Arn and Elmer Towns (Wheaton, IL: Tyndale House, 1986), 43-46.

2   R. K. Orchard, *Missions in a Time of Testing* (London: Lutterworth Press, 1964), 92.

3   "A minister should not present any candidate for baptism and church membership until he can satisfy the church by a public examination that the candidate has been well instructed and is ready to take such a step. . . . The minister's work is not completed until he has thoroughly instructed the candidates, and they are familiar with and committed to all fundamental beliefs and related practices of the church and are prepared to assume the responsibilities of church membership." General Conference of Seventh-day Adventists, *Seventh-day Adventist Church Manual* (Silver Spring, MD: General Conference of Seventh-day Adventists, 2005), 30.

4   Ibid., 41. Similar ideas in John R. W. Stott, "The Biblical Basis of Evangelism," in *Mission Trends No. 2: Evangelization,* ed. Gerald H. Anderson and Thomas (New York: Paulist Press, 1975), 4-23.

5   Summarized and adapted from Ralph D. Winter, "The New Macedonia: A Revolutionary New Era in Mission Begins," chap. in *Perspectives on the World Christian Movement: A Reader*, ed. Ralph D. Winter and Steven C. Hawthorne (Pasadena, CA: William Carey Library, 1999), 339-53.

6   Ibid., 342.

7   Adapted from Nancy Vhymeister and Madeline S. Johnson, *Go! A Student Missionary Manual* (Berrien Springs, MI: Department of World Mission, Andrews University, 1984), 20-21.

8   John R. W. Stoot, "The Great Commission," in *One Race, One Gospel, One Task* (Minneapolis: Word Wide Publications, 1967), 1:37.

PART II

RELIGIONS OF SOUTH ASIA

5. **HINDUISM**

6. **CHRISTIAN WITNESS TO HINDUS**

7. **JAINISM**

8. **SIKHISM**

CHAPTER 5

Hinduism

1. *Introduction*

a. Hinduism could be regarded as an evolving religious tradition, rather than a simple, separate "religion" in the sense that the term is usually understood. Hinduism displays few of the characteristics that are generally expected of a religion. It has no founder and is not prophetic. It is not creedal, nor is any particular doctrine, dogma, or practice held to be essential to it. It is not a system of theology, it does not have a single moral code, and the concept of a god is not central to it. There is no specific scripture regarded as being uniquely authoritative, and it is not sustained by an ecclesiastical organization.

The use of the word "hindu" is itself complex. Both "India" and "Hindu" derive from "Sindhu," the traditional name for the Indus River. In ancient inscriptions and documents, "Hindu" refers to the people of "Hind," the Indian subcontinent. In the Muslim-ruled empires of medieval India, it was used for many non-Muslim Indian communities. Although the term is found in Hindu literature earlier, it was only after the late eighteenth century that it became popular as a name for the dominant religion of the Indian people.[1]

b. Hinduism evolved by the two processes of evolution and assimilation over a period of several thousand years. This produced an enormous variety of religious systems, beliefs, and practices. It is possible to find groups of Hindus whose respective faiths have almost nothing in common. It is also almost impossible to identify any universal belief or practice that is common to all

Hindus. What makes Hinduism a single religious tradition is the common Indian origin, the historical continuity, the sense of a shared heritage, and a family relationship between the various parts. Most important, and somewhat ironic, is the fact that Hindus affirm their faith as one single religion.

> It is Hindu self-awareness and self-identity that affirms Hinduism to be one single religious universe, no matter how richly varied its content, and which makes it a significant and potent force alongside the other religions of the world.[2]

c. The Census Commission of India provides the following marks of a Hindu: accept the supremacy of Brahmins, receive a mantra from a recognized Hindu guru, accept the authority of the Vedas, worship Hindu gods, be served by Brahmins as family priests, have access to the interior of a Hindu temple without causing pollution, cremate their dead, and do not eat beef.[3]

2. *The Hindu Population*

a. It is estimated that there are 837 million Hindus worldwide,[4] accounting for 13.4% of the earth's population (for comparison, Protestant Christians account for 10.4% of the world). Generally speaking, a Hindu is born, not made. Except for recent trends of conversion to Hinduism, the growth of Hinduism has been mostly biological.

b. The vast majority of Hindus live in India, where they account for 80.5% of the population (Christians account for 2.3%).[5] More than two million Hindus live on the Indonesian island of Bali. Nepal is the only nation where Hinduism is the state religion. Hindus comprise a significant portion of the population in other countries:[6]

1) Nepal	89%	Asia
2) Mauritius	52%	Indian Ocean
3) Guyana	40%	South America
4) Fiji	38%	Pacific Ocean
5) Suriname	30%	Caribbean/America
6) Trinidad and Tobago	24%	Caribbean/America
7) Bhutan	25%	Asia
8) Sri Lanka	15%	Asia
9) Bangladesh	11%	Asia

c. By 2004 the number of Hindus in the United States was approximately 1,478,670, or 0.5% of the population.[7] "People from India live in all fifty of the

United States and now represent the fourth-largest Asian ethnic minority (after Chinese, Japanese, and Filipinos)." The largest concentrations of Asian Indians are in the states of California and New York and in such major urban areas as New York City, Chicago, Los Angeles, Houston, Philadelphia, and the San Francisco Bay area.[8]

3. *The Rise of the Hindu Religion*

"Some Hindus would argue there can be no historical treatment of Hinduism; it is *sanatana dharma*, 'the eternal religious teaching.'"[9] However, in order to develop a fuller understanding of Hinduism, we are going to take a brief look at its origins and development.

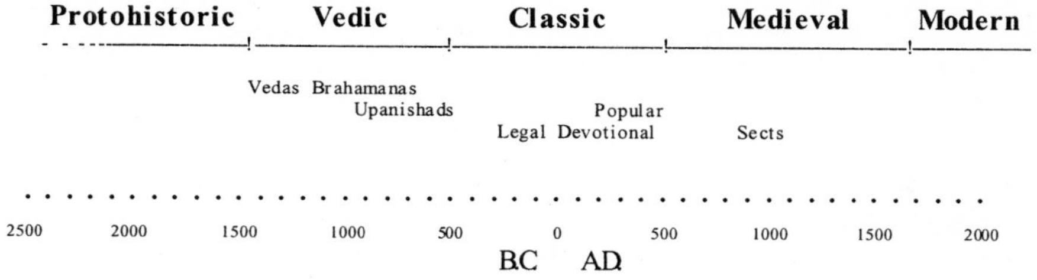

Protohistoric	Vedic	Classic	Medieval	Modern

```
                    Vedas Brahamanas
                          Upanishads                      Popular
                                        Legal Devotional        Sects

 . . . . . . . . . . . . . . . . . . . . . . . . . . . . . . . . . . . . . . .

2500      2000       1500      1000      500      0      500     1000     1500     2000
                                              B.C.   A.D.
```

Figure 5.1

a. Protohistoric Hinduism (2300-1500 B.C.).

1) Early inhabitants were part of the immigration which took place right after the Flood (about 2500 B.C.). These early inhabitants, known as Dravidians, built up large cities in the Indus valley: Mohenjo-Saro and Harappa. People who became established by the Indus River were known as "Hindus."[10] They were a dark-skinned race, but their ethnic origin is unknown.[11] The fact that their civilization was akin to that of the Sumerian and Egyptian civilizations[12] is significant since Sumeria is another name for Mesopotamia (Ararat, Ur, Nineveh, Babylon). Historians affirm that civilization started in Sumeria.[13]

2) The Harappan civilization developed the earliest stage of religious life in India. Archaeologists have found statuettes of one male god, several

female goddesses, and phallic symbols. Their religion was based on animal sacrifices and domestic rites, including ritual purification with water.[14]

b. Vedic Hinduism (1500-500 B.C.). This period saw the arrival of the semi-nomadic, light-skinned, Aryan, Indo-European tribes moved to Iran/Afghanistan and then into India. They included the Scythians (west coast) and the Mongoloids (northern mountain). These race types fused, not only genetically but ideologically, as a new religious identity evolved into what is known today as Hinduism.[15] Religious literature written during that period includes:

1) The *Vedas* (1200-1000 B.C.). They are Hinduism's earliest sacred writings, related to the Aryans. The centuries of movement and the seizure of lands by the Aryans were accompanied by a growing oral tradition of folk tales, epics, and adventures, known as the *samhitas* ("collections"). They were written in Sanskrit and convey revealed knowledge.[16] It is believed that the truth of the *Vedas* is eternal and that it existed ontologically before it was written or spoken. "Sacrifice, the making of blood and non-blood offerings as worship to a particular deity, was central to Vedic religion."[17]

2) The *Brahamanas* (1000-800 B.C.). They are commentaries on sacrificial rites, in which favors are acquired from the gods. This appears as a modified development of Vedic thought since the sacrifice and the priest now take on more significant roles. Thus, the need of a specialized priestcraft is mandatory since the gods themselves are dependent upon the sacrifice. Therefore, the multiple deities are subordinate to the ultimate power behind the sacrifice. This ultimate power is known as Brahaman.[18]

3) The *Upanishads* (800-700 B.C.). These writings emphasize inner contemplation. They elaborate upon true reality as Brahaman. Brahaman is incomprehensible, unknowable, and impersonal. All phenomena within the world, including one's own self, is illusory (*maya*).[19]

c. Philosophic Hinduism (800-600 B.C.). It is based on the *Upanishads*. Salvation is not based on sacrifices but on having union with Brahma.

d. Classical Hinduism (500 B.C.-A.D. 500) has been divided into three periods:

1) Legal Hinduism. The *Code of Manu* (250 B.C.) explains Indian ethical and social standards, demands strict obedience to religious duties,

explains that liberation is attained through transmigration, and gives divine endorsement to the caste system.

2) Devotional Hinduism (by first century A.D.). This period adds worship to Krishna. Devotional Hinduism is based on the *Bhagavad-Gita* ("Song of the Lord"), "the most famous and influential text of Hinduism."[20] Mythological tales of Aryan heroes provided illustrations for moral principles and devotion in life. They evolved into an existential branch in Hinduism noted for love and devotion (*bhakti*).[21]

3) Popular Hinduism (A.D. second and fifth centuries). It was marked by a diffusion of religious duties. It was established on the *Mahabharata*. The *Mahabharata* is the longest poem in the world–it includes the *Bhagavad Gita* (the most popular Hindu writing), *Ramayana* (teachings in the form of allegories), and the *Puranas* (legends of the gods).

e. Medieval Hinduism (A.D. 600-1800). This was a period marked by advanced development of religious philosophy. There was a proliferation of sectarian movements and reforms that arose in India during this time:[22]

1) Caitanyaism in the northwest emphasized conversion and love to Krishna.

2) The Lingayats, or "*lingam*-carriers," were found in the south central region.

3) Tantric Saivism in the far north (Kashmir) included sexual intercourse as a means to attaining the highest state of bliss and knowledge.

4) Sri Vaisnavism in the south (Tamil Nadu) expressed fervid devotion to Vishnu.

f. Modern Hinduism. During this period much of India came under British control. In the 1930s and 40s, Mahatma Gandhi led a nonviolent civil disobedience movement. In 1947 the British Indian Empire came to an end. Virtually all forms of Hinduism are currently practiced throughout India in different degrees.

4. *Major Gods of the Hindu Religion*

a. Brahaman.

1) Monism, the idea that there is but one unified reality in the universe, is the foundation of Hindu philosophy. Brahaman is the ultimate reality or impersonal absolute, also known as the "universal soul."[23] Brahaman is seen as the unchanging reality, which is beyond the universe, yet unifies it. Its nature is unknowable by humans.

2) Brahaman is everywhere and dwells therein but is not captured in everything simultaneously. The universe is continuous with and extends from the being of Brahaman. This is known as "pantheism." Our human essence is identical to that of Brahaman.

b. The Hindu triad (*trimurti*) consists of Brahma, Vishnu, and Shiva. The most important Hindu gods have consorts and means of transportation, called "vehicles." The gods of the Hindu triad correspond with the cyclical system of rebirth through creation, preservation, destruction, and recreation.

c. Brahma, the Originator or Creator of all things.

1) Brahma's origin lies in the desire of Brahaman to create a world of beings. He first created water into which he cast his seed. From this was born Brahma, the earliest progenitor of all creatures. Since his work is already accomplished, Brahma no longer needs worship. He is worshiped only at two temples in India.[24] Interestingly, in a Buddhist country like Thailand, Brahma is a popular object of worship.[25] During one hour, when I was in a temple in Bangkok, I saw about one hundred Buddhists bowing before Brahma's image. Buddhism is essentially atheistic, and people need an object of worship.

2) Brahma's *murti* ("image," "representation") shows him with four faces and four arms, holding a drinking vessel, a walking stick, a scepter (sometimes two spoons), and a book. Brahma's vehicle is a swan. Sarawasti, the Hindu goddess of learning and fine arts, is sometimes regarded as the second wife of Brahma, though she is also associated with Vishnu as his consort.[26] In contrast with Brahaman, who is only mind, Brahma is material.

Figure 5.1

d. Vishnu, the Preserver.

1) He is represented in sculpture and painting in human form, with a dark bluish complexion. In his four hands he holds a lotus flower, a round weapon, a sea shell, and a discus. Vishnu wears a precious jewel around his neck. His vehicle is Garuda, the eagle.

2) He came down to earth in many *avatars* ("descents," incarnations) in order to preserve humanity from impending calamities. The best known *avatars* are

Figure 5.2

the fish, the tortoise, the boar, the man-lion, the dwarf, and four fully human forms–Purusarama, Dasaratharma, Krishna, and Buddha. Kalki, the tenth incarnation, still to come, is supposed to destroy evil people and build a new world.[27] The most popular *avatar* is Krishna, a folk-figure who lives a pastoral life while being lavished with many mistresses; they are seen as symbolic of devout admiration.

3) Vishnu is believed to be a benevolent god and is accompanied by his wife, Lakshmi. He is one of the most popular gods in India. Vishnu's identity is understood through mythical stories, which show his wisdom, judgment, and superiority over demons.

e. Shiva, the Destroyer (sometimes the Regenerator).

1) He is close to the creation and seems to use *maya* (the illusion of matter) to his advantage. He initiates destruction in order to make room for a new creation.[28] This idea of a new creation brings sexual symbolism into Hindu worship through the *lingam* and *yoni,* which represent male and female reproductive organs. Shiva is very often represented by the *lingam/yoni* as a symbol of his creative side.[29]

2) As the "Lord of the Dance," Shiva controls the movement of the universe. He dances to destroy ignorance and create understanding. Shiva is represented with one face and four arms. The two upper hands hold a small hand-drum controlling the rhythm of creation, and a flame of the fire of destruction. He offers protection with his lower right hand and indicates salvation with the left hand. He dances on the demon of ignorance with his right foot,

Figure 5.3

while his left foot is raised. His whole body is surrounded by an arch of flames. Shiva's vehicle is the bull. The weapon of Shiva is the *tyrisul* or trident.

3) Shiva is popular among ascetics who "destroy" their body in order to gain spiritual life. In Kathmandu, Nepal, I saw an ascetic, or *sadhu* ("holy man"), who for several years had guarded a temple of Shiva. Every few minutes he smoked marijuana (also called "hashish"). His bloodshot eyes, unkempt hair, weak complexion, and the dirt of his body reflected the destructive nature of the object of his devotion.

5. *Lesser Deities of the Hindu Pantheon*

a. Each member of the Triad has a wife, who is an important goddess in the Hindu Pantheon. They are worshiped in their own right and not merely as consorts of a male deity.

1) Sarawsati, the wife of Brahama, is the goddess of wisdom and the arts. She is white in color and shown as a graceful woman with two arms, holding a stringed musical instrument and riding a peacock (Figure 5.4).

2) Lakshmi, the wife of Vishnu, is a beautiful woman with four hands, rising from a lotus. In two hands she holds lotus flowers, with the third she bestows wealth in the form of gold coins, and with the fourth she blesses the worshiper (Figure 5.5). Her vehicle is the owl.[30]

3) Parvati is Shiva's consort (Figure 5.6). Like him, she has a peaceful and a fearful side. She is known in her terrifying form holding a variety of weapons. Her vehicle is the lion. Sacrifice of animals take place in her temples. The "Mother Goddess," Shakti, is the female principle in creation. Among female deities, Parvati, Amba, Durga, and Kali are the main recipients of the title "Mother."[31]

Figure 5.4   Figure 5.5   Figure 5.6

b. Ganesha, the son of Shiva and Parvati, is the elephant-headed god of wisdom and success.

1) The Ganesha mythology is given in many *Puranas*. Although the reasons vary, they all agree that Shiva cut off his son's head in anger. Shiva promised Parvati that he could replace the head and sent his attendants to bring the head of anyone found sleeping with their head pointing north. They found a baby elephant in that position and brought its head, which Shiva attached to the torso, bringing the boy back to life.[32]

2) The Ganesha *murti* ("representation") shows him with a large human body of pink complexion and an elephant's head with one tusk (Figure 5.7). His vehicle is a rat. He has four hands, each hand carrying a symbol which differs from the symbols in other hands. With one hand he offers protection and blessing to his devotees.

3) He is the defender and remover of obstacles and has to be propitiated first, before the worship of other gods. He is one of the most popular figures in Hinduism.[33]

Figure 5.7

c. Krishna, an avatar of Vishnu.

1) Krishna is presented quite often in dark blue or black images. The name *Krishna* in Sanskrit literally means "black"; nevertheless, the deity has been worshiped in India for more than two thousand years without any pejorative meaning attached to his color.[34]

2) For devotees, Krishna is a personal God, not an impersonal force, and the most important of all *avatars*. He is commonly worshiped as a baby, a powerful ruler, or most often as an attractive young cowherd who tends the cows and plays erotically with Radha and other cowherdesses.

Figure 5.8

Krishna is described as a child and as a lover who has all the qualities and elicits all the emotions associated with such roles.

As a child, he plays mischievously and wildly, stealing butter, playing with his shadow, rolling in the dirt, playing pranks on his companions. He is the flute-playing lover of incredible beauty, grace and joy who, when the lotus is in full blossom on clear autumn nights, entices his lovers to abandon their responsibilities and dance with him in the forest.

Sensuous love poetry describes the courtship of Krishna and Radha or others of his lovers. They fall in love at first sight, arrange to be introduced, meet in secrecy, dance and sing, love ecstatically; they quarrel, are jealous, forsake each other, and agonize over the separation. In many of the stories the themes of extramarital love are present: risking one's reputation and life if caught, the impossibility of a permanent relationship, brief moment of shared ecstasy, separation, and longing for reunion.[35]

3) Modern devotion to Krishna is known as the Hare Krishna movement. The Beatles made it popular in the West when they became devotees of Krishna.[36] The pastimes of the adolescent cowherd are of greatest importance to the Hare Krishna movement. While Krishna's sexual pleasures[37] may appear materialistic to a common observer, devotees say that "just listening to them causes the hearer to lose his lust as he becomes more spiritual."[38]

d. Rivers.

1) Hindus have regarded rivers as deities since Vedic times. They are personifications of goddesses. They are invoked as deities capable of bestowing wealth, abundance, nourishment, and offspring on their worshipers. Bathing in sacred rivers is one of many religious duties required of all Hindus. Many places along the banks of the sacred rivers are considered *tirthas*, or holy bathing places. It is believed that the rivers wash away people's sins.[39]

2) While all rivers in India are sacred, there are seven that are regarded as the most sacred: the Ganges, Jumma, Godavari, Saravasti, Narmanda, Indus, and Kaveri. Allahabad and Varanasi are some of the well-known *tirthas*. Crematory ashes are ceremoniously thrown in the Ganges, especially at Varanasi (Benares), in the belief that the spirit of the cremated person will sail to higher worlds.[40]

e. Hinduism is sometimes known by the high regard of the cow. While Hindus are averse to taking animal life, it is only in the case of cattle that they have a great repugnance. To kill a cow is not only a crime but a sacrilege. Many different animals are killed in sacrifices, but the cow is a notable exception.[41] Though cattle in India are regarded as sacred animals and treated with veneration, they are not actually worshiped, and the veneration stops short of deification.[42] In the *Rig-Veda*, the cow already bears the epithet *aghnya*, meaning "not to be killed."[43] The reason for this prohibition is not necessarily related to their value but to totemistic ideas. Cows were believed to embody the Fertility-Spirit.

f. In addition to these principal deities, there are an almost innumerable number of gods in the Hindu system, commonly estimated at 330,000,003.[44] Lakes, trees, animals, birds, flowers, statues, and tombs are also revered objects. When we look at Hinduism from the Hindu's point of view, all gods are but representations of the one true God. Hinduism insists that God is one, though He is many. He is one in the same way that humanity is one.

6. *Basic Beliefs of the Hindu Religion*

a. The Hindu doctrine of man.

1) The essential essence of man is the spiritual self or *atman* ("self"), which is distinct from the material body. The real and innermost self is hindered by the physical body and must strive to be one with Brahaman (the "universal soul") if he is to have a fully authentic existence and attain *moksha* ("liberation").[45]

2) As for man's present existence, it is derived from and dependent upon what he does and has done. This is influenced by the law of cause and effect known as *karma*. Hinduism is clearly a religion that has retribution at the center of man's moral nature.

b. *Karma* ("action"). The Law of *Karma* indicates that every responsible decision must have its consequences. This is an ethical interpretation of the law of causation. The effects of our actions follow us, not only in the present lifetime but from lifetime to lifetime (reincarnation). Even in a state of bondage and suffering, the Hindu does not think his present situation unjust, but a reward resulting from the law of *karma*.

c. *Samsara* ("reincarnation"). It refers to the ever-revolving wheel of life, death, and rebirth. It is often symbolized as a circle of flame kept moving through the combined effect of divine action and natural law (including the law of *karma*). The created universe periodically comes in and out of being; these periods of evolution and devolution stretch over immensely long periods (3.1536 x 10^{14} human years). Within these cycles, the soul transmigrates from one body to another in reincarnation, carrying its load of *karma* from previous lives.[46]

d. *Moksha* ("liberation").

1) Hindus want to be liberated from reincarnation. "To be free is to be free from all attachments and dependencies. It is to be free to do what one

wishes to do; but it is also to be free from limiting factors around oneself. Attaining such a state is the major preoccupation of Hindu religious thinkers."[47]

2) Ignorance is the cause of human misery and separation from Brahaman. Liberation is attained through realizing that the concept of the individual self is *maya* ("illusion") and that only the undifferentiated oneness of Brahaman is real. With that realization, one must strive to detach oneself from the desires of the ego.[48]

3) Actions performed without any attachment to their results lead to spiritual freedom. This is achieved by performing *dharma*, religious duties. Actions performed with a desire for rewards bind the soul to the wheel of existence.

4) The final necessity to attain *moksha* is total abandonment. Three things are required: a) A *guru* ("teacher") who helps a person distinguish reality from illusion; b) renunciation to the material world, since all nature is unreal; and c) complete control of the body, mind, and senses.

e. *Yoga* ("union through discipline").

1) *Yoga* consists of disciplinary exercises which produce control of mind over body and perfect confidence. It is the process or path of discipline leading to oneness with the divine or with one's self.

2) *Yoga* provides escape from reincarnation. There are several ways to liberation:[49] a) The way of knowledge, or *Jnana Yoga*, strives to get an individual to recognize one's equality with Brahaman and thus actualize *moksha* ("liberation"). By attaining scriptural knowledge, one may achieve a transforming wisdom. b) The way of action, or *Karma Yoga*, focuses on a renunciation of personal benefits. It is the path of unselfish action. c) The way of devotion, or *Bhakti Yoga*, is the most popular since it allows for the expression of emotions toward a deity. d) In the way of meditation, or *Raja Yoga*, the goal is to empty the mind. The steps are restraint, observances, bodily posture, regulatory breathing, withdrawing of the senses, concentration, meditation, and trance (*samadhi*).[50]

3) In *Yoga*, every desire is subdued, all activity stilled. No fresh round of *karma* is set in motion, so release comes. The body is thought to exist within a field of energy, which is concentrated at subtle centers (*chakras*) along the spine. Breath is thought to be the key to controlling the flow of invisible life energy. The goal of yoga is to raise the energy from the lowest *chakra*, located

at the base of the spine, to the highest, located at the crown of the head. The opening of the highest *chakra* leads to the bliss of union with the Sublime.[51]

4) The practice of *Raja Yoga*, very popular in the West, is related to the concept of the *kundalini*. The *kundalini* has a serpent nature; it "is curled up in the back part of the root *chakra* in three and one-half turns around the sacrum." The *kundalini* moves upward through different techniques. "The practice of Kundalini Yoga consists of a number of bodily postures, expressive movements and utterances, characterological cultivations, breathing patterns, and degrees of concentration. The movements and the body-work should not . . . be considered mere stretching exercises."[52]

7. *The Hindu Scriptures*

a. Hindu sacred literature is divided into two categories: 1) *Shruti* ("what is heard") is the message that the sensitive seers heard through revelation and is only applicable to the authoritative *Vedas*; and 2) *smriti*, the other texts that "are remembered" but are of secondary importance.[53]

b. *Shruti* is the foundation of Hindu scripture. The *Vedas* ("knowledge") are the earliest and most important of the Hindu Scriptures and are considered to be revelations.[54] The *Vedas* (1500-500 B.C.) are divided into "four layers":

1) *Rig Veda*: Composed of 1028 hymns of praise. The oldest collection.

2) *Sama Veda*: A book of songs used in sacrifices.

3) *Yajur Veda*: Sacrificial formulas for the priests.

4) *Atharva Veda*: Contains incantations, spells, and magic formulas.

c. Each *Veda* is divided into four parts:

1) *Mantras*: Basic verses sung during the rituals.

2) *Brahamanas*: Explanation of the verses. They introduce the ideas of transmigration and reincarnation (written between 1000-800 B.C.).

3) *Aranyakas*: Reflections on the meaning of verses.

4) *Upanishads*: Mystical interpretations of verses. They describe ways of release from transmigrations. These books are analogous to the "New Testament" of Christianity. They are a collection of 108 poems written between 800-600 B.C. They emphasize inner contemplation and self-denial, or asceticism.

d. *Smriti* ("remembered") are secondary scriptures. However, they are more popular than the Vedas because they are easy to understand, explain universal truths through symbolism and mythology, and contain some of the most beautiful and exciting stories in the history of world religion literature.[55]

1) *Ramayana*: "The journey of Rama." It contains the teachings of the ancient Hindu sages and presents them through allegory.

2) *Mahabharata*: "The great story." It consists of 220,000 lines in 12 books (four times the size of the Bible), making it the world's longest poem.[56] Within this epic is the *Bhagavad-Gita* ("Song of the Lord"), the most popular of all Hindu Scriptures.[57] The main character of the *Gita* (short form of the name) is Krishna, a disguised incarnation of Vishnu.

3) The *Vedangas* are codes of law, including the *Code of Manu* (250 B.C.). They offer an explanation of Indian ethical/social standards. They justify and explain the division in social classes, or caste system.

4) The *Puranas* ("old tales") consist of legends of the gods (A.D. 500).

5) *Sutras* are a collection of proverbs dealing with social conduct (between 250 B.C. and A.D. 250).

6) *Tantras* deal with mystical teaching, spells, and yoga (A.D. 500-1800).

8. *The Caste System*

a. Caste (*varna*) refers to the division of social ranks and tasks of traditional Indian society.[58] Social classes are fixed at birth and not allowed to change from one generation to another. Its origin lay largely in the color difference between the fair-skinned Aryan invaders and the dark-skinned Dravidian aborigines, whom they conquered.[59]

b. Religion plays a key role in its continuation. The system is supported by two major philosophical presuppositions: the idea of rebirth (*samsara*) and the causal law of *karma*. One is born into a *varna*, or caste, as a reward for his previous *karma*. The general assumption is that the higher the caste, the better the spirituality in previous life.

c. The four major castes are:

1) *Brahmans*	priests and religious teachers
2) *Kshtriyas*	kings, nobles, and warriors
3) *Vaisyas*	cultivators, artisans, and merchants
4) *Sudras*	servants, unskilled workers, and peasants

d. The four *varnas* are first mentioned in the *Rig Veda*, which describes the castes coming forth from the body of the cosmic, primal Man, Purusha. "His mouth became the Brahmin; his arms were made into the Warrior, his thighs the People, and from his feet the Servants were born."[60]

e. Each caste has many subdivisions. There are as many as 25,000 additional sub-castes.[61] Outside the four castes are the "untouchables" or "outcasts," whose occupations rendered them unclean (e.g., cleaning human waste, removing dead animals, and tanning hides). The untouchables usually live in segregated areas outside of a main village or town. However, Mahatma Gandhi called them *Harijans* ("the children of God"). The constitution of India now rules against discrimination on the basis of caste, and the government is granting special benefits to members of the low castes.[62]

f. Syrian Christians, who entered India very early, received a high caste degree, which protected them but did not allow them to proselytize.[63] However, most recent Christian converts in India come from the low castes and the outcasts.[64] Christianity has a relatively low status in India.

9. *Hindu Diversity*

Hinduism is so diverse internally that the only way of defining it acceptably is externally, in terms of people and places. In fact, it is a conglomeration of ideas, beliefs, convictions, and practices (varying from people to people and from region to region).

a. Religious Hinduism, already described.

b. Intellectual Hinduism is heavily dependent on nationalism, patriotism, and traditions. Intellectually-oriented Hindus develop their worldview and the scheme of salvation through *karma*, reincarnation, and performing of caste duties. This form of Hinduism is dominated by the authority of the *Vedas* and *Upanishads*. In intellectual Hinduism there are different schools concerning the Ultimate Reality.[65]

c. Popular or Folk Hinduism is far removed from philosophy and Brahmanism. Millions of Hindus do not even know the existence or names of their ancient scriptural texts. Folk Hindus are influenced by ancestral tradition, animal worship, magic, exorcism, and the occult.[66] Adherents of popular Hinduism are indifferent to the authority of the Vedas and are concerned only about the god who protects them, blesses them, and makes them prosperous. The majority of Hindus adhere to this form.

d. Mystic Hinduism is centered around the claims of gurus that they are avatars, have supernatural gifts of healing, claim the ability to perform miracles, read the inner thoughts of people, and prophesy the future. Some prominent gurus are Sathya Sai Baba, who has millions of followers and claims to be an *avatar* of Vishnu,[67] and Maharishi Mahesh Yogi, founder of the Transcendental Meditation program (TM).[68]

e. Secular Hinduism. Secular Hindus are generally nominal in their beliefs and indifferent to religious practices. They may accept the identity of Hinduism but are primarily concerned with the social and economic development of the Hindu masses, or simply interested in their own and their family's economic progress.

f. Sectarian Hinduism. These are some of the most notorious sects:

1) Shaivism: Worship of Shiva. The worshiper has three horizontal white lines on the forehead.

2) Vaishnavism: Worship of Vishnu. The worshiper has three vertical white lines on the forehead.

3) Tantrism: Worship based on the occultic religious practices and observances of the *Tantras*.

4) Ramaism: Worship of Rama.

6) Krishnaism: Worship of Krishna.

10. *Hindu Culture and Religious Life*

a. It would be impossible to cover the rich variety of Hindu cultural expressions within the confines of this book. India contains over 500,000 villages. In these villages live approximately seven out of ten Indian citizens. There are no "standard" rural Indians. To understand a single village and the people in it is to begin to understand India, but it is no more than a beginning.[69]

b. Red is a symbol of joy and happiness and the color used for marriage ceremonies. Married women are expected to wear a lot of red, but widows are forbidden to do so. White is the color of mourning.[70]

c. Except for the Brahmins, Hindus have no fixed time of worship, and only a few people visit the village temple for daily devotions. The gods are appealed to only at times of difficulties and during village festivals.

d. In most villages, Hinduism is not the classic metaphysical system, but a rather mechanical religion of fasts, feasts, festivals, and prescribed rituals which cover critical periods of life. Many castes, localities, and families form unique cult groups in any given community. Folk beliefs include ghosts, demons, ancestor spirits, and the practice of witchcraft.[71]

e. A variety of feasts, festivals, and rituals concerned with the major crises of birth, a child's first solid meal, puberty, marriage, and death of one of the members bring the families, castes, or villagers together.[72]

f. Each temple is really a house for its particular god. It is the priest's job to look after the image of the god and to treat it like a royal guest. In the morning the priest dresses the image of the god in fine clothes and garlands it with fresh flowers. Food is offered to the god, which worshipers share later on.

g. Inside a Hindu home, regardless of how rich or poor the family is, there is a shrine to the family's chosen god. The shrine may be just a small corner or a whole room. On a shelf or table is a small image of the family god or some colorful pictures. Near it stands a bell, which is rung before prayers. Early in the morning before going to work or school, members of the family will visit the shrine to say prayers and to honor their god. Often the mother performs *puja* (worship) on behalf of the rest of the family.[73]

h. At the time of worship in a temple, Hindus will receive a mark on their forehead, called *tilaka*. These marks are made in various ways with sacred clay, ashes, or sandal-paste.

i. No Hindu eats beef. High castes do not eat any meat, but amongst the lower castes and outcast communities it is fairly common. In Bengal, however, Brahmans are allowed to eat the flesh of goats, deer, and certain varieties of fish. The milk of cows and buffaloes is also popular in the diet of Hindus.[74]

j. Vegetarianism has been related to the concept of non-violence.[75] Hindus need to maintain a pure life in order to be liberated from *samsara* (rebirth) and be united with Brahaman in the next life. They do not intend to harm animals,[76] particularly the cows. They fear that their beloved ones may have been reincarnated as animals.

k. Music is a necessary feature of all marriages, initiations, and other religious ceremonies. In order for the atmosphere to be purified by its auspicious sound, a small orchestra is installed before the entrance of the house or temple where the ceremony is to be held and plays almost continuously. Certain traditional musical themes, called *ragas*, are recognized as creating a mood for meditation when played properly on stringed instruments.[77]

l. The women, in general, are expected to serve their husbands and take care of the home.[78] Indian society emphasizes the changed status that individuals possess at different periods of their lives. Marriage and begetting children is part of the Hindu way of life. Unmarried men are not given positions of importance or considered able to perform sacrifices. Brides are chosen by family elders and parents. It is the "duty of women to perpetuate her race and continue the family line and this is achieved by remaining a loyal and chaste wife."[79] "Women do not go to observe the Vedic worship and they are not allowed to use the sacred mantras."[80]

m. Hindus do not bury corpses but practice cremation on a pyre. The corpse is place on top of a pile of wood. The mound is lit on fire, which consumes the wood and the deceased.

11. *Glossary of Selected Hindu Terms*

a. *Aum.* The most sacred *mantra,* contains the first and last sounds of the Sanskrit alphabet, similar to Alpha and Omega in Greek language. This *mantra* contains all the other *mantras*, all the Vedas,[81] and all the meaning of the universe.[82] This *mantra* is used as the symbol of Hinduism.

b. *Avatar.* An incarnation. The descending of Vishnu to the world in different forms in order to correct growing evils.

c. *Brahman.* A person belonging to the highest caste. The word is derivative from "Brahaman," the Supreme Being or Soul. Originally "*brahman*" meant "one possessed of Brahama" (a god in the *trimurti*). The term is conventionally spelled "*brahmin*" in order to establish more difference with "Brahama" and the *Brahamanas* (sacred writings).

d. *Dharma.* The Hindu word for religion, also translated "duty" or "appropriate action." It is the way a Hindu should live, especially with respect to performing the duties of one's caste. To live according to the *dharma* is to live in harmony with the universe.

e. *Karma.* The law of cause and effect. You will suffer in this life or in future lives for the consequences of your decisions in the past.

f. *Mantra* ("thought form"). A single- or multi-syllable phrase (usually in Sanskrit) on which one meditates. Each *mantra* is identified with a particular deity to the extent that the correctly pronounced *mantra* embodies that deity. The point of repeating the *mantra* is to invoke the powers of that deity and to invite it to enter you.[83] For instance, *Hare Krishna, Hare Krishna, Krishna Krishna, Hare Hare/Hare Rama, Hare Rama, Rama Rama.*[84]

g. *Maya.* The doctrine that the visible world is an illusion that clouds the reality of absolute oneness.

h. *Namaskar.* The Indian word for "greeting."

i. *Nirvana.* The individual self merging into the impersonal and undifferentiated oneness of the Ultimate Self. *Nirvana* is the goal of enlightenment.

j. *Sanskrit.* The language of the Hindu scholars and scriptures.

k. *Vedas.* The earliest Hindu Scriptures. *Veda* means "knowledge" and has the same root as the English word "wisdom" and the Greek *oida* ("to know").[85]

Notes

1   Vasudha Narayanan, "Hinduism," in *Eastern Religions*, ed. Michael D. Coogan (New York: Oxford University Press, 2005), 10.

2   Simon Weightman, "Hinduism," in *A Handbook of Living Religions*, ed. John R. Hinnells (Middlesex, England: Penguin Books, 1985), 192.

3   Sunder Raj, *The Confusion Called Conversion* (New Delhi: Traci, 1986), 130.

4   "Hinduism: The World's Third Largest Religion," *Ontario Consultants on Religious Tolerance*, 2005 [article online]; retrieved on January 10, 2006, from http://www.religioustolerance.org/hinduism.htm.

5   Census of India 2001, "Data on Religion," *Office of the Registrar General, India*, 2004; retrieved on December 27, 2005, from http://www.censusindia.net/ religiondata/ Summary%20Hindus.pdf and http://www.censusindia.net/religiondata/ Summary%20Christians.pdf.

6   "The Largest Hindu Communities," *Adherents*, 2005 [article online]; retrieved on January 28, 2006, from http://www.adherents.com/largecom/com_hindu.html.

7   "Hinduism in the United States," *Wikipedia, the Free Encyclopedia*, 2005 [article online] retrieved on January 13, 2006, from http://en.wikipedia.org/wiki/ Hinduism_in_the_United_States.

8   Gerald James Larson, "Hinduism in India and in America," in *World Religions in America*, ed. Jacob Neusner (Louisville, KY: Westminster John Knox Press, 2003), 125.

9   Roger Schmidt, Gene C. Sager, Gerald T. Carney, Albert C. Muller, Kenneth J. Zanca, Julius J. Jackson Jr., C. Wayne Mayhall, and Jeffrey C. Burke, *Patterns of Religion*, 2nd edition (Belmont, CA: Wadsworth, 2005), 123.

10   William A. Young, *The World's Religions: Worldviews and Contemporary Issues*, 2nd ed. (Upper Saddle, NJ: Pearson Prentice Hall, 2005), 59.

11   *Grolier: The 1996 Multimedia Encyclopedia* (Danbury, CT: Grolier Electronic Publishing, 1996), s.v. "Ancient India." Also see *New Twentieth Century Encyclopedia of Religious Knowledge*, s.v. "Indian Religion."

12   *New Catholic Encyclopedia*, s.v. "Hinduism."

13   Robert A. Guisepi, "Ancient Sumeria," *History World International*, 1985-2005 [article online]; retrieved on December 28, 2005, from http://history-world.org/sumeria.htm.

14   "The Ancient Indus Valley," *Harappa*, 1995-2005 [article online]; retrieved on December 5, 2005, from http://www.harappa.com/har/har0.html.

15 Some of the traditional religious practices of India include an emphasis upon cultic baths, ritual purity, fertility goddesses, animals with anthropomorphic features, and phallic symbolism. These non-Aryan emphases were incorporated into the developing tradition which was directed primarily by the Indo-European people. Alf Hiltebbeitel, "Hinduism,"*The Encyclopedia of Religion*, ed. Mircea Eliade (New York: Macmillan, 1989).

16 John B. Noss, *Man's Religions*, 6th ed. (New York: Macmillan, 1980), 74.

17 Schmidt et al., *Patterns of Religions*, 126.

18 Griffiths, "Hinduism," 1124.

19 Lewis M. Hopfe, *Religions of the World* (New York: Macmillan, 1983), 100.

20 "Selections from the *Baghavad-Gita*," in Robert E. Van Voorst, *Anthology of World Scriptures*, 5th ed. (Belmont, CA: Wadsworth, 2006), 52.

21 S. A. Nigosian, *World Religions* (London: Edward Arnold Publisher, 1975), 107-8. See also Louis Renove, ed. *Hinduism* (New York: George Brazilller, 1961), 27.

22 Nimian Smart, *Religions of India* (Englewood Cliffs, NJ: Prentice Hall, 1993), 57-60.

23 "*Brahaman* (neuter substantive) is pure Being, pure Consciousness, the Unlimited, or, according to another triad, pure Being, pure Consciousness and Beatitude." Madeleine Biardeau, *Hinduism: The Anthropology of a Civilization* (Delhi: Oxford University Press, 1989), 17.

24 V. P. Hemant Kanitkar and W. Owen Cole, *Hinduism*, Teach Yourself Series (Berkshire, England: Cox & Wyman, 1996), 40.

25 Board of Directors, Than Tao Mahaprom Foundation Erawan Hotel, "History of the Brahma of Erawan Hotel Shrine" (Bangkok: Than Tao Mahaprom Foundation, Buddhist Era 2532). Robin Fowler, "Spirits at Home in Modern Thailand," *Dallas Times Herald*, April 5, 1987, D-5.

26 Kenneth W. Morgan, *The Religion of the Hindus* (New York: The Ronald Press Company, 1953), 75.

27 Hemant Kaniotkar and W. Owen Cole, *Hinduism*, Teach Yourself Books (London: NTC Publishing Group, 1995), 24-26.

28 An illustration is of a chick that breaks an egg in order to have life. The egg is destroyed, but life continues. This principle is seen to permeate all of the natural order.

29 "Lingam," *Wikipedia: The Free Encyclopedia*, 2005 [article online]; retrieved on January 8, 2006, from http://en.wikipedia.org/wiki/Lingam.

30 Kanitkar and Cole, *Hinduism*, 27.

31 See David Kinsley, *Hindu Goddesses: Visions of the Divine Feminine in the Hindu Religious Tradition* (Los Angeles: University of California Press, 1988).

32 Kantikar and Cole, *Hinduism*, 31. Raj says that Shiva "returned to his wife Parvati after a journey lasting 14 years. Arriving home at night, he found Parvati asleep with a young boy beside her. Suspecting her of infidelity he immediately lopped off the boy's head and then discovered it was his own son." Prakash A. Raj, *Kathmandu & the Kingdom of Nepal* (Victoria, Australia: Lonely Planet, 1983), 16.

33 Jnan Bahadur Sakya, *Short Description of Gods, Goddesses and Ritual Objects of Buddhism and Hinduism in Nepal* (Kathmandu, Nepal: Handicraft Association of Nepal, 1995), 37.

34 Larry D. Shinn, *The Dark Lord: Cult Images and the Hare Krishnas in America* (Philadelphia: The Westminster Press, 1987), 23.

35 C. George Fry and others, *Great Asian Religions* (Grand Rapids: Baker, 1984), 54.

36 John Lennon and George Harrison [Beatles], *Chant and Be Happy: The Power of Mantra Meditation* (Los Angeles: The Bhaktivendanta Book Trust, 1983), 1-10.

37 Krishna participated in "sports" with his seven wives and other16,100 married girls, although their love is seen as moral, respectable, and approved. William George Archer, *The Love of Krishna in Indian Painting and Poetry* (New York: Macmillan, 1957), 70.

38 Prabhupada, *Krishna: The Supreme Personality of Godhead*, xxi.

39 Morgan, *The Religion of the Hindus*, 112-14.

40 Narayanan, "Hinduism," 71-73.

41 The chief sacrificial victims are the sheep, the ox, and the goat. Morgan, *The Religion of the Hindus*, 111.

42 "Sacred Cow," *Wikipedia: The Free Encyclopedia*, 2005 [article online]; retrieved on January 5, 2006, from http://en.wikipedia.org/wiki/Sacred_cow.

43 Sandhya Jain, "Did Vedic Hindus Really Eat Cow?" *The Hindu Universe*, 2001 [article online]; retrieved January 21, 2006, from http://www.hindunet.com/forum/showflat.php?Cat=&Board=beef&Number=59176&Main=11992.

44 Ibid., 43.

45 Mary McGee, "Hinduism," in *The Sacred Path: Understanding Eastern Religions*, ed. C. Scott Littleton (London: Thornsons, 2003), 18-19.

46 Tinu Ruparell, "Hinduism," in *Encountering Religion*, ed. Ian S. Markhan and Tinu Ruparell (Oxford: Blackwell, 2001), 170.

47 David L. Johnson, *A Reasoned Look at Asian Religions* (Minneapolis: Bethany, 1985), 83.

48 McGee, "Hinduism," 30.

49 Narayanan, "Hinduism," 63-65.

50 "Introduction: Four Main Paths," *ISKCON Educational Services*, 2004 [article online]; retrieved on January 7, 2006, from http://hinduism.iskcon.com/practice/.

51 Mary Pat Fisher, *Living Religions*, 5th ed. (Upper Saddle River, NJ: Prentice-Hall, 2002), 97-98.

52 "Kundalini," *Wikipedia: The Free Encyclopedia*, 2005 [article online]; retrieved on January 25, 2006, from http://en.wikipedia.org/wiki/Kundalini#Kundalini_rising.

53 Alex Smith, "Religion and Scripture: The Function of the Special Books in Religion," in *Encountering Religion*, ed. Ian S. Markham and Tinu Ruparell (Oxford: Blackwell, 2001), 82.

54 Van Voorst, *Anthology of World Scriptures*, 26-27. "Shruti: The Four Vedas," *ISKCON Educational Services*, 2004 [article online]; retrieved on January 8, 2006, from http://hinduism.iskcon.com/ tradition/1106.htm.

55 Van Voorst, *Anthology of World Scriptures*, 27-31; "Smriti," *Wikipedia: The Free Encyclopedia*, 2005 [article online]; retrieved on January 8, 2006, from. http://en.wikipedia.org/wiki/Smriti.

56 Ruparell, "Hinduism," 187.

57 "The Bhagavad-Gita Online," *Bhagavad-Gita* [book online, with commentaries]; retrieved on January 6, 2006, from http://www.baghavad-gita.com/; original translation by Abhay Charan De Bhaktivedanta Swami Prahhhupada, *Bhagavad-Gita as It Is* (Los Angeles: The Bhaktivedanta Book Trust, 1976).

58 Denise L. Carmody and T. L. Brink, *Ways to the Center: An Introduction to World Religions* (Belmont, CA: Wadsworth, 2006), 88-89.

59 The actual word used for "caste" in Sanskrit is *varna*, meaning "color." Selvaraj Muthiah, "Approaching and Retaining Brahmin Converts in the Hindu Context: A Case Study," (D.P.Th. diss., Adventist International Institute of Advanced Studies, Silang, Cavite, Philippines, 1998), 39.

60 "The Creation of the Caste System," from *Rig-Veda* 10.90, in Van Voorst, *Anthology of World Religions*, 37.

61 John Renard, *The Handy Religion Answer Book* (Canton, MI: Visible Ink Press, 2002), 284.

62 "Hinduism," *Refuge-Outreach*, 2005 [article online]; retrieved on November 28, 2005, from http://refuge-outreach.org/religions/hinduism.htm.

63 Kenneth Scott Latourette, *The Thousand Years of Uncertainty: 500 A.D. to 1500 A.D. , Vol. 2, A History of the Expansion of Christianity* (Grand Rapids: Zondervan, 1970), 282.

64 See Sender Raj, "Why the Untouchables Seek Christ," chap. in *The Confusion Called Conversion* (New Delhi: Traci, 1986), 81-85.

65 Stephen A. Grunlan and Marvin K. Mayers, *Cultural Anthropology: A Christian Perspective*, 2nd ed. (Grand Rapids: Zondervan, 1988), 135.

66 S. M. Michael, *The Cultural Context of Evangelization in India* (Pune, India: Ishvani, 1980), 96.

67 "Sathya Sai Baba," *Wikipedia: The Free Encyclopedia,* 2005 [article online]; retrieved on January 22, 2006, from http://en.wikipedia.org/wiki/Sathya_Sai_Baba.

68 "Maharishi Mahesh Yogi," *The Transcendental Meditation Program*, 2005 [article online]; retrieved on January 12, 2006, from http://www.tm.org/main_pages/maharishi.html.

69 Grunlan and Meyers, *Cultural Anthropology*, 184.

70 P. Raj, *Kathmandu & the Kingdom of Nepal*, 17.

71   Elman E. Service, "A Village in India," chap. in *Profiles in Ethnology*, rev. ed. (New York: Harper & Row, 1971), 479.

72   David M. Knipe, "The Journey of a Lifebody," *Hindu Gateway*, 2005 [article online]; retrieved on January 8, 2006, from http://www.hindugateway.com/library/rituals/.

73   Morgan, *The Religion of the Hindus*, 176-84.

74   Ibid., 111, 112.

75   David W. Shenk, *Global Gods: Exploring the Role of Religions in Modern Societies* (Ontario: Herald Press, 1995), 102.

76   This means no animal slaughter beyond the needs of sacrifice. Madeleine Biardeau, *Hinduism: The Anthropology of a Civilization*, trans. Richard Nice (Delhi: Oxford University Press, 1989), 31.

77   Ibid., 172.

78   "Hindu religious texts sometimes imagine a woman as a snake, hell's entrance, death, a prostitute, or an adulteress. In Manu's code, slaying a woman was one of the minor offenses. In the Hindu family, the basic unit of society, woman therefore carried a somewhat negative image. . . . India mainly honored women for giving birth and serving their husbands." Carmody and Brink, *Ways to the Center*, 114.

79   Ranjana Kumari, *Female Sexuality in Hinduism* (New Delhi: ISPCK, 1988), 14.

80   Parrinder, *Introduction to Asian Religions*, 50.

81   According to Upanishad 1.1.1-10, in Van Voorst, *Anthology of World Scriptures*, 51.

82   *Aum* is believed to be the first primordial sound. Ross, *Hinduism*, 131.

83   See Rice, *Eastern Definitions*, 247.

84   Lennon and Harrison, *Chant and Be Happy*, title page.

85   David Frawley, "Hindu and Vedic Knowledge in Modern Age," *Hindu Books Universe*, 1994-2003 [book online]; retrieved on January 7, 2006, from http://www.hindubooks.org/david_frawley/riverheaven/hindu_and_vedic_knowledge_in_modern_age/veda_and_yoga.htm.

CHAPTER 6

Christian Witness to Hindus

1. *Introduction*

a. Witnessing among Hindus is not an easy task. Missionaries must overcome many obstacles, one of them being prejudice. Mahatma Gandhi wrote: "When I was a youth, I remember a Hindu having become a convert to Christianity. The whole town understood that the initiation took the shape of this well-bred Hindu partaking of beef and brandy in the name of Jesus Christ. These things got on my nerves."[1] In time, Gandhi rectified his statement, admitting that it was only a prejudiced rumor, but this statement was reprinted in most of the subsequent editions of his autobiography.

b. Christian witnesses must remember that a change of presuppositions is a miracle. How can we demonstrate that there is only one God? Conversion is a change of assumptions that only the Holy Spirit can produce. Missionaries must depend on prayer as they do cross-cultural evangelism.

2. *Hinduism and Christianity Contrasted*

HINDUISM	CHRISTIANITY
GOD Impersonal. Many gods and goddesses	Personal. One God.
HUMANITY Continuous in the sense of being extended from the Being of God.	Discontinuous in the sense of being separate from the Being of God; continuous in the sense of being made in God's image.
HUMANITY'S PROBLEM Ignorance.	Moral rebellion.
THE SOLUTION Liberation from illusion and ignorance	Forgiveness of sin and reconciliation with the personal holy God.
THE MEANS Detachment from desire and awareness of unity with the divine through self-effort.	Repentance from sin and trusting in the completed and substitutionary work of Jesus.
THE OUTCOME Merge into Oneness; the individual disappears.	Eternal fellowship with God; the person is fulfilled in a loving relationship with God.
DEATH Man is born again and again, 8.4 million times, in a cycle of birth and rebirth.	Resurrection to receive reward.
SOCIETY Divided into four divinely instituted castes, not to intermingle.	All one family in Christ, who is the head.
HISTORY Cyclic. Everything is repeated age after age.	Linear. The present world order to be destroyed. New earth to continue forever.
SALVATION To be earned by knowledge, devotion, and good works.	Free, given by God as a gift.

Table 6.1

3. *Biblical Framework for a Basic Christian Witness*

The following list of doctrines is not exhaustive, nor are the passages mentioned a full representation of biblical teachings. This section intends to provide a biblical background of some Christian doctrines, which will then be compared and contrasted with the beliefs of Hindus.

a. Since eternity, the Father, the Son, and the Holy Spirit (1 John 5:7; Matt 28:19; 2 Cor 13:14) have shared a unique, loving, and personal relationship (John 17:24), existing as one God (Isa 43:10; Eph 4:6). In contrast with pantheistic ideas, the Bible presents God as distinct from His creation (Rom 1:20-23). The Bible also condemns polytheism (Deut 6:4, Exod 20:3), idol worship (Exod 20:4-6; Isa 44:6-20), and self-deification (Eze 28:2-9; Isa 47:8-11).

b. It is essential to establish that everyone is a sinner (Rom 3:9,23). Some Hindus, like Krishna devotees, will not object to this, but others will reject this view. However, biblical understanding of sin (Psalm 51, Rom 14:23; Jas 4:17; 1 John 3:4, etc.) will be necessary in order to testify that Christ is the sole Redeemer (Heb 10:10). Once sin is understood, Christ and *avatars* can be compared and contrasted.

c. The Christian witness must know by experience what it means to accept Jesus as the only Savior (Acts 4:12). Furthermore, he must know and understand the biblical teachings of Christ. In Jesus Christ is the fullness of the Godhead (Col 2:9). In the beginning He existed with God (John 1:1) and was God (John 5:18, 8:58, 20:28; Titus 2:13; Rom 9:5; 1 John 5:20; Heb 1:8). The unique and sufficient incarnation of Christ is in sharp contrast with the multiple incarnations of Vishnu.

d. Salvation is not a result of works (Eph 2:8-9) and rests solely on what Jesus Christ did on the cross (Heb 9:9-14). He lived a sinless life (2 Cor 5:21; Heb 4:15; 1 Pet 2:22), died on the cross (Heb 12:2), rose from the dead (1 Cor 15:4; Rom 4:25; Eph 1:20), and now lives to intercede for those who believe (Heb 7:25; 2 Tim 2:5). In Him, Christians look forward to resurrection (1 Tim 4:16) with Jesus Christ as Forerunner (1 Cor 15:23). Hindus, on the other hand, expect many lives of slavery to immutable *karma*.

e. The Bible calls Christians to live holy lives (1 Pet 1:16; Rom 12:1-2) and to keep their behavior excellent among unbelievers so that they may glorify God (1 Pet 2:12; Matt 5:16). The body is the temple of the Holy Spirit (1 Cor 6:19-20) and must be properly kept for God's glory (Rom 12:1-2; 1 Cor 10:31).

Human relationships play an important role in a Christian's life (Luke 2:52; Rom 12:10-20). Unlike Hindu ideas, Christianity upholds the quality of women and men before God (Gal 3:28). Hindus identify externals as reflective of holiness.

4. *Hindrances to the Evangelization of Hindus*

The following are some of the issues that have alienated Hindus and proved a hindrance to evangelism:[2]

a. Food habits among Christians, such as beef consumption, are totally contrary to Hindu practices.

b. The Christian way of worship is predominantly Western in form.

c. Excessive social mingling of boys and girls in Christian families and in religious activities go against Hindu culture.

d. The practice of Christians forbids the use of the *tilaka* [the red spot on the forehead], which symbolizes devotion to a Hindu god.

e. Christianity appears as a foreign religion–Western.

f. Christianity is seen as a threat to Indian culture and identity because of the prevailing thought that "Indian" means "Hindu."

g. Hindus share the wrong notion that Christians are not patriotic.

h. Hindus tend to assume that only "untouchables" (*Harijans*) embrace Christianity.

i. The caste system is the Hindu's strongest forte of social security. Conversion to Christianity destroys this, leading to excommunication from the community, damage to family reputation, termination of marital prospects, physical assault, and persecution.

j. Due to superstition, many Hindus live in constant fear of invoking the wrath of the Kula Devata (family god) if they accept the gods of other religions.

k. Hindus fear the of loss of property upon conversion to Christianity.

l. Privileges and positions in society are lost because of the non-recognition of caste distinction in the Christian faith.

m. Low-caste people hesitate to mingle with Christians (even socially) because Christians are perceived as a middle-class people.

n. Students converted to Christianity may suffer the loss of economic privileges, such as withdrawal of financial aid by the government.

5. *Theological Bridges*

a. It is necessary to understand that Hinduism revolves around a different center than does Christianity, asking fundamentally different questions and supplying different answers. Therefore, the use of any theological bridge is fraught with difficulty. No concept of Hinduism can be accepted into Christianity without change, but there are some bridges that can be grouped into two categories:1) Bridges that may be used with minor adjustments and 2) those that require radical changes.[3]

b. Bridges that need minor adjustments:

1) The concept of God. Even though Hindus hold a pantheistic world view, it is not necessary to defend the existence of God.

2) Respect for Scripture. Hindu respect for sacred writings can be applied towards the unique authority of the Bible. Unlike any other religious community, Hindus will listen attentively to an exposition of scripture.

3) The person of Christ. The quality of Christ's relationship with people, his teachings (particularly the Sermon on the Mount), and his unique vicarious self-giving and suffering have a strong appeal to the Hindu.

4) The doctrine of *karma*. The Hindu seeks freedom from the cycle of rebirths which his sin causes. He must be told of Jesus Christ who, His suffering and death on the cross, triumphed over sin and has taken upon Himself the penalty of the sins of mankind.

c. Bridges which require a radical, conceptual redefinition:

1) Christianity and Hinduism differ radically in their understanding of history. The biblical teaching that God created the world is an utterly foreign

idea to the Hindu mind. The witness can use this dissimilarity as a bridge by stressing the purposes of God in time, creation, the historical resurrection, and the coming judgment.

2) Spirituality is very noticeable among those who stress devotion, such as the Hare Krishnas. The emphasis on devotion and austerity are very commendable aspects of the Hindu way of life, but the Christian communicator must stress that spirituality is not an end in itself, nor is it merely by spiritual exercises that one inherits the Kingdom.[4]

3) The belief in the incarnation of God must be radically redefined in Christian communication. Hindus believe in incarnations, but this is not enough. Christ was not just one more *avatar*. They believe that avatars came to the world to destroy sinners, and this requires repeated *avatars*. The incarnation of Christ is unique, sufficient for all time, and is rooted in the love of God's saving sinners.

4) Their distorted views of the Trinity. The Hindu triad is radically different from the Christian concept of three persons in one God. Thorough dialogue, clarification, and redefinition are indispensable.

6. *Christian Witness*

a. Generally, during the initial contact, Hindus will speak. The Christian must listen patiently and attentively. Do not assume you know what your friends believe. Hinduism allows many varied interpretations. Ask questions and listen carefully to the answers. Dialogue will help you to know their thoughts on religion. The knowledge of their background and thinking will be useful while sharing the gospel with them.

b. Christians should avoid condemning Hinduism. Hindus will be able to see the truth for themselves after it has been presented.

c. Christians should not argue; they might win a point but lose a soul. Differences should be handled with respect after a friendship has been established.

d. Through love and friendship a Christian may earn the right to share the gospel with Hindus. "The true heart-expression of Christlike sympathy, given in simplicity, has power to open the door of hearts that need the simple, delicate touch of the Spirit of Christ."[5]

e. Christian witnesses should be willing to adopt as much as possible from the Hindu culture without compromising the integrity of the Christian message. We should enunciate the gospel in Indian categories so that the Hindu can understand the message. In order to achieve this, we should make continuous applications to daily life. We should deal with the problems, questions, and needs of the listeners by communicating the gospel through drama, discourse, dialogue, Indian music, etc.

f. Offer Jesus' forgiveness.[6] A convert from Hinduism who became an evangelist said: "I have never yet failed to get a hearing if I talk to them about forgiveness of sins or peace and rest in your heart."[7] Forgiveness is a real need for Hindus because it is not available in their system.

g. Keep God's personhood in mind. A personal God must be related to in terms of morality, obedience, and trust. If God is personal, then sin is not a matter of ignorance but of moral rejection and the breaking of a relationship. Using familiar images of interpersonal relationships will help you find ways to illustrate the Christian perspective on spiritual issues. For instance, the parable of the prodigal son can help to explain the meaning, the consequences, and the resolution of sin. The way to restore a relationship is by confessing your guilt and requesting forgiveness. God's love is more powerful than the wrath of the gods of Hinduism.

> We must tell them that the fruit of worshiping the true God is 'love, joy, peace patience, kindness, goodness, faithfulness, gentleness, and self-control' (Galatians 5:22-23). *They know this intuitively and also through the sayings of the sages of their own religion*, and yet they continue to worship the gods and spirits that lead them astray and only enslave them.[8]

h. Speak to the context of the listeners. Be deeply involved in their lives. Deal openly with their problems, questions, and needs. Health is one of the natural bridges to reach the Hindus. They will be open to the gospel as Christians seek to alleviate suffering through medical missionary work. Vegetarian missionaries will definitely gain the respect of many Hindus.

i. Have a humble spirit. In many respects, Hindus see Christians as spiritually inferior. Eating meat is seen as a proof of this. Recognize what Hindus consider essential qualities in a spiritual leader (*guru*): willing to wait, willing to mortify his body and desires, willing to suffer pain, and willing to fast. Christian leaders with these types of spiritual qualifications are a powerful means of communication.

j. Focus on Jesus. Present them with the New Testament. Let your friend know that Gandhi said: "Your lives will be incomplete unless you reverently study the teachings of Jesus."[9]

k. Be aware of differing definitions. When you speak of God, man, salvation, or sin, your Hindu friends will hear their own versions of your presentation of the gospel, based on their own worldview. "Born again" will refer to reincarnation, which is something from which they want to be liberated.

l. It is not correct to ask a Hindu about which caste he belongs to. Modern education discourages such questions, unless you are well acquainted with the person. Such a question could be compared to asking Americans how much salary they make annually.[10]

7. *Responding to Hindrances and Objections*

a. "Christianity will disrupt our culture and my family."[11]

1) There are several cultural factors that might prevent Hindus from considering Christianity. Many Hindus think they must reject their culture before they can accept Christianity. Proper contextualization (adaptation to the context) will help Christians remain one with their people.[12]

2) Second, there is a cultural/religious pride among educated Hindus that prevents them from considering other religions.

3) The third reason arises from the association that Christianity had with colonial exploitation. We must always keep focused on Jesus Christ and His salvation and separate that message as much as possible from Western culture. After all, Jesus was an Asian, and Christianity has its roots in Asia, not in the West.

4) Fourth, the extended Indian family does not allow individuals to make their own decisions.[13] The actions of one member of the family affect the family as a whole.

5) Ghandi was right when he said that "conversion must not mean denationalization."[14] The task of a cross-cultural evangelist is not to preach the Western culture, but to preach Jesus and His truth as revealed in biblical doctrines. Indians can be Christians and still be proud of their national heritage.

6) The price for accepting Christ might indeed be high, but Jesus has promised that those who pay such a price "will receive a hundred times as much and will inherit eternal life" (Matt 19:29).

b. "Jesus Christ is not unique."

1) Hindus view Jesus as an *avatar*. They may be willing to incorporate Jesus into their pantheon without accepting Him as the exclusive incarnation of God. Gandhi represented typical Hindu thinking when he said, "I . . . do not take as literally true the text that Jesus is the only begotten Son of God. God cannot be the exclusive Father and I cannot ascribe exclusive divinity to Jesus."[15]

2) There are distinct differences between the incarnation of Jesus and that of Vishnu:[16]

VISHNU	JESUS
At least nine incarnations (some claim more) in both animal and human form.	One incarnation in human form.
The stories of the *avatars* are mythical in nature. If it were shown that there were no historical basis to the stories, it would have no effect on their meaning and influence.	History is very important to the veracity of Jesus' claims and to the salvation that He accomplished on our behalf (1 Cor 15:14, 17; 1 John 1:1-3).
The purpose of Vishnu's incarnations was "for the destruction of evil-doers." *Bhagavad-Gita*, 4:8.	The purpose of Jesus' incarnation was to "seek and to save what was lost" (Luke 19:10; also see John 3:17; John 10:10).
The *avatars* pointed to a way by which we can attain enlightenment over a period of many lifetimes: "But striving zealously, with sins cleansed, the disciplined man, perfected through many rebirths, then (finally) goes to the highest goal" *Bhagavad-Gita*, 6:45.	Jesus points to Himself as the way by which to receive eternal life immediately (John 6:29; 40; 10:9-10; 14:6; 11:25-26; 1 John 5:10-13).

Vishnu incarnates periodically as an *avatar* when the need arises, and then the *avatar* dies and is reabsorbed back into Brahman.	Jesus' incarnation was a unique event. His sacrifice was "once for all" (Heb 9:26-28). He died and rose from the dead.

Table 6.2

c. "There are many paths to God."

1) This is probably the most common Hindu objection to Christianity. Since the ultimate reality is an undifferentiated oneness and is contained in each person, an individual can choose whichever way is best suited for him or her. This idea is reflected in the often-repeated "All paths lead to the top of the mountain" and "All religions are one."

2) Do not argue about this issue in initial contacts. Emphasize that the gospel of Jesus Christ is intended for the whole world. This all-embracing Christ will naturally appeal to the Hindu. Little by little the Hindu will understand the uniqueness of Jesus.

d. "I must pay for my own karmic debt."

1) Hindus believe that actions have consequences both now and in subsequent lives, and that each person bears the consequences of his or her own actions alone. In one sense, the law of *karma* is true in that the one who sins will personally reap the consequences of that sin. Paul wrote, "A man reaps what he sows" (Gal 6:7).

2) One must put this issue in the context of God's being personal. If God is personal, then our sin is ultimately an affront to the moral authority of a holy God. If God is an impersonal force, then moral laws become more like the laws of nature; an impersonal nature cannot offer forgiveness when we break its laws. Again, the way to restore a relationship is by confessing your guilt and requesting forgiveness.

3) Forgiveness is a radical alternative to *karma*, with the difference that when we forgive the one who has wronged us, we bear on ourselves the hurt and the consequences caused by the other's action. This is precisely what Jesus accomplished on the cross.

Notes

1   Mahatma K. Gandhi, *The Story of My Experiment with Truth* (Navjeevan, India: Ahmedabad, 1927), 85; quoted in Sunder Raj, *The Confusion Called Conversion* (New Delhi: Traci, 1986), 37.

2   The Lausanne Committee for World Evangelization, "Christian Witness to Hindu People: Lausanne Occasional Paper # 14," *The Lausanne Committee for World Evangelization* [document online]; available on January 30, 2006, at http://www.lausanne.org/Brix?pageID=14650.

3   Most materials for this section on theological bridges have been adapted from The Lausanne Committee, "Christian Witness to Hindus," 632-38.

4   Lausanne, "Christian Witness to Hindus," 646.

5   Ellen G. White, *Testimonies for the Church* (Mountain View, CA: Pacific Press, 1948), 9:30.

6   Unless otherwise stated, the rest of these suggestions are taken from Dean C. Halverson, "Hinduism," in *The Compact Guide to World Religions*, ed. Dean C. Halverson (Minneapolis, MN: Bethany, 1996), 92-95.

7   David Hesselgrave, *Communicating Christ Cross-Culturally* (Grand Rapids: Zondervan, 1978), 169.

8   Madasamy Thirumalai, *Sharing Your Faith with a Hindu* (Minneapolis, MN: Bethany, 2002), 73. Italics in original.

9   Ananad Hingorani, *The Message of Jesus Christ by M. K. Gandhi* (Bombay: Bharatiya Vidya Bhavan, 1964), 23.

10   Thirumalai, *Sharing your Faith with a Hindu*, 75.

11   The following responses to hindrances and objections are from Halverson, "Hinduism," 95-100.

12   Donald A. McGavran, *Ethnic Realities and the Church* (Pasadena, CA: William Carey Library, 1979), 95.

13   "The two main pillars supporting the whole structure of Hindu society are the caste system and the joint family." S. M. Michael, *The Cultural Context of Evangelization in India* (Ishvine, Pune: Satprakashan Indore, 1980), 24.

14   Swami Aksharananda, "Mahatma Gandhi on Conversion," *Stephen Knapp*, 2001 [article online]; retrieved on January 7, 2006, from http://www.stephen-knapp.com/ mahatma_gandhi_on_conversion.htm.

15   Hingorani, *The Message of Jesus Christ*, 53.

16   Halverson, "Hinduism," 98.

CHAPTER 7

Jainism

1. *Introduction*

a. A contemporary of Gautama Buddha, Vardhamana Mahavira launched a movement that eventually became known as Jainism. He adopted the title "*Jina*," meaning "conqueror." The religion draws its name from the experience of conquering the mundane. The Jina's basic message was that self-denial would win salvation for the devotee. Jainism is a religion of strict ethics and self-control, leading to a purification of the self.

b. Together with Buddhism, Jainism was one of the two major attempts to reform Hinduism. If one was a form of relaxation of Hindu ideals, the other made the path even more rigorous. While Buddhism is a "Middle Way" between affluence and asceticism, Jainism revolves around an extreme ascetic ideal. The message and example of 24 teacher-conquerors was that the human being, without supernatural aid, is capable of conquering the bondage of physical existence and achieving freedom from rebirth. This conquest is to be achieved only by the most rigorous renunciation of all physical comforts and social constraints.

c. This ethnic religion–mostly confined to India–is in a process of extinction. Today they comprise about 4.5 million followers.[1]

2. *The Rise of the Jain Religion*

a. The Jain teachings are not thought to have originated with Mahavira. Followers of the Jain religion believe that the Jain "way of life" has always existed.[2] Mahavira is not considered the founder but, rather, the preacher of this religion. Supposedly, Mahavira had 23 divine precursors called *tirthankaras*, a title meaning "crossing-maker," which point to their role as teachers and examples for others who seek the same goal. With the exception of the twenty-third *tirthankara*, the descriptions concerning the others is fantastic. For instance, the first Jina, Rishabha, was more than one mile high. The twenty-second, Aristanemi, lived 84,000 years. Pasava, the twenty-third precursor about 250 years before Mahavira, died when he was one hundred years old.

b. Vardhamana Mahavira (599-527 B.C.)

1) The last great *tirthankara* was born Jnatrputra (also spelled as Nataputta) Vardhamana in northeast India, near modern Patna. Like Siddartha Gautama, the founder of Buddhism, Vardhamana was born in the warrior class and raised in luxury.

2) At thirty years of age, Vardhamana renounced his caste privileges and took up the life of a possessionless mendicant (a begging monk). For more than twelve years he devoted himself to renunciation and detachment from worldly desires. Among other things, he spent several days squatting without moving, meditating uncovered in the intense summer heat, enduring fire lit under him while meditating, etc. At the end of this time, having reached complete understanding of the nature of the universe and absolute detachment from worldly desires, he took the titles of *Jina* and *Mahavira*, and began teaching others. "*Mahavira*" is an honorary title meaning "great hero." "*Jina,*" meaning "conqueror," is also an honorary term, but not a proper name.[3]

3) His rules were the Three Jewels: Right Faith, Right Knowledge, and Right Conduct.[4] He gave much importance to meditation and penance, both for monks and laymen.

4) In about 527 B.C. he died of voluntarily starvation, the ultimate act of self-denial. By the time of his death at the age of 72, he had gathered about 500,000 followers, including 14,000 monks, 36,000 nuns, 159,000 laymen, and 318,000 laywomen.[5]

3. *Jain Development*

a. By Christ's time, Jains were divided into two groups. The issue of nudity was the preeminent source of disunity.[6]

1) *Shvetambaras* ("white-clad"), so named because its monks and nuns dressed in white. They were located in the northern and western India.

2) *Digambaras* ("sky-clad"), so named because their male ascetics went naked. Today some use a loin cloth, imposed by Muslim rulers in the past. Unlike Shvetambaras, Digambaras do not allow women to take full monastic vows (they must await rebirth as males in order to pursue full ascetic careers and thus attain liberation). They have only two possessions: a broom of feathers dropped by peacocks and a gourd for drinking water.[7] There are only about sixty-five Digambara ascetics left in India; they are located in south and central India.[8]

b. Jains were experiencing rapid growth until the thirteenth century when membership began to recede because of competition with Islam. From this time onward, Jainism went through movements of reform and renewal. Two were very influencial:

1) *Sthanakavasis* resulted from the fifteen and sixteenth century reform movement among the Shvetambaras. Still active today, its members are recognizable by their practice of wearing a cloth or mask over their mouth and nose. They objected to the veneration of images.

2) *Taranapanthas* resulted from a similar movement of reform in the seventeenth century among the Digambaras by also objecting to the veneration of images.

c. Though relatively small in numbers, Jains notably influenced the history of their country. Its adherents are generally very rich. "Jains today constitute one percent of the Indian population. And yet, Jains are said to contribute a proportionately considerable share of all Indian philanthropic donations. Their money comes predominately from environmentally sound, non-violent occupations–banking, real estate, diamonds, pawning, computer technology, law and adjudication, accounting, medicine, government positions, publishing, teaching, ecological science, aesthetics, astronomy, physics and engineering."[9]

4. *Jain Texts*

a. All scriptures considered sacred are called *Agamas*, "tradition." Most Jains call their scripture the *Siddhanta*, "doctrine."[10]

b. Before the division between Shvetambaras and Digambaras, they did not have major scriptures. Digambaras began to write their own soon after the division, by Christ's time. Shvetambaras had a council during the 5th century A.D. and, as a result, produced the *Siddhanta*. The Shvetambaras scriptures include the remembered sermons and discourses of Mahavira. "The Digambaras hold that the original teachings are lost, but maintain that in their texts the essence is preserved."[11]

5. *Basic Beliefs of Jainism*

a. The human being can conquer the limitations of physical existence and attain immortality by means of rigorous ascetic discipline.

b. Jainism's key beliefs about *samsara* and *karma* are related to Hinduism. As in Hinduism and Buddhism, Jainism also believes in *karma*. Unlike Buddhism, Jains affirm the existence of individual selves, or *jivas* (often translated as "souls"). The *jiva* is innately omniscient and eternal.

c. In the Jain view, *karma* is a subtle form of sticky matter–minute particles that individuals accumulate as they act and think.[12] *Karma* clings to the *jiva*, obscuring the *jiva*'s innate capacities. This obscuring of its faculties causes the *jiva* to be reborn into an infinite series of physical existences. One must start the path to liberation by avoiding the acquisition of more *karma*, especially through acts that cause pain to other beings. The only way in which the *jiva* can be set free of this karmic bondage and resultant rebirth involves the ascetic life, which reduces the *karma* one accumulates.[13]

d. Jainism perceives life of any form on earth to be of equal worth to the human. The compassion resulting from this belief is the first step in rectifying the endless unhappiness that assails all organisms.

> Every organism possesses a soul, known as *jiva*, from a minute amoeba virus, to the enormous redwood tree with its 36,000 cubit feet of life. That soul is independent, endowed with a strong personality and individual destiny. Every organism is capable of achieving salvation, happiness, and must be allowed to continue its path.[14]

e. Related to the concept above, Jains stress *ahimsa* ("non-injury" or "non-violence"). Although a similar principle can be found in many religions, Jainism adheres to this in an extreme form. It involves the willingness to separate oneself from acts of injury, aggression, and killing. *Ahimsa* also includes thoughts and language. Language can be violent and therefore cause negative *karma*. When walking, Jains avoid killing or injuring as many forms of life as they can. When drinking water, there are life forms that are ingested and therefore killed. This accrues karmic residue and is therefore not good. So water is often strained to remove as many of these life forms as possible. The goal is to avoid violence in all forms–ahimsa–thus eliminating *karma* and making liberation easier. Jains, obviously, are strict vegetarians. A Shvetambara' scripture (*Sutrakritanga*, 1.7.1-9) says:

> He who lights a fire kills living beings; he who extinguishes it kills the fire. Therefore a wise man who well considers the Law should light no fire. Earth contains life, and water contains life; jumping or flying insects fall in the fire; dust-born vermin and beings live in the wood. All these beings are burned by lighting a fire.
> Plants are beings that have a natural development. Their bodies require nourishment, and they all have their individual life. Reckless men who cut them down for their own pleasure destroy many living beings. By destroying plants, when young or grown up, a careless
> man does harm to his own soul.[15]

f. A raised hand is the symbol of the Jain religion, symbolizing its main tenet, the doctrine of *ahimsa*, non-violence. The raised hand means "stop." The word in the center of the wheel is *"Ahimsa."* The symbol reminds Jains to stop for a minute and think twice before doing anything. Through this symbol, Jains are encouraged to examine their behavior to be sure that they will not hurt anyone by words, thoughts, or actions. The wheel in the hand reminds Jains that if they are not careful and carry on violent activities, they will go endlessly through the cycles of birth and death.[16]

Figure 7.1

g. Before a layman becomes a monk, he must practice the eight *mulangas*, or basic restraints. These *mulangas* include the renunciation of all meat, alcohol, unboiled water, honey, and eleven *pratimas*. *Pratimas* are strict instructions concerning activity (no trampling of grass, no food or drink at night, no sexual activity during the day), limitations on enjoyment, and instructions on charity and meditation.[17]

h. In this religious system there is no room for the concept of a Creator God. "In Jainism, unlike Christianity and many Hindu cults, there is no such a thing as a heavenly father watching over us. To the contrary, love for a personal God would be an attachment that could only bind Jains more securely to the cycle of rebirth. It is a thing that must be rooted out."[18] Nevertheless, Jainism acknowledges the divinity within the twenty-four *tirthankaras*, or precursors, and elaborate patterns of worship, ritual, and devotion have emerged in the course of its history. They are supposed to have attained omniscience in virtue of their ascetic detachment from all physical things. Since the *tirthankaras* cannot hear prayers nor grant favors, the rationale for worship is that "it elevates one's soul to dwell on their ideal perfection."[19]

i. Once a person (monk) has been liberated from *karma*, he must avoid its re-entry by making five *anuvatras*, or vows:

1) *Ahimsa* (non-violence).
2) Truthfulness. Not to lie, even in jest.
3) Honesty. Not to steal.
4) Sexual abstinence. Perfect chastity, even in thought.
5) Non-possession. Renouncement of all belongings.[20]

j. Related to the last vow above, another key teaching is *aparigraha*, "non-attachment." Jains believe that possessions are an obstacle to liberation. Believers should live with the minimum requirements and not be attached to material possessions. As long as people are attached to things, those things exert a power over people. When those things are relinquished–when "non-acquisitiveness" is realized–there is a sense of personal peace.[21]

k. Jainism also stresses *anekantwad*, which means "relativity." The story of the blind people describing an elephant is instructive here. Each blind person feels a portion of the elephant–the trunk, the ear, the leg–and describes the elephant based on that limited, relative perception. Jains remember this story, avoid judgmentalism, and remain open to seeing an issue from many perspectives.[22]

l. Mahavira taught the three jewels of Jainism: *Samyak Darshan* (Right Faith), *Samyak Jnan* (Right Knowledge), and *Samyak Charitra* (Right Conduct). The right knowledge means having the knowledge that soul and body are separate and that the soul, not the body, attains the salvation. The right faith means one must have faith in what is told by Jinas, who were omniscient. The right conduct means that our actions should be void of attachment and hatred

m. There are about eighteen points of divergence between Shvetambaras and Digambaras, but they still are in complete agreement upon the core concepts of the Three Truths, the major vows, and the underlying assertion of *ahimsa*.[23]

6. *Jain Practices*

a. Monastic asceticism is the only way to salvation. It will take many lifetimes of asceticism to attain disassociation from the bonds of *karma*. Ideally, the monk will choose to die voluntarily by fasting.

b. Monks carry a small broom with which to gently brush away any living creature before they sit or lie down. For the same reason, the Sthanakavasi wear a mask to prevent even the accidental ingestion of invisible creatures. The entire Jain community is strictly vegetarian and opposes animal slaughter.

c. For Jains, ejaculation is akin to genocide, in that a few hundred million sperm will die.[24]

d. Temple worship is centered around images of the *tirthankaras*. Temples are outside the domain of monastic control.

e. Throughout India, all Jain villages and major cities have animal sanctuaries. In these veterinary oases, stray animals are brought in, cared for, loved, and visited at least once a week by veterinarians.[25]

f. Jain laypersons do not engage in occupations that could end in the destruction of living things (plowing the soil, for instance, could kill insects). Jains consider it absolutely forbidden to accept a livelihood involving wood, carts, animal byproducts, insect secretions, alcohol, poisonous articles (professions using chemicals), activities that involve fire, and draining of swamps.[26] As a result, most Jains are members of mercantile or professional classes.

g. It is meaningful that Mahatma K. Ghandi was raised in a Jain area. "The Jain principle of *ahimsa*, or nonviolence, was embraced by Ghandi as a principle of personal and social transformation during the Indian movement for independence."[27]

7. *The Jain Conception of the Universe*

Jain *pratika*, the symbol of Jain faith, was officially adopted in 1975 by all sects of Jainism while commemorating the 2500th anniversary of Mahavira's *nirvana*.[28]

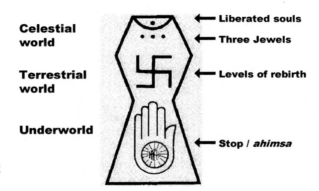

Celestial world

Terrestrial world

Underworld

← Liberated souls

← Three Jewels

← Levels of rebirth

← Stop / *ahimsa*

Figure 7.2

    a. The curved arc at the top represents the dwelling place of liberated *jivas*.

    b. The three dots are the Three Jewels: religious virtues of faith, knowledge, and conduct.

    c. The four arms of the *swastika* represent the four possible levels of rebirth: divine, human, animal (including birds, bugs, and plants), and underworld beings.

    d. The raised hand means "stop." The palm of the hand carries a stylized version of the word *ahimsa*.

8. *Christian Witness*

    a. Most approaches to Hindus may be useful in reaching Jains, and vice versa.

    b. There is very little similarity between Christianity and Jainism. Common ground is minimal. Most approaches by Christians to reach Jains have not been successful. Since they do not accept the Bible, there is little basis for beginning, other than friendship and philosophical reasoning.

c. Establish a personal friendship. Invite them for dinner. They will appreciate a vegetarian meal. This is one point of contact. Talk about the sanctity of life.

d. Attempt to reason that if God's creation is personal, intelligent, and rational, God must be a personal, intelligent, loving Being. If He is not a Being, how could something impersonal create someone personal? How could the non-intelligent produce the intelligent? How could something non-loving produce someone loving? Ask, "Where does the source of love originate?"

e. After a few visits, share a study on the inspiration of the Bible.

f. Proceed with your personal testimony regarding Jesus.

g. Carefully review the plan of salvation.

9. *The Most Serious Jain Objection*

"The crucifixion goes against *ahimsa*, non-violence to all life."

a. The crucifixion was not a proof that Christians uphold death, but a demonstration of God's desire for us to have life (John 3:16-27; 10:10). God is the source of all life. He abhors death. God hates sin because sin destroys His creatures. That is why He was motivated to give His one and only Son as a sacrifice for their sins. Christ also lived a life of renunciation and non-injury. He practiced no violence in thought and action. He allowed Himself to be crucified as an example of non-violence. Christ's death does not uphold killing; instead, it demonstrates the extent of God's love for sinners (Rom 5:8).

b. Many in India believe in going to the extreme to demonstrate their love for someone. A mother, for example, would go hungry to feed her children. A father would deprive himself of everything so that his children could go to school. Jains may be moved by the sacrifice of Jesus on the cross to validate His love for those whom He loved.

Notes

1   Timothy L Gall, ed., *Worldmark Encyclopedia of Culture & Daily Life: Vol. 3 - Asia & Oceania* (Cleveland, OH: Eastword Publications Development, 1998), 325.

2   The University of Michigan Jains, *A Jain Study Guide*, [book online, 1997], 4; retrieved on January 17, 2006, from http://www.umich.edu/~umjains/jainbook.doc.

3   William A. Young, *The World's Religions: Worldview and Contemporary Issues*, 2nd ed. (Upper Saddle River, NJ: Pearson-Prentice Hall, 2005), 99.

4   Mircea Eliade and Ioan P. Couliano, *The HarperCollins Concise Guide to World Religions* (New York: HarperCollins, 2000), 164.

5   Paul Dundas, *The Jains* (London: Routledge, 1992), 49.

6   Michael Tobias, *Life Force: The World of Jainism* (Fremont, CA: Jain Publishing Company, 1991), 62.

7   Mary Pat Fisher, *Living Religions*, 6th ed. (Upper Saddle River, NJ: Prentice-Hall, 2005), 117.

8   Tobias, *Life Force: The World of Jainism*, 62.

9   Ibid., 29.

10   Robert E. Van Voorst, *Anthology of World Scriptures*, 5th ed. (Belmont, CA: Wadsworth, 2006), 107.

11   Young, *The World's Religions*, 100.

12   Fisher, *Living Religions*, 119.

13   Roger Schmidt, Gene C. Sager, Gerald T. Carney, Albert C. Muller, Kenneth J. Zanca, Julius J. Jackson Jr., C. Wayne Mayhall, and Jeffrey C. Burke, *Patterns of Religion*, 2nd ed. (Belmont, CA: Wadsworth, 2005), 449.

14   Tobias, *Life Force: The World of Jainism*, 29.

15   Van Hoorst, *Anthology of World Scriptures*, 115.

16   "Jain Symbol," *Jainism Global Resource Center*, 2005 [article online]; retrieved on January 6, 2006, from http://www.jainworld.com/education/jainsymbol.htm.

17 Tobias, *Life Force: The World of Jainism*, 92.

18 Padma Agrawal, quoted by Fisher, *Living Religions*, 123.

19 Theodore M. Ludwig, *The Sacred Path of the East*, 4th ed. (Upper Saddle River, NJ: Prentice-Hall, 2006), 182-84.

20 Tobias, *Life Force: The World of Jainism*, 91.

21 "Jain Living," *British Broadcasting Corporation*, 2005 [article online]; retrieved on January 15, 2006, from http://www.bbc.co.uk/print/print/religion/religions/ jainism/living/living5.shtml.

22 "Introduction to Anekantwad," *Ahimsa Foundation*, 2005 [article online]; retrieved on January 20, 2006, from http://www.jainsamaj.com/literature/ anekantwad.htm.

23 Ibid., 62.

24 Tobias, *Life Force: The World of Jainism*, 88.

25 Ibid., 34.

26 Ibid., 58.

27 Schmidt et al., *Patterns of Religion*, 450.

28 "Jain Symbol," *Jainism Global Resource Center*.

CHAPTER 8

Sikhism

1. *Introduction*

a. It is quite likely that the man you saw at the airport with the turban on his head was a follower of Sikhism, the fifth largest religion in the world. Sikhs are neither Hindus nor Muslims; rather, they combine elements from both religions. Like Islam, Sikhism is strictly monotheistic. Like Hinduism, Sikhism believes in *karma* and reincarnation. Unlike Hinduism, Jainism, and Buddhism, the lifestyle promoted by this religion does not involve denial. Sikhs may marry, live an ordinary life, and still expect to escape the cycle of rebirth.

b. The word *Sikh* literally means "a disciple." Sikh faith and teaching can only be understood in terms of the role of the Guru. Sikhs explain *Guru* as a word that means "remover of darkness."[1] The Sikh is the learner; the Guru is the teacher. The Sikhs, originally from India, follow the teachings of the ten Gurus and the *Guru Granth Sahib*, their holy book.

c. Sikhism is the fourth most important world religion born on Indian soil. It is different from the other three–Hinduism, Buddhism, and Jainism–in two major ways:

1) First, it began much later. While the other three religions had their genesis in the fifth century B.C. or earlier, Sikhism arose in the fifteenth century A.D.

2) Second, it represents a conscious attempt to combine two major world religions into one: Hinduism and Islam. Sikhism blended *bhakti* (devotional) Hinduism with *Sufi* (mystical) Islam.

2. *Founder*

a. Sikhism arose in Punjab, India, as a result of the preaching of Nanak. Nanak's life span (A.D. 1469-1539) corresponds approximately with that of the reformer Martin Luther (1483-1546).[2]

b. Nanak was born in the Punjabi Indian village of Talwandi, in what today is Pakistan. His father was the village's accountant and was also a farmer. His parents were Hindus and his schoolmaster was a Muslim. He married when he was 19 years old, and his wife bore him two sons, Lakmi Das and Siri Chand.

c. Some time after his thirtieth birthday, he went to Sultanpur to find a job. He disappeared while bathing in a nearby river. He was thought to have drowned, but reappeared three days later, claiming to have been transported into the presence of God, who commissioned him to call men to meditate upon His name.

d. His first proclamation after reappearing was, "There is neither Hindu nor Muslim." This began Nanak's life as a traveling teacher. It is almost certain that he traveled outside the Punjab, but his whereabouts are uncertain. Traditions indicate that he went on a pilgrimage to diverse religious centers in India. Some even believe that he went to Mecca and Medina. His travels occupied a period of about two decades, culminating with his return to the Punjab between 1520 and 1526.

e. Upon his return, Nanak founded (or at least made prominent) a city, Harttarpur, where he spent the rest of his life. He organized his followers into a close-knit community with himself as *guru*. They rejected caste and religious ritual. His community (*panth*) was developed around private and public devotion (*kirtan*), a common kitchen (*langar*), family life, and community service (*seva*).

f. Before his death in 1539, Nanak appointed one of his disciples to succeed him as Guru.

3. *The Ten Gurus*

a. Guru Nanak's successors are sometimes referred to as Nanak 2, Nanak 3, and so on. Like Guru Nanak, his first four successors were all poets, and their compositions are found in their holy book.[3] The first four gurus after Nanak developed the Sikhs into an organized community of faith.[4]

b. Guru Angad (1504-1552) was appointed by Nanak to succeed him. He was an organizer. He compiled a hymnal and collected information on the travels of Nanak.

c. Guru Amar Das (1479-1574) began the creation of a religious structure. He organized the Sikhs into 22 "bishoprics" for the purpose of collecting funds for the support of the place of worship.

d. Guru Ram Das (1534-1581) began the transformation of the Sikhs into a civic community. He bought land where the most important Sikh shrine was later built. He established the tradition of *langar*, the provision and sharing of free food by all who come together for worship, with no concessions of rank.[5]

e. The remaining Gurus ruled while suffering persecution from the Muslim emperors. The fifth, Guru Arjun (1563-1606), completed the compilation of the *Adi Granth* (works of the first four Gurus), and installed it as the sacred scriptures of the Sikhs.

f. Guru Hargobind (1595-1644) maintained a cavalry and bodyguard of three hundred. The next three gurus, Guru Har Ral (1630-1661), Guru Har Krishan (1656-1664), and Guru Tegh Bahadur (1621-1675) died without making a significant contribution to the development of the Sikh faith.

g. The tenth Guru, Gobind Rai (1666-1708), completed the transformation of the Sikhs into a regional military force of great courage and skill that is respected until today.[6] Under pressure from the emperor, he took steps to organize the Sikhs into a fighting force that could resist imperial power. He also founded the *khalsa*, or the "brotherhood of the pure." This brotherhood is the name given to those who wish to follow the teachings of the historical gurus, live moral lives, defend the faith, and establish a moral society.[7] Guru Gobind Rai initiated five men, and then he himself requested baptism. He changed his name to Guru Gobind Singh; since then all members of the brotherhood will adopt the name Singh ("lion").

h. Before his death, Guru Gobind Singh installed the scriptures as Guru, thus completing a process which had been developing for well over a century. "The distinction between the human Guru and the Gurbandi [the words contained in the Granth Sahib] now became complete with his decision to appoint no human successor."[8]

i. The Sikh Gurus are described as perfect in the Sikh Scriptures. Guru Nanak himself said, "Everybody else is subject to error; only the Guru and God are without error. . . . The Guru is sinless."[9] However, they are not divine. The Gurus made it very clear that they were only human beings and were not to be worshiped.[10]

4. *The Sacred Book*

a. After ten Gurus, the scriptures became the living Guru. The last human Guru did not appoint a human successor but installed the collection of sacred writings as the living Guru.[11] The holy book of Sikhism is known by different names: the *Granth* ("the book/scriptures"), the *Adi Granth* ("the first/original book"), *Granth Sahib* ("the book personified or revered"), and *Guru Granth Sahib* ("the book which is a revered teacher"). The book is the embodiment of the soul of the gurus, the statement of the essence of Sikhism, and the final authority for the faith.[12] He is the living Guru of Sikhism.

b. The *Guru Granth Sahib*, the work of several dozen authors, was compiled primarily by the fifth Sikh Guru Sri Arjun Deo in 1604. He wrote 2,216 songs and compiled the songs of his four predecessors, including 976 hymns composed by Guru Nanak. Later, hymns of the ninth Guru were added.[13] The *Granth* contains 12,480 rhymed verses that extol the name of God and exhort followers to proper daily life. It is not arranged by subject but, rather, according to the musical measure (*raga*) in which a hymn is sung. There are 31 such musical measures (*ragas*). The *Granth* is written in six different languages and several dialects, with the result that few can read it in its entirety.[14] It reads largely like the Old Testament psalms. There is little historical narrative or doctrinal exposition.

c. Sikhs venerate the *Granth* in worship and give it a prominent place in their religious life. They look upon the *Granth* as the symbolic representation of all ten Gurus and treat the book as a person. It is "roused" in the morning and placed under an awning or canopy draped in fineries. Devotees bow down to it and place their offerings in front of it. In the evening it is put to rest for the night.[15]

d. Most Sikhs read the *Guru Granth Sahib* every day and meditate upon it, and full cover-to-cover readings are done frequently. Great respect is shown to the *Granth* when opening, reading, or closing it. It is kept in silken and/or clean cloths, and a fly flicker is always at hand to wave over it. When it is brought in, all those present must stand with bowed heads, showing extreme reverence to the *Granth*. Some Sikhs may have a copy of the book in their homes, but (as is required) they give it a room of its own and create an altar of pillows and beautiful cloths on which to place it.[16]

5. *The Sikh Concept of God*

a. Sikh religion stands out because of its mysticism. God cannot be studied, only experienced. He is unknowable, yet chooses to reveal Himself to man. Sikhism reveres its god so formally that they will avoid calling it "God" and instead call the being "True Name" since they believe all other names to be limiting.[17]

b. The most significant words in the Sikh teachings are *Ek Onkar*, the first two words of the *Granth*. The first twelve words contain the core teachings of Sikhism and are known as the "*Mool* [or *Mul*] mantra," (meaning "root formula/basic sacred chant"). "With the brevity of a text message, they sum up Guru Nanak's essential teaching. They also pose an immediate challenge to the translator. The twelve words are nouns and adjectives: they include no verbs or pronouns. To compound the challenge, the nouns have no exact counterpart in European languages."[18]

c. *Ek* means "one," emphasizing the oneness of God, which is the essence of Sikhism. *Onka*r (Figure 8.1) is "derived from the Sanskrit word *Om*, which consists of three syllable sounds representing the trinity of Brahma, Vishnu and Shiva. *Onkar* therefore means GOD in His entirety."[19] The *Mool* mantra is the mirror of the Sikh conception of God:

Ek Onkar	[There is only] one God,
Sat Naam	truth [by] name,
Karta Purkh	the creator,
Nirbhau	without fear,
Nirvair	without hate,
Akaal Moorat	without time [and] form,
Ajooni	without birth [and] death,
Sabhang	self existent,
Gur Parsaad	[known by] the Guru's grace.[20]

Figure 8.1

d. The name of God commonly used among the Sikhs is *Wah Guru*, meaning "Wondrous Teacher." In the *Grant Sahib*, God is remembered by almost all the names known to Hindu mythology or scriptures and the Semitic religions, notably Islam. For instance, He is called Rabb, Allah, Khuda, and Sahib, with all the attributes with which the Qur'an endows the one absolute God. He is referred to in Hindu terms such as Rama, Mohan (Krishna), Hare (Lord), Shiv (Shiva), Braham (Brahama), and Paramatma (supreme soul).[21] Even God is known by the name Jesus.[22]

e. Sikhs repeat the name of God in order to obtain enlightenment and liberation from the endless cycle of rebirths. This allows the devotee to achieve union with God through the power of *bakhti* (devotion, act of worship). Repeating God's name, to the Sikh, aids one in conquering the ego, or self-interest, which Nanak saw as the greatest evil. The ritual of repeating God's name, often with the aid of rosary beads, requires realization of the truth, its expression in prayer, and detachment from worldly things. Salvation is absorption in God, the True Name.[23]

f. Sikhs strongly oppose any idol worship. Most Sikh homes have framed pictures of Guru Nanak and the tenth Guru, Gobind Singh, but they do not worship them. Idol worship is condemned in the *Granth*.

g. Like Hinduism, Sikhism accepts the doctrine of *karma* and the transmigration of the soul from one life into another until it finally merges with the eternal, all-pervading Supreme Soul. Thus, in the final stage the soul loses its identity within the Supreme Soul. The *Granth* reads, "When man obtains the 'sangat' [fellowship of saints and true seekers of God] the divine light shines in his heart and he sings his glories and praises. He becomes one with God as water mixes with water. This is where transmigration ends and man gets true rest by becoming one with eternal God."[24]

6. *Sikh Worship*

a. In worship, as in Islam, there is no official clergy in Sikhism; instead, someone leads the worship and manages temple affairs. Professional scripture readers are known as *granthis*. Sikhs assemble in the mornings and evenings at the Sikh temples to hear the singing of hymns, known as *kirtan*, which is done by professional singers. Meditation and prayer chanting are an integral part of their faith.[25]

b. Places of worship are called *gurdwaras* ("gates to the gurus"). Services, held on Sundays, consist of singing, meditation (an important part of their communication with God), and readings from the *Guru Granth Sahib*. Since Sikhs recognize no day of the week as more holy than others, the fact that worship services, take place on Sunday is solely out of convenience. After worship services they offer *langar*, the community meal, which is freely offered to all who come, regardless of caste.[26]

c. In every Sikh worship service, the *Guru Granth Sahib* is the central focus. They usually read it without explanation. While in its presence, Sikhs must remove their shoes and cover their heads out of respect. In worship services, the *Granth* is placed on a pedestal of pillows, and is opened and closed ceremoniously. It is transported with the utmost care. On special occasions as a token of thanksgiving and gratitude, the *Granth* is read continuously, which takes about two days and two nights. "The spiritual power of the Granth only reaches its full potential when it is sung."[27]

d. Sikhs believe that the repetition of the name of the Gurus cleanses the mind of impure thoughts and the soul of sin. Often chanted are "*Wah Guru*," "the True Name," and "the Wondrous Guru."[28]

7. *Sikh Practices*

b. The *khanda* (Figure 8.2) is the symbol of the Sikhs. The symbol derives its name from the double-edged sword (also called a *khanda*), which appears at the center of the logo. This double-edged sword is a metaphor of divine knowledge; its sharp edges separate truth from falsehood. The *chakar* is a circle without a beginning or an end around the *khanda* that symbolizes the perfection of God, who is eternal. The *chakar* is surrounded by two curved swords called *kirpans*. These two swords symbolize the twin concepts of temporal and spiritual authority. They signify that a Sikh must place on spiritual aspirations as well as obligations to society.[29]

Figure 8.2

c. Sikhs have several annual festivities. Three are Hindu: *Baisakhi*, New Year's Day in Punjab; *Diwali*, the Hindu "Festival of Lights"; and *Hola Mohalla*, a spring festival on the day after *Holi*, one of the most popular Hindu festivals. The rest are *gurpurbs*, anniversaries associated with the Gurus.[30] For these festivals, Sikh families gather in a *gurdwara,* which is properly decorated and illuminated. The *Granth* is usually read in its entirety.[31]

d. There are several ceremonies associated with the Sikh religion: the naming of a baby, weddings, funerals, and initiation into the faith. At birth, the *Mool* mantra is whispered into the baby's ear. The baby is named at the local *gurdwara.* The *Guru Granth Sahib* is opened, and the first letter of the first word on the page gives the first letter of the baby's name. At death, the body is cremated and the ashes thrown into running water.[32]

e. The *Khalsa* (meaning "pure") is the Order of Sikh initiates founded by the tenth Guru, Guru Gobind Singh, in 1699.[33] The *Khalsa* "baptism," or *Amrit* ceremony, is undertaken as part of one's own personal spiritual evolution when the initiate is ready to fully live up to the high expectations of Guru Gobind Singh. All Sikhs are expected to join the *Khalsa* or be working towards that objective. The ceremony involves drinking of *amrit* (sugar water stirred with a dagger) in the presence of five *Khalsa* Sikhs as well as the *Guru Granth Sahib.* The initiate is instructed in the *Khalsa* Code of Conduct and then *amrit* is sprinkled into his eyes and his hair five times.[34] Initiated men receive the name *Singh* ("lion") and women *Kaur* ("princess").

f. *Khalsa* Sikhs are supposed to be distinguished by the wearing of the "Five Signs of Sikhism" at all times.[35] These five signs symbolize purity, submission to God's will, and fearlessness. They are also known as "the five K's":

   1) the *kesh*–uncut hair (with turbans and beards for men),
   2) the *kangha*–a comb to keep the hair clean,
   3) the *kara*–a steel wrist bracelet that symbolizes their bond with God,
   4) the *kirpan*–a dagger (which may be a miniature or an engraving),
   5) and the *kach*–white underwear, signifying readiness for action.[36]

g. Although their faith does not consider any place, river, or mountain sacred, Sikhs do go on pilgrimages to the temples associated with the Gurus. Birthdays and death anniversaries are celebrated by every devout Sikh, and large gatherings take place on these occasions.[37]

h. Sikhism has a firmly entrenched militaristic tradition. Sikhs are seen as a soldier caste. They were used by the British as soldiers and constabulary. The emphasis on militant tradition and community service in Sikhism continues even today, and many Sikhs serve in the Indian army or police.[38]

i. In contrast to the low status of women in Indian society, the Gurus accorded considerable respect to women. In 1996 women were allowed to perform sacred services in Sikh *gurdwaras*.[39]

8. *Most Sacred Shrines*

a. The *Harimandir Sahib* (meaning "Temple of God") is also commonly known as the Golden Temple. It is situated in the city of Amritsar in Punjab. The Golden Temple is a source of inspiration for all Sikhs and their chief place of pilgrimage. The temple, with its glistening gold covered exterior, stands in the middle of a square tank known as the Pool of Nectar. A causeway traverses the pool to reach the Temple itself.

b. On the other end of the causeway and outside the pool is the Akal Takht. *Akal Takht* literally means "Eternal Throne." It is part of the Golden Temple complex in Amritsar. During the day the *Guru Granth Sahib* is kept in the Golden Temple, while at night it is kept in the Akal Takht. While the Golden Temple stands for spiritual guidance, the Akal Takht symbolizes the dispensing of justice and temporal activity.

9. *Sikhs Today*

a. In India, Sikhs number about twenty million, close to 2% of the population. In 2001 more than 75% of India's Sikhs lived in Punjab, and this is the only state in which they form a majority (approximately 60%).[40]

b. The largest Sikh community outside India is in the United Kingdom, where the 2001 census counted 336,000 Sikhs.[41] By 2000 there were about 175,000 adherents in the United States and 225,000 in Canada.[42] Smaller communities are in Australia, New Zealand, Fiji, and many African countries.

c. The Indian army assaulted the holiest shrine of the Sikhs, the Golden Temple, in June 1984. The reaction of the Sikhs was one of anger, vengeance, and hatred toward the Hindu government. In October 1984, a Sikh assassinated Prime Minister Indira Gandhi. Within two days, in New Delhi alone, three thousand Sikhs lost their lives and millions of dollars' worth of property in property was burned and looted. It seems that the crisis has forever altered the relations of Hindus and Sikhs.[43]

d. Sikhs believe that their religious and political identity is threatened in India. Although the majority of Sikhs are peaceful citizens, they support the movement for a separate state known as *Khalistan* ("the land of the pure"). They believe that their interests, identity, and religion will be best served in an independent homeland. It is interesting to note that all overseas Sikhs seem to be in favor of *Khalistan.*

e. As happens in all religions, secularism is making an impact on Sikhism. "Third and fourth generation Sikhs in England and Canada are more likely to be into drinking beer, smoking, cutting their hair, and living a non-Sikh way of life than being a practicing Sikh."[44]

10. *Christian Witness*

a. First befriend them by showing genuine concern and interest. Be prepared to give and receive help in practical ways. Once the friendship is established, talking about God flows naturally from the lips of these people. This is called "friendship evangelism."

b. As the friendship grows, you may be invited to attend birthday parties and weddings. This would be an indication that you have earned the trust and confidence of your Sikh friend. From this point on, sharing the gospel becomes easy. Invite them into your home and family circle for fellowship and conversation–this they will understand and appreciate.

c. Use God's Word; however, do not give them the entire Bible. Present them with a copy of the Gospel of John or Luke in the language they prefer. Request that they read it, mark it, and indicate what impresses them by an asterisk and what they do not understand by a question mark. Offer to dialogue with them on these items.

d. Respect their customs and sensitivities. For example, beef or pork should never be offered to them. Always explain that the drink is non-alcoholic.

e. Use Christian pamphlets written by former Sikhs. Sikhs are curious to read something written by one of them and in their native language.[45]

f. As your Sikh friend learns to trust you more and more, he might also like to know about your personal matters, which you may not understand right away. For instance, he may ask, "where does your wife work and how much does she earn?" In India and within the Sikh community, discussing personal details is an accepted way of life; this is how East Indians converse.

g. Be modest in dress and reserved in manner. Men should witness to men, and women to women.

h. Recognize the importance of being a good listener. Everyone wants to be heard and understood. Seek to discover heart needs. Ask your Sikh friends about their faith; this is a good way to begin a conversation.

i. Avoid debate and philosophical discussion like the plague. This is a field where they shine and where real issues are seldom raised.

j. Keep in mind similarities and differences between both religions.

1) Points of similarity between Christianity and Sikhism include the facts that both believe in one creator God, emphasize meditation on God's truth, reject idol worship, and emphasize a life of service to humanity.[46] Both are a people of "the book," and both religions emphasize divine grace.[47]

2) Differences between Christianity and Sikhism include the possibility of a divine incarnation. Sikhs regard Jesus as a great teacher but do not accept Him as God in human flesh.[48] They believe in salvation based upon human efforts, virtues, and *karma*. Bad *karma* is overcome by good *karma*. The idea of someone else's death atoning for a man's sin is totally foreign to their works-oriented religious background.

k. Build bridges, not barriers. Differences in theology are profound, but initially emphasize agreement about the fact of one true God.

l. The best way to talk to a Sikh about the incarnation of Jesus Christ is to read the scriptures with him. Since the Sikh highly respects the scriptures, he may see for himself that the teaching of an incarnate God is not propagated by human scholars but is based upon the written Word. A recommended passage is Matthew 1:18-23. Never forget to emphasize the resurrection of Christ

l. Pray with them if possible and keep the door open for future contact. Sikhs are won to Christ by painstaking effort over a period of time.

m. Do not forget to share your personal testimony. A Punjabi proverb says, "Only the man who has tasted a mango can tell you its flavor."

n. Many prefer Christian schools over the public school system. After they become independent from their families, they may become vocal about their faith in Christ.

o. Show the "Jesus" video to them in Punjabi.[49]

Notes

1   Eleanor Nesbitt, *Sikhism: A Very Short Introduction* (New York: Oxford University Press, 2005), 3.

2   Warren Mathews, "Sikhism," in *World Religions*, 4th ed. (Belmont, CA: Wadsworth-Thomson, 2004), 185-88.

3   Nesbitt, *Sikhism: A Very Short Introduction*, 28.

4   "Biographies of Gurus," *History of the Sikhs*, 2004 [article online]; retrieved on January 8, 2006, from http://www.sikh-history.com/sikhhist/gurus/index.html.

5   Nesbitt, *Sikhism: A Very Short Introduction*, 29.

6   Even though today Sikhs compose less than 2% of the Indian population, roughly 30% of the Indian army is Sikh. William A. Young, *The World's Religions: Worldview and Contemporarry Issues*, 2nd ed. (Upper Saddle River, NJ: Pearson-Prentice Hall, 2005), 242.

7   Douglas Davis, "Religion of the Gurus: The Sikh Faith," in *Eerdmans' Handbook to the World's Religions* (Grand Rapids: Eerdmans, 1982), 201.

8   W. Owen Cole and Piara Singh Sambhi, *The Sikhs: Their Religious Beliefs and Practices* (London: Routledge & Kegan Paul, 1978), 50.

9   Teja Singh, *Sikhism: Its Ideals and Institutions*, revised (Amristsar, Punjab, India: Khalsa Bros., 1978), 19.

10   Santosh Raj, *Understanding Sikhs and Their Religion* (Hillsboro, KS: Kindred Press, 1991), 6.

11   When Guru Gobind Singh (the tenth Guru) was fatally stabbed at Nander (in the state of Maharashtra), his followers inquired who was to succeed him. The Guru replied, "Believe in One God who will always protect you. The work of the Gurus is completed. Henceforth their spirit would live in the sacred Granth and the

Khalsa. Wherever five Khalsas are assembled and abide by the teaching of the Gurus, I am in their midst. The Khalsa is the Guru and the Guru is the Khalsa, for in the Khalsa is found the spirit of the Gurus. To get inspiration with the presence of the Guru, the Holy Granth, the divine words, is your Guru from today. Obey the Granth, it is the visible body of the Guru. Let Him who desires to meet me diligently search its hymns." Quoted by ibid., 5.

12   Robert E. Van Voorst, *Anthology of World Scriptures*, 5ᵗʰ ed. (Belmont, CA: Thomson Wadsworth, 2006), 120.

13   Raj, *Understanding Sikhs*, 4, 8.

14   Josh McDowell and Don Stewart, *Understanding Non-Christian Religions* (Sydney: Here's Life Publishers, 1982), 182-83.

15   Raj, *Understanding Sikhs*, 9.

16   Davis, "Religion of the Gurus," 201-2.

17   Young, *The World's Religions*, 170.

18   Nesbitt, *Sikhism: A Very Short Introduction*, 22.

19   "Ekonkar–One God," *Sikh.net*, 1998-2004 [article online]; retrieved on January 15, 2006, from http://www.sikh.net/sikhism/ekonkar.htm.

20   Raj, *Understanding Sikhs*, 1.

21   Gopal Singh, "On the Compilation of the Guru Granth," in *Sri Guru Granth Sahib (International Edition)* (New Delhi: Gondals Press, 1984), xviii.

22   Padshahi X Chaupai, Rahiras Sahib; quoted by Raj, *Understanding Sikhs*, 7.

23   "*Sikhism,*" *Reference.com*, 2005 [Encyclopedia online]; retrieved on January 27, 2006, from http://www.reference.com/browse/wiki/Sikhism.

24   Ashtapadi XI:8; quoted by Raj, *Understanding Sikhs*, 13.

25   Hardit Singh, "Langar: Its Ideal and Concept," *History of the Sikhs*, 2004 [article online]; retrieved on December 26, 2005 from http://www.sikh-history.com/sikhhist/archivedf/feature-dec.html.

26   Sandeep Singh Brar, "What is a Gurdwara?" *The Sikhism Home Page*, 2005 [article online]; retrieved on January 12, 2006, from http://www.sikhs.org gurdwara.htm.

27 Alex Smith, "Sikhism," in *Encountering Religion* (Malden, MA: Blackwell, 2001), 88, 89.

28 Ibid., 4.

29 "Khanda," *Wikipedia: The Free Encyclopedia*, 2005 [article online]; retrieved on January 6, 2006, from http://en.wikipedia.org/wiki/Khanda.

30 "Gurpurbs," *Shiromani Gurdwara Parbandhak Committee* [article online]; retrieved on January 7, 2006, from http://www.sgpc.net/festivals/index.asp.

31 "Sikh Festivals," *Gateway to Sikhism*, 1999-2005 [article online]; retrieved on January 23, 2006, from http://www.allaboutsikhs.com/way/sikhfestivals.htm.

32 "Sikh Worldview," *Instructional Systems*, 2002 [article online]; retrieved on January 23, 2006, from http://www.teachingaboutreligion.org/SingleWorldview/sikh_worldview.htm.

33 Sundeep Singh Shergill, "Baptism," *Ikonkar* [article online]; retrieved on January 15, 2006, from http://www.ikonkar.com/sikhism/sikhsm/phanjk/baptism.htm.

34 "Amrit Sanskar," *Gateway to Sikhism*, 1999-2005 [article online]; retrieved on January 6, 2006, from http://allaboutsikhs.com/way/amrit.htm.

35 Maurice Smith, "Sikhism," in *Beliefs of Other Kinds*, ed. Everett Hullum (Atlanta: Home Mission Board of the Southern Baptist Convention, 1994), 132.

36 Vinay Lal, "Five Symbols of the Sikh Faith," *Manas* [article online]; retrieved on January 25, 2006, from http://www.sscnet.ucla.edu/southasia/Religions/paths/fivesymbols.html.

37 Santosh Raj, *Understanding Sikhs and Their Religion* (Hillsboro, KS: Kindred Press, 1991), 2.

38 Charles Samuel Braden, *The World's Religions*, revised (New York: Abingdon Press, 1954), 111.

39 Mary Pat Fisher, *Living Religions*, 6th ed. (Upper Saddle River, NJ: Pearson-Prentice Hall, 2005), 428-29, 433.

40 Census of India 2001, "Data on Religion," Office of the Registrar General, India, 2004; retrieved on December 27, 2005, from http://www.censusindia.net/religiondata/Summary%20Sikhs.pdf.

41 Nesbitt, *Sikhism: A Very Short Introduction*, 3.

42   "Ministering to Sikhs," *Ethnic Harvest*, 2004 [article online]; retrieved on December 26, 2005, from http://www.ethnicharvest.org/peoples/sikh.htm.

43   Summer McCoy, "Sikhism," *New Religious Movements*, University of Virginia, 2001 [article online]; retrieved on January 22, 2006, from http://religiousmovements.lib.virginia.edu/nrms/sikhs.html.

44   "Sikhism: History, Beliefs, Practices, Etc." *Ontario Consultants on Religious Tolerance*, 1996-2005 [article online]; retrieved on January 23, 2006, from http://www.religioustolerance.org/sikhism.htm.

45   The following websites offer Christian literature in Punjabi: http://www.multilanguage.com/ pun/Default.htm and http://www.ethnicharvest.org/peoples/countries/india.htm.

46   Raj, *Understanding Sikhs*, 42.

47   Nesbitt, *Sikhism: A Very Short Introduction*, 7.

48   Nikky Singh, "Jesus through Sikh Eyes," *British Broadcasting Corporation*, 2005 [article online]; retrieved on January 15, 2006, from http://www.bbc.co.uk/religion/ religions/sikhism/features/sikh_eyes/.

49   The following websites offer the "Jesus" video in Punjabi: http://www.thejesusvideo.com/ languages.htm; http://www.jesusfilmstore.com/; http://www.christcenteredmall.com/bible/ video.htm, and http://christianvideos.org/punjabi_videos.html.

PART III

BUDDHISM

CHAPTER 9

Buddha and His Teachings

1. *Introduction*

a. Brahmanism underwent two major reform attempts around the fifth century B.C. that resulted in the formation of two independent religions: Jainism and Buddhism. Jainism moved to extreme asceticism, while Buddhism adopted a "middle way" between self-indulgence and self-mortification.

b. No other religion has existed in such disparate cultures as a major influence for so long. About half of the world's population lives today in areas where Buddhism has at some time been the dominant religious force. Today Buddhism is the religion of about four hundred million people who live in lands stretching from Sri Lanka to the islands of Japan and throughout large areas of the Asian mainland. It is the state religion of Thailand, Sri Lanka, and Laos; the religion of the majority in Myanmar (Burma) and Kampuchea (Cambodia); and the faith of a very great number of Chinese, Japanese, and Koreans.

c. All forms of Buddhism today arise from the same roots. No two schools of Buddhism will agree on the classification of the states of mind related to the path to liberation nor with the methodology of spiritual training; however, they share the same main goal and have similar methods to attain it. "The ultimate goal of Buddhism is to put an end to suffering and rebirth."[1] They do not normally speak of "Buddhism," but of "Buddha-*Dharma*," or simply "*Dharma*" ("teachings, "doctrine").[2]

e. As Christians, we study Buddhism to reach its people, very few of whom have responded to the gospel of Christ.

2. *The Founder of Buddhism*

a. The Period of Enjoyment (563-534 B.C.)

1) Siddhartha Gautama was born to the noble warrior Suddhodana and the Princess Maya, of the Gautama clan. They belonged to the Kshatriya (warrior) caste of the Sakya tribe. This is why Siddhartha (meaning, "Aim Attained") is sometimes called "*Sakyamuni*," "the sage of the Sakya tribe." He is referred to as Siddhartha or Gautama.

2) In many Buddhist countries, the most important holiday is "Buddha Day," which falls on the full-moon day of the month of Vesak, corresponding to April-May in our calendar. This festival is thrice sacred, for in Buddhist tradition it is the date of the Buddha's birth, enlightenment, and death.[3]

3) Siddhartha's birthplace was the town of Kapilavastu, which was then in northeastern India but is now part of Nepal, 130 miles to the north of Vanarasi or Benares. Many signs accompanied his birth.[4] The details of his career are uncertain since no biography was written until hundreds of years later.[5] It appears, however, that his early life was spent in ease and luxury.

4) During his teens, Siddhartha married his cousin, Yasodhara, and moved into a palace which his father had built for him, where he continued to enjoy the comfortable life of the elite. His wife bore him a son who received the name of Rahula. One day, however, at the age of 29, Siddhartha ventured away from his palace and encountered all four kinds of suffering: an old man, a sick man, a dead man, and a begging monk. This experience profoundly affected him. He became disillusioned with his wealth and deeply concerned with the issue of suffering.

b. The Period of Enquiry (534-528 B.C.)

1) As a result of his encounter with suffering, one night Siddharta left his sleeping family—including his wife and child. That night is known as the "Blessed Night of the Great Renunciation." He committed himself to

discovering and eliminating the source of suffering and how to eliminate it. Convicted by the monk he had seen, Siddhartha began to practice asceticism. To begin with, he put himself under the instructions of two famous Brahmin hermits, Alara and Uddaka, but he was unable to find satisfaction in their teaching, for they could not tell him how to eliminate reincarnation and the suffering that accompanies it.

2) Next, Siddhartha with five companions withdrew to Uruvela and underwent a life of extreme asceticism in the jungle. It is said that in the fashion of Jainism, Siddhartha survived on a mere grain of rice a day, until his delicate body was almost reduced to a skeleton. After six years, his body became so weak he almost drowned while bathing in a river. He realized that extreme asceticism did not produce the enlightenment that he was seeking.

c. The Period of Enlightenment (528-483 B.C.)

1) Siddhartha then decided to turn away from such limitations and devoted himself to a simple life of intense mental activity. He ate some food and walked to a city named Bodh Gaya (also Buddagaya), where he sat under a fig tree (a *bodhi* tree) by the edge of a river. Siddhartha vowed not to rise again until he had attained enlightenment, and thereupon went into a deep state of meditation. During his meditation, he was severely tempted by Mara, the evil one. Siddhartha resisted the temptations, and after a period of time (some say one night, others one week, and others as many as 49 days) he attained enlightenment. After that, Siddhartha Gautama was called "*Buddha*," which means "the enlightened one."[6]

2) During one memorable night, Buddha gained three pieces of knowledge: remembrance of his former lives, knowledge of the birth and death of beings, and the certainty of having finally cast off the ignorance and passions which until then had bound him to successive rebirth. This threefold knowledge brought with it perfect insight into the cycle of the causation of all phenomena of life. The Buddha mentally examined, first forward and then in reverse, the causes which condition birth and death. He then acquired the certainty of having escaped from the ever-spinning wheel of rebirths and of finally living his very last life. Bodh Gaya is now the site of the holiest shrine in the Buddhist world, the Mahabodhi Temple. The fig tree is now known as the *Bo*, or Wisdom Tree.

3) It took one year for Buddha to develop a methodology out of the concepts he got at the time of enlightenment.[7] Then Buddha traveled to Benares, and in the Deer Park he preached his first sermon–the content of which is now known as the "Four Noble Truths." Eventually he won thousands of followers,

who formed communities called *sanghas*. Buddha called his path to enlightenment the "Middle Way," because it avoided the extremes of affluence and asceticism.[8]

3. *The Four Noble Truths*

a. Although there are extreme variations within Buddhism, most Buddhists share the same basic beliefs, contained in the "Four Noble Truths." According to Buddha, all forms of life have three characteristics in common: suffering (*dukkha*), impermanence (*anicca*), and the fact that nothing has a permanent or immutable essence (*anatta*).[9]

b. The First Noble Truth: Life consists of suffering (doctrine of *dukkha*). All forms of existence are subject to it. Buddha's concept of suffering includes all experiences of pain, misery, sorrow, and unfulfillment.[10]

c. The Second Noble Truth: Everything is impermanent and ever changing (the doctrine of *anicca*). Suffering has a double root: one is our ignorance (*avidya*) of the true nature of reality, and the other is our attachment (*tanha*) to things that are impermanent.[11]

> All that exists passes through the cycle of birth, growth, decay, and death. Life is one and indivisible; its ever-changing forms are innumerable and perishable, for though in reality there is no such thing as death, every form must die and give place to a different one. The world of phenomena, the very universe itself, has a purely relative existence, and this impermanence, this lack of absolute objective reality, applies to the individual's "self."[12]

d. The Third Noble Truth: The way to liberate oneself from suffering is to eliminate all desire. We must stop craving for that which is temporary.[13]

e. The Fourth Noble Truth: Desire can be eliminated by following "The Eightfold Path," which consists of eight points that can be categorized according to three major sections.[14]

    1) Wisdom (*Panna*)

        a) Right Understanding
        b) Right Thought

    2) Morality (*Sila*)

c) Right Speech
d) Right Action
e) Right Livelihood

3) Meditation (*Samadhi*)

f) Right Effort
g) Right Awareness
h) Right Meditation

f. These eight points are not steps to be taken in sequential order, but are attitudes and actions to be developed simultaneously.[15] The first two points under *panna*, or wisdom, serve as the foundation from which the other points flow.

1) Right Understanding covers an intellectual grasp of the "Teaching of the Dhamma." With Right Understanding (or right views), one sees that the universe is impermanent and illusory and that the "I" (or "self") does not, in reality, exist. This is known as the doctrine of *anatta* ("no-self" or "no-soul"). Ultimately, no phenomenon in this world has substantial reality (doctrine of the "Void").[16]

2) Right Thought (or right aspirations, right motives) follows Right Understanding in that it means to renounce all attachment to the desires and thought of this illusory self. Freeing his thought from such things as lust, ill will, and cruelty, a man should have a firm resolve to achieve the highest goals.

g. The *sila*, or moral precepts, form the basis for ethical conduct.

1) Right Speech: Speak well of others. Words must be gentle, soothing to the ear, penetrating to the heart, useful, rightly timed, and according to the facts. All idle gossip and unprofitable talk must be stamped out.

2) Right Action: Obey moral commands or abstentions. Avoid making your living through an occupation that breaks the moral precepts of Buddhism. These moral commands are known as "The Five Precepts" (*Pancha Sila*). They require abstinence from 1) the taking of life (all forms, not just human), 2) stealing, 3) immoral sexual behavior (Buddhist monks are celibate), 4) lying, and 5) intoxicant liquor or drugs. Monks are required to add five additional abstentions, resulting in "The Ten Precepts." 6) Eating moderately and not after noon, 7) avoiding entertainment such as singing or dramas, 8) not using flowers,

perfumes, or jewelry, 9) using simple beds, and 10) accepting no gold or silver.[17]

3) Right Livelihood: Earn your living in a righteous way. Wealth should be gained legally and peacefully. There are four specific activities one should avoid because they harm other beings: using weapons, dealing with living beings (including slave trading, prostitution, and raising animals for slaughter), working in meat production and butchery, and selling intoxicants and poisons, such as alcohol and drugs.

h. *Samadhi* deals with the remaining points of the Eightfold Path. *Samadhi* is a deep state of consciousness and absorption into the spiritual. After reaching this stage, *nirvana* is at hand.[18]

1) Through Right Effort, one prevents evil thoughts from entering the mind. The efforts are in four directions: avoiding the uprising of evil; overcoming evil; developing meritorious conditions such as detachment, investigation of the law, and concentration; and last, maintaining these meritorious conditions and bringing them to maturity and perfection. The climax of this achievement is universal love.

2) Through Right Awareness, one is especially conscious of the events in one's life. One should aim for the complete mastery of one's mental process by contemplating the transitoriness of the body, the feelings of oneself and of others, and all other mental phenomena.

3) Through Right Meditation, one can attain the bliss of enlightenment. Once all hindrances have been overcome, right concentration aims to complete one-pointedness of thought, concentrating the mind on a single object. Such arduous mind development is the principal occupation of the more enlightened Buddhist and an integral part of the daily life of the humblest follower of Gautama. It leads to trances where the devotee is purified from all distractions and evils and is filled with rapture, happiness, and equanimity. Finally, he passes beyond sensation of either pleasure or pain into a state transcending consciousness and ultimately attains full enlightenment, which is the highest possible state of perfection.

4. *The Beliefs of Buddhism*

a. *Dharma*

1) Buddha's doctrine received the name of *"Dharma"* or *"Dhamma"* ("Doctrine" or "Law"), a doctrine of self-deliverance, not of salvation by any external agency.

2) Buddha retained some basic Hindu teachings, like the concepts of *karma* (law of cause and effect) and *samsara* (the cycle of death and rebirth). However, in many respects Buddha revolted against Hinduism. He reacted against the caste system, the Vedic sacrificial system, and the leadership of the Brahmin.

b. *Karma*

1) *Karma* signifies action-reaction and denotes the law of cause and effect. What you sow, you reap. Nobody can suspend the operation of this law or withhold the consequences of a deed. The law of cause and effect is an unbroken chain through the ages. You are what you are and your behavior is a result of your actions in all previous incarnations; similarly, your future rebirths will be conditioned precisely by what happens in your present life.

2) As soon as an individual's present existence terminates, a new being appears by the sheer force of his *karma*. This new being is not identical, but has continuity with the one that has just passed away. The *karma* link preserves a certain individuality through all the countless changes that take place. In fact, "all living beings are nothing but karma."[19]

3) This belief in *karma* and the inexorable succession of cause and effect through successive rebirths produces fatalism in the thinking of the Buddhist. People are held accountable for a past they do not remember and are victims of a fate they cannot elude.

c. *Nirvana*

1) Buddha's immediate goal was to eliminate the cause of suffering. His ultimate goal was to become liberated from the cycle of death and rebirth (*samsara*) by teaching how we can cease craving and thus eliminate our attachment to and belief in the existence of the illusory self.

2) As we eliminate such attachment, the effects of *karma* will have nothing to attach themselves to, which in turn means that they cannot cause the individual to return to the realm of illusion. At that moment of enlightenment, we will have achieved the state of *nirvana* (in Pali, *nibbana*)[20]–the ultimate goal for the Buddhist, and Buddhism's equivalent to salvation. Buddha described *nirvana* with the following words:

> There is a sphere which is neither earth, nor water, nor fire, nor air, which is not the sphere of the infinity of consciousness, the sphere of nothingness, the sphere of perception, or non-perception, which is neither this world, neither sun nor moon. I deny that it is coming or going, enduring, death, or birth. It is only the end of suffering.[21]

3) It has been said that Buddha would have us get rid of the problems of life by getting rid of life itself. However, Buddhist scholars argue that *nirvana* does not mean that the person is annihilated.[22] And yet, at the same time, the Buddhist denies that *nirvana* means continued existence.[23]

4) For many Buddhists there is no such thing as "entering into Nirvana after death." The word *parinibbuto,* used to denote the death of Buddha, does not mean "entering into Nirvana." *"Parinibbuto* simply means 'fully passed away,' 'fully blown out,' or 'fully extinct,' because the Buddha or an *Arahat* has no re-existence after his death."[24] For these Buddhists the goals of Buddhism are virtually opposite to the eternal life of which Christians preach.

5) Some Buddhists speak of a "Pure Land," very similar to the Christian understanding of heaven. This is the "Pure Land Buddhism."[25]

6) The modern Buddhist scholar insists that a true description of *nirvana* is impossible. The concept of *nirvana* does not fit into human categories, so it is difficult for men to understand.[26]

d. Rebirth

1) While Hinduism teaches of an individual essence that is continuous from lifetime to lifetime, Buddhism does not teach that such a continuous essence exists. There is nothing eternal or immortal about man nor any part of him. Buddha denied the existence of the self as a separate entity (doctrine of *anatta*).[27]

2) According to Buddha, no self exists that is continuous throughout the *samsara* cycle. Instead, each individual consists of a combination of five aggregates, called *skandhas*, which include the physical body, emotions,

perception, volition, and consciousness.[28] Death causes these aggregates, or parts, to be dismantled, and much like a car, it ceases to be a cohesive unit when it is taken apart piece by piece.

3) Buddhism stresses the idea of "rebirth," rather than the Hindu concept of "transmigration."[29] It rejects the notion of a soul's forming the connecting link between successive incarnations. What lives on after death is not some invisible part of the individual, but simply *karma*.[30] It has been compared to the flame of a nearly spent candle's being used to light a new one.

"The King said: 'Where there is no transmigration, Nagasena, can there be rebirth?'"
"Yes, there can."
"But how can that be? Give me an illustration."
"Suppose a man, O king, were to light a lamp from another lamp, can it be said that one transmigrates . . . to the other?"
"Certainly not."
"Just so, great King, is rebirth without transmigration."[31]

4) A true Buddhist believes that what lives on after death is not some invisible part of the individual, but simply *karma*, the results of what has happened before.[32] In spite of this, in practice many Buddhists hold to the view of transmigration.

e. God

1) Buddhism has been described as "an atheistic religion"[33] and as a "non-theistic ethical discipline."[34] It is hardly a religion in the generally accepted sense of the word as connoting some contact between man and divinity. It is, rather, a moral philosophy. But it is religious in the sense that it provides an explanatory system to the same questions religions ask.

2) The Buddhist concepts of impermanence (*anicca)* and the fact that nothing has a permanent soul (*anatta*) virtually eliminate the idea of an eternal Being. "According to Buddhism . . . everything is relative, conditioned and impermanent, and that there is no unchanging, everlasting, absolute substance like Self, Soul, or *Atman* within or without."[35] Buddhism

is purely man-centered, a system of self-training, stressing ethics and mind-culture to the exclusion of theology. God, in the objective personal sense, does not fit into the Buddhist system. Buddhism, as taught by its founder, is in no sense a system of faith and worship as understood in the Christian view. Buddha left no room for prayer or praise; he offered neither forgiveness nor heaven, he warned of no judgment and no hell. It must be pointed out, however, that many followers of Buddha have turned him into "God," to whom they offer homage and supplication.[36]

5. *The Later Career of Buddha*

a. After attaining enlightenment, Buddha was tempted to keep his discovery to himself. Having overcome this reluctance, he sought out the five men with whom he had formerly experimented in the way of austerity. He found them in the Deer Park at Banaras and preached his first sermon to them. It was received with such success that they became the original members of the Order, which he established on the basis of his moral and philosophical principles. Rules and regulations for this community of believers were gradually formulated and became a part of the Buddhist canon of scripture.

b. Within three months their number had grown to sixty, most of them being wealthy young noblemen satiated with luxury and pleasure. Buddha then sent them out in all directions as missionaries.

c. For more than forty years Gautama lived as a mendicant preacher. It was his custom to spend the three wet months of the year in retreat and the nine dry ones itinerating. After 45 years of spreading his message, Buddha suffered an attack of dysentery when he was 80 years old, probably as a result of food poisoning. He died in the Upavart Grove, just outside of the town of Kusingari, lying between two trees. "Unlike others, he was 'utterly extinguished' (*parinibbuto*), for he would never be reborn to suffer again."[37] His last words were, "Decay is inherent in all component things! Work out your salvation with diligence."[38]

d. He was cremated and the neighboring population shared his relics, which they placed in commemorative monuments known as *stupas*.[39] Of the ten *stupas* said to have been erected over the ashes of the Buddha, few have been identified with any certainty.[40]

e. Among the more famous relics in Sri Lanka are a reputed cutting from the original Bodhi Tree,[41] a collar-bone of Gautama, the imprint of his foot from a lonely mountain peak, and one of his teeth, to which immense reverence is paid in the Temple of the Tooth at Kandy.[42]

Notes

1   Damien Keown, *Buddhism: A Very Short Introduction* (New York: Oxford University Press, 2000), 44.

2   Chris Pauling, *Introducing Buddhism* (New York: Barnes & Noble, 2001), 3.

3   Malcolm David Eckel, "Buddhism," in *Eastern Religions*, ed. Michael D. Coogan (New York: Oxford University Press, 2005), 184.

4   These signs allegedly included a dream the night he was conceived, soothsayers announcing that he would become either a monarch or a Buddha, talking and walking right after birth, and miracles all around the world at the very moment of his birth. Ornan Rotem, "Buddhism," in *The Sacred East: Understanding Eastern Religions*, ed. C. Scott Littleton (London: Thorsons, 2003), 59.

5   Even the date of his death is not precisely identified. Two independent chronologies are used in the old documents. Etienne Lamotte, "The Buddha, His Teachings and His Sangha," in *The World of Buddhism: Buddhist Monks and Nuns in Society and Culture*, ed. Heinz Bechert and Richard Gombrich (London: Thames and Hudson, 1993), 41.

6   "No one, it is said, can possibly explain enlightenment. It does not lend itself to description or explanation in words. The man who has awakened, however, is in no doubt about the occurrence. . . . As a term, enlightenment signifies a direct, dynamic spiritual experience brought about, in the Buddhist view, through the faculty of intuition, a faculty developed and sharpened by such spiritual disciplines as intensive meditation and contemplation." Nancy Wilson Ross, *Buddhism: A Way of Life and Thought* (New York: Vintage Books, 1981), 14, 15.

7   Ryuho Okawa, *The Essence of Buddha: The Path of Enlightenment* (London: Timwarner Books, 2002), 19.

8   Michael Carrithers, *Buddha: A Very Short Introduction* (New York: Oxford University Press, 2001), 49.

9   Walpola Rahula, "The Doctrine of No-Soul: Anatta," *What the Buddha Taught*, Foreword by Paul Demieville, rev. ed. (New York: Grove Press, 1974), 51-66.

10   "It is true that the Pali word *dukkha* (or Sanskrit *duhkha*) in ordinary usage means 'suffering', 'pain', 'sorrow' or 'misery', as opposed to the word *sukha* meaning 'happiness', comfort' or 'ease'. But the term *dukkha* as the First Noble Truth, which represents the Buddha's view of life and the world, has a deeper

philosophical meaning and connotes enormously wider senses. It is admitted that
the term *dukkha* in the First Noble Truth contains, quite obviously, the ordinary
meaning of 'suffering', but in addition it also includes deeper ideas such as
'imperfection', 'impermanence', 'emptiness', 'insubstantiality'." Ibid., 17.

11 Eugene R. Swanger, "The Buddhist Tradition," in *Great Asian Religions* (Grand
Rapids: Baker, 1984), 70.

12 David Bentley-Taylor, "Buddhism," in *The World's Religions*, ed. Sir Norman
Anderson (Grand Rapids: Eerdmans, 1989), 176.

13 A true Buddhist "is always calm and serene, and cannot be upset or dismayed by
changes or calamities, because he sees things as they are. The Buddha was never
melancholy or gloomy. He was described by his contemporaries as 'ever-smiling'
(*mihitapubbamgama*). In a Buddhist painting or sculpture the Buddha is always
represented with a happy countenance, serene, contented and compassionate. Never
a trace of suffering or agony or pain is to be seen." Rahula, *What the Buddha
Taught*, 27.

14 Keown, *Buddhism: A Very Short Introduction*, 55.

15 Theodore M. Ludwig, *The Sacred Paths: Understanding the Religions of the World*,
4ᵗʰ ed. (Upper Saddle River, NJ: Pearson Prentice Hall, 2006), 153.

16 Okawa, "The Idea of the Void," chap. in *The Essence of Buddha*, 52-68. Emptiness
(*shunyata*) is one of the most important concepts and yet the most elusive notion to
be grasped in Mahayana philosophy.

17 Warren Mathews, *World Religions*, 4ᵗʰ edition (Belmont, CA: Wadsworth, 2004),
130.

18 William A. Young, *The World's Religions: Worldviews and Contemporary Issues*,
2ⁿᵈ ed. (Upper Saddle River, NJ: Pearson Prentice Hall, 2005), 92-93.

19 [Albert Charles Muller,] "Buddhism," in *Patterns of Religion*, ed. Roger Schmidt
(Belmont, CA: Wadsworth, 2000), 194.

20 Originally, *nirvana* was connected with the verb *nibbati*, "to cool by blowing"; a
related term is *nibbuta*, a past participle used to describe the early Buddhist ideal
man, "he who is cooled." "The 'cooling' here refers to a state of being cooled from
'fever' of greed, hatred, and delusion, the three principal forms of evil in Buddhist
thought." S. G. F. Brandon, A *Dictionary of Buddhism: A Guide to Thought and
Tradition* (New York: Charles Scribner's Sons, 1972), 196-97.

21 Ibid.

22   However, this was what early translators of the *Sutras* thought, because the word
can be literally translated as "going out," as a fire dies out when it lacks fuel. Ibid.,
128.

23   "Nirvana is definitely no annihilation of self, because there is no self to annihilate."
Rahula, *What the Buddha Taught*, 37.

24   Ibid., 41.

25   "Pure Land Buddhism," *Wikipedia, The Free Encyclopedia*, 2006 [article online];
retrieved on November 15, 2006, from http://en.wikipedia.org/wiki/
Pure_Land_Buddhism.

26   Paul Lairon, "Buddhism 101," *The Buddhist Channel*, 2004 [article online];
retrieved on January 29, 2006, from http://www.buddhistchannel.tv/
index.php?id=10,188,0,0,1,0.

27   Denise L. Carmody and T. L. Brink, *Ways to the Center* (Belmont, CA: Wadsworth,
2006), 256.

28   Etienne Lamotte, "The Buddha, His Teachings and His Sangha," in *The World of
Buddhism: Buddhist Monks and Nuns in Society and Culture*, ed. Heinz Bechert and
Richard Gombrich (London: Thames and Hudson, 1993), 42.

29   "Rebirth maintains that there is a causal connection between one life and another.
The following life is completely new but is conditioned by the old one." Jane Hope
and Borin Van Loon, *Introducing Buddha* (New York: Totem Books, 1995), 145.

30   Bentley-Taylor, "Buddhism," 175.

31   B. R. Ambedkar, *The Buddha and His Dhamma* (Bombay: Government Central
Press, 1995), Book 4, Part 2, Section 4, 7-19 [book online]; retrieved on February
23, 2006, from http://www.columbia.edu/itc/mealac/pritchett/00ambedkar/
ambedkar_buddha/04_02.html.

32   Another explanation is that energies do not die. "When this physical body is no
more capable of functioning, energies do not die with it, but continue to take some
other shape or form, which we call another life." Rahula, *What the Buddha Taught*,
33.

33   Young, *The World's Religions*, 94. Young explains that Theravada Buddhism "is
atheistic in a functional rather than a theoretical sense. Theoretical atheism denies
that gods exist. Functional atheism is not concerned about the question of the
existence of gods; it only knows that whether they exist or not, they are irrelevant to
human destiny." Ibid..

34 Buddhism is "a non-theistic ethical discipline, a system of self training, anthropocentric, stressing ethics and mind-culture to the exclusion of theology." Davis Taylor and Clark Offner, "Buddhism," in *The World's Religions*, ed. Norman Anderson (Grand Rapids: InterVarsity, 1975), 177. Also see Pat Zukeran, "Buddhism," *Probe Ministries*, 1996-2006 [article online]; available on February 26, 2006, at http://www.leaderu.com/orgs/probe/docs/ buddhism.html.

35 Rahula, *What the Buddha Taught*, 39.

36 John T. Seamands, *Tell it Well: Communicating the Gospel Across Cultures* (Kansas City, MO: Beacon Hill Press, 1981), 171.

37 Carrithers, *Buddha: A Very Short Introduction*, 3.

38 According to Rahula's translation, "Transient are conditioned things. Try to accomplish your aim with diligence." See Rahula, "The Last Words of the Buddha," in *What the Buddha Taught*, 136-138; text translated from *Mahaparinibbana-sutta* of the *Digha-nikaya, Sutta* No. 16.

39 Lamotte, "The Buddha, His Teachings and His Sangha," 42. *Stupas* are commemorative monuments usually housing sacred relics associated with the Buddha or saintly persons. Originally they had a hemispherical form, but eventually they evolved into bell-shaped monuments (Sri Lanka), terraced temples (Borobudur, Java, Indonesia), and multistoried pagodas (China, Korea, and Japan).

40 Humphreys, *Buddhism*, 42.

41 When Ashoka introduced Buddhism to modern Sri Lanka, a cutting of the Bodhi Tree was brought to that island. The original tree in India died in the 12th century. In about 1884 a cutting of the newer tree was brought back to replace it. Jean Boisseller, *The Wisdom of the Buddha* (New York: Harry N. Abrams, 1994), 68.

42 Bentley-Taylor, "Buddhism," 180.

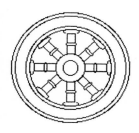

CHAPTER 10

Major Buddhist Divisions

1. *Introduction*

a. For two centuries Buddhism did not spread beyond the borders of India. Then came the warrior King Ashoka Maurya, who ruled India from 274 to 232 B.C. During a battle he felt such revulsion to the bloodshed that he renounced all such fighting. He converted to Buddhism and devoted himself and his resources to its propagation. It is Ashoka who may be credited with making Buddhism a world religion. He commissioned Buddhist missionaries to go to the other parts of India, as well as to Syria, Egypt, Cyrene, Greece, and Sri Lanka.[1]

b. Around Ashoka's time a major division began to develop within Buddhism. The primary issue was whether enlightenment is accessible to everyone or to only a few.

1) Buddhists who said enlightenment was available to everyone were called *Mahayana*, or "the greater vehicle."[2]

2) Those who said that enlightenment is accessible only to the committed few (for instance, monks) were called *Hinayana*, or "the lesser

vehicle."[3] Being offended by the negative connotation of the term *Hinayana*, they began to refer to themselves as *Theravada* Buddhists, which means "the teaching of the elders."

3) The canon was also an issue of contention. The Theravada canon is a collection of Buddha's doctrinal discourses and was fixed early; in Mahayana areas the concept of "canonicity" was quite loose, and their canon comprises a monastic library called "*sutras*." The Theravada "attacked the Mahayana by claiming that its *sutras* were not the actual teachings of the Buddha. The Mahayana responded by saying that the teaching of the [Theravada] Schools was merely a preparatory teaching which the Mahayana superseded."[4]

c. Ashoka sought to establish a realm of righteousness in northern India, but gradual corruption by local superstition and magic led to the decline of the religion by the seventh century A.D. The death blow was delivered by the Muslim invaders of the eleventh century, and since that time there have been few Buddhists in the land that gave it birth.

d. Generally speaking, Buddhism reached Sri Lanka in the third century before Christ, China soon after the time of Christ,[5] Central Asia in the first century A.D., Thailand in the second, Korea and Indonesia in the fourth, Japan and Tibet in the sixth.[6]

2. *Theravada Buddhism*

a. Theravada Buddhists pride themselves on keeping to Siddhartha Gautama's original teaching as found in the earliest Buddhist writings (hence, "teachings of the elders"). In the views of Theravada Buddhism, Buddha was just a great teacher; he was a superior person but nevertheless only a man. The ideal of Theravada Buddhism is the condition of the *arhat*, one who has reached *nirvana*.[7]

b. Theravada Buddhism is conservative and has legalistic teachings, involving a narrow, austere path to spiritual enlightenment.[8] It emphasizes the individual's effort toward salvation and recognizes no divine help in this; rejects all rituals and images, even frowning on statues of the Buddha; emphasizes the life of the *sangha* (monastery); considers prayer as meditation rather than petition; and its key virtue is wisdom.[9]

c. From India, Theravada Buddhism eventually spread into the southeastern regions of Asia: Sri Lanka, Burma, Thailand, Cambodia, and Laos. Because of their spread in this area, Theravada Buddhism is sometimes referred to as "Southern Buddhism."

d. Theravada Buddhist scriptures

1) Theravada Buddhism considers the canon to be closed with the *Pali Tripitaka*. *Pali* refers to the language in which it was written, and *Tripitaka* (also spelled *Tipitaka*) means the "three baskets"[10] of teachings, which include 1) Buddha's sermons, 2) rules for monks, and 3) later doctrinal elaborations.[11] The length of the *Tripitaka* is around seventy times that of the Bible, providing abundant opportunity for a variety of interpretations.

2) The words of Buddha were not committed to writing until he had been dead for several centuries. The third basket was completed around the second century B.C. During the first 250 years following Buddha's death, four major Councils were convened with the purpose of reciting aloud and thus fixing in the minds of the *sangha* members (monks) the contents of the Tripitaka.[12]

3. *Mahayana Buddhism*

a. In contrast with Theravada, this later development within Buddhism is a more liberal branch with a broad path to enlightenment. "*Mahayana* means the 'Great Vehicle,' so called because it regards itself as the universal way to salvation."[13]

> A potent factor in the expansion of Buddhism has been the tolerance with which it has incorporated ideas and practices which were really alien to its spirit. . . . This compromise is especially clear in Mahayana, [that produced] systems of thought which seem far removed from the relative simplicity of Gautama's message.[14]

b. There are three elements in Mahayana Buddhism which represent striking innovations: 1) postulation of an Absolute or Supreme Reality, 2) the development of a pantheistic world-view, and 3) the recognition of an individual "soul" which survives death and may pass through various heavens and hells en route to *nirvana*.[15]

c. Within the Mahayana communities, Gautama is not seen as merely a human being. Rather, he is understood to have been and to be the absolute, supreme, and only reality. They see Gautama as essentially sacred.[16] Mahayana Buddhism developed elaborate pantheons which have elevated the Buddha and other great Buddhist teachers into deliverers. These transcendent divine beings offer more than a way of enlightenment. They offer grace to those who have faith in them and give them devotion. There are an infinite number of Buddhas saving people.[17]

    d. Salvation does not depend necessarily upon individual effort, but may be an unmerited blessing, granted or attained suddenly, even in this present worldly existence. Mahayana Buddhists allow for redemption to occur through an individual's own effort, but self-effort is no longer necessary. One can appeal to the Absolute for emancipation from the sufferings of life.

    e. The development of Mahayana Buddhism was related to a change in the ideal of Buddhist perfection. Mahayana's key virtue is compassion rather than wisdom. In contrast with Theravada, with its idealization of the *arhat,* "worthy one" or "saint," in Mahayana the ideal is the *bodhisattva,* a term referring to one who renounces his own salvation out of compassion for his fellow man. This concept introduces peculiar Mahayanist elements such as altruistic activity, vicarious suffering, and transferable merit, which are in clear contrast with Theravada thought.[18]

    f. The Mahayanan concept of *bodhisattva*

      1) When one is ready to attain *nirvana* through ethics, enlightenment, and the compassion and mercy of a Buddha, one may become a *bodhisattva,* a savior who helps others. "The word Bodhisattva means one whose essence of being (*sattva*) is perfect Wisdom (*Bodhi*), but historically it meant one who has dedicated his life to the welfare of mankind, delaying thereby his entry into Nirvana, the reward of his own Enlightenment."[19]

      2) Mahayana Buddhism teaches that one's own redemption cannot be fully realized until all are redeemed; in contrast with Mahayana monks and nuns, most Theravada monks see their immediate goal as reaching *nirvana* and exiting this life. For Mahayana Buddhism, the primary goal must be to bring mercy to those in suffering. Hence, the *bodhisattva* is the Mahayana ideal. The following is a commonly told Mahayana parable.

> Four men lost in the desert had become weak and emaciated and were slowly dying of hunger and thirst. Barely able to move, they stumbled upon a stone wall. It rose high above them. After some consideration, one of them, with the last bit of energy he could muster, slowly climbed the wall. At the top he peered over, let out a scream of delight, leaped to the other side, and disappeared from sight. The three who remained were puzzled and looked silently at each other. Finally after some time had passed and nothing was heard from the other side, the second person made the arduous climb with his

last reserve of strength. He too looked over the top of the wall, shouted for joy, and disappeared from sight. The third man also did the same. Then the fourth person slowly pulled himself, stone by stone, up the wall. At the top his eyes gazed upon a cool green oasis filled with fruit and bubbling springs of water. Having momentarily refreshed himself, he climbed back down on the desert side of the wall and wandered off into the dessert looking for others who were lost among the rocks, the sand, and the heat.

3) An important *bodhisattva* in the Mahayana pantheon is Kwan-yin (Figure 10.1). In the Hindu pantheon is a male known as Avalokiteshvara ("hearer of cries" or "hearing the world's cries"). In East Asia, this *bodhisattva* became female to fit her position as a protector of women.[20] When someone meets difficult situations or calamities and praises her name, *bodhisattva* Kwan-yin will save them. For Mahayana Buddhists, Kwan-yin holds the place which the Virgin Mary holds for the pious Catholic.[21]

Figure 10.1

4) Another important *bodhisattva* is Amitabha (Figure 10.2), known as Omitofo in Chinese and Amida in Japanese. Buddha Amitabha, Lord of the Western Paradise, will deliver those who recite *Nan-Wu A-mi-To-Fo* (praise to Buddha Amitabha) for one to seven days, with true faith and devotion at the time of death.[22]

5) Although Kwan-yin (Avalokiteshvara) and Amitabha are the most important deities in the Mahayana pantheon, Maitreya is the earliest cult *bodhisattva*. He is called Milofo in Chinese and Miroku in Japanese, and his devotees anticipate his imminent coming to earth. Images of the corpulent and happy Maitreya are popular in East Asia.[23] Since absolutely nothing endures, in time Buddhist teachings and practices will decline and life will become very difficult for the faithful. When that occurs, Maitreya will come and reestablish the form and means of the Buddhist faith.[24]

Figure 10.2

6) A common sight in Mahayana temples is a form of Trinity. "Samantabhadra, representing the love aspect of the Buddha-principle, and Manjusri, representing the wisdom aspect, are to be found on either side of a thousand 'trinities', with the Buddha in some cosmic aspect in the centre."[25]

h. Mahayana Buddhism spread toward the northeastern parts of Asia: China, Vietnam, Korea, and Japan. Because of their spread in this area, Mahayana Buddhism is sometimes referred to as "Northern Buddhism."

g. Mahayana Buddhist scriptures

1) The canon remains open. Thus, they include writings from Indian, Chinese, Japanese, and Tibetan sources in their scriptures, although Sanskrit is the language of the oldest scriptures.

2) In contrast to the comparatively limited scope of the Pali canon used by Theravada Buddhists, Mahayana scriptures have multiplied to the point where standard editions of the Chinese canon encompass over five thousand volumes.[26]

3) Some of the more popular Mahayana scriptures include the *Lotus Sutra* and the *Perfection of Wisdom*, which in turn includes the *Diamond Sutra* and the *Heart Sutra*.

4) Most Mahayana sects have chosen certain favorite scriptures exclusively. Such selection is necessary, for this extreme bulk and breadth of the scriptures make it impossible for believers to be acquainted with, let alone understand and practice, the often contradictory teachings found in them.

4. *Vajrayana or Tantrayana Buddhism*

a. The third vehicle, latest and least numerous of the three branches, is called *Vajrayana*, "the thunderbolt vehicle," or "the diamond vehicle." The name *Vajrayana* implies the sexual symbolism (*vajra*, "thunderbolt," symbol of the phallus) that pervades the structure of this form of Buddhism.[27] Vajrayana Buddhism incorporated Mahayana principles. The devotee worships the transcendent *bodhisattvas* with whom he identifies himself. It spread mainly in Tibet, Bhutan, Nepal, and Mongolia.

b. Other names for this form of Buddhism are "Tantraism," "Tantric Buddhism," and "Tantrayana Buddhism." The main importer of Tantraism into Tibet was Padma Sambhava, a Tantric sorcerer. Tantraism was blended with Bon, the indigenous religion of Tibet.[28] The name is derived from a form of Hinduism called *tantra*,[29] which emphasizes occultic techniques for the development of spiritual power. Liberation is achieved through "seed formulas," using liturgical rites which stress *mantras* (magic words),[30] *mudras* (specific gestures and postures assumed while practicing),[31] and *mandalas* (cosmic diagrams).[32]

c. Sometime in the fifth century A.D. a number of Buddhist books were brought into Tibet from India. It was not until King Srongtsen Gampo was converted by his two chief wives in the middle of the seventh century that Buddhism became a force in Tibet. He is considered to be the founder of this form of Buddhism. It has been described as "a priestly mixture of Sivaite mysticism, magic, and Indo-Tibetan demonolatry, overlaid by a thin varnish of Mahayana Buddhism."[33]

d. This branch is also known as "Lamaism." *Lama* means the "superior one." It is a term that should be reserved for the heads of monasteries and the highest dignitaries, but for courtesy is given to all of the *gelong*, or fully ordained rank. Atisha, a famous Mahayanist monk from India, reformed the Buddhism of Tibet in the eleventh century. New monasteries were built and new scriptures translated. Tsong-ka-pa (1358-1419) from China created the Gelugpa Order, or Yellow Hat sect, from which the Dalai ("Great Ocean") Lamas are chosen.[34] The Dalai Lama is probably today's most recognizable living symbol of Buddhism, at least in the West.

e. Tibet is a region in Central Asia and the home of the Tibetan people; today most of the area is administered by the People's Republic of China. With an average elevation of 4,900 meters (16,000 ft), it is often called the "Roof of the World." The Dalai Lama is Tibet's exiled spiritual and political leader. Due to his influence, this branch of Buddhism is also known as "Tibetan Buddhism." Tibetan Buddhists consider the current Dalai Lama to be the fourteenth reincarnation of Avalokiteshvara, the *bodhisattva* of compassion.[35] Until the Chinese Communist invasion of 1959, the Dalai Lama ruled from the great Potala, one of the most magnificent buildings in the world. After leaving Lahasa, capital of Tibet, the Dalai Lama moved to Dharsalama in India.

f. Vajrayana/Tibetan Buddhist scriptures seem to be the codification of a monastic library. The Tibetan Canon consists of two parts: (1) the *Kanjur*, 108 volumes ("Translation of the Word of the Buddha"), and (2) the *Tanjur*, 225 volumes ("Translation of the Teachings"). Because this latter collection contains works attributed to individuals other than the Buddha, it is considered only semi-canonical. Some portions of the *Tanjur* are not even Buddhist in character. They deal with logic, grammar, lexicography, poetry and drama, medicine and chemistry, astrology and divination, painting, and biographies of saints. Their inclusion in the Tibetan Canon is justified by the fact that they are necessary aids in the practice of the religion.[36]

g. Tibetan Buddhism uniquely established the principle of succession by reincarnation among its religious leaders, made possible by the recognition of *tulkus*, children who are identified as reincarnations of noted religious personages. The discovery or recognition of a *tulku* often comes between the ages of two and five. Various tests of confirmation are followed.[37]

h. The use of paranormal energies, or supernatural powers, is another unique aspect of this form of Buddhism. By combining special powers of concentration, breathing exercises, and yogic or gymnastic training, the body may reach amazing physical capacities. These include withstanding extremes of unrelieved cold, including total immersion in the icy waters of high mountains, ability to travel in trance hundreds of miles in a single day, and levitation.[38]

i. Prayer wheels, known as *mani*, are common sights in areas where Tibetan Buddhism prevails. Tibetans carry hand-held prayer wheels around for hours, spinning them any time they have a hand free. Larger wheels, which may be several feet high and five to six feet in diameter, can contain myriad copies of the *Om Mani Padme Hum* mantra, and may also contain sacred texts, up to hundreds of volumes.[39] A "Dharma Wheel Cutting Karma" has been turning at the Library of Congress since 1997. The *mani* contains 208 repetitions of 42 Tibetan scriptures, and it is said "to generate compassion, prevent natural disasters, and promote peace in the world."[40] Prayer flags are also typical of Tibetan Buddhism. They are inscribed with auspicious symbols, invocations, prayers, and mantras. Tibetans set these flags outside their homes and temples for the wind to carry blessings, long life, and prosperity to the flag planter and those in the vicinity.[41]

5. *Zen Buddhism*

a. The Zen school accepts the Mahayanan doctrines but adds some distinctive elements: 1) A close relationship between master and disciple, 2) disciplined effort aimed at bringing body and mind into the condition conducive to attaining *satori*, "enlightenment," and 3) adjusting one's daily routine and surroundings to what contributes to enlightenment (e.g., beautiful gardens).

b. Although the roots of Zen reach back to India, its historical origins are in China as a meditation school of Mahayana Buddhism. Buddhism entered into China during the third century B.C. Zen appeared after a long period of development in Chinese Buddhism. It was founded by Bodhidharma, who reached China from South India in A.D. 520.[42] This form of Buddhism met the first waves of Christianity coming into China and they influenced each other.

c. The original Sanskrit term means meditation, contemplation, tranquilization, or concentration. "Zen" is an abbreviation of *Zazen*, which is Japanese. The root of the term can be traced to Sanskrit, passing through different languages:[43]

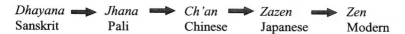

Dhayana ➡	*Jhana* ➡	*Ch'an* ➡	*Zazen* ➡	*Zen*
Sanskrit	Pali	Chinese	Japanese	Modern

d. This direct path to enlightenment passed to Japan in the twelveth century, where it took root and commands the largest following today. Japanese scholar D. T. Suzuki was largely responsible for introducing Zen Buddhism to the West during the early part of the twentieth century.[44]

e. Zen beliefs

1) "If a Zen Buddhist were asked what Zen teaches, he would answer that Zen teaches nothing. Whatever teachings there are in Zen come out of one's own mind. One teaches oneself; Zen merely points the way."[45]

2) There are no scriptures in Zen Buddhism. Since the truth gained through *satori* is beyond expression in human language, Zen emphasizes its independence from written scriptures or literature of any kind. "Anything that has the semblance of an external authority is rejected by Zen."[46] Because of these beliefs, even Zen cannot believe that Zen's own doctrine is more true than the doctrine of other religions. This is a dilemma. "If it is believed that truth cannot be known, it cannot be believed that the premises of Zen are true. Therefore, to think Zen is true means to think Zen is not true."[47] These perspectives sound appealing to post-moderns, and this may be a reason for the conversion of many Westerners to Buddhism.

3) *Satori*, spiritual enlightenment, comes as a sudden flash of spiritual insight. *Satori* can be brought on by meditation and mind control, which prepare one for the awakening of the dormant mental faculties. In order to achieve this *satori*, one must be still for hours–as long as it takes. Before starting meditation, Zen Buddhists will carefully arrange their bodies, as in *yoga*, to prepare the mind and correct the breathing. By doing so, the mind becomes "sharpened by concentration to the point of freedom from all bondage to thoughts or imaginations of any kind," resulting in a state of "absolute emptiness."[48]

4) There are four steps taken to free oneself from the bonds of present thought: 1) Unthink: The Zen follower begins to de-condition himself mentally. He cuts ties to his old views of religion, politics, social problems, male or

femaleness, youth or age, etc. 2) Stop thinking: He learns to let the waves of thought die down until silence is all that is left. He chooses to dwell at "the center of the turning world" and remains in this state even when back in the noisy world. 3) Re-think: This phase concentrates on the thought forces which emanate from the Buddha-mind. 4) Beyond thought: This is the stage where enlightenment takes place.[49]

5) The subject for meditation is the *Koan*, a paradoxical problem that is kept before the mind's eye until one eventually breaks through to enlightenment. The following are some examples of *Koan*:

> Reveal the true nature of the universe while washing bowls.

> If you meet someone in the street who has attained the truth, you must pass him neither speaking nor in silence. How would you meet him?

> We know the sound of two hands clapping, but what is the sound of one hand clapping?[50]

When one wrestles long enough with the *Koan*, an answer comes. Meditation on these paradoxes often brings about great anguish until one breaks through to the joyful solution, which has nothing to do with logic.

> A monk asked Chao-chou, "What is the meaning of the first patriarch's visit to China?" "The cypress tree in the front courtyard," came the answer.[51]

> "Am I right when I have no idea?" asked another enquirer. "Throw away that idea of yours," was the reply. "What idea?" asked the bewildered pupil. "You are free, of course," said the Master, "to carry about that useless idea of no idea."[52]

6. *Folk Buddhism*

a. Buddhists may profess one of the "official" branches of Buddhism, or they may practice popular Buddhism. Those involved in the folk version usually know very little about the official version taught in their area.

b. The following are some distinctive aspects of popular Buddhism:[53]

1) *Karma*. Buddhism teaches that only the consequences of deeds are transmitted from one incarnation to another. However, the popular conception of *karma* is practically indistinguishable from the Hindu idea of transmigration of the soul. The chief concern of the average Buddhist layman is that he will

have to reckon with the fruit of his actions committed in present, former, and future lives. He is oppressed by the fear of being born as an animal or in one of the terrible Buddhist hells, the horrors of which are plainly shown in the temple pictures.

2) Merit. The folk Buddhist believes that in order to be born in a happier sphere in the next incarnation, he must store up the necessary merit. "By one's own good deeds salvation must be won" is axiomatic in popular Buddhism. The salvation aimed at is rebirth in happier conditions than those of the present life. The hope of entering *nirvana* fades into an indefinite future.

3) Fear of demons and spirits. Folk Buddhists believe that spirits influence and control people's lives. In the thought of the masses, the law of *karma* does not suffice to account for the ills of life. They believe that people must appease the spirits in order to have success, and that they should seek the guidance of the spirits through various forms of divination.

4) Worship and prayer. Although contrary to Gautama's teaching, he is popularly worshiped as a god, and prayers for material benefits are mostly addressed to him. Clearly, the human heart has deep longings for fellowship with the Eternal.

c. Folk Buddhists attribute magical power to the sacred writings of Buddhism. They are the embodiment of the truth of the Absolute, and are effective against illness, demons, traffic accidents, and so forth. Thus in China, Korea, or Japan it is not uncommon for people to carry a portion of a *sutra* as protection, nor is it unusual to see them hanging from rearview mirrors in automobiles.[54]

7. *A Comparison of the Major Branches*

a. There is hardly any difference among Buddhists with regard to the fundamental teachings.[55]

1) All accept Buddha as the Teacher.
2) The Four Noble Truths are exactly the same in all schools.
3) The Eightfold Path is exactly the same in all schools.
4) All reject the idea of a supreme being who created this world.
5) All accept the doctrines of *anicca*, *dukkha*, and *anatta*.

b. The differences within Buddhism may be compared to those within Christianity between Greek Orthodox, Roman Catholicism, and Protestantism, including the many movements and groupings which each of these contains.

c. A comparison of the three major branches of Buddhism:[56]

THERAVADA	MAHAYANA	VAJRAYANA
"The teaching of the elders" Conservative Buddhism	"The greater vehicle" Liberal Buddhism	"The diamond vehicle" A special form of Mahayana
Southern Buddhism. Spread mainly in Burma, Cambodia, Laos, Sri Lanka, and Thailand.	Northern Buddhism. Spread mainly in Mainland China, Hong Kong, Korea, Japan, Taiwan, and Vietnam.	Tibetan Buddhism. Spread mainly in Bhutan, Mongolia, and Tibet. Also known as "Lamaism."
Ideal: The *arhat*. One who is more concerned with his own enlightenment than with that of others. His primary concern is to attain enlightenment for himself by forsaking all.[57]	Ideal: The *bodhisattva*. One who has attained enlightenment but, out of compassion for the unenlightened masses, refuses to enter *nirvana* in order to come back and guide others along the path.	Ideal: One who uses *tantra*. Occultic techniques to develop pure spiritual power and the ability to cut through illusions so as to gain enlightenment quickly.
Buddha was only a man and not a god. Buddha was a teacher.	Buddha is a historical manifestation of a universal Absolute, or Buddha essence. Buddha is a savior.	Same understanding of Buddha as in Mahayana.
Attainment requires constant commitment and is primarily for monks and nuns.	Religious practice is relevant to life in the world and therefore available to lay people.	Same as in Mahayana.
Minimizes ritual	Emphasizes ritual	Emphasizes ritual.

There can be only one Buddha.	There have been many manifestations of the Buddha essence and there will be at least one more, the "Maitreya Buddha."	There have been many manifestations of the Buddha essence.
Human beings are emancipated by self-effort, without supernatural aid.	Human aspirations are supported by divine powers and the grace they bestow.	Humans are supported by divine powers.
One must attain enlightenment solely through one's own efforts. *Karma* cannot be forgiven.	*Bodhisattvas* can help along the path and can even transfer their own extra karmic merit to seekers.	*Boddhiastvas* transfer their own merit to seekers.
Canon closed with the *Pali Tripitaka.*	Open canon. *Sutras.* Indian, Chinese, Japanese, and Tibetan sources.	Open canon. *Kanjur* (108 volumes) and the *Tanjur* (225 volumes).
They do not ordain nuns. Monks are celibate.	Monks and nuns. Some Korean orders allow marriage, but in Japan most monks are married.	Monks and nuns. One of the four Tibetan monastic orders permits marriage.
Nirvana is extinction, the end of reincarnation and suffering.	For some Mahayana schools, *nirvana* is close to the Christian concept of Paradise. For Zen Buddhism, the goal is to attain *satori.*	*Nirvana* is the cessation of karma, ignorance, and delusion.
Key virtue: wisdom.	Key virtue: compassion.	Key virtue: compassion.

Table 10.1

8. *Buddhist Monasticism*

a. From the beginning, Buddhism was a religion of monks. Gautama himself established the *sangha*, the Buddhist Order. The *sangha* is one of the "Three Jewels" (*Triratna*): Buddha, the *dharma* ("law" or "doctrine"), and the *sangha* ("monastic order"). Upon entering the *sangha*, new recruits are required to pronounce the formula of the "Three Refuges": "I take refuge in the Buddha; I take refuge in the Doctrine; I take refuge in the Order."[58]

b. Members vow to observe the "Ten Precepts." Most practicing Buddhists are committed to the first five. The first five precepts forbid 1) murder, 2) theft, 3) sensuality, 4) deceit, and 5) the use of intoxicants. The remaining five precepts are for monks. They require the avoidance of 1) food after midday and 2) sleeping on a mat on the ground, and prohibit 3) dancing, 4) theatricals, and 5) the use of gold and silver, including any form of self-adornment. Criminals, soldiers, debtors, slaves, or those afflicted with such diseases as consumption, leprosy, and epilepsy are disqualified. Applicants must also be over twenty years of age and have their parents' consent. In Buddhist monasticism, physical labor has been discouraged, and there are few celebrations to divert them from seeking their own salvation.[59]

c. Monasteries were built in Gautama's lifetime, and with great reluctance he yielded to the request of his foster mother to admit women to the Order. The Order of Nuns, which has in some countries ceased to exist, was made subject to the Order of Monks.[60]

d. Conservative Therevadas do not allow nuns, and all monks must remain celibate while they are in the *sangha*. While one of the four Tibetan monastic orders permits marriage, as well as some Korean orders, Japan is the only Buddhist country where the majority of religious specialists are married.[61] In some Mahayana areas, "the fully ordained monk resembles the English parish priest. . . . He may marry, and he is responsible for a parish."[62]

9. *Schools of Buddhism*

a. Theravada is virtually non-existent in the areas of northern Buddhism. In modern times Theravada Buddhism is highly unified. The most noticeable Theravada schools were Mahasanghika and Sarvastivada.[63] In time, however, they lost their separate identity.

b. Mahayana ideas spread mostly in the area of influence of China, including Korea, Japan, Mongolia, Hong Kong, and Taiwan. The following are among the best-known Buddhist schools:

1) The Pure Land school (Chinese *Ching-t'u*) was established in the fourth century and is known in Japan as Jodo Buddhism. The school aimed at "simplification." The Pure Land is a transitional realm from which it is easier to

attain *nirvana* than from the earth realm. One enters the Pure Land through faith in Amitabha or Amida Buddha, Lord of the Western Paradise, and by chanting his name. "Here, free from earthly distractions, the devotee can prepare for *nirvana*, which is guaranteed to all who attain the Pure Land."[64] Descriptions of the Pure Land are extremely material, equating more with the Islamic Paradise than Buddhist descriptions of Nirvana.[65]

2) Tendai Buddhism (Chinese *T'ien-t'ai*) emphasizes the essential unity of all Buddhas, times, places, and teachings. All Buddhist scriptures are considered to be an authentic teaching of Buddha. This progressive revelation, however, is considered to have reached its culmination in the *Lotus Sutra*.[66]

3) In the Zen school, liberation is achieved by realizing the primacy of meditation, seeing that everything is mind only. Zen, or Ch'an Buddhism, uses a technique of meditation on the "Vast Emptiness" within oneself.[67]

4) The Nichiren school was the foundation for the Soka Gakkai sect in Japan. Nichiren Daishonin studied in the Tendai school and arrived at the conclusion that he had to launch a vigorous campaign based on "returning to the Lotus Sutra." The violence of his methods awakened much persecution.[68]

11. *Glossary of Common Buddhist Terms*

a. *Anatta*, "no self." The doctrine that no continuous self exists.

b. *Anicca*. The doctrine that everything is impermanent, changing, and in a constant state of flux.

c. *Arhat*. In Theravadha Buddhism, a sage who has overcome all attachments and has attained *nirvana*.

d. Ashoka (274-232 B.C.). Great Buddhist king in India, the "second founder" of Buddhism.

e. *Bodhisattva*. In Mahayana Buddhism, an enlightened person who is ready to enter *nirvana* but does not, in order to relieve others of suffering.

f. Dharma, "doctrine." The teachings of the Buddha.

g. *Dukkha*, "suffering." Life consists of suffering. The cure for *dukkha* is the way of discipline found in the ethic of the Eightfold Path.

h. Eightfold Path. The fundamental path toward *nirvana* as taught by the Buddha.

i. Four Noble Truths. Basic teachings presented in Buddha's first sermon.

j. *Lama*. A Tibetan teacher.

k. *Mantra*, "thought form." A mental aid for meditation.

l. *Mandala*. Painting of cosmic Buddhas or symbolic cosmos, used in Tibetan Buddhism.

m. *Nirvana*, literally, "to extinguish," as in blowing out a flame. The goal of enlightenment.

n. *Pali*. Language of the scriptures of Theravada Buddhism. Pali is a descendant of Sanskrit, the classical language of India.

o. *Samsara*. The cycle of life, death, and rebirth. Reincarnation.

p. *Satori*. The state where all thought ceases through Zen meditation.

q. *Skandhas*. The combination of five elements, or aggregates, that come together to form a person.

r. *Stupa*. Memorial Buddhist shrine or reliquary.

s. *Tanha*. The desire and craving that causes rebirth.

t. *Tantras*. Scriptures describing the rituals, spells, and formulas of esoteric traditions which followed magical and occultic practices (esoteric refers to that which is known by a restricted number of people).

u. Three Refuges. Phrases by which one becomes a monk or nun: "I take refuge in the Buddha; I take refuge in the *Dharma*; I take refuge in the *Sangha*."

v. *Tripitaka*, "three baskets." The scriptures of the Pali canon of Theravada Buddhism.

w. *Yana*. A "vehicle" or a "way" of spiritual progress (as in Mahayana).

Notes

1   Theodore M. Ludwig, *The Sacred Paths: Understanding the Religions of the World*, 4th ed. (Upper Saddle River, NJ: Pearson Prentice Hall, 2006), 134.

2   *Maha* means "great," as in Mahatma (*Maha-atman,* "Great Soul") Gandhi.

3   *Hinayana* (small raft) assumes that "each individual has to cross the river of suffering by his own efforts: Buddha only provides an example of how to do it." Denise L. Carmody and T. L. Brink, *Ways to the Center* (Belmont, CA: Wadsworth, 2006), 232.

4   Malcolm David Eckel, "Buddhism," in *Eastern Religions*, ed. Michael D. Coogan (New York: Oxford University Press, 2005), 149.

5   According to tradition, Buddhism is said to have been introduced in China in 67 A.D. during the reign of King Ming of the Latter Eastern Han Dynasty (25-220 A.D.). In fact, it was 84 years later that the Buddhist scriptures were introduced to and translated in China (in A.D. 151) by King Huan of the same dynasty. Nukkyo Dendo Kyokai ["Buddhist Promoting Foundation"], *The Teaching of Buddha* (Tokyo: Kosaido Printing, 1966), 558.

6   Carl Olson, *The Different Paths of Buddhism: A Narrative-Historical Introduction* (New Brunswick, NJ: Rutgers University Press, 2005), 9.

7   Christmas Humphreys, *Buddhism: An Introduction and Guide* (London: Penguin Books, 1990), 127.

8   David Bentley-Taylor, "Buddhism," in *The World's Religions*, ed. Sir Norman Anderson (Grand Rapids: Eerdmans, 1989), 170.

9   Wulf Metz, "The Enlightened One: Buddhism," in *Eerdmans' Handbook to the World's Religions* (Grand Rapids: Eerdmans 1982), 223.

10   Pali is a language related to Sanskrit and close to that spoken by the Buddha. The *Pali Tripitaka* was written in Sri Lanka. The word *pitaka* ("basket") refers to the baskets in which palm-leaf manuscripts were stored. Nancy Wilson Ross, *Buddhism: A Way of Life and Thought* (New York: Vintage Books, 1981), 45.

11   Robert E. Van Voorst, *Anthology of World Scriptures*, 5th ed. (Belmont, CA: Thomson Wadsworth, 2006), 68-70.

12 Carl Olson, *Original Buddhist Sources: A Reader* (New Brunswick, NJ: Rutgers University Press, 2005), 2-9.

13 Damien Keown, *Buddhism: A Very Short Introduction* (New York: Oxford University Press, 2000), 58.

14 Clark B. Offner, "Mahayana Buddhism," in *The World's Religions*, ed. Sir Norman Anderson (Grand Rapids: Eerdmans, 1989), 180.

15 Ibid., 181.

16 Christmas Humphreys, *Buddhism: An Introduction and Guide* (London: Penguin Books, 1990), 155.

17 George W. Braswell Jr., *Understanding World Religions* (Nashville: Broadman Press, 1983), 14, 87, 88.

18 Mircea Eliade, Ioan P. Couliano, and Hillary S. Wisner, *The Harper Collins Concise Guide to World Religions* (New York: Harper San Francisco, 2000), 32.

19 Humphreys, *Buddhism*, 55.

20 Chain, Wing-Tsit, "Religions of the Chinese," in *The Great Asian Religions: An Anthology* (New York: Collider Macmillan, 1969), 199, 201. See also Swanger, "The Buddhist Tradition," 79. According to folk beliefs in Taiwan, Kwan-yin was a famous princess during the Yuan dynasty (1271-1368). Doong, Fan-yuan, ed. *Essays on Taiwan Folk Beliefs* (Taipei: Charng Chin Cultural Company, 1980), 62, 63. Among the Chinese, the male aspect of this *bodhisattva* is Kwan Shau-yin, but the later female version is Kwan-yin. In Japanese Buddhism she is known as Kwannon. Humphreys, *Buddhism*, 156.

21 T. Patrick Burke, *The Major Religions: An Introduction with Texts*, 2nd ed. (Malden, MA: Blackwell, 2004), 199.

22 Richard C. Bush, *Religion in China* (Niles, IL: Argus Communications, 1977), 41, 51; Chain, "Religions of the Chinese," 195, 197.

23 John L. Esposito, Darrel J. Fasching, and Todd Lewis, *World Religions Today*, 2nd ed. (New York: Oxford University Press, 2006), 378.

24 Eugene R. Swanger, "The Buddhist Tradition," in *Great Asian Religions* (Grand Rapids: Baker, 1984), 81-83.

25 Humphreys, *Buddhism*, 156.

26 Offner, "Mahayana Buddhism," 181.

27 Eliade, Couliano, and Wiesner, *Concise Guide to World Religions*, 34.

28 Bon is the shamanistic religion of Tibet. "The original features of Bon seem to have included a cult of divine kingship, the kings being regarded as manifestations of the sky divinity (reformulated in Buddhism as the reincarnation of lamas); an order of oracular priests (their counterpart, the Buddhist soothsayers); a cult of the gods of the atmosphere, the earth, and subterranean regions (now lesser deities in the Buddhist pantheon); and the practice of blood sacrifices (transmuted into more conventional offerings." *The New Encyclopedia Britannica,* 15th ed., s.v. "Bon."

29 Tantraism is a path to liberation that combines opposites (such as male and female) and permits illicit sexual behavior such as intercourse between son and mother and using in sexual acts bodily fluids that are normally considered polluting. "Due to the illicit, powerful, and dangerous nature of its practice, Tantric teachings are secret and esoteric." Carl Olson, *Original Buddhist Sources* (New Brunswick, NJ: Rutgers University Press, 2005), 225. In Tibetan literature *Vajra* is the name for the male sexual organ.

30 "The syllable *man*, related to our word 'mental,' connotes 'to think or to have mind'; the suffix *tra* is used to form substantives denoting 'instruments or tools.' A *mantra* can therefore be defined as a 'tool in sound,' a tool designed to be used by the mind as an aid in meditation and in the eventual attainment of Buddha Wisdom." Ross, *Buddhism*, 130.

31 See a traditional list of *mudras* in Jean Boisseller, *The Wisdom of Buddha* (New York: Harry N. Abrams, 1993), 152-53.

32 The Sanskrit word *mandala* means "circle" in the ordinary sense of the word. They are "highly complex symbolic and pictorial designations that must be 'read' or 'penetrated.' The goal is to use the mandala to influence the mind in order to establish altered states of consciousness." John Ankerberg and John Weldon, *Encyclopedia of New Age Beliefs*, 1996 ed., s.v. "Mantras and Mandalas." Also see Ross, *Buddhism*, 132-34.

33 L. A. Waddell, *The Buddhism of Tibet*, 30; quoted by Humphreys, *Buddhism*, 190.

34 For a history of Tibetan Buddhism, see Humphreys, *Buddhism*, 190-95.

35 See John R. Hinnells, *Handbook of Living Religions* (Middlesex, England: Penguin Books, 1985), 336.

36 "The Tibetan Canon," *Buddha Dharma Education Association*, 2004 [article online]; retrieved on February 7, 2006, from http://www.buddhanet.net/e-learning/ history/s_tibcanon.htm.

37 Ross, *Buddhism*, 107.

38 Ibid., 126. Many additional examples in T. Lobsang Rampa [pseudonym for C. H. Hoskin], *The Third Eye* (New York: Doubleday, 1957).

39 "Spiritual Technology from Tibet," *Dharma Haven*, 2004 [article online]; retrieved on February 20, 2006, from http://www.dharma-haven.org/tibetan/prayer-wheel.htm.

40 Voorst, *Anthology of World Scriptures*, 67.

41 "Prayer Flag," *China Tibet Information Center* [article online]; retrieved on February 25, 2006, from http://zt.tibet.cn/english/zt/religion/200402004518143923.htm.

42 Olson, *The Different Paths of Buddhism*, 225-26.

43 "Zen," *Answers.com*, 2006 [encyclopedia online]; retrieved on February 25, 2006, from http://www.answers.com/topic/zen.

44 Olson, *The Different Paths of Buddhism*, 252-54.

45 Karen Bullock, "The Way of Zen Buddhism," paper for the seminar "Religions of the East 591-763," Southwestern Baptist Theological Seminary, Fort Worth, TX, Spring 1990, 6.

46 D. T. Suzuki, *An Introduction to Zen Buddhism* (New York: Random House, 1964), 44.

47 Tucker N. Callaway, *Zen Way: Jesus Way* (Rutland, VT: Charles E. Tuttle, 1976), 157-59.

48 Offner, "Mahayana Buddhism," 187.

49 Bullock, "The Way of Zen Buddhism," 19-20.

50 Genjo Marinello, "Zen Koan Practice," *Zen Project*, 2001 [article online]; retrieved on February 20, 2006, from http://www.zenproject.faithweb.com/zen_teachings/koan_practice.html.

51 William Johnston, *Christian Zen* (New York: Harper & Row, 1971), 58.

52 Humphreys, *Buddhism*, 181.

53 Paul A. Eakin, *Buddhism and the Christian Approach to Buddhists in Thailand* (Bangkok: Rung Ruang Ratana, 1960), 24-26.

54 Swanger, "The Buddhist Tradition," 76.

55 Walpola Rahula, "Theravada - Mahayana Buddhism," *Buddhasasana*, 2006 [article online]; retrieved on February 22, 2006, from http://www.saigon.com/~anson/ebud/ebdha125.htm.

56 Adapted from Huston Smith, *The World's Religions: Our Great Wisdom Traditions, revised and updated edition of The Religions of Man* (New York: HarperSanFrancisco, 1991), 126. Adapted from Dean C. Halverson, "Buddhism," in *The Compact Guide to World Religions,* ed. Dean C. Halverson (Minneapolis, MN: Bethany House, 1996), 61.

57 Christmas Humphreys, *Buddhism: An Introduction and Guide* (London: Penguin Books, 1990), 127.

58 Mary Pat Fisher, *Living Religions*, 6th ed. (Upper Saddle River, NJ: Pearson Prentice Hall, 2005), 144.

59 Bentley-Taylor, "Buddhism," 179.

60 D. Amarasiri Weeraratne, "Buddhism and Women," *Buddha Dharma Education Association & Buddhanet*, 2004 [article online]; retrieved on June 18, 2006, from http://www.buddhanet.net/e-learning/history/nunorder.htm.

61 "Buddhist Monasticism," *Wikipedia: The Free Encyclopedia*, 2006 [article online]; retrieved on February 24, 2006, from http://en.wikipedia.org/wiki/Buddhist_monasticism.

62 Humphreys, *Buddhism*, 139. Also see Soko Morinaga, "Celibacy: The View of a Zen Monk from Japan," *Vatican*, 2006 [article online]; retrieved on February 24, 2006, from http://www.vatican.va/roman_curia/congregations/cclergy/documents/rc_con_cclergy_doc_01011993_zen_en.html.

63 Olson, *The Different Paths of Buddhism*, 6, 12.

64 Eckel, *"Buddhism,"* 198.

65 Humphreys, *Buddhism,* 162.

66 Ibid., 168.

67 Ross, *Buddhism*, 141-73.

68 "Nichiren Shoshu," *New Religious Movements*, 2001 [article online]; retrieved on January 16, 2006, from http://religiousmovements.lib.virginia.edu/nrms/ nichiren.html. William O. Woodward stated: "Followers are obliged to engage in forced conversions, and in doing so, they force themselves into private homes and refuse to leave when asked. They disrupt public meetings and threaten nonbelievers. Leaders encourage violence." Woodward, "Japan," *Look,* 10 September 1963, 24; quoted by Pat Means, "Nicherin Shosu/Soka Gakkai," *The Mystical Maze: A Guidebook Through the Mindfields of Eastern Mysticism,* Foreword bo Josh McDowell (San Bernardino, CA: Campus Crusade for Christ, 1976), 176.

CHAPTER 11

Buddhism and Christianity

1. *Historical Similarities*

a. Both Buddhism and Christianity arose in the East. Both are ancient and Asiatic. Though the time was different by five centuries, the customs and atmosphere are clearly oriental. The founders of both religions used the proverb, aphoristic beatitude, parable, nature simile, and the sermon styles that denote the East.[1]

b. Both were reforms of an established religion. Buddhism came from Brahmanism, as Christianity came from Judaism. Both were a protest against legalism, ceremonialism, and sacerdotalism of a traditional system. Buddha broke with the Brahmans, confounded them in argument, denounced their worship, summoned them to discipleship, discredited their sacrificial system, repudiated their gods, and announced himself the authoritative revealer of truth.

c. The founders of both religions left no writings. Both taught through spoken word, deed, and character. Both called and instructed disciples. The sacred canons which preserve their teachings were composed after their ministry had ceased, from the memorial data handed down by their disciples.

d. Both religions resulted in a structured organization. Gautama created the *Sangha* (community of followers), and Christ established His Church. In each case the organization proceeded according to the necessities that arose and after forms that were already in existence. Both societies were composed of disciples for purposes of spiritual growth and propagation.

e. Both religions were missionary in character. Both founders had the consciousness of a message for all mankind. Both Gautama and Jesus gave commissions. During the first three centuries, each faith spread over a vast empire and then went beyond to reach distant peoples.

f. Both religions became state religions--Buddhism under Ashoka, and Christianity under Constantine.

g. Both suffered division. In a rough way, the Buddhist division into the Mahayana and Hinayana schools corresponds to the great schism which split the Church into Eastern and Western, and later into Catholic and Protestant, while the minor Buddhist sects are suggestive of the Christian denominations. The causes of division in both religions have largely been questions of doctrine, ritual, and forms of government.

h. Both developed monasticism. The *sangha* was monastic from the beginning and has remained so. Christianity developed ascetic communities very early and monastic orders in the Middle Ages.

i. Both underwent decline and corruption. Departure from the simple original teachings, corruption of life, and decline of power mark the history of both religions. Both religions disappeared almost totally from the lands of their origin, so that India is now a foreign mission field for Buddhists, as Palestine is for Christians.

j. Both became hierarchical and ritualistic. This is strikingly evident from a comparison of Tibetan Lamaism with Roman Catholicism.[2]

2. *Buddhism Encounters Christianity*

a. Buddhism entered China in the first century A.D. by way of trade routes.[3] While Buddhism was making its way into China, it was undergoing a transformation.[4] This happened just at the time when Christian missions first made their way to China following the trade routes of the Silk Road. Alopen, an Nestorian Bishop from Assyria, began his mission in Xian in A.D. 635. By the time of his arrival, there were so many Christians that emperor T'ai-Tsung (A.D. 627-649) sent an escort to the western outposts of the Chinese Empire to meet Alopen. The emperor granted him permission to translate the gospel sutras in the Imperial Library. The famous Xian-fu monument, known as the "Nestorian monument" (erected in A.D. 781 and unearthed in 1623), states that Emperor Kao-Tsung (A.D. 650-683) ordered the construction of a monastery and furthered Christianity by imperial decree.[5]

b. Christianity made an impact in China and affected Buddhism. The religion of Buddha offered no god to be worshiped, no hope, no savior, no eternal life, no paradise. Man was left to find within himself the solution to his sin. In sharp contrast with Theravada Buddhism, Chinese and Japanese Buddhism developed the concept of worship, the concept of trinity, mediators (*bodhisattvas*) between sinners and the gods, the concept of forgiveness, the doctrine of the second coming of Buddha as Maitreya, and the doctrine of paradise, or heaven. Shan-tao, a prominent Chinese Buddhist priest who died in A.D. 681, began to proclaim salvation by faith in Buddha under the name Amitabha. He preached a form of Buddhist trinity, a vicarious savior, grace, forgiveness, and eternal life by faith in Amitabha. Shan-tao insisted so much on a concept of trinity that it was said of him that "when he preached, the three Buddhas appeared in his breath."[6] As a result of its encounter with Christianity, the "doctrine of salvation through faith alone . . . appeared in Buddhism about a thousand years after the death of its founder."[7]

c. In turn, Buddhism affected Christianity. Many practices among Christians were not taken from the Bible. The use of the rosary, holy water, processions, repetitions of short prayers, tonsure (shaving the crown of the head by priests or members of a monastic order), relic worship, candles in worship, images, worship in a tongue unknown to the bulk of the worshipers, and the halo (or "aureole"), all predated Christianity and are found in Buddhism. Abbe Huc traveled through Tibet and China around 1845. Among the Tibetan priests, he found not only many characteristic doctrines of the Roman Church, but even many of their rituals, vestments, and sacred implements. Huc includes the Roman Catholic infallible head and grades of clergy corresponding to popes, cardinals, bishops, abbots, presbyters, deacons, and priests. He found that in China and Tibet they used mitre, censer, holy water, confession, tonsure, relic worship, lights and images before shrines and altars, the worship of the queen of heaven, the use of religious books in a tongue unknown to the majority of the worshipers, the aureole or nimbus, penance, and flagellations–religious elements that were not originated in biblical teachings but in pre-Christian Buddhism.[8]

3. *Doctrinal Contrasts*[9]

THERAVADA	MAHAYANA	CHRISTIANITY
God Nirvana, an abstract void.	Nirvana, an abstract void, but also an undifferentiated Buddha essence.	A personal God who is self-existent and changeless.
Humanity An impermanent collection of aggregates.	A temporary collection of aggregates. For Jodo Buddhists, personal existence continues for a while in the Pure Land.	Man in God's image. Personal existence has value.
The Problem We suffer because we desire that which is temporary, and we continue in the illusion of the existence of the self.	Same as Theravada.	We suffer the consequences of sin. We also suffer because, being made in God's image, we are fulfilled only when we are in a relationship with God. Sin has separated man from God.
The Solution To cease all desire and to realize the nonexistence of the self, thus finding permanence.	To become aware of the Buddha-nature within.	To be forgiven by and reconciled with God. We find permanence in the immutability of God.
The Means Self-reliance. We must follow the Middle Path and build up karmic merit.	Self-reliance. Means vary from following the Eightfold Path, to emptying the mind, to accruing merit by performing rituals, to realizing the Buddha-nature within, and to depending on the merits of a *bodhisattva*.	Reliance on God. We must repent of our sins and trust in the saving work of Jesus Christ.

The Outcome		
To enter *nirvana* where the ego is extinguished.	It varies from that of returning as a *bodhisattva* in order to guide others, to entering *nirvana*, to living in a Pure Land from which one can enter *nirvana*.	Our existence as individuals will continue after the resurrection. Immortality in an earth made new. No more death.

Table 11.1

4. *Hindrances to Evangelism*

a. Objection to "Jesus is not unique."

1) Theravada Buddhists see Jesus as a spiritual master on a par with Buddha.   See the following comparisons to understand better the uniqueness of Jesus:[10]

BUDDHA AND JESUS	
THERAVADA BUDDHISM	**CHRISTIANITY**
Buddha did not claim to have a special relationship with God. He he did not consider the issue of God's existence to be important because it did not pertain to the way to escape suffering.	Jesus did claim to have a special relationship with God (John 3:16; 6:44; 10:30; 14:6,9).
Buddha claimed to point to the way by which we could escape suffering and attain enlightenment.	Jesus claimed to be the way by which we could receive salvation and eternal life (John 14:6; 5:35).
Buddha taught that the way to eliminate suffering was by eliminating desire.	Jesus taught that the solution to suffering is found not in eliminating desire but in having right desire (Matt 5:6; 6:33).

Table 11.2

2) Mahayana Buddhists see Jesus as one more *bodhisattva*. Notice the following comparison:[11]

THE BODHISATTVAS AND JESUS	
MAHAYANA BUDDHISM	**CHRISTIANITY**
There are many *bodhisattvas*.	There has been only one incarnation of the Son of God.
The *bodhisattvas* were motivated out of a sense of their own compassion for the world. Their compassion is not a reflection of the Void's feelings toward the world.	Jesus is the unique demonstration of God's love for the world (John 3:16; Rom 5:8; 1 John 4:10).
The *bodhisattvas* had to overcome their sin (i.e., attachment, ignorance) over a process of numerous lifetimes.	Jesus was sinless from the very beginning (Matt 17:4; Luke 23:41; 2 Cor 5:21; Heb 4:15).

Table 11.3

b. Difficulties in understanding Christianity. It is not easy for a Buddhist to understand some basic teachings of Christianity, such as a God who has emotions, anger, and love. Emotions indicate attachment to the ego. The Christian speaks of eternal life, but the Buddhist interprets the hope of life after death as having its source in the ego's continuing to thirst after personal existence.

c. The emphasis in the statement "Just as there are many paths to the top of the mountain, so there are many paths to God" is placed on the *path* that *we* must walk. In other words, salvation is based on human effort in that we are the ones who must strive to make it up the mountain. In order to counter this, explain the biblical reasoning behind the exclusivity of the biblical way of salvation through the concept of reconciliation. The only way to restore a broken relationship is by confessing our guilt and requesting forgiveness.[12]

5. *Contextualization Efforts in the Buddhist Context*

a. Contextualization is the process of making the biblical text and its context meaningful and applicable to the thought patterns and situations of a given people. However, there are acceptable and unacceptable contextualizations.[13] Asian scholars have developed contextualized theologies that put more emphasis on the "context" than on the "text," making them unacceptable for Christians with a high view of scripture. Among them, pain of God theology (Japan), water buffalo theology (Thailand), third-eye theology (for the Chinese), *minjung* theology (Korea), theology of change (Taiwan), and a score of other national theologies, such as Indian theology, Burmese theology, and Sri Lanka theology.[14] Any attempt to do contextualization must preserve the fundamental doctrines intact.

b. In Thailand I visited a Christian display developed as an effort to seek common religious ground and artistic expressions. Following the advice of an interdenominational consultation, some Christians developed an approach that seeks nonconfrontational ways to reach the educated middle class. In order to make the "teachings be as authentically Thai as possible," they hired secular artists to paint Christian motifs.[15] Another aspect of that experiment with contextualization in Thailand relates to external matters. In a Buddhist temple the highest platform in the building is for the image of Buddha, and the second highest is for the preaching monk. Worshipers sit on the floor, surrounding the preacher. Instead of following a Western model, a local architect designed a preaching hall for a Christian church. The church was built three feet from the ground, because only beasts sit on the ground. No pews were built for the congregation. The church had a Malay-styled roof. Villagers began to attend church because it looked like a religious building. Preachers do not stand when preaching because that is considered to be rude. They use the *Wai* gesture (bringing the palms of their hands together, fingers extended and joined, in front of their face). The order of worship is according to the Buddhist temple: they do not sing during services but use local instruments and Thai music.[16]

d. In December 2000 I conducted an evangelistic series in Darhan, the second largest city in Mongolia. The country had been under Communism for more than seventy years and has a Buddhist background; both belief systems deny the existence of God. After much reflection, I decided the following sequence of topics for my first presentations:

1) Is there a God?   The five irrefutable proofs of the existence
                                      of God. God reveals Himself in different
                                      ways.

2) Buddha and Jesus.   A sympathetic comparison of Buddhism and Christianity. Two great teachers. An introduction to the Bible.

3) Nirvana   To end suffering, Buddhism offers a Void. Christianity offers eternal happiness. A review of the Christian "nirvana."

4) The Law of Karma   Karma demands suffering the consequences of actions. God offers forgiveness and a new start.

Hundreds of non-Christians attended. As a result, two churches were established.

6. *Christian Witness*

a. General guidelines[17]

1) Workshops on how to reach Buddhists should be held regularly in areas where there are adherents to this religion. Both pastors and church members need to be properly trained and equipped.

2) Asians under the influence of Buddhism have close ties with their siblings. They usually maintain strong connections with their extended families. "Evangelism of whole families, rather than evangelism of individuals, is vital. Social solidarity demands that whole families and groups of families be won for Christ if viable churches are to be planted and are to make an adequate impact on the community. The individual should be used to win the family."[18]

3) Remember that listening is the way to earn the right to be heard.

4) Determine the type of Buddhism you are encountering. Buddhism is complex, and beliefs have different implications and emphases according to the sect or faction involved.

5) The Christian must overcome many barriers as he attempts to share the gospel with Buddhists, no matter what sect of Buddhism he encounters. Therefore, the believer must rely upon the guidance and power of the Holy Spirit. Because the issue of sin is not clear in Buddhism, Christians who witness

to Buddhists should pray for the effectual ministry of the Holy Spirit in convicting unbelievers of sin, righteousness, and judgment.

b. Even though Christianity and Buddhism have irreconcilable differences, it is best to start on what may be identified as common ground. The following are some significant similarities on which you can build:[19]

1) Both agree that desire can cause suffering.
2) Both emphasize the fact of impermanence.
3) Both have high standards of ethics.
4) Both emphasize self-discipline.
5) Both place a strong emphasis on meditation and prayer.
6) Both commend compassion for others.
7) Both speak of inner peace.

c. Buddha stressed the issue of desire. To eliminate desire is a goal difficult to attain because it requires the desire not to have desire. Gently point out that Jesus said, "Blessed are those who hunger and thirst for righteousness, for they will be filled" (Matt 5:6). The important thing is to have the right desire. God puts new and right desires in a converted heart.

d. As a Christian witness, be open about your faith in a personal God. Buddhists find it difficult to understand the existence of a God who has emotions such as anger or love, for emotions indicate too much attachment to the ego. Your testimony of a personal relationship with God, as well as His answers to your prayers, are very powerful. A Void would not be able to do such things. Share how you have found peace and joy in the knowledge that God loves you and wants you to bring your cares and concerns to Him.

e. Buddha taught that permanence can be found only in the Void. The problem is that when we find permanence in the Void (*nirvana*), we as individuals cease to exist. The God of the Bible is permanent in two ways: He is permanent in that He is changeless in His character (Mal 3:6; Jas 1:17) and He is permanent in that He is faithful in all that He promises (Lam 3:23; Heb 13:5).

f. Both Christianity and Buddhism have a set of moral precepts. The moral precepts of Buddhism, called *sila*, are similar to the Ten Commandments. However, in Buddhism the breaking of moral precepts does not have consequences of vertical dimension. Sin is a matter both of ignorance (a mental issue) and of *karma* (an issue of an impersonal moral principle). As such, sin carries no consequences with respect to breaking our unconditional connection to the Void. Since sin is ignorance, it is something that we alone must deal with.

According to Buddhism, an action against the law of *karma* cannot be forgiven. According to Christianity, the Creator was willing to give His creatures a second chance by paying with His own death the penalty for their sins. In Christianity, God is willing to forgive and restore.

g. Use bridges to introduce the Good News

1) A *bodhisattva* is one who, out of compassion, has refused to enter *nirvana* in order to assist others along the way to enlightenment. According to Mahayana Buddhism, a *bodhisattva* is able to transfer his extra karmic merit to the one who believes in him. The differences, however, must be made plain. The *bodhisattva*s had to overcome their own attachments and ignorance over a long period of time involving several lifetimes. In sharp contrast, Jesus was sinless from the very beginning (Matt 17:4; Luke 23:41; 2 Cor 5:21; Heb 4:15).

2) Parables, symbols, and analogies are generally more acceptable to the Buddhist mind than are strictly focused arguments. Their minds are conditioned by a way of thinking that requires elaborate and continuous illustrations. Understanding the way they communicate will be critical to effective evangelism.[20]

h. In witnessing, Christians should avoid terms such as "new birth," "rebirth," "regeneration," or "born again." Instead, they should use alternatives such as "endless freedom from suffering, guilt, and sin," "new power for living a whole life," "promise of eternal good life without suffering," or "gift of unlimited merit."[21]

i. While Buddhists believe that *nirvana*, the idea of unreality, is the highest thing in the universe, Christians say that God is a reality and that He is a person. Instead of saying that God is a person, we should say that God is a Spirit and a Spirit that ordinary men cannot see at all, either with the eye or with the mind; He can only be seen when He reveals Himself to us.[22]

j. In Buddhism, anyone who has severed himself from all love and does not love his children, his wife, his money, his possessions, not even himself, is on high level of attainment in Buddhism. In response, it should be stressed that there is a kind of love which gives. The love of God seeks no gain for itself but only the good of the beloved. This is an important point in Christian witnessing that people may easily acknowledge as valid.

k. One aspect of the Christian faith that does not fit with Thai life is its zeal and enthusiasm. Buddhism teaches the extinguishing of zeal. When Buddhists walk, they walk slowly; when they move, they move gently, and when they speak, they speak softly. All this is to indicate that they are in complete control of themselves. We have to keep this in mind as we try to communicate with Buddhists.

l. In popular Buddhism, the hope of attaining Nirvana fades into an indefinite future. Some say that *nirvana* will be unattainable until the coming of Maitreya, the Buddha of kindness, who will appear in about twenty-five centuries from now (five thousand years from the death of Buddha Gautama). In sharp contrast, the Christian witness is called to proclaim the provisions of salvation by grace in this earthly life and for eternity.[23]

m. Buddhism does not offer forgiveness or eternal life. Buddhists hope to enter into the state of Nirvana, but even Buddha himself was not certain about death or *nirvana*. All Buddhists have is hope in a teaching that Buddha was not sure of. Today the body of Buddha lies in a grave in Kusinara, at the foot of the Himalaya Mountains, and some of his remains are scattered in different countries. Christianity is "the religion of the empty tomb."

n. The founder of Christianity amazed His audience because He taught eternal truths with authority (Matt 7:28, 29). His authority came from the fact that He existed before creation (John 1:1-3), and He proved His claims by rising from the dead. "The resurrection of Jesus Christ is a proven fact of history and clearly demonstrates Christ's authority over sin and death."[24]

Notes

1   Paul A. Eakin, *Christian Approach to Buddhists in Thailand* (Bangkok: Rung Ruan Ratana, 1960), 27-30.

2   "Lamaism indeed with its shaven priests, its bells and rosaries, its images and holy water, and gorgeous dresses; its services with double choirs, with processions and creeds, mystic rite and incense, in which the laity are spectators only; its abbots and monks, and nuns of many grades; its worship of the double Virgin, and of the saints and angels; its fasts, confessions, and purgatory; its images, and idols, and its pictures; its huge monasteries and its gorgeous cathedrals; its powerful hierarchy, its cardinals, its pope, bears outwardly at least a strong resemblance to Romanism in spite of the essential difference of its teachings and its mode of thought." Rhys Davis, *Buddhism*, trans. Peter Pardue (New York: MacMillan, 1971), 250.

3   "Buddhist Art and the Trade Routes," *Asia Society Museum*, 2003 [article online]; retrieved on April 10, 2006, from http://www.asiasocietymuseum.com/buddhist_trade/ chinamongolia.html.

4   Benjamin George Wilkinson, *Truth Triumphant: The Church in the Wilderness* (Mountain View, CA: Pacific Press, 1944), 368-69.

5   Dale A. Johnson, *The Asian Faces of Jesus*, 2004 [book online], 23; retrieved on February 22, 2006, from http://video.lulu.com/items/volume_1/83000/83798/3/ preview/asian9x6.pdf.

6   Yoshiro Saeki, *The Nestorian Monument in China* (London: Society for Promoting Christian Knowledge, 1916), 148.

7   Wilkinson, *Truth Triumphant*, 368.

8   Huc and Gabit, *Travels in Tartary, Tibet and China (1844-1846)*, translated by William Hazlitt; reprint; first published in 1928 (New Delhi: Asian Educational Services, 1988), 2 vols, 846 pp.

9   Slightly modified from Dean C. Halverson, "Buddhism," in *The Compact Guide to World Religions*, ed. Dean C. Halverson (Minneapolis, MN: Bethany House, 1996), 61.

10   Ibid., 63.

11   Ibid.

12   Ibid., 62.

13   Carlos G. Martin, "What Constitutes 'Acceptable Contextualization'?" *Asia Adventist Seminary Studies* 1 (1998): 19-25; retrieved on January 27, 2006, at http://www.aiias.edu/academics/seminary/aass/vol1-1998/martin_what_constitutes. html.

14   B. R. Ro, "Asian Theology," in *Evangelical Dictionary of Biblical Theology*, ed. Walter A. Elwell (Grand Rapids, Baker, 2006); retrieved on January 20, 2006, at http://mb-soft.com/believe/txo/asian.htm.

15   "Thailand Mission Reevaluates Its Approach to Buddhists," *Adventist Review*, January 23, 1986, 19.

16   Class notes from Dr. Cliff Maberly, MSSN 672 "Buddhism and Christianity," Summer 1995, Adventist International Institute of Advanced Studies, Silang, Cavite, Philippines.

17   Kenneth Boa, *Cults, World Religions, and You* (Wheaton, IL: Victor Books, 1977), 31.

18   Lausanne Committee for World Evangelization, "Lausanne Occasional Paper 15: Christian Witness to Buddhists," *Lausanne Committee for World Evangelization* 2004 [document online from the 2004 Forum for World Evangelization]; retrieved on December 6, 2005, from http://www.lausanne.org/Brix?pageID=14724.

19   Halverson, "Buddhism," 64.

20   Lausanne, "Christian Witness to Buddhists," 2004.

21   Daniel R. Heimbach, "Buddhism," *Interfaith Evangelism Belief Bulletin*, 2001 [article online]; retrieved on January 22, 2006, from http://www.namb.net/atf/cf/{CDA250E8-8866-4236-9A0C-C646DE153446}/BB_Buddhism.pdf.

22   Wan Petchsongkram, *Talk in the Shade of the Bo Tree: Some Observations on Communicating the Christian Faith in Thailand*, trans. and ed. Frances E. Hudgins (Bangkok: Thai Gospel Press, 1975), 13, 14.

23   Eakin, *Christian Approach to Buddhists*, 26.

24   Pat Zukeran, "Buddhism," *Probe Ministries*, 1996-2006 [article online]; retrieved on February 26, 2006, at http://www.leaderu.com/orgs/probe/docs/buddhism.html.

PART IV

RELIGIONS OF EAST ASIA

CHAPTER 12

Introduction to Chinese Religions

1. *Overview*

a. East Asia is a vast region that includes the peoples of China, Korea, and Japan. This is a very diversified cultural area with many ethnic and linguistic groups that comprise about one-fourth of the world's population. East Asia shares a common religious vision. One key element of this vision is a "functioning harmony of a cosmos filled with sacred forces." East Asians believe in a close interrelationship between natural and sacred forces–gods, spirits, *kami*, and *yin-yang* forces. The highest good comes from maintaining harmony and balance within this unified cosmos.[1] While Jainism and Buddhism were emerging as religions in India, three other religions were developing in East Asia. Taoism and Confucianism grew largely in China, and later spread to Japan and Korea. Shinto was distinctively Japanese. In time, Buddhism spread to all of East Asia. East Asians may turn to different parts of their religious tradition (Buddhism, Confucianism, Taoism, Shintoism) to answer different needs at different times. This unit will refer to this trait as "eclecticism."

b. China is the mother culture of East Asia. China has a continuous historical record extending over three thousand years. In spite of wars, invasions, and revolutions, a distinctively Chinese culture stretched from the first settlements in the Yellow River valley in the second millennium B.C. to the present day.[2] China is the world's most populous country with about 1.3 billion people–20% of the earth's population.

c. A brief outline of the history of China will help to show the overall scope of this unit.[3]

Shang Dynasty (ca. 1750-1122 B.C.)	Chinese writing is developed.
Chou Dynasty (ca. 1122-222 B.C.)	Wars. Emergence of Confucianism and Taoism.
Ch'in Dynasty (221-206 B.C.)	First central government in China.
Han Dynasty (202 B.C.-A.D. 220)	Confucianism became foundational.
Three Kingdoms (A.D. 220-618)	Buddhism spread througout the land.
Tang Dynasty (618-907)	Chinese schools of Buddhism were developed.
Sung Dynasty (907-1279)	Neo-Confucian school receives endorsement.
Yuang Dynasty (1279-1368)	Controled by Mongols. Marco Polo arrived.
Ming Dynasty (1368-1644)	Stability and prosperity. Christianity rejected.
Ch'ing Dynasty (1644-1911)	Opium Wars (1839-42). Boxer rebellion (1900).
Nationalistic Party (1912-1949)	Republican Revolution. Chiang Kai-Shek.
Communist Revolution (1949-Present)	Mao Tse Tung.
Cultural Revolution (1966-1976)	Extreme persecution of all religions.
Student Democracy Movement (1989)	Since then, economic modernization.

d. In the first chapters of this unit, Chinese words are transliterated according to the old Wade-Giles system and by the more contemporary Pinyin system. Wade-Giles was the standard for the Romanization of Mandarin Chinese for the majority of the twentieth century.[4] Although Wade-Giles is linguistically sound, it has proved largely ineffective in popular use. It has largely been supplanted by Pinyin. When only one transliteration is offered, it is according to Wade-Giles, and when two or more transliterations are used, the ones in parentheseis are according to the Pinyin system.

2. *Major Periods of Chinese Religious History*

Chinese religious history is divided into four major periods, listed traditionally as the spring, summer, autumn, and winter of cultural development.[5]

a. The Spring, Birth of Chinese Religions

1) The earliest recorded Chinese practices begin with the Shang Dynasty (ca. 1750 - 1100 B.C.).[6] Early myths do not have much to say about the origin of things, but legendary heroes are said to have invented fire, iron, fishing with nets, music, and writing. The records are hundreds of thousands of fragments of oracle bones, with divination enquiries. They were addressed to the spirits for guidance. The request having been inscribed, the diviner then applied

heat to holes bored in the bone, and the resultant heat cracks were interpreted as being either "auspicious" or "inauspicious" responses from the spirits.[7] The spirits of the deceased kings, the spirits of the ancestors, and the deities of the hills and streams were consulted for guidance in matters of conduct and to ensure the fertility of men and women, crops, and beasts.

2) The later spring of China's religious history extends from the beginning of the Chou kingdom, ca. 1100 B.C., to the beginning of the Han dynasty in 206 B.C. During this extended period, ancient worldviews developed religious systems based on the assumption that all reality operates through the "five elements" which act and transform things: water, fire, wood, metal, and earth. They also believed in the importance of the balancing forces of *yin* and *yang* within the *Tao*, the ultimate sacred reality and the eternal way of the universe. Several patterns of thought are recognized to have formed the core of the Chinese cultural/religious system. They were not called "religion" but *chiao* (*gjiao)*, "teachings." [8]

3) The following are the two major schools of thought during this period: (1) *Ru-chiao*, the Confucian way, or the Confucian school, was formed by the collected moral/ethical directives of Confucius (551-479 B.C.) and Mencius (Mengzi, 371-289 B.C.), and the penal codes of the Legalists–they believed that the use of harsh penal law would deter political opposition and enhance and maintain power.[9] (2) *Tao-chiao*, the Taoist way, included religious Taoism, based on the works of Lao-tze (Laozi, sixth/fifth centuries B.C.) and Chuang-tze (Zhuangzi, fourth century B.C.) and the Mohist school, that stressed the brotherhood of man and universal love.[10] Like two sides of the same coin, Confucian social ethics and Taoist communion with nature formed the core of the Chinese religious spirit. "Like *yin* and *yang*, they interpenetrate and complement each other."[11]

b. The Summer, the Maturity. The period between 206 B.C. and A.D. 900 witnessed the introduction of Buddhism into China from India, the formation of liturgical or spiritual Taoism as the priesthood of the popular religion, and the supremacy of Confucianism as custodian of the moral/ethical system of Chinese social culture. The rites of passage summarized by the Confucian New Text of the Han period and the grand Taoist liturgies of renewal became standardized for all China.

c. The Autumn, the Reformation

1) This period covered from the beginning of the Sung dynasty, ca. 960 B.C., to the end of the Ch'ing dynasty and the imperial system, A.D. 1912. During this period a true reformation of the religious spirit of China occurred under Mongol rulers, some five hundred years before the reformation of European religious systems.[12] The Chinese religious reformation was typified by lay movements in both Buddhism and Taoism; a syncretism, even ecumenism, between Buddhist and Taoist spiritual elements; and the growth of local popular cultures.

2) Secret societies (*yu-hsieh*), religious cults, clan and temple associations, and merchant groups flourished throughout China. Well-trained Confucians were the only men capable of handling public affairs. After A.D. 631 the sole qualification for holding public office was a successful examination in the Confucian classics. It was the influence of these scholars which lay behind the strong conservatism and opposition to progress which characterized China before the 1911 Revolution that ended with the empire.

3) Christianity was brought to China by Nestorians in the seventh century, by Franciscans in the thirteenth century, by Jesuits in the sixteenth century, and by increasing waves of missionaries in the nineteenth and twentieth centuries. However, due to the inability of Christian missionaries to adapt to the religious cultural system of China, it never equaled the popularity of Buddhism in the Chinese context.

d. The Winter, Modern Chinese Religious History.

1) With the fall of the empire in 1911, Confucianism suffered a severe blow. The empire cult came to an end. In spite of periodic attempts to reinstate Confucian morals, there has been no comeback and Communists denounce Confucianism as pure feudalism and therefore a bar to progress. They have even attempted to break up the intense family loyalty which Confucius inculcated and have had a measure of temporary success.[13]

2) After the Cultural Revolution, religion is experiencing rebirth in the People's Republic of China.[14]

3. *Characteristics of Chinese Religion*

a. It is eclectic and not dogmatic, inclusive and not exclusive. Eclecticism means the free selection and borrowing of ideas and beliefs from diverse sources. Chinese philosophy teaches that no one can claim to comprehend the whole truth. Therefore, many traditional Chinese are animists and Confucianists, who also practice Buddhism and Taoism with no sense of incongruity. It is common in Taiwan for Buddhist or Taoist priests and monks to follow popular religious practices as the common religionist does.[15] He might be a devout Buddhist, a Taoist, and an admirer of Confucius, without any sense of inner conflict. In addition, he might also be a practitioner of popular religion. These four categories are intermixed.[16] The right question to ask is not whether an individual is Confucian or Taoist, but to what extent Confucian and Taoist traditions make that person's life relevant.[17] This eclecticism/syncretism moves them to be highly polytheistic. This polytheism contrasts sharply with the nature of the Christian faith, which asserts that "there is salvation in no one else, for there is no other name under heaven given among men by which we must be saved" (Acts 4:12).

b. It is pragmatic rather than theological. To the Chinese, the purpose of religion is not primarily to understand the unknown, explain the mysteries of life, or trace the origins of the universe. Religion is a formulation of rules and principles for dealing with life here on earth. Chinese religion is also humanistic. In Christianity, God is revealing Himself to man. In Chinese religions, man is seeking and finding God through spiritual piety and good deeds. The Chinese character for 'faith' (*xin*) includes the word 'man' (*ren*). Chinese religion is man-centered.[18]

c. It is both communal and personal. On the public side, religion consists of ceremonies and rituals that an individual is obligated to observe as a responsible member of the family, clan, or society. An individual may even participate in the outward form of the religion without actually believing it. However, religion is strictly private and personal. Piety is a personal accomplishment. Congregational worship and fellowship as we understand it in Christianity does not exist.

4. *The "Yin-Yang" Principle*

a. A very ancient Chinese belief which may date back to 1000 B.C., but its origins are uncertain. Its development deeply permeated Chinese thought, especially in its Taoist form. The concept of a basic dualist essence in the universe represented by two cosmic principles: *yang*, positive, and *yin*, negative. Beauty implies ugliness. Goodness implies evil. Darkness and light compete with each other. Voice and tone wed each other.[19] The interaction of these forces does not reflect a passive balance, but an eternal variability or flux in things. The following are some of the contraries represented by *yang* and *yin*:

Yang	*Yin*		*Yang*	*Yin*
Male	Female		Sun	Moon
Good	Evil		Summer	Winter
Active	Passive		South	North
Light	Darkness		Positive	Negative
Warmth	Cold		Life	Death
Expansion	Contraction		Strength	Weakness
Heaven	Earth		Mountain	Lake

b. In the symbol for *yin* and *yang*, the curving line symbolizes the dynamic interaction between the two forces. The two dots indicate that the *yin* is present

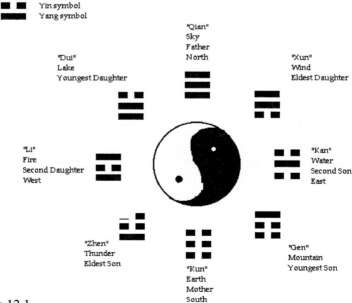

Yin symbol
Yang symbol

"Qian"
Sky
Father
North

"Dui"
Lake
Youngest Daughter

"Xun"
Wind
Eldest Daughter

"Li"
Fire
Second Daughter
West

"Kan"
Water
Second Son
East

"Zhen"
Thunder
Eldest Son

"Gen"
Mountain
Youngest Son

"Kun"
Earth
Mother
South

Figure 12.1

in the *yang*, and vice versa. The system was finally elaborated on by both Confucianists and Taoists, and the form, completed during the Sung Dynasty (A.D. 907-1279), was Neo-Confucianism.[20] It was an endeavor to express the phenomena of nature. Under the Taoists, it grew to be more than a speculative theory as to the order of the universe. The system became a science applied to geomancy, medicine, etc.

c. The symbol of this system is the *pa kua* ("eight trigrams"), which comes from the appendices of the *I Ching* (*Yijing, Ee jing*, "the Book of Changes").[21] The trigrams are composed of combinations of an unbroken line (*yang*) and two short dashes (*yin*). The trigrams may be paired to yield 64 possible hexagrams (Figure 12.1 offers a summarized version). Heaven, for instance, is totally male with three long dashes, while earth is totally female with six short dashes. The trigrams are arranged around the *T'ai Chi* symbol of the two "fish" (*yin* and *yang*) which was added in the Sung Dynasty.[22] The *I Ching*, composed about 800 B.C., is a common source for both Taoism and Confucianism, and is regarded as a classic text in both traditions.[23]

5. *"The Unknown God" of the Chinese*

a. The Chinese had early notions of a personal God. According to the earliest records, during the Shang Dynasty (ca. 1750-1122 B.C.), God was conceived as the original or Great Ancestor of the Shang clan, the supreme *Ti*. During the Chou Dynasty (ca. 1122-222 B.C.), God was spoken of as a personal Being, a High God, under the name *Shang Ti* (*Shangdi*, "the Supreme Ruler") or *Ti* "on high." In their own tradition, the Chou clan referred to God as a *Tien*, meaning "Sky" or "Heaven." Even though *Tien* and *Shang Ti* were identified as the same, the usage of names indicated different connotations, *Shang Ti* being thought of as a personal Being and *Tien* as having an impersonal character.[24]

b. In the past, only the emperor was allowed to worship *Shang Ti* through a number of sacrifices and rituals.[25] The most solemn and impressive of these was on the Altar of Heaven at the winter solstice.[26] In subordination to him are numerous gods responsible for the various areas of heaven and earth. These lesser gods must be appeased and pacified. They are like emissaries of the supreme being, and report to him regarding the behavior of men and women on earth. Some gods would help men in their journey through life, while others would try to thwart their plans. The fact is that the common people eventually gave more importance to the lesser gods.[27]

c. Most elderly Chinese believe in the one supreme God who rules the whole universe. This supreme being maintains, sustains and controls the order of the universe. Although they do not worship this God, this is a bridge that Christians can use in their preaching.[28]

6. *Selected Practices of Chinese Religions*

a. An important aspect of social life is a large variety of rites of passage, rituals that mark the transition from one stage in life to another. These rites have been regulated from the Han period onward by the ritual law of the Confucian tradition.[29]

b. The annual cycle of festivals follows the farmer's almanac. Cyclical festivals fall in the off-numbered, or *yang* months, and farming activity in the even-numbered, or *yin* months. The first day of the first lunar month is the lunar New Year, or Spring Festival. It usually falls between January 21 and February 19. The Chinese traditionally offer a family banquet in honor of the ancestors and the living members of the family, who assemble from distant places to affirm identity. Women wear flowers in their hair, children receive presents and cash in a red envelope, new clothes are donned, and fireworks signal the beginning of the New Year. Good-luck characters are posted by the door and the lintels.[30]

c. Divination has long roots, as evidences of this practice are among the earliest records of Chinese history.[31] Both Buddhist and Taoist temples offer a modernized version of the method of prognostication for reading one's fortune for common sense advice in practical home and business matters. Usually, numbered wooden sticks are drawn from a wooden container by chance, and the corresponding hexagram is read by a monk or nun in the temple.

d. Geomany is a blend of divination and magic. This practice is called *feng-shui*. Common usage is to determine the site of a grave, the design of a building, and the decoration of a room. The diviner determines which forces, good and evil, are at work, and with proper tools establishes the different circles of power for those forces.[32]

e. Ancestor worship became an established practice under Confucianism. After the parent's death, the eldest son of the family sets up the tablet for the deceased in the guest room cabinet, together with the other ancestor's tablets. The burning of incense is practiced in the evening and the morning. When the family reunion takes place, the sacrifice will be offered to the ancestor. To have a son is very important for the family because this son will take care of the parents not only when they are old, but also after their deaths.[33]

7. *Present State of Chinese Religions*

a. The term for religion in China, *tsung-chiao*, refers literally to a *tsung* ("lineage") of *chiao* ("teachings"). The common men and women of China have traditionally admitted three basic teachings: the Confucian system of ethics for public life, the Taoist system of rituals and attitudes towards nature, and the Buddhist salvational concepts concerning afterlife.[34] "More than one author has suggested that the Chinese relate to nature through Taoism, to society through Confucianism, and to transcendent reality through Buddhism."[35]

b. "One of the great surprises of China after Mao has been the efflorescence of religious belief and practice."[36] The Chinese Communists have not abandoned their Marxist interpretation of religion; however, great progress has been made in restoring religious activities, including the recovering, repairing, and reopening of churches, temples, mosques, and monasteries.

Notes

1   Theodore M. Ludwig, *The Sacred Paths: Understanding the Religions of the World* (Upper Saddle River, NJ: Pearson Prentice Hall, 2006), 204.

2   Geoffrey Hudson, "China," in *Asia: A Handbook*, ed. Guy Wint (New York: Frederick A. Praeger, 1966), 139.

3   William A. Young, *The World's Religions: Worldviews and Contemporary Issues* (Upper Saddle River, NJ: Pearson Prentice Hall, 2005), 109-110.

4   "Wade-Giles," *Pinyin.info*, 2004 [article online]; retrieved on January 8, 2006, from http://www.pinyin.info/romanization/wadegiles/.

5   John R. Hinnells, *A Handbook of Living Religions* (Middlesex, England: Penguin Books, 1985), 346.

6   Julia Ching, *Chinese Religions* (Maryknoll, NY: Orbis, 1993), 15-32.

7   Michael D. Coogan, *The Illustrated Guide to World Religions* (New York: Oxford University Press, 2003), 204.

8   Ibid., 234.

9   Ching, *Chinese Religions*, 80.

10   Ibid., 70.

11   Mary Pat Fisher, *Living Religions*, 6th ed. (Upper Saddle River, NJ: Prentice-Hall, 2005), 178.

12   Roger Schmidt, Gene C. Sager, Gerald T. Carney, Albert C. Muller, Kenneth J. Zanca, Julius J. Jackson Jr., C. Wayne Mayhall, and Jeffrey C. Burke, *Patterns of Religion*, 2nd ed. (Belmont, CA: Wadsworth, 2005), 240.

13   Fisher, *Living Religions*, 199.

14   Donald E. MacInnis, *Religion in China Today: Policy and Practice* (Maryknoll, NY: Orbis, 1989), xvii.

15   Henri Maspero, *Taoism and Chinese Religion*, trans. Frank A. Kierman Jr. (Amherst, MA: University of Massachusetts Press, 1981), 78. From the middle of the first century A.D. onward for at least 150 years, Buddha and Lao Tze were worshiped together. Wing-tsit Chan, "Religions of the Chinese," in *The Great Asian Religions: An Anthology* (New York: Collier Macmillan, 1969), 179.

16   Robert J. Bolton, *Treasure Island: Church Growth among Taiwan's Urban Minnan Chinese* (South Pasadena, CA: William Carey Library, 1976), 42-43. More than 90% of the people practice Folk Religion. The Chinese perceive that the three religions are "harmonious" and "the three systems are one." Chan, "Religions of the Chinese," 220.

17   Denise Lardner Carmody and T. L. Brink, *Ways to the Center: An Introduction to World Religions* (Belmont, CA: Thomson Wadsworth, 2006), 165.

18   Lee Chong Kau, "The Chinese View of Christianity," chap. in *How to Speak to Our Elders about Christ* (Singapore: Overseas Missionary Fellowship, 1972), 6-7.

19   Young, *The World's Religions: Worldviews and Contemporary Issues*, 112-14.

20   Cyrille Javary, *Understanding I Ching*, trans. Kirk McElhearn (Boston: Shambala, 1997), 67-76.

21   The *I Ching* (*Yijing*, *Ee jing*, "The Book of Changes") probably existed at the time of Confucius, and was attributed to the sages of old. Commentaries were later added to the oracles. Ching, *Chinese Religions*, 55-56. Some scholars suggest a very early date. "Its basic text–the sixty-four hexagram descriptions–dates from around the year 1000 B.C.; its line by line commentaries from a little later." Martin Palmer, *The Elements of Taoism* (Rockport, MA: Element, 1991), 28.

22   James Norman Anderson, *The World's Religions* (Grand Rapids: Eerdmans, 1989), 224; Hinnells, *Handbook of Living Religions*, 354.

23   Fisher, *Living Religions*, 178.

24   T. Patrick Burke, *The Major Religions: An Introduction with Texts*, 2nd ed. (Malden, MA: Blackwell, 2004), 124-26.

25   Ludwig, *The Sacred Paths*, 207.

26   Fisher, *Living Religions*, 198.

27   Ibid., 178.

28   Lee Chong Kau, *How to Speak to Our Elders*, 8.

29   See Ann Wan Seng, *Chinese Customs and Taboos* (Shah Alam, Malaysia: Penerbit Fajar Bakti, 1995); Marie-Luise Latsch, *Traditional Chinese Festivals* (Singapore: Graham Brash, 1988).

30   Jennifer Oldstone Moore, "Chinese Traditions," in *The Illustrated Guide to World Religions*, ed. Michael D. Coogan (New York: Oxford University Press, 2003), 225.

31   Kuang Yu Chen, "Chinese Oracle Bone Incriptions," *Rutgers: The State University of New Jersey*, 2006 [article online]; retrieved on June 20, 2006, from http://rutchem.rutgers.edu/~kyc/Chinese%20Oracle%20Bone%20Inscriptions.html.

32   Carmody and Brink, *Ways to the Center*, 166.

33   Anderson, *The World's Religions*, 223.

34   Hinnells, *Handbook of Living Religions*, 344.

35   C. George Fry et al., *Great Asian Religions* (Grand Rapids: Baker, 1984), 22.

36   MacInnis, *Religion in China Today*, 34.

CHAPTER 13

Confucianism

1. *Introduction*

a. In speaking of Confucianism and Taoism as religions, it is important to remember that in the Chinese mind they are *chiao* ("teachings"). They are not exclusively or specifically religious, though they are concerned with much that we should think of as religion.

b. Confucianism and Taoism have been thought of by the Chinese themselves as manifestations quintessential of the national ethos, and not specifically as religious faiths inviting conversion, membership, and personal commitment. However, there are religious elements present in many facets of family and social organization, the practices of economic groups, and political theory. The multiplicity and varieties of temples and shrines in every city and village across the land, and their presence in countless households of the domestic gods and their altars provide tangible evidence of this.

c. Confucianism has influenced Chinese culture for five thousand years. In present Taiwan, Hong Kong, Singapore, and Macao societies, this predominance is challenged by the Western industrial culture. However, Confucianism is still part of the Chinese mindset and rules the majority of life choices and daily activities.

2. *Confucius*

a. Confucius' (ca. 551-479 B.C.) real name was K'ung Ch'iu (Kong Qiu). Disciples referred to him as *K'ung fu-tze* (*Kongfuzi; Kung Fuzi,* or *Kong Fuzu*), meaning "Master K'ung." *Tze* means "teacher." Confucius is the latinized form of K'ung fu-tze.

b. Confucius was born around 551 B.C. in the state of Lu, modern Shantung. The Chinese Empire was at this time ruled by the Chou Dynasty, which was composed of a small number of semi-independent feudal states, often engaged in internal wars. It was a troubled period of oppression, luxury, and lust. But against this background it was also a time of intense intellectual activity, the classical age of Chinese literature. Confucius believed that a "return to the classical rites and standards of virtue was the only way out of the chaos." [1]

c. From a young age Confucius showed a desire for learning. He became China's first professional teacher. At the age of 15 he began taking tuition-paying students, and he was employed by the state of Lu when he was seventeen. Two years later he married and at the age of 20 had a son. But he eventually divorced. At this time he left his position with the state of Lu and wandered about China seeking a prince who would offer him employment. At age 50 Confucius was invited to return to Lu as chief magistrate of the town of Chung-tu and as the minister of justice. As the ruler of Lu rejected his advice of not accepting a gift of dancing girls from another state, Confucius resigned his position. For the next 14 years he wandered from state to state. Finally he settled down and gave himself to research in ancient history, poetry, and ritual. His last five years were devoted to writing. He died in 479 B.C.[2]

d. Basically, Confucius asserted that government must be founded on virtue, and that all citizens must be attentive to the duties of their positions. He was not an innovator, but someone who called for a return to ancient traditions and values.[3]

3. *Confucian Literature*

a. The underlying concern of the Confucian canon is harmony in the social order. The canon consists of the "Four Books" and the "Five Classics."[4] Confucius asserted that to be a cultivated, "superior person," one must be immersed in music, poetry, divination, and etiquette. For Confucius the wisdom of the sage kings of antiquity was accessible primarily through the study of the "Five Classics." [5]

1) The *Classic of History* is an anthology of narrative history from ancient China.

2) The *Classic of Poetry* is an anthology of three hundred poems from ancient China.

3) The *Book of Changes*, also known by the Chinese name of *I Ching*, is a system of divination. It is based on a combination of eight trigrams, devices made up of broken and unbroken lines that represent the opposing yet complementary forces of *yin* (broken) and *yang* (unbroken). The trigrams are combined in pairs to form a total of 64 hexagrams. They are taken to represent all possible situations and developments in the constantly changing universe.

4) The *Classic of Rites* is an anthology of ancient ceremonial and ritual teachings.

5) The *Annals of Spring and Autumn* compiles chief events in the history of Lu.

6) Some add a sixth, the lost *Classic of Music*.

b. The "Four Books" describe ways to achieve virtuous government and a harmonious society. They are built on what Confucius and his followers taught about the earlier "Five Classics." [6]

1) The *Analects* is a collection of Confucius' sayings as remembered by his followers. It is very similar to the Book of Proverbs, consisting of sayings and aphorisms. It is the most reliable source for knowledge of Confucius himself. It consists of 12,700 ideograms, loosely organized and repetitive at times.

2) *The Great Learning* is a treatise on higher education. It served as a text for young men to learn the basics of becoming gentlemen.

3) *The Doctrine of the Mean* describes the middle way between two extremes, the way of compromise.

4) *The Works of Mencius*. He was the greatest interpreter and preserver of Confucius' thoughts.

4. *The Teaching of Confucius Becomes an "Ism"*

a. After the death of Confucius, his disciples, as in other religions, broke into groups, each stressing a separate aspect of their master's teaching mission.

b. Mo-tzu, Mo Tse, Mo Ti (Mozi, ca. 478-382 B.C.) was the first reformer of Confucianism. His name was Latinized as Micius. He was the founder of a school referred to as the "Mohist School." He had a theistic view of God--He was a personal God who was both loving and righteous. Micius taught universal and equal love on the basis that God loves all equally. He understood that the Confucian five formal relationships were too narrow.[7] His followers created a religious brotherhood, called *yu-hsieh*, which was a strictly disciplined organization that was capable of military action. They were defenders of the oppressed and champions of the distressed.[8]

c. Mencius (ca. 371-287 B.C., a contemporary of Plato and Aristotle) is the latinized form of Meng-tzu (Mengzi, "Master Meng"). He was Confucius' major interpreter and preserver of his thoughts. His birth name was Meng Ko or Meng Ke. Mencius was even less interested in religion than his master was. He elaborated Confucius' teachings about human virtue and good government, and emphasized even more than Confucius the inherent goodness of man. Humans are evil only because they forgot their original nature.[9] The *Book of Mencius* became one of the Four Books of Confucianism.

d. Hsun Tzu (Xunzi, 335-288 B.C.) rejected the concept of basic goodness of humankind. His school, or line of thought, is sometimes known as Legalism. He believed that only strong law could motivate human nature to right action; training, laws, and restraint are necessary in order that society might survive. This made rites all the more important, because it is through rites that people are trained in proper living. He insisted that education can train nature to seek goodness.[10]

e. Confucianism became the state religion of China during the Han Dynasty (206 B.C.-A.D. 220) and remained so for over two thousand years, until the Republic was established in 1912.

f. Chu-Hsi (Zhu Xi), Chu-fu-tzu ("Master Chu"), also known as Chufucius (A.D. 1130-1200), developed "Neo-Confuciansim." This movement was the result of the impact that Buddhism and Taoism had made on the Chinese society; it resulted in a synthesis of these religious systems. Chufucius was the most authoritative spokesman for Confucianism, after Mencius.[11]

5. *Basic Teachings: Human Nature*

a. The original state of man concerns man's humanity and the spirit of man. According to Confucius, "there are good and evil potentialities within human personality."[12] His "princely man" was equal to the modern idiom "perfect gentleman," which was characterized by "kindness, sincerity, graciousness, loyalty, and self-denial."[13] Confucius believed that the human problem is basically intellectual rather than moral. His philosophy was very simple: namely, virtue is the foundation of happiness. Man can be virtuous only if he makes up his mind to do it.

b. The teachings of Confucius were based around certain central themes. One of them is represented by the word *li*. It has been translated into English in a variety of forms such as "propriety," "ritual," "protocol," "etiquette," "ceremony," and "courtesy." Basically, the word seems to mean "the course of life as it is intended to go." It has both religious and social connotations. It encourages politeness in social interactions and awareness of the different social ranks.[14]

c. Confucian ethics are directed toward the creation of a harmonious society and a virtuous, benevolent state. It can be brought about, Confucius believed, if everyone is reflective and sincere, and practices *ren (jen)*, "humanity," "benevolence," a deep-seated altruism.[15] Confucius described *ren* as treating all people with respect, and living according to the "silver rule" (a negative version of the "golden rule"): "Do not do unto others what you would not have them do to you" (*Analects* 12:2).[16] A person who practices *li,* or propriety, in daily life, performing the proper rituals and ceremonies, develops inwardly the quality of *ren*.[17]

d. Mencius, Confucius' major expounder, stressed that "man's nature is good; and it is as water flows down."[18] This good nature should be developed and exercised; otherwise, the heavenly human nature will be lost and humans will become one with the beasts.[19] Mencius also emphasized that a real man should experience the feeling of commiseration, shame, modesty, and a sense of right and wrong, because all of these are the beginnings of benevolence [*jen*], righteousness [*I*], propriety [*li*], and wisdom [*chih*]. Mencius pointed out that evil develops due to lack of proper nourishment and care, so he stressed the importance of love [*ren* or *jen*] and righteousness [*I*] in government, in education, and within the circle of the family. In order to cultivate the good human nature, education was regarded with supreme importance.[20] This concept of the goodness of man inoculated the Chinese educated classes against the acceptance of Christian teachings that emphasized the concept of a human nature ruined by sin.

e. On the contrary, Hsun Tzu (Xunzi) emphasized the negatives of human nature which were tendencies toward evil and selfishness; and only through the help of a positive education and a powerful, legally enforced environment, would humans be able to overcome evil. In short, Hsun Tzu believed that human beings would become good through education.[21] So, Confucian scholars on both sides emphasized education. It is not surprising, then, that East Asians normally value education and aim to excel.

6. *Basic Teachings: Filial Piety*

a. According to Confucius, there are five constant relationships in life (*wun Lun*). If *li* (propriety) were present in these relationships throughout society, then the social order would be ideal.[22] The Five Relationships correspond to the Five Constant Virtues. The responsibilities of filial piety (*Hsiao*) are the priorities of life:

1) Father to son. There should be kindness in the father and filial piety in the son. This is the prototype of all other relationships.

2) Older brother to younger brother. There should be gentility in the senior and respect in the younger.

3) Older friend to younger friend. There should kind consideration in the older and deference in the younger.

4) Husband to wife. There should be righteous behavior in the husband and obedience in the wife.

5) Ruler to subject. There should be benevolence in the ruler and loyalty in the subject.

b. The father and son's relationship is the first and most important relationship. The father treats his son with kindness, and the son should obey his father implicitly and respect his parents even after death. Thus, Confucianism emphasizes filial piety. Confucius said,

> The body, the hair and skin are received from our parents, and we dare not injure them: this is the beginning of filiality. [We should] establish ourselves

in the practice of the true way, making a name for ourselves for future generations, and thereby bring glory to our parents: this is the end of filiality. Filiality begins with the serving of our parents, continues with the serving of our prince [current civil ruler], and is completed with the establishing of our own character.[23]

c. Filial piety includes caring for one's own body, serving the civil authorities faithfully, and honoring one's parents. While the parents are still living, the son does all he possibly can to make them feel happy. When the parents die, the son buries them with grief, and brings sacrifices to them with a solemn heart.

d. When Confucianism met Indian Buddhism, the concept of the immortality of the spirit of man combined with filial piety, and thus ancestor worship was established among the Chinese. Confucius said that worship and sacrifice to ancestors will bring abundant blessings.[24] Furthermore, ancestor worship is an extension of human sympathy. It is through ancestorship that the family members may serve and respect the dead as if they were still alive and abiding in the family.[25] All of this has resulted in the ancestor worship system of today.

7. *Basic Teachings: Man and Government*

a. Hsun Tzu thought that the state, as the civilizing influence, should act on the evil characteristics of human beings through legislation, regulation, and punishment, in order to restrain and redeem. Moreover, Mencius identified the relationship between ruler and subject as the second class among the five classes. The state is only an enlarged family.[26] The ruler is to be a kind man; the subjects are to be loyal. The king's authority is received from *Tien* ("heaven"), so he is called *Tien Tzu* or "Son of Heaven." The government must provide sufficient food for the people and an efficient militia, to gain the people's confidence.[27] As the population grows, the state should provide education for the people.[28]

b. According to Li Chi, the ideal world is portrayed as a state characterized by a "great similarity," which is described as follows:

The men do not regard as . . . parents only their parents, nor treat as . . . children only their own children. A competent provision is made for the aged until their death, employment for the able bodied, and means of education for the young. The widowers, widows, orphans, childless men, and those who are disabled by disease are all sufficiently maintained. Each man has his proper work and each woman has her proper home.[29]

c. This is fulfilled when a good government supplies a wealthy, peaceful, equal, and economic society. Without these a revolution is justified because the ruler has forfeited "the mandate of Heaven" and could thus be dethroned.[30]

d. In other words, the purpose of the state is to offer a stable society to meet the needs of the people. The people should support this type of government. "Most emperors after Confucius gravitated toward Confucianism rather than Buddhism or Daoism because Confucianism offered social thought more likely to produce docile subjects."[31]

8. *Basic Teachings: Man and God Relationship*

a. The Confucian ethics are preserved in the *Analects*, which consist of questions by his disciples and the appropriate answers. This is in no sense a religious work, but an expression of the views of a pragmatic moralist with an interest in religion. Confucius emphasized the importance of virtue, propriety, and correct ritual, while accepting the current religious beliefs in *Tien*, "heaven," and in spirits. His references to the deity are in impersonal terms. But he recognized this impersonal power as a sanction for moral conduct. His interest was in this world rather than in the next.[32]

b. Confucius accepted *Tien* ("Heaven") as the expression of the Ultimate. He spoke of it in impersonal terms, as the moral order that underpins the cosmos.[33] The characteristics of Heaven are loving and righteous.[34] *Tien* reveals its will through its appointment, decree, and commissioning to communicate with humans.[35] *Tien* assigns a country to a sovereign and chooses humans and trains them through hardship, to empower them to be able to share the future's great responsibilities.[36]

c. The will of Heaven can be discerned. Confucius said, "At fifty I comprehended the will and decrees of heaven. At sixty my ears were attuned to them."[37] The requirement of the nobleman was that he knew heaven's appointment.[38] Confucius taught that during the temple ceremony the ritual is more important than sacrifices. When he answered Tzu-Kung's question regarding the dispensing of the sheep on the temple service of the first day of the new moon, Confucius said, "Ah! You grudge the loss of the sheep; I grudge the loss of the ceremony."[39] Regardless of this, Confucius denied that he had any knowledge regarding the spiritual realm. Chi Lu, a disciple of Confucius, asked how to serve the ghosts and spirits. Confucius said, "Where there is scarcely the ability to minister to living ones, how shall there be ability to minister to the spirits?" On his venturing to ask a question concerning death, he replied,

"Where there is scarcely any knowledge about life, how shall there be any about death?"[40]

d. Thus, Confucius was concerned about human beings, but he had no interest in the sphere of their spirituality. Nevertheless, he respected Heaven as a supreme God. After the Han Dynasty (A.D. 220), Confucianism lost its prestige and became only a conservative, moral, and social tradition. But in the eleventh century a few thinkers started to revive the Confucian philosophy. The best known of these new Confucianists was Chufucius (Chu-Hsi, Zhu Xi, 1130-1200). He accepted ancestor worship and respected the spirit of the Chinese heroes. However, he opposed Taoism, Buddhism, and especially denied that there was a supreme Creator deity. This meant that after neo-Confucianism was established, many educated people became more skeptical of religion.[41]

9. *Confucianism: A Religion or an Ethical System?*

a. Is Confucianism a religion, or merely an ethical system? The answer to this question obviously depends on how one defines religion. While Confuciansim prescribes a great deal of ritual, little of it could be construed as worship or meditation in a formal sense. With its close attention to personal conduct and the moral order, Confucianism sees life from a different angle than do other Eastern religions. However, this does not imply that it should not be considered a religion. "If religion is taken in its widest sense as a way of life woven around a people's ultimate concerns, Confucianism clearly qualifies." However, if religion is an effort to put man in contact with God, "Confucianism is still a religion albeit a muted one."[42]

b. To understand the total dimensions of Confucianism as a religion, it is important to see that Confucius shifted the emphasis from Heaven to Earth without dropping Heaven out of the picture entirely.

The extent to which Confucius shifted emphasis from Heaven to Earth should not blind us, however, to the balancing point; namely, that he did not sunder man from Heaven altogether. He never repudiated the main outlines of the world view of his time–Heaven and Earth, the divine creative pair, half physical and half more-than-physical, ruled over by the supreme *Shang Ti.* Reticent as he was about the supernatural, he was not without it. Somewhere in the universe there was a power that was on the side of right. The spread of righteousness was, therefore, a cosmic demand, and 'the will of Heaven' the first thing a gentleman would fear. Confucius believed he had a personal commission to spread his teachings.[43]

c. Confucius himself eventually became an object of worship. Although his own descendants and disciples have worshiped him since he died, in 195 B.C. the first of the Han emperors gave him that honor. By the early Middle Ages, Confucian temples were erected, his tomb in Shantung became a national shrine, and official worship continued until the revolution of 1911. Even under Communism, August 27 was to be his birthday and a national holiday.[44]

d. Confucius' teachings are intimately related to the cult of the ancestors. Ancestor worship has been highly developed in China, Korea, and Japan. Ancestor worship "goes back into antiquity and Confucius certainly did not invent it. But recognizing the importance of filial piety for the stability of society, he carried over this reverence to the dead as well as the living." He said that children should spend three years mourning for their departed parents and established a complex ritual for the veneration of the dead, which until the advent of Communism, "was practiced by every devoted son, often at a cost he could not afford which might involve him in debt for life."[45]

10. *Christian Witness*

a. Confucianism teaches that "the feeling of right and wrong is found in all men."[46] Heaven, as an impersonal principle, cannot not have moral laws. The human sense of sympathy about the suffering of others is rooted in a personal God who is capable of caring.[47]

b. Even though Confucius depersonalized the Ultimate by speaking of *Tien* ("Heaven") rather than in terms of a personal *Shang Ti*, he attributed to Heaven personal characteristics.[48] This opens a door for Christian witness. If the five basic relationships provide a context for meaning on the human level, our relationship to the Ultimate Reality should not be anything less than personal. If there is a Person in Heaven, He could speak to humanity and desire to do so. In fact, this Person reveals Himself through nature, conscience, providental acts, prophets, and ultimately through His Son.

c. Some Confucianists stress that human nature is evil, and others affirm that it is good. Nevertheless, Confucius himself said in the *Analects* that "the way of the superior man is threefold, but I have not been able to attain it."[49] The Bible says that humans were made in the image of a holy God, but that they rebelled against Him. What drives humans now is not a good nature within, but a spirit of independence, a broken relationship. What humans need is reconciliation with a personal God through the means that in His love and grace He provided for humans–the person of Jesus Christ.

11.   *ssary of Confucian Terms*

icestor Worship. This practice is based on the assumption that after
erson becomes deified. This enables them to watch over their living
nts and to intercede for them with more powerful divine beings. The
rship them, usually at a household shrine, to show their respect for

octrine of the Mean. The Confucian ideal of avoiding the extremes, of
way between two conflicting, radical solutions. In life situations this
ns a tendency to negotiation and compromise instead of confrontation
ict.

ial Duty or Filial Piety, *Hsiao*. The term is broad enough in meaning
covers not only a son's duty to his father, but also his obligations as a
l a citizen.

ve Relationships, *Wun Lun*. They are applied and oftentimes expressed
below, in reverse. The Five Relationships are the duty of

) a ruler to his subject,
) husband to his wife,
) older friend to younger friend,
) elder brother to younger brother, and
) father to son.

The Confucian notion of proper behavior. It refers to both
the right thing to do–and the notion of the proper rites or rituals.

icius. Next to Confucius himself, he was perhaps Confucianism's
tant teacher. Living one hundred years after Confucius' death, he
d his master's teachings.

Jen). This is the most important Confucian virtue. While it
leans "humanness," it is perhaps better understood as the respect for
umanity. Another way to understand it is as a person's dignity,
mbination of self-respect, and respect and sympathy toward others.

Ti. This means, literally, the "Lord of Heaven." It is the oldest
nation of the supreme god. In some stories he is considered to be
estor of the Shang Dynasty (roughly 1700-1000 B.C.). Usually, he
le god of rulers and those who wield power.

i. Superior Man, *Chiun-Tze* (*Chun Tzu, Jiun Tze*). This is the Confucian ideal of a perfected human being. This is a person who is mature, magnanimous, respectful, and helpful towards others. He or she is poised, always in control of him or herself. The term is variously translated as Superior Man, Princely Man, Higher Man, etc. In the *Analects*, he is often contrasted to the *Siao Yun*, or mean man: that is, one whose nature is unenlightened and unregenerate.

j. *Tien*, Heaven. In Confucius' usage, this is an impersonal term for God. It is used in the same way that Christians speak of the "kingdom of Heaven": that is, a realm, an order of existence governed by laws .

Notes

1   Mary Pat Fisher, *Living Religions*, 6th ed. (Upper Saddle River, NJ: Prentice-Hall, 2005), 194.

2   "Biography of Confucius," *Sacklunch* [article online]; retrieved on April 15, 2006, from http://www.sacklunch.net/biography/C/Confucius/html.

3   Denise Lardner Carmody and T. L. Brink, *Ways to the Center* (Belmont, CA: Thomson Wadsworth, 2006), 166.

4   D. Noss, *A History of the World's Religions*, 10th ed. (Upper Saddle River, NJ: Prentice Hall, 1999), 288.

5   See a more complete description in Julia Ching, *Chinese Religions* (Maryknoll, NY: Orbis, 1993), 55-57.

6   Robert Van Voorst, *Anthology of World Scriptures* (Belmont, CA: Thomson Wadsworth, 2006), 139.

7   Carmody and Brink, *Ways to the Center*, 177.

8   Ching, *Chinese Religions*, 70.

9   Carmody and Brink, *Ways to the Center*, 177.

10   Ching, *Chinese Religions*, 76.

11   "Zhu Xi," *Wikipedia, the Free Encyclopedia*, 2006 [article online]; retrieved on April 15, 2006, from http:///www.en.wikipedia.org/wiki/Zhu_Xi.

12   C. George Fry, "Confucianism," in *Great Asian Religions* (Grand Rapids: Baker, 1984), 97.

13   Norman Anderson, *The World's Religions* (Grand Rapids: Eerdmans, 1975), 221.

14   Carmody and Brink, *Ways to the Center*, 166.

15   B. A. Robinson, "Confucianism," *Religious Tolerance*, 2004 [article online]; retrieved on January 7, 2006, from http://religioustolerance.org/confuciu.htm.

16   Carmody and Brink, *Ways to the Center*, 167.

17   Theodore M. Ludwig, *The Sacred Paths: Understanding the Religions of the World* (Upper Saddle River, NJ: Pearson Prentice Hall, 2006), 212.

18   Anderson, *The World's Religions*, 222; Mencius believed that righteousness is also innate in all human beings, so human nature is good. Hsu Cho-yun, "The Unfolding of Early Confucianism: The Evolution from Confucius to Hsun-tzu," in *Confucianism: The Dynamics of Tradition*, ed. Irene Eber (New York: Macmillan, 1986), 34.

19   Lawrence G. Thompson, *Chinese Religion: An Introduction* (Belmont, CA: Wadsworth, 1979), 15.

20   D. Howard Smith, *Chinese Religions* (New York: Holt, Rinehart and Winston, 1968), 50, 52.

21   Fisher, *Living Religions*, 196.

22   Huston Smith, *The Illustrated World's Religions: A Guide to Our Wisdom Traditions* (New York: Harper San Francisco, 1995), 111.

23   Hsiao Ching I, quoted in Thompson, *Chinese Religions*, 40.

24   Confucius, "Shu Ching," in *The Book of Songs*, trans. Arthur Waley (London: Allen & Unwin, 1937), 127. But if the person neglects to worship his ancestors, he will be punished, and that will cause disaster in the family. Since Chinese people consider their ancestors to be lesser gods, they will not ask for help from them when facing big issues such as business or marriage. Arthur P. Wolf, "God, Ghosts, and Ancestors," in *Religion and Ritual in Chinese Society*, ed. Arthur P. Wolf (Stanford, CA: Stanford University Press, 1974), 160, 165-67.

25   Shih-Lieu Hsu, *The Political Philosophy of Confucianism* (New York: Harper & Row, 1975), 72. Filial piety is the sons' (and/or daughters') way to repay their debt to their parents, who gave life and raised them. George J. Jennings, *All Things, All Men, All Means to Save Some* (Le Mars, IA: Middle East Mission Research, 1984), 161.

26 Hsu, *The Political Philosophy of Confucianism*, 40.

27 *Analects* 12:7, quoted in Confucius, *Analects*, in *The Wisdom of Confucius*, trans. Ephiphanius Wilson (New York: Avenel Books, 1982), 63.

28 *Analects* 13:9, quoted in ibid., 65.

29 Li Chi, 7:12, quoted in Hsu, *The Political Philosophy of Confucianism*, 237.

30 Hsiao Ching, 5:4, quoted in ibid., 75.

31 Carmody and Brink, *Ways to the Center*, 171.

32 Confucius, *The Analects of Confucius*, trans. Arthur Waley (New York: Vintage Books, 1989).

33 Jennings, *All Things, All Men, All Means to Save Some*, 151.

34 Smith, *Chinese Religions*, 37, 52.

35 Ibid., 36.

36 Mencius 6:15, quoted in Smith, *Chinese Religions*, 53.

37 *Analects* 2:4, quoted in Confucius, *Analects*, 12.

38 *Analects* 20:3, quoted in ibid., 108.

39 *Analects* 3:17, quoted in ibid., 19.

40 *Analects* 11:12, quoted in ibid., 57.

41 Daniel L. Overmyer, *Religion of China: The World as a Living System* (San Francisco: Harper & Row, 1986), 48-50.

42 Huston Smith, *The Religions of Man* (New York: Harper & Row, 1958), 187-88.

43 Ibid., 190-91.

44 Fry, "Confucianism," 108.

45   Anderson, *The World's Religions*, 223.

46   One of the many online editions of the *Analects* is posted by Daniel C. Stevenson, "The Analects," *Internet Classics Archive*, 1994-2000 [book online]; retrieved on January 28, 2006, from http://classics.mit.edu/Confucius/analects.html.

47   These suggestions for witnessing are summarized from Thomas I. S. Leung, "Confucianism," in *The Compact Guide to World Religions*, ed. Dean C. Halverson (Minneapolis, MN: Bethany, 1996), 76-84.

48   In the *Analects*, Confucius is quoted as saying, "Heaven knows me." "The Analects of Confucius," *Association Française de Professeurs of Chinois* [book online]; retrieved on April 15, 2006, from http://www.afpc.assoc.fr/wengu/wg/ wengu.php?1=Lunyu&no=382&m =NOzh. To "know" someone is one of the characteristics of a personal Being, not of an impersonal principle.

49   James Legge, trans., "English Translation of Holy Confucian Analects," *Ishwar* [book online]; retrieved on April 10, 2006, from http//ishwar.com/confucianism/ holy_confucian_analects/part_15.html.

CHAPTER 14

Taoism

1. *Introduction*

   a. Taoism is the most important religion among all of the religions practiced in Taiwan and Hong Kong. It is deeply rooted in the Chinese mind and rules the Chinese daily lifestyle, instruction, and worldview. However, it cannot be clearly delineated as a religion with a certain body of doctrines and rituals in the same way as Islam or Christianity. Little is known of its founder, Lao-tze. Despite the vaguely theistic teachings of the earliest teachers of Taoism, by the time of Christ Taoism had evolved into a complex belief system with gods, priests, temples, and sacrifices. During this process many popular beliefs flowed into mainstream Taoism. This resulted in a somewhat mysterious branch of Taoism called Folk Taoism, which is focused mainly on charms, exorcisms, and magical attempts to prolong life.

   b. The name "Taoism" is taken from the title of a book, *Tao-te King* or *Daode jing*, and is probably best translated as "the way" or "the way of nature." Original Taoism is the religion of nature, with a special emphasis on the relationship between man and nature.[1]

2. *The Life of Lao-tze*

   a. Lao-tze (ca. 604-517 B.C.) was born "Li-poh-yang." His disciples gave him the title Lao-tze, Lao Tse, or Lao Tzu (Lao-zi, Laozi, "Old Master") as an expression of respect.[2] He was a contemporary of Confucius, another famous Chinese.

b. It is said that he was the keeper of royal archives in the court of the Chou Dynasty during the tumultuous period when order was breaking down. As a custodian of the secret archives of the state, it is reasonable to assume that Lao-tze must have been a scholar, learned in the literary legacy of the ancients.

c. Lao-tze eventually became tired of the artificial life in the court and retired from his post. Journeying to the West, he reached a pass in the mountains at the northwest boundary of China where he sought to leave the country. The guard at the pass recognized him as being a wise man and refused to allow him to leave until he had committed to writing the sum of his wisdom. So Lao-tze sat down and wrote the *Tao-te King* (Tao te Ching, Daodejing, Dao De Jing, Daode jing). When this was completed, the guard allowed him to leave the country. He was never seen again. Considering that this is all we know about Lao-tze, it is safe to say that we know less about the founder of Taoism than we know about any of the other founders of world religions.

3. *The Tao-te King*

a. The literary sources of Taoism are the same as those from Confucianism. They both presume, in their background, the ancient classics as a spiritual legacy. From the many references to the Tao in the Chinese writings, it is evident that Lao-tze did not invent this term.

b. The title, *Tao-te King*, is translated in various ways, but for all practical purposes, it is something along the lines of "The Way and the Power of the Higher Life." Since *Tao* and *Te* are words filled with meaning, many translators prefer to leave the title untranslated.

c. This little volume only has about five thousand Chinese characters; each is an ideograph. For comparison, it is shorter than the Gospel of Mark. Very few translations resemble each other because suggestiveness rather than explicitness is the quality of Eastern symbols. It has been the object of at least a thousand commentaries, and it is second only to the Bible in the number of Western translations.[3] With exception to the writings of Mao, it is probably the best known of all Chinese books.

4. *Chuang-tze*

a. Chuang-tze, Chuang tzu, or Chuang tse (Zhuang Zi, Zhuangzi, "Master Chang"), lived from ca. 369 to 286 B.C. and was a contemporary of the Confucian apologist, Mencius. Chang-tze was the most famous of the disciples of Lao-tze and his most intelligible expounder.[4] He thought of himself primarily as a commentator, and his writings are compiled into a work which is also known as *Chuang-tze*. The *Chaung-tze* is second in importance only to the *Tao-te King*. Under Chuang-tze, the religious philosophy of Taoism became systematized, explained, and formalized.

b. Chuang-tze advised people to "return to nature." By this he meant the original nature, the "god inside each of us" whose reality we must awaken. His reference to a sage, the Perfected Man, led to the development of the religious belief that there are "Immortals" who are no longer dependent on a diet of grains and have conquered death.[5]

5. *The Texts of Taoism*

a. The Taoist canon as a whole is known as the *Tao Tsang*.[6] It consists of more than one thousand volumes. Only the *I Ching,* the *Pao-p'u-tze*, and the *Tao-te King,* from the books listed below, are recognized by most Taoists.

b. The *I Ching* (Yijing, Ee jing, ca. 800 B.C.) is an ancient book of divination cherished by Taoists and Confucianists.

d. The *Pao-p'u-tze* (317 B.C.) is a compendium of techniques of immortality and Taoist alchemy.

c. The *Tao-te King* (ca. 500 B.C.), attributed to Lao-Tze, is a short book of Taoist philosophy written in semipoetic style.

e. The *Chuang-tze* (ca. 300 B.C.), is a collection of anecdotes and essays attributed to Chuang Tze. It attempted to convince the Chinese to accept Lao-tze instead of Confucius as their main teacher.

f. The *Huai-nan-tze* (ca. 140 B.C.) is an encyclopedic collection of Taoist teachings.

g. The *Ling Piao* (ca. A.D. 400) are revelations from the Celestial Worthies who personify the Tao. Many present liturgies followed today are adaptations of its legacy.[7]

6. *The Teachings of the Early Taoist Philosophers*[8]

a. The beliefs of Taoism are difficult to ascertain and come mostly from the *Chuang-tze*. Original Taoism was not a religion concerning God or gods. It was essentially atheistic. It was a philosophy, a way of life, and a way of self-cultivation.[9] Two of the dominant concepts in this philosophy are those of *Tao* and *Wu-wei*.

   b. *Tao (Dao)*

   1) The basic unity behind the universe is a mysterious and indefinable force called the *Tao*. The true *Tao* is impossible to define. Nameless and indefinable though it may be, the *Tao* is the source of the universe.[10] Even the gods seem to have evolved from the flow of *Tao*. *Tao* has many different definitions, including Way of Moral and Physical Order, Way of Thinking, Rule of Living, Path of Reason, Ultimate Reality, Way of Nature, Truth, Virtue, and the Way both approved and followed by heaven itself.[11]

   2) Lao-tze pointed out that Tao means the Way, the Great, and Nature.

> Something undifferentiated was born before heaven and earth; still and silent, standing alone and unchanging, going through cycles unending, able to be mother to the world. I do not know its name; I label it the Way. Imposing on it a name, I call it Great. . . . Humanity emulates earth, earth emulates heaven, heaven emulates the way, the way emulates Nature.[12]

   3) Moreover, Lao-tze taught that *Tao* means "the creator." He stated, "The way gives birth." "The way produces one; one produces two, two produce three, three produce all beings: all beings bear *Yin* and embrace *Yang*, with a mellowing energy for harmony."[13]

   c. *Wu-wei*

   1) Another central aspect of Lao-tze's philosophy is *wu-wei*, "noninterference" with the *Tao*. To achieve order and harmony in one's own life and in the cosmos, a person must learn to perceive the *Tao* in nature and to act, or refrain from acting, in accordance with it. *Wu-wei* has been described as "the art of being."[14]

2) *Wu-wei* can be translated as "the way of non-action," "nonselfishness," and "teaching without words."[15] According to some Western scholars, *wu-wei* is "Lao Tzu's most difficult idea."[16] When we cultivate our natures with the principle of heaven as our guide, we will fulfill the way.[17] One is better off moving with the flow of things. "A life based on *wu-wei* is a life of spontaneity, simplicity, naturalness, tranquility, and virtue."[18]

3) In addition, Lao-tze's *wu-wei* refers to a return to harmony with nature. The human being does not do anything through his own ego but depends on a power he does not possess, which is nature. He used the characteristic of water to illustrate his philosophy by saying, "Higher good is like water: the good in water benefits all, and does so without contention. It rests where people dislike to be, so it is close to the way."[19] *Wu-wei* is likened unto water, which looks weak but is still strong. Water is clear when it is still; similarly, one may have peace of mind through *wu-wei*.

4) To sum up, *wu-wei* means "teaching without words," no action, non-activity, and harmony with natural law. When a person practices *wu-wei*, then he follows *Tao*.

d. Life

1) Life is to be lived simply. Believing that all life originated from the *Tao,* the early Taoists turned their backs upon civilization with all its ills and benefits and sought to live as simply as possible. They considered education, wealth, power, and family ties all worthless and, in fact, impediments to living, according to the principles of *Tao*. In general, Taoists were concerned about the quality of life as it is lived on a day-to-day basis without much interest in the heavens, the gods, rituals, or life after death.

2) Life is the greatest of all possessions. This led Taoists to search for means whereby life might be lengthened, and eventually they employed various health and magical practices in an attempt to prolong and enrich life.[20] Their attempts to use the five elements in order to produce an elixir of life resulted in what later became known as alchemy.[21]

7. *Metamorphosis of Taoism*

a. Most scholars prefer to distinguish between the ancient "philosophical Taoism" and the later "religious Taoism."[22] Taoist scholars distinguish even further between "religious Taoism" and "folk Taoism." They say that the gods of folk Taoism were once humans, but that the gods of religious Taoism are special divine manifestations of the Tao. They insist that the gods of folk Taoism reside in the lower heavens or on earth, while those of philosophical Taoism dwell in the higher or "stellar" heavens.[23] However, this section will not focus on these subtle differences and will use interchangeably the terms "religious Taoism," "folk Taoism," and "Folk Chinese Religion." The development of Taoism may be divided into three periods: philosophical Taoism, developmental Taoism, and Folk Chinese Religion.[24]

1) Philosophical Taoism (500-300 B.C.) is considered to be ancient or "primitive" Taoism–"primitive" in the sense that it followed the uncorrupted teaching of Lao-tze. Ancient Taoism was a time of relative purity. However, its religious philosophy remained for the most part unexplained. Chuang-tze (Zhuang Zi, "Master Chuang"), a successor to the first Taoist teachers, expounded on their basic teachings during the fourth century B.C.[25]

2) The "developmental" period (300 B.C.-A.D. 300) reached its height in the work and activity of Chuang-tze and his school. After Chuang-tze's death, Taoist believers became fascinated with diets, elements of magic, yoga, and alchemy in order to prolong life as well as to gain immortality after death.[26] Chinese alchemists tried to pursue immortality through chemical experiments and yogic techniques. They sought the patronage of the noble and wealthy by promising to produce an "elixir of immortality."[27]

3) Folk Chinese Religion (A.D. 200-Present) of later centuries, with the addition of *Hatha Yoga* practices, good luck charms, fortune-telling, and magical ceremonies, is far removed from the teachings of Lao-tze. By degrees Taoism descended from spiritual heights to gross superstition and demonology.[28]

b. The breathing exercises of *Hatha Yoga*[29] were introduced in Taoism as a means to purify the mind and to accelerate the formation of the psychic plasma which builds up the body of the Immortal. *Yoga* in Taoism is referred to as *kung-fu*, or work. Kung-fu includes external and internal aspects. The outer work, *wai-kung*, involves 1) moral conduct, adherence to the ethical commandments, 2) worship, including reading of the sacred writings and prayers and meditation upon the divine Immortals of the Taoist pantheon, and 3) performance of good works, such as repairing roads or doing acts of mercy. The inner work, *mei-kung*, is open for those whose hearts are restless because of a higher calling, or who are willing to dedicate themselves to the higher quest. The final goal of the inner work is to bring man to immortal life, to oneness with the spiritual realities.[30]

c. The man given credit for formally establishing Taoism as a "religion" is Chang-Tao-Ling, born about 34 B.C. He claimed that Lao-tze appeared to him and decreed that the high priesthood should belong perpetually to his family. Since that time the Primate of Taoism has almost always come from the Chang clan.

d. Around the beginning of the second century of the Christian era, Mayahana Buddhism was introduced and established in China. Taoists were attracted by its concept of *bodhisattva* (one who has attained enlightenment but decided not to enter into *Nirvana*). Eventually Taoism accepted Buddhist ideas related to rebirth and retribution, and incorporated into its pantheon various Buddhist deities and *bodhisattvas*. From that time on, Folk Chinese Religion was characterized by a pantheon of gods and evil spirits, as were many other religions.[31] In spite of the mutual influence of religions, "Taoists never accepted the basic starting point [of Buddhism]: that all existence is suffering. Indeed, the quest for physical immortality presupposes a contentment with life in this world."[32]

e. The last forerunner of Taoism was Ko Hung (A.D. 254-334), an alchemist. He emphasized that the right drugs and foods, combined with gymnastics, special sexual techniques for the conservation of vital fluids, and alchemy, would enable a person to reach immortality. The development of Taoism ended with the work of Ko Hung. He and several members of his clan claimed that they had received revelations from the Celestial Masters that were codified and later became the basis of present doctrines and rituals of Folk Chinese Religion. By A.D. 444 Emperor Wei made Taoism the state religion of China.[33]

8. *Folk Chinese Religion*

a. What today is called "Folk Chinese Religion" or "Folk Taoism" is mainly a collage of the traditional beliefs of the immigrants from Miin-nan (the Southern Fukien Province) and Yeh-dong (Kwangtung Province).[34] Most of these immigrants escaped to Taiwan when MaoTse Tung took over the government and established the People's Republic of China. President Chiang Kai-Shek maintained the Republic of China in Taiwan. They comprise about 85% of the Taiwan Chinese population.[35] It is in Hong Kong and Taiwan–sites peripheral to the Chinese mainland–that Chinese Folk Religion is most alive at the present time.

b. As mentioned before, one of the characteristics of Chinese religions is their eclecticism. Folk Chinese Religion is based on a foundation of ancient Chinese animism and blended with the essential beliefs of Confucianism, Taoism, and Buddhism.[36] In Folk Chinese Religion, gods from all these religions are accepted and are worshiped together in the same temples. Even the Taoist priests find it difficult to distinguish between them.[37] Nevertheless, Taoist gods are the bulk of the Folk Chinese Religion pantheon.

c. The gods of Folk Chinese Religion/Folk Taoism

1) The Folk form of Taoism teaches that the world runs smoothly and regularly by itself. It is unnecessary for the gods to operate it. The gods just act out their responsibilities in their assigned positions. The administrative system of the Taoist gods closely adopted the social and political hierarchy of the Chinese.[38]

2) There are numberless gods who occupy various positions, from the celestial Taoist heaven down into earthly households and into individual physical bodies. These gods are believed to have been men who after death were promoted because of their merits and for various other reasons.[39] There are three categories of Folk Taoist gods: the gods of nature, the gods who are responsible for the living, and the gods who are responsible for the dead.[40]

d. The way of immortality and salvation in Folk Chinese Religion incorporates elements from Confucianism, Buddhism, and Taoism. However,

1) Folk Taoists seek eternal life in two ways: first, during this life; and second, after death. To obtain immortality during this life, a Taoist must do good works, practice alchemy, perform asceticism, and exercise yoga respiration. There are 96 good works and 34 recompenses. When a person has performed three hundred good deeds, he becomes immortal on the earth. If a person has accomplished twelve hundred merits, then he becomes immortal in heaven. On the other side, each sin will take away three days of life, while the more serious crimes reduce life by up to three hundred days.[41]

2) Folk Taoists believe in judgment. A person will be saved after he dies if he has invoked Amitabha's name, a Buddhist *bodhisattva*. These souls will be reborn for eternity to enter the heavenly palaces.[42] In addition, there are some souls who pass through nine of the ten judgments of Hell's kings. After staying in Hell for 28 months, the soul will appear before the tenth king of Hell to be reborn and become either a human being or an animal, according to the merits of the soul.[43]

3) Folk Taoists believe in several possible destinies. One might suffer eternal punishment by demons in hell; could become a ghost, hovering over the grave; could continue existence in this world, nourished by filial survivors; or become an immortal and enjoy the freedom of those unique beings; or even become gods.[44]

9. *Christian Witness*

a. First of all, demonstrate appreciation for their culture. At a minimum, become acquainted with the main points of their philosophy. Do not dismiss the contribution of Lao-tze or Chuang-tze as irrelevant for the twenty-first century; after all, they try to answer the same ultimate questions that people have today.[45]

b. Examine evidences that God must have personal attributes such as will, emotions, creativity, and moral standards, which are not perceived as being part of the impersonal Tao. The fact that there are personal differences among people is in itself an evidence of a creative personal God and of an intelligent Designer. The fact that people have moral sensitivity is an evidence of a decision of a Creator with moral authority, not of a *Tao* void of moral distinctions. The fact that the *Tao* is described as being capable of "deep love"[46] may be an indication that "the God of the Bible and the God of ancient China are One and the same,"[47] and that in time the Chinese lost their knowledge of the True God.[48]

c. The issue of sin must be solved before a Taoist can understand the Christian message. Taoists understand the concept of disharmony. However, they attempt to solve this problem by themselves. They aim to attain immortality and understand that not meeting the standards of the Tao means death.[49] They are also aware of the fact that they cannot meet those standards: "All the world knows that the weak overcomes the strong and the soft overcomes the hard. But none can practice it."[50] Help them to see that a personal God wants to give them victory over sin. Taoism cannot provide a satisfactory solution. The *Tao-te King* speaks of the need of forgiveness,[51] but an impersonal *Tao* cannot offer it. The sage foreshadowed the need for One who would suffer in our place.[52] It is likely that Taoists will empathize and appreciate the "soft" way in which Jesus dealt with the problem of sin.

10. *Glossary of Taoist Terms*

a. *Chi.* The idea of the vital energy of the Tao, which a person cannot only use but also enhance and increase. This can be done in several ways, including the eating of particular substances, meditation, dance, and other types of movement.

b. Chuang-tze. Next to Lao-tze, the most significant Taoist sage. His writings extended and developed the *Tao-te King*–providing important ideas that were later developed into Religious Taoism and attacked Confucianism.

c. Philosophical Taoism. This is a reflective form of Taoism, whose practitioners seek to understand the *Tao* in order to make more efficient use of its power, or *te*. It is organized into a school with teachers and students. The students learn an attitude toward life which enables them to live within the flow of *Tao* through the practice of *wu-wei*.

d. Religious Taoism, also known as Folk Taoism, and Chinese Folk Religion. The popular form of Taoism that seeks to extend followers' lives, even to reach physical immortality. The idea is that if a person can achieve a perfect fit with the *Tao*, then such feats can be accomplished. Religious Taoism uses feats of magic, meditation, and rituals to enhance the believers' lives. It was developed in the second century A.D.

e. *Tao.* *Tao* cannot be conceptualized nor expressed in concrete terms. In translating the *Tao-te King* or "Book of the *Tao*," however, the word is variously rendered in many ways, including Divine Reason, the Way, Nature, the Law of Life, and Being.

f. *Tso-wang.* The term literally means "blank mind." In Taoist meditation practices, it is a type of ecstasy, when the inner dweller has left his body and lower mind and has entered into higher states of contemplation. It is a form of occultism.

g. *Wu-wei.* Although this Taoist term is literally translated as "inaction," the concept actually emphasizes the notion of accomplishing things by "going with the flow" rather than working against it. The idea is to align the self with the *Tao* and in that position to act spontaneously or, more aptly, to act with the *Tao*. *Wu-wei* is when a person allows the *Tao* to carry oneself along its path.

h. *Yin-yang.* The Taoist concept of opposites. Life's opposites, such as male and female, light and dark, are always in tension. But even within that tension, each term has some of its counterpart within it, as represented in the Tai Chi symbol found in the center of the Korean flag. The *yin-yang* symbol represents the interlocking of opposites, because every place where a diameter line can be drawn across the circle, it intersects both white and black.

Figure 14.1

Glossary of Folk Taoist Terms

a. Alchemy. A reputed spiritual science that links the heating and ㄱting of metals with belief in healing powers and even immortality.

. Divination. Forecasting the future, usually through casting wooden and then linking the result to a place in a collection of divinatory sayings, s the *I-Ching*.

c. Gate Guardians. Two Guardians stand on both sides of the main sᴄᴗhern gate of a temple to ward off evil spirits or thieves. They are believed by Buddhists to represent two opposing forces of the universe.

d. General Kuang-kung (Guan-gong). He is honored everywhere in China as the righter of wrongs and supporter of justice.

e. Immortals. Humans that attained a high state of development. Perhaps originally intended to be allegorical, the nature and abilities of these beings became a practical goal for later Taoists. They are described in the *Chuang-tze*.

f. Jade Emperor. A Chinese deity viewed by Taoists as the executor of orders from the Three Pure Ones.

g. *Shen*. While generally associated with the "spirits" and divinities of the ordinary world, the deeper significance of *shen* is the spiritual self in man, which inhabits the temple of the body (*kung*).

h. Three Pure Ones. The three highest gods in the Folk Taoist pantheon. Also called Lords of Worthies. They are the Lord of Heaven, the Lord of Earth, and the Lord of Humanity

Notes

1 Huston Smith, *The Religions of Man* (New York: Harper & Row, 1958), 214. See also Wing-tsit Chan, "Religions of the Chinese," in *The Great Asian Religions: An Anthology* (New York: Collier Macmillan, 1969), 162.

2 Martin Palmer, *The Elements of Taoism* (Rockport, MA: Element, 1991), 34-38.

3 Mary Pat Fisher, *Living Religions*, 6th ed. (Upper Saddle River, NJ: Prentice-Hall, 2005), 180.

4 Theodore M. Ludwig, *The Sacred Paths: Understanding the Religions of the World* (Upper Saddle River, NJ: Pearson Prentice Hall, 2006), 214.

5 Later, the use of mercury and sulfur characterized the development of an immortality cult within Taoism. Julia Ching, *Chinese Religions* (Maryknoll, NY: Orbis, 1993), 91.

6 Robert Van Voorst, *Anthology of World Scriptures* (Belmont, CA: Thomson Wadsworth, 2006), 162.

7 Roger Schmidt, Gene C. Sager, Gerald T. Carney, Albert C. Muller, Kenneth J. Zanca, Julius J. Jackson, Jr., C. Wayne Mayhall, and Jeffrey C. Burke, *Patterns of Religion*, 2nd ed. (Belmont, CA: Wadsworth, 2005), 239.

8 Lewis M. Hopfe, *Religions of the World* (New York: Macmillan, 1983), 235-40.

9 John Blofeld, *Taoism: The Road to Immortality* (Boulder, CO: Shambhala Publications, 1978), 90. Furthermore, Lao-tze and Chuang-tze were not interested in the supernatural aspects of Taoism. Ibid., 92. See also Chan, "Religions of the Chinese," 150.

10 Schmidt et al., *Patterns of Religion*, 231.

11 Denise Lardner Carmody and T. L. Brink, *Ways to the Center: An Introduction to World Religions* (Belmont, CA: Thomson Wadsworth, 2006), 168. Modern scholars concur that *Tao* means road, path, way, method, principle, doctrine. Arthur Waley, *The Way and Its Power* (London: Allen & Unwin, 1956), 30. According to Huston Smith, there are three meanings of *Tao*: (1) the way of ultimate reality, (2) the way of the universe, the norm, the driving power in all nature, the ordering principle behind all life, (3) the way man should order his life to gear in with the way the universe operates. Huston Smith, *The Religions of Man* (New York: Harper & Row, 1958), 199-200. According to Dolitella, *Tao* is equivalent to the Greek *hodos* (a

road or a way), and to *Logos*. Joseph Dolitella, *Taoism and Confucianism* (Iowa City, IA: Sernoll, 1967), 22-23.

12 Lao-tze, *The Essential Tao: An Initiation into the Heart of Taoism through the Authentic Tao Te Ching and the Inner Teaching of Chuang-tzu*, trans. Thomas Cleary (San Francisco: Harper & Row, 1991), 24.

13 Ibid., 40, 35.

14 Palmer, *The Elements of Taoism*, 49.

15 Ibid., 8.

16 Ibid., 49.

17 Chan, "Religions of the Chinese," 222.

18 Schmidt et al., *Patterns of Religion*, 231.

19 Lao-tze, *The Essential Tao*, 12.

20 See a discussion on alchemy in Taoism in Ching, *Chinese Religions*, 104-111.

21 Ludwig, *The Sacred Paths*, 217.

22 Jen Cairns, "General Essay on Taoism," *Philosophy, Theology and Religion*, 1999 [article online]; retrieved on April 20, 2006, from http://philtar.ucsm.ac.uk/ encyclopedia/taoism/ geness.html.

23 Schmidt et al., *Patterns of Religion*, 247-48.

24 Cairns, "General Essay on Taoism."

25 Dolitella, *Taoism and Confucianism*, 45. McDowell and Stewart point out that Taoism as a philosophy began around 300 B.C. John McDowell and Don Stewart, *Handbook of Today's Religions* (Nashville: Thomas Nelson, 1992), 346.

26 William A. Young, *The World's Religions: Worldviews and Contemporary Issues* (Upper Saddle River, NJ: Pearson Prentice Hall, 2005), 117.

27 Denise L. Carmody and T. L. Brink, *Ways to the Center*, 6th ed. (Belmont, CA; Thomson Wadsworth, 2006), 175.

28 Chang's successors used the title *T'ien Shih* as a respect title for many centuries, until the Tang Emperor Hsuan Tzung (A.D. 713-56) bestowed it officially to them. Later on, the Yuan Emperor Khubilai confirmed it as a perpetual title for his successors. In 1949 the title of *Tien Shih* was censored by the Communist government of People's Republic of China but it is used in Taiwan. See Blofeld, *Taoism: The Road to Immortality*, 27-28, 35 and Schmidt et al., *Patterns of Religion*, 235.

29 "Hatha Yoga," *Wikipedia: The Free Encyclopedia*, 2006 [article online]; retrieved on June 20, 2006, from http://en.wikipedia.org/wiki/Hatha_yoga.

30 Adam Hsu, "The Real Difference between Internal and External Kung Fu," 1998 [article online]; retrieved on April 8, 2006, from http://www.adamhsu.com/spr/int_vs_ext.html.

31 Dolitella, *Taoism and Confucianism*, 48 and Blofeld, *Taoism: The Road to Immortality*, 93. Emperor Huan erected a temple to honor Lao-tze, where offerings were made to him. This indicates that Taoism had already become a religion. John McDowell and Don Stewart, *Handbook of Today's Religions* (Nashville: Thomas Nelson, 1992), 346.

32 Ching, *Chinese Religions*, 118.

33 Schmidt et al., *Patterns of Religion*, 237-39.

34 Fan-yuan Doong, *Essays on Taiwan Folk Beliefs* (Taipei: Charng Chin Cultural Company, 1980), 12.

35 Ibid.

36 Ibid., 40. The essence of ancient animism included totemism (for example, the twelve animals of the Chinese year), magic, taboo, and mythology (for example, Parn-guu, the creator of heaven). Ibid., 13-14.

37 John Meskill, *An Introduction to Chinese Civilization* (New York: Columbia University Press, 1973), 65.

38 Jennifer Oldstone-Moore, "The Celestial Empire," in *The Illustrated Guide to World Religions*, ed. Michael D. Coogan (New York: Oxford University Press, 2003), 209.

39 For example, the god of the Yellow River was a man who drowned while he was crossing the river in the third or fourth century A.D.; the god of Che River was an unjustly killed prince, Wu Tzu-hsu, and so on. Henri Maspero, Taoism and Chinese Religion, trans. Frank A. Kierman (New York: Collier Macmillan, 1969), 86, 183. In this way there is a series of new divinities appearing in the Chinese world continuously. In 1975 the former president, Chiang Kai-shek, passed away. Even though he was a Methodist Christian, he has become a god, and a temple has been erected to honor and worship him in Kaohsiung.

40 Maspero, *Taoism and Chinese Religion*, 93.

41 Chan, "Religions of the Chinese," 167-68; 173-77.

42 If serious crimes are discovered when his soul is judged, the grace of *Ti-tsang* will save him. See Chan, "Religions of the Chinese," 188, 190, 193; Doong, *Essays on Taiwan Folk Beliefs*, 136.

43 Doong, *Essays on Taiwan Folk Beliefs*, 136, 139. On the fifteenth day of the seventh month of the year, the *Chung-yuan* ceremonies are assigned to provide food for the wandering souls and to guide them to re-enter the way of transmigration. Maspero, Taoism and Chinese Religion, 187.

44 Schmidt et al., *Patterns of Religion*, 249.

45 These suggestions for witessing are summarized from Kent Kerdl and Dean C. Halverson, "Taoism," in *The Compact Guide to World Religions*, ed. Dean C. Halverson (Minneapolis, MN: Bethany, 1996), 223-33.

46 "When Heaven is to save a person, Heaven will protect him through deep love." *Tao-te King*, 67.

47 Samuel Wang and Ethel R. Nelson, *God and the Ancient Chinese* (Dunlap, TN: Read Books Publisher, 1998), 45.

48 Ibid., 271.

49 "Not to suit the Way is early death," *Tao-te King,* 30. This idea is similar to what the Bible says in Rom 6:23, "The wages of sin is death."

50 *Tao-te King,* 78. This is close to Rom 3:23, "All have sinned and fall short of the glory of God."

51 "Why did the ancients so treasure this Tao? Is it not because it has been said of it: 'Whosoever asks will receive; whosoever has sinned will be forgiven'? Therefore Tao is the most exquisite thing on earth." *Tao-te King*, 62.

52 "Therefore said the Holy Man: 'He who is disgraced for the kingdom is the Lord of the kingdom; he who suffers for the Kingdom is the King of the universe." *Tao-te King*, 78. Wang and Nelson provide an extended explanation of how the Chinese were provided with light in *God and the Ancient Chinese*, 117-19.

CHAPTER 15

Shintoism

1. *Introduction*

a. Before the arrival of the Christian faith in Japan, two religious traditions had already been institutionalized–Shintoism and Buddhism. The Shinto tradition, indigenous to Japan, is prehistoric in origin. The Buddhist tradition, on the other hand, arrived relatively late: that is, in the sixth century A.D., after one thousand years of evolution on the Asian mainland. There has been relatively little conflict between the two traditions–to the point that it is difficult to tell where one ends and the other begins.

b. Since the Japanese islands are bound on all sides by seas, a somewhat unified cultural and religious sphere developed around Shinto. Shinto is the only religion indigenous to Japan. It is essentially an animistic religion that worships gods and goddesses in various aspects of nature. In contrast with most world religions, Shinto has neither a founder nor a written canon; so it is not surprising that it has never developed a systematic theology.

c. Shinto is an amalgam of attitudes, ideas, and ways of doing things that throughout time have become an integral part of the way of the Japanese people.

Shinto is both a personal faith in the *kami* and a communal way of life according to the mind of the *kami*, which emerged in the course of the centuries as various ethnic and cultural influences, both indigenous and foreign, were fused, and the country attained unity under the Imperial Family.[1]

d. Until the advent of a cultural invasion from the Chinese mainland which forced the Japanese to consciously reflect upon their own traditions, there was no entity known as "Shinto." The Japanese created the term *Kami-no-michi* or *Shinto* (in Chinese) to distinguish their traditions from the Way of Buddha or the Teaching of Confucius. In Japanese, *Kami-no-michi* means "the way (s) of (the) *kami*," "the *kami* way," "the way of the gods," "the way of those above." When translated into Chinese, the words emerge as two characters: *shen* ("spirit," "gods") and *tao* ("path," "way"), or *Shinto*. The initial character in both languages (*shen* in Chinese and *kami* in Japanese) may be either singular or plural. *Kami* may refer to gods, spiritual beings existing today, mythological entities of ancient times, natural phenomena (including both inanimate and living things), physical objects of worship, or ancestral spirits. The second character (*michi* in Japanese) is the Chinese character *Tao* with its historical significance from both Taoism and Confucianism. "Shinto" has been commonly translated as "the way of the gods."[2]

2. *The History of Shinto*

a. The "prehistoric period" is the Shinto religion before A.D. 552.

1) Japanese history goes back to the Jomon period (ca. 4000 [around the time of the Flood]-250 B.C.), when early settlers lived as hunters and fishers. The sun was very important to these early Japanese. During the Yayoi period (ca. 250 B.C.-A.D. 250) the Japanese initiated wet-rice cultivation, and their religious life was concerned with fertility, growth, birth, and renewal. The formation of Japanese society and religion was completed under the Kofun period (ca. A.D. 250-500). As one clan attained dominance over the others, the figure of the emperor became central. The emperors built huge mound-tombs for their burials.[3]

2) According to mythological tradition, the first Japanese emperor, Jimmu Tenno, was enthroned in 660 B.C. In the prehistoric period, shrines were established all over the Japanese islands for the worship of the various *kami*. Shrines were built in individual homes for ancestor and *kami* worship. Amaterasu, the powerful sun goddess, and Susanoo, her brother, were the most popular gods.[4]

b. The "historic period" is related to the influence of Chinese religions upon Japan.

1) After the fourth century A.D. the Japanese came under the influence of Buddhism, Taoism, and Confucianism. The *Kojiki*, "Chronicles of Ancient Events," records the entrance of Chinese culture into Japan. The *Kojiki*, written in Chinese characters in A.D. 712, is the earliest historical record available.[5] The presence of other religions caused the Japanese to collect their various myths and rituals under the title of *Kami-no-michi* to distinguish their native religion from those brought in by the Chinese and Koreans.[6]

2) According to these records, Mahayana Buddhism was first introduced from what is now Korea, in A.D. 552.[7] Between the sixth and the ninth centuries there was a strong syncretism between Shinto and Buddhism, called *Ryobu Shinto* ("double aspect Shinto").[8] Buddhist priests officiated in Shinto sanctuaries.

3) Eventually the Japanese developed their own forms of Buddhism, such as Pure Land and Nichiren. These and other forms became so popular in Japan that even though Shinto was intermingled with them, it was almost forgotten as a viable religion for the Japanese people.

c. The Revival of Shinto[9]

1) From the eighth century onward, Shinto and Buddhism were submerged into a syncretistic form of religion to the point that Shinto was almost obliterated. During the eighth century, Buddhists developed a system of temples centering around Nara (southwest of Tokyo). This is known as the "Nara Period" (A.D. 710-84). As the Japanese moved their capital from Nara to Kyoto (784-794), their culture was moving toward feudalism. The imperial court developed a highly stylized, aesthetic cultural life. The Japanese consider the Heian Period (794-1185) as the epitome of classical Japanese culture. The Buddhists considered the Shinto gods to be guardians, pupils, or expressions of Buddhist gods.

2) During the Kamakura Period (1185-1333) the *samurai* defeated the old order and established a new capital in Kamakura. Shintoism in this era experienced something of a revival through the development of a school that aspired to be a pure Shinto. During the Muromachi Period (1333-1600) aesthetic pursuits blossomed under the influence of the different religious traditions, including poetry, painting, drama, calligraphy, tea ceremony, flower arranging, gardening, martial arts, sword fighting, and archery. Toward the end

of this period, the country became involved in political and religious violence. Under these circumstances, Christianity made its entrance in Japan. St. Francis Xavier (1506-52) first introduced Roman Catholicism to Japan. Initially he met with great success. According to estimates, as much as 10% of the population was Christian during that era.[10]

3) During the Tokugawa regime (1600-1867) military leaders sought to isolate the nation from outside influences. The capital city was moved to Edo (now Tokyo). Shinto was supported by the national government. A terrible persecution, fueled by anti-foreign and anti-Western passions, wiped out the Christian movement. Christianity did not return to Japan for over two hundred years. One of the most colorful aspects of Japanese life during the Tokugawa era was the formation of a class of feudal knights called the *samurai*. The *samurai* is a man of honor bound to the ethical and discipline of the Bushido Code.[11] He preferred death to dishonor and was expected to take his own life rather than face a situation in which he was dishonored. *Harakiri*, which means "belly slitting," is suicide by disembowelment, a common form of suicide for the *samurai*. [12]

d. During the Meiji Period (1868-1945) Japan combined two different stances. On the one hand, it became a modern nation. In 1853 Commodore Perry of the United States forced Japan to open its nation to foreigners. After a period of confusion, it was decided in the Constitution of 1889 that the nation would follow the pattern of many Western nations in establishing a state-supported religion. On the other hand, the government attempted to restore a kind of "pure" Japanese society. The emperor was thought of as the father of the nation. The government declared that Shinto was not a religion but, rather, the cultural heritage of all Japanese. Even Buddhists and Christians were expected to participate in Shinto rituals to show loyalty to the emperor and the nation.

1) During the Meiji Restoration the state took over the support of some 110,000 Shinto shrines and approximately 16,000 priests who tended these shrines throughout the nation. However, all other religions were allowed to exist and propagate freely. In the late nineteenth century, missionaries reintroduced Roman Catholicism and introduced Protestantism for the first time.

2) In the first half of the twentieth century, Shinto became such an inseparable part of Japanese militarism that the American occupation forces felt it necessary to direct the abolition of the state support for Shinto in December of 1945. Emperor Hirohito officially disclaimed his divine status. Immediately following World War II, attendance at state-supported shrines dropped off and many fell into disuse.

3) An important phenomenon in the recent history of Japanese religion is the growth of the *Shinko Shukyo* ("New Religions"), a broad term used to cover the many sects that appeared in the early nineteenth century as a result of the collapse of feudalism and in the twentieth century after the collapse of the State Shinto.[13]

4) Lately, Shinto has been regaining strength and now claims more than 100,000 priests and 85,000 shrines, together with some 100,000,000 adherents. Its priests are now being trained to transmit to their parishioners a growing body of Shinto doctrine, along with much of the traditional ethics that are no longer taught in schools.[14]

3. *Shinto Beliefs*

a. The word *kami* is often translated as "deity," but in reality it designates an extremely wide range of spirit-beings, together with a host of supernatural forces, natural phenomena, and the essences of prominent geographical features. The *kami* are the spirits that abide in and are worshiped at the shrines. It is also applied to anything or anyone inspiring awe, respect, and devotion. All nature may be *kami*, including human beings, birds, trees, mountains, and oceans.[15] A common Japanese expression is that there are "eight hundred thousand" forms of *kami*: this is to say, an innumerable amount. "The polytheism of Shinto is inexhaustible."[16]

b. The creation myths are intimately related to the beginning of imperial Japan. They are found in the *Kojiki*, which was written as an attempt to revive Shinto in the imperial court. The creation myths in the *Kojiki* describe a primal chaos, which then separated into heaven (male) and earth (female). From this source emerged the *kami*. Seven generations of the *kami* culminated in the marriage of Izanagi (a male *kami*) and Izanami (a female *kami*). These two went down to an ocean, thrust a spear into the waves, and pulled it out. At every place where a drop fell from the spear, a Japanese island appeared. Izanagi and Izanami then descended into the ocean and produced other *kami*. After several generations, Amaterasu, the Sun Goddess, appears; she in turn becomes the great grandmother of Jimmu Tenno, the first emperor.[17] Amaterasu is the most revered deity in Japan. These myths say that land, emperor, and people are bound together in the sacredness of Japan.[18]

c. According to Shinto, the Japanese people descended from the *kami*. "Japanese differ completely from and are superior to the peoples of . . . all other countries of the world, and for us to have called our country the Land of the Gods was not mere vainglory." All "gods were without exception born in Japan."[19] This worldview eventually led Japan to make war on other nations.

d. Shintoism does not have a sense of sin as Christianity has. A major reason for this view is that, according to Shintoism, humans have a divine nature.

> Unlike the creation stories of the Abrahamic religions, the creation of humans does not receive special attention in the Japanese myths. Humans are 'children of the *kami*,' just like the mountains, rivers, animals, and all the rest. There really is no sharp line separating humans from *kami*, for in a sense all humans have the *kami* nature. . . . Since humans received life from the *kami*, they have the *kami* essence within themselves. They are originally pure and clean.[20]

e. For Shintoism, anything that disrupts harmony, *wa*, is bad. "Humans are not at war with *kami*, there is no fall into sin, and evil is not a cosmic force overpowering us. But evil and pollution are accumulated in the ordinary course of living, like dirt and dust."[21] Individualism and lack of reverence for the *kami* bring on chaos, disharmony with the *kami*, and pollution, from which people must be cleansed through rites of purification.[22] The necessity of living by *wa* is even seen in a variety of customs that at first do not seem to be religious, such as removing one's shoes before entering a house, taking a daily bath (*ofuro*), or leaving an object in the place and position where it is supposed to be.[23]

4. *Types of Shinto*

The term "Shinto" has been used for various religious forms:[24]

a. Imperial Shinto, *Koshitsu*: Special rites followed by the imperial family. These rites were private, but they exerted a strong influence on the other forms of Shinto.

b. State Shinto or National Shinto: Term used prior to the disestablishment of Shinto in 1945, which referred to ritual observances enforced through state control.

c. Shrine Shinto, *Jinjam*: The present form of primitive clan ritual and beliefs that have continued throughout the ages. Rites center around the numerous shrines found in every locality of the country, which must be rebuilt every twenty years.

d. Sectarian Shinto, *Kyoha*: A general term for a number of sects founded by private persons and based on various interpretations of traditional Shinto.

e. Domestic Shinto: Particular rituals performed at homes rather than at the communal shrines. Traditionally, a Japanese house possesses a *kamidama*, or private altar, which usually has a miniature shrine.

f. Folk Shinto, *Minkan*: Rites borrowed from other religions, festivals, and superstitious practices of the Japanese hinterland involving shamans.

5. *Shinto Practices*

a. Shrines[25]

1) In early times there were no buildings, but through the centuries, buildings have been erected on nearly all of the ancient sacred sites. Shrines vary in size from several thousand acres to minor ones as small as beehives. Many are located in places where manifestations of the *kami* are said to have occurred. A manifestation can happen via a dream, a vision, or most often as a subtle sense of beauty or serenity that evokes an awareness of *kami* in that place.

2) A distinguishing feature of Shinto shrines is the presence of the *torii,* a gate composed of two vertical posts joined at the top by two horizontal beams. They vary in height from ten to fifty feet, and some of the large ones measure up to four feet in diameter. Draped from the lower horizontal beam of the *torii* is a heavy rope called *shimenawa*.[26] The word *torii* literally means "a bird perch" and is associated with the rooster. Thus the *torii* is also a symbol of a sacred moment described in mythology, when the sun *kami*'s return from a cave made life possible once again. According to the same mythology, a *shimenawa* was hung in order to prevent the sun *kami* from withdrawing into the cave again. The *shimenawa* and the *torii* are symbols of trust and hope in the ongoing prosperity given to the people through the creative energies of the sacred. The Japanese people therefore associate both symbols with longevity, strength, plenty, and purity.

3) The more important shrines have three *torii*. The first one marks the entrance to the sacred ground. The other two mark the progression to the most sacred spot on the holy ground, where the *kami* resides. After walking under the

first *torii*, a visitor can expect to cross a small stream, which is understood to be a barrier to the profane. By walking across the bridge, the visitor leaves behind a portion of whatever within himself might be undesirable.

4) In addition to the *torii* and the bridge, there are fences to protect the sacred areas of the shrine. The most important have between two and four fences. The approach to the most sacred area in the shrine complex ought not to be straight. For religious, aesthetic, and ethical reasons, after passing under the first *torii*, the visitor will find a bend in the pathway (*sando*).[27]

5) The most important building in the shrine is the *honden*, or "Holy of Holies," where the *kami* resides. Because the *kami* is within, no lay person is allowed to look into it. Within the *honden* there is still a more sacred place, a cabinet which contains an object, the *mitama-shiro* (literally, "divine soul-body"), in which the *kami* is present. It may be a sword or a mirror or more often a natural object. In nearly all shrines the cabinet is never opened. In some important shrines there is no *honden*, because a natural geographical feature such as a mountain or a waterfall is the *mitama-shiro*.

b. Worship

1) Shintoism does not have regular services, but ardent Shintoists may worship before the *kamidana* (a household altar) in their homes every day, while the less devout may visit a shrine occasionally, especially on religious holidays and festivals. Acts of devotion at a shrine consist of rinsing the hands and mouth at the ablution basin, clapping the hands twice in front of the sanctuary to get the attention of the *kami*, bowing, ringing a bell, praying silently, and dropping a coin in the offering box. Sometimes worshipers leave a prayer written on a piece of paper or a wooden tablet.[28]

2) Purification rituals are an important way of honoring the *kami*.

Although there is no concept of sin in Shintoism, there is a notion of ritual impurity that may offend the *kami* and bring about unfavorable experiences, such as death, disease, or drought. *Tsumi* is the name of the quality of impurity and it requires purification. There are personal ways of cleansing *tsumi*, ways that are idiosyncratic to the individual. There are also ritual forms of purification. One of these is called *misogi*, ritual purification by standing beneath a waterfall.[29]

3) Prayers are generic expressions of appreciation and awareness of the bond between the living and the dead, and between the individual, his community, and his nation. The worshiper does not specify his sins and ask

forgiveness, nor does he request certain blessings in return for which he will mend his ways. The central belief of Shinto is that man (e.g., Japanese man) is innately good and that he should follow his genuine natural impulses.[30]

4) At the shrines, worshipers may request special protections from the *kami*. I witnessed the ceremony of a Shinto priest purifying and blessing a brand new car to insure against accidents. The priest chanted in front of all open doors and dispelled all evil *kami* by using a wand, and with sparks that he produced using flint. Then he affixed a talisman reflector to the back bumper.

c. Shinto is basically imageless, but symbols are abundant. The *kami* dwells in the symbolic objects of the shrine. These are rarely displayed but kept inside the shrine's main building. The mirror, the sword, and the jewel are important symbols for many shrines. The sacred sword was used by Susanoo (brother of the sun goddess) to defeat an eight-headed dragon. The jewel (*magatama*) is a necklace like the one that belonged to Amaterasu, and the mirror (*kagami*) is sacred because it holds her image. Another popular Shinto symbol is the *sakaki* tree, a perennial tree related to pines which ensures the safe delivery of babies, maintains a happy marriage, prevents diseases and, if planted at the corner of fields, ensures a bumper crop. Water symbolizes new life, growth, vitality, health, and cleanliness. The use of the color red or red-orange by many Shinto shrines was adopted from the Chinese and has virtually the same meanings associated with it as water. The fox is regarded as a messenger of the *kami* and is also the symbol of fertility.[31]

d. Annual festivals, or *matsuri*, are offered in every village.[32] The word *matsuri* is translated "festival," but its full meaning is closer to "live in an attitude of constant prayer and obedience to the will of the *kami*." The *matsuri* represent a special time of prayer and obedience. There are three kinds of *matsuri*: those intended to give new life to the people and their village (this includes Oshogatsu, the New Year's Festival which is the most significant and joyous), those intended to revitalize the agricultural and fishing cycles, and those connected with local traditions.

6. *New Religions*

a. One of the most significant religious phenomena in Japan is the sudden rise of new religious movements. These religions are more concerned with temporal problems than with spiritual matters. Most emphasize the coming of a new age, but at the same time they stress worldly benefits, healing, prosperity, and happiness. "Though often criticized for eclecticism, vulgarity, and magicoreligiosity, they have activated the spiritual life of many people who had little to do with traditional religions."[33]

b. New religions constitute the most vital sector of Japanese religion today and include about 25 percent of the nation's population in their membership.[34] According to one estimate, there are some 200,000 new religions today, although many have a very small number of adherents.[35]

c. These religions claim to have solutions to everyday life problems. Their message very often relates to happiness, success, healing, and wealth. Their teaching is syncretistic and often combines elements of shamanism, animism, ancestor worship, Buddhism, Shintoism, and Christianity. The following is an example of one new religion in Japan:

> The Institute for Research in Human Happiness is Japan's fastest growing sect. The five-year-old institute is the creation of Ryuho Okawa, who claims to be Buddha reincarnated, and before Buddha, to have been the Greek god Hermes. He says he has talked with Picasso, Jesus Christ, and Newton, all of whom helped him devise a four-pronged approach to happiness: love, intellect, self-reflection, and development. About 1 million people subscribe to the institute's monthly magazine, *Monthly Miracle*. More than 27 million copies of Okawa's books are in circulation. Last year, sales of his 130 books and cassette tapes totaled $2.2 million.[36]

d. There were three waves in the development of new religions:

1) The first wave took place at the end of the Edo era or during the Meiji restoration, which started in 1868. At this time people ran to new religions looking for worldly profits.

2) The second wave began after World War II, when Shinto lost its status as the state religion. People simply became disoriented and disappointed with their traditional religion.[37]

3) The third wave began with the oil shock of 1973 and is related to the New Age movement. This is noticeable in magazines of the time which contain many references to fortune-telling, charms, exorcism, inspiration, spiritualism, supernatural power, divination, protecting deities, ancestral spirits, mediums, yoga meditation, magic, astrology, and the occult.[38]

7. *Soka Gakkai*

a. Even though Soka Gakkai is related to Buddhism rather than to Shintoism, it is considered here because it is the largest of all new religions. School teacher Tsunesaburo Makiguchi (1871-1944) founded Soka Gakkai in the 1930s as the lay auxiliary of the Orthodox Sect of Nichiren Buddhism. Soka Gakkai is based on the teachings of Nichiren (1222-82), a monk that claimed to be the *bodhisattva* heralded in the Buddhist *Lotus Sutra*.[39]

b. The growth of this organization has been formidable. It was launched during a public meeting in 1937 with about sixty members.[40] It was said in the early 60s that *Soka Gakkai* ("Value-Creating Society") was "the most vigorous, dogmatic, exclusivistic, belligerent, self-confident, and fastest-growing group in Japan today."[41] By 2005 the organization had grown to more than twelve million members in more than 190 countries and territories. A *Time* magazine article (November 20, 1995) claimed over 8.1 million members in the United States, even though the number could be much lower.[42]

c. To the fundamental question "What must I do to be saved?" Soka Gakkai answers, "Believe only in the *Dai-Gohnozon* and recite the *Daimoku*, and you will be saved."[43] In 1297 Nichiren wrote a short sentence called the *Daimoku* ("invocation") on the *Dai-Gohnozon,* a wooden box which Soka Gakkai considers the most valuable object in the universe. The *Daimoku* reads, "*Nam-Myoho-renge-kyo,*" meaning "Homage to the *Lotus Sutra*."[44] The *Dai-Gohnozon* is considered to contain the universal power of all Buddhas and *bodhisattvas* and is the equivalent of the supreme god. It is owned by the organization, but copies are given to families on a lifetime loan. While Nichiren was alive, he said he was the highest incarnation of the Buddha, but after his death that power was attributed to the *Dai-Gohnozon*. The daily ritual of Soka Gakkai consists in chanting the *Daimoku* while kneeling before the *Dai-Gohnozon*. By chanting the *Daimoku*, devotees dedicate their life to the *Dai-Gohnozon* and all it represents. Early each morning eager believers chant the prayer formula several hundred times.[45]

d. According to Soka Gakkai, happiness is not related to the pursuit of truth, but in the creation of value. Positive value consists of beauty, profit, and good. Negative values are ugliness, harm, and evil. A life devoted to good guarantees both beauty and profit.[46] Soka Gakkai offers distinctly "worldly" benefits in the form of healing, long life, solutions to family problems, freedom from personal habits and adversity, and material prosperity.[47]

8. *Christian Witness*

a. Although 112 million out of 120 million Japanese say that they follow Shinto, 65 to 75% of Japanese claim no personal religion. For the majority, religious allegiance is nominal. To be Shinto, in the minds of many Japanese, is simply to be Japanese. It is just part of their culture.[48] The Japanese, as other East Asians, may accept beliefs of different religions without a sense of incongruity. For many Japanese, religions do not offer a personal faith–they provide ceremonial services. For example, it is quite popular in Japan to have a "Christian" wedding. This means only that the dress, format, and setting are Western and churchlike. A popular phrase which sums up Japanese eclecticism is that "Japanese are Shintoists at the birth of a child or at the opening of a business, Christian for a wedding ceremony, and Buddhist at the death of a loved one."[49] As an illustration of how the Japanese share more than one religion, compare the total population with the total number of believers in the table below.

	1978	1996[50]
Population of Japan	115,174,112	120,030,000
Shinto	98,545,703	111,800,000
Buddhist	88,020,880	93,100,000
Christian	950,491	1,400,000
Other	13,729,376	11,400,000
Total of believers	201,246,450	223,700,000

b. The Japanese culture has some built-in hindrances to witnessing. Most Christian denominations are not growing well in Japan, and one of the main causes has to do with the Japanese culture. In 1997 I conducted a two-week evangelistic series in Japan, with an average of 150-200 in attendance every night. After a few days I learned that many in the audience had faithfully attended church services for 3 to12 years; however, they had not been invited to join the church. It is very difficult for a Japanese pastor to confront an individual with an invitation to join the church because if there is an objection, both the pastor and the prospective member may lose face. As in most foreign cultures, although perhaps more so in Japan, it is not always easy for outsiders to understand the native worldview; outsiders need to be sensitive and aware of cultural differences.

c. Japanese who wonder what their families will think if they decide to follow Christ need to be encouraged that, in the long run, their family life will be better because of their relationship with Christ. Introduce him to other Christians. By modeling what it is like to live in a Christian home, you inspire him with hope for change in his family.[51]

d. Japanese men are extremely dedicated to their work, spending long hours on the job and even cultivating business relationships after hours. Introduce your friend to other Christians with similar professional interests. Model close and fun relationships within a network of Christian men, so that he can see that Christian friendship can replace unhealthy relationships.

e. Every New Year is preceded by parties called *bo-nen-kai*, or "forget-the-year parties," when groups of people from a given company or social club engage in heavy drinking. Show your friend how it is possible to celebrate New Year's and other holidays in a Christian way. One church in Japan plans "remember-the-year parties," a Christian alternative to the drunken *bo-nei-kai*. At these times people are encouraged to share publicly how God has helped them during the preceding year. These parties are often held in conjunction with a community dinner.

f. Ancestor worship is an integral part of filial piety in Japan. Help your friend see that one can be a very loyal son or daughter without worshiping at the family shrine. Model good family relationships for your Japanese friend. Invite him along when you go to place flowers on the grave of a loved one. Explain that your actions are a way of remembering the deceased person, but they do not involve the worship of that person's spirit.

g. Every summer the Japanese celebrate a festival related to the return of the ancestral spirits with a dance held in the evenings, called *bon-odori* ("dance for ancestors"). Many Japanese engage in it simply for fun. As someone from another culture, be cautious about telling your Japanese friend to stop participating in this dance. Pray together that God would guide your friend in a clear way regarding the *bond-odori*.

9. *Introducing Biblical Doctrines*

a. Japan is a patriarchal society; therefore, the Japanese people know what it means to have a human father. Since the Bible describes God as a Father, emphasize this connection. The Shinto gods or various conceptions of Buddha do not have this theme of fatherhood. Another point to remember is that since there are millions of gods and goddesses in Shinto, monotheism is a strange concept to the Japanese. One way to approach this concept is to explain the attributes of the one true God according to the Bible (Exo 20:3-6; 34:6-7).

b. The nature of the Japanese gods (*kami*) as contrasted with the God of the Bible:[52]

Shinto	**Christianity**
There are many gods (*kami*)	There is one true God
The *kami* are procreated by other gods	God created all things and persons
The *kami* dwell in the natural world	God transcends the world in His being
The *kami* may be either helpful or hurtful	God is loving and absolutely good
The *kami* are the gods of Japan	God is the Creator and Lord of all peoples

Table 15.1

c. While most Japanese do not have a clear idea of sin, they do acknowledge that self-centeredness is wrong. You can explain the Fall as a self-centered move away from the true Father, who took delight in creating and providing for humanity. This Fall is lived out in our own lives when we pursue self-centered ends instead of God. This explanation will inevitably entail an explanation of God's standards as shown through the Ten Commandments. The parable of the prodigal son is also effective in illustrating this concept.

d. Moral standards in Japan are enforced by shame. "Losing face," i.e., losing reputation and honor, is one of the worst things that can happen to an individual, and it may even lead him to commit suicide. When a whole group is stigmatized, a collective act of atonement is made. For example, if the Shinkansen "Bullet Train" or a Japanese airline is late, every available employee will form a line where passengers can see them and bow as a form of apology to delayed passengers. Once atonement is made, the shame is removed. When you discuss the concept of sin, be sure to acknowledge the shame that sin causes.

You can show from Gen 2:25 and 3:5-11 how shame came upon humanity with sin. Let them talk about the impact shame has on our lives. It is your job to describe how God in Christ has delivered and is delivering you from sin and the shame it brings in your own life. When your friend comments on being ashamed of something, encourage him or her to follow Christ and allow Him to solve this shame problem. However, they must eventually understand that shame is not the real problem, but sin. Sin is the root of feelings of shame.

e. The Japanese understand the need of purification to remove defilement. The *kami* are offended by ritual or ceremonial pollution related to blood or death. As ritual pollution separates humans from *kami*, so moral pollution keeps humans from God. Keep in mind that the Japanese notion of pollution is ritual, not moral. Explain that disloyalty to God is the cause of our pollution. Only as we experience forgiveness for our disloyalty do we become pure.

f. Introduce Jesus as the ultimate "go-between." The concept of having mediators is natural to Japanese society. The biblical concept, therefore, makes perfect sense to the Japanese, once the condition of human alienation from God has been accepted.

10. *Glossary of Shintoist Terms*

a. Amaterasu. The sun goddess, the chief deity worshiped in Shintoism.

b. Bushido Code, "the warrior-knight-way." A code practiced by the *samurai* during the feudal period, which has held a fascination for the Japanese people since its inception. The code is an unwritten system of behavior, stressing loyalty to emperor and country.

c. Emperor Meiji. The Japanese emperor who established Shinto as the state religion of Japan.

d. *Harakiri*, "belly slitting." Suicide by disembowelment, a common form of suicide for the *samurai*, performed as an atonement for failure or bad judgment.

e. *Honden*. The inner sanctuary of a Shinto shrine that houses the object in which the *kami* is present.

f. Izanagi, "female-who-invites." The female deity who, according to Shinto Myth, gave birth to the eight islands of Japan.

g. Izanami, "male-who-invites." The male deity who, along with the female deity Izanagi, helped produce the Japanese islands and the Japanese people.

h. *Kami.* The sacred power found in both animate and inanimate objects. This power is deified in Shintoism.

i. *Kojiki.* The "records of ancient matters" composed in A.D. 712, charting the imperial ancestors and the imperial court.

j. Mikado. A term used by foreigners to designate the emperor of Japan.

k. Shinto. The term is derived from the Chinese term *Shen-tao*, meaning the "way of the higher spirits." Shinto is the designation for the religion that has long characterized Japan and its people.

l. Shinto Myth. The belief that the islands of Japan and the Japanese people are of divine origin.

m. State Shinto. The patriotic ritual, established in 1882, which worshipped the emperor as the direct descendant of the gods. State Shinto was abolished at the end of World War II.

n. *Torii,* "bird perch." Portal to enter a Shinto sanctuary.

Notes

1   Sokyo One, *The Kami Way* (Rutland, VT: C. E. Tuttle, 1962), 3-4.

2   David A. Raush and Carl Hermann Voss, *Religions: Our Quest for Meaning* (Valley Forge, PA: Trinity Press International, 1993), 101.

3   This section has heavily depended on Theodore M. Ludwig, *The Sacred Paths: Understanding the Religions of the World*, 4th ed. (Upper Saddle River, NJ: Pearson Prentice Hall, 2006), 278-92.

4   "Amaterasu and Susanoo," *Wikipedia, the Free Encyclopedia*, 2006 [article online]; retrieved on April 15, 2006, from http://en.wikipedia.org/wiki/Japanese_mythology#Amaterasu-and-Susanoo.

5   Robert E. Van Voorst, *Anthology of World Scriptures*, 5th ed. (Belmont, CA: Thomson Wadsworth, 2006), 177.

6   There are many questions about the accuracy of the documents of "early Shinto" because they were written much later than the actual period they purport to describe. David Clark, "Shinto," in *The Compact Guide to World Religions*, ed. Dean C. Halverson (Minneapolis, MN: Bethany, 1996), 198.

7   Jack Seward, *The Japanese* (Chicago: Passport Books, 1992), 189.

8   The term refers to the mixing of Shintoism with Buddhism and Confucianism. Josh McDowell and Don Stewart, *Handbook of Today's Religions* (Nashville: Thomas Nelson, 1983), 355.

9   Ian Markham, "Shintoism," in *Encountering Religion*, ed. Ian S. Marham and Tinu Ruparell (Malden, MA: Blackwell, 2001), 299-303.

10   Clark, "Shinto," 206.

11   Denise L. Carmody and T. L. Brink, *Ways to the Center*, 6th ed. (Belmont, CA: Thomson Wadsworth, 2006), 192-93.

12   Jack Seward, "Colorful Ways of Departing this World," chap. in *The Japanese*, 69-83.

13   C. Scott Littleton, "Shinto," in *Eastern Religions*, ed. Michael D. Coogan (New York: Oxford University Press, 2005), 512-15.

14   Seward, *The Japanese*, 197.

15   William A. Young, *The World's Religions: Worldviews and Contemporary Issues*, 2nd ed. (Upper Saddle River, NJ: Pearson Prentice Hall, 2005), 154.

16   Roger Schmidt, Gene C. Sager, Gerald T. Carney, Albert C. Muller, Kenneth J. Zanca, Julius J. Jackson Jr., C. Wayne Mayhall, and Jeffrey C. Burke, *Patterns of Religion*, 2nd ed. (Belmont, CA: Wadsworth, 2005), 458.

17   Find selections from the *Kojiki* in Van Voorst, *Anthology of World Scriptures*, 178-83.

18   Schmidt et al., *Patterns of Religion*, 458.

19   Kodo Taii, quoted by Littleton, "Shinto," 446.

20   Ludwig, *The Sacred Paths*, 296.

21   *Ibid*, 298.

22 Warren Matthews, *World Religions*, 4th ed. (Belmont, CA: Thomson Wadsworth, 2004), 239.

23 Littleton, "Shinto," 473.

24 Mircea Eliade and Ioan P. Couliano, *The Harper Collins Concise Guide to World Religions* (New York: Harper San Francisco, 2000), 221-23.

25 Littleton, "Shinto," 479-87.

26 Motosawa Masashi, "Shimenawa," *Encyclopedia of Shinto*, 2005; retrieved on December 2, 2006, from http://eos.kokugakuin.ac.jp/modules/xwords/ entry.php?entryID=317.

27 Edan Dekel, "Sacred Spaces in Shinto: The Shrine Complex," Teaching Comparative Religion Through Art and Architecture, *University of California, Berkeley*, 2001; retrieved on December 4, 2006, from http://ias.berkeley.edu/orias/visuals/japan_visuals/ shintoB.HTM.

28 Schmidt et al., *Patterns of Religion*, 459.

29 Pearson Education, *The Sacred World: Encounters with The World Religions*, "Shintoism," 2004 [CD-ROM]; available from Pearson Prentice Hall, Upper Saddle River, NJ.

30 "Shinto," *Refuge Outreach* [article online]; retrieved on April 15, 2006, from http://www.refuge-outreach.org/religions/shintoism.html.

31 "The Three Sacred Treasures and 108," *Geocities*, 1997 [article online]; retrieved on April 15, 2006, from www.geocities.com/Tokyo/Temple/5105/sjcc-10.html.

32 Littleton, "Shinto," 493-96.

33 "Religion in Japan," *Asian Studies Network Information Center*, 1995-2005, The University of Texas at Austin [article online] retrieved on January 20, 2006, from http://asnic.utexas.edu/asnic/countries/japan/japreligion.html.

34 Rausch and Voss, *Religions: Our Quest for Meaning*, 111. Eloise Armstrong, "Japan: Land of the Rising Sun," *Operation World* [book summarized online]; retrieved on February 26, 2006, from www.24-7prayer.com/ow/country2. php?country_id=30.

35 Robert Garran, "Japan's Rush Hour of the Gods," *The Australian Magazine*, September 28, 1996 [article online], *The Rick A. Ross for the Study of Destructive*

Cults, Controversial Groups and Movements; retrieved on January 20, 2006, from http://www.rickross.com/reference/gakkai/gakkai28.html.

36   "The Happiness Sect," *The Wall Street Journal*, August 1, 1991. Quoted in *Mamoru Billy Ogata*, "What We Can Learn from Japan's New Religious Movements," *Evangelical Missions Quarterly* 27 (October 1991): 369.

37   Ian Baruma, "Lost Without a Faith: In the Spiritual Vacuum of the Postwar Years, Some Japanese Seek New Gods," *Time*, Special Edition: World Religions, 2004, 17.

38   Inoue Nobutaka, "Recent Trends in the Study of Japanese New Religions," in *New Religions: Contemporary Papers on Japanese Religion*, trans. Norman Havens, ed. Inoue Nobutaka (Tokyo: Institute for Japanese Culture and Classics, Kokugakuin University, 1991) [book online]; retrieved on February 25, 2006, from http://www2.kokugakuin.ac.jp/ijcc/wp/ cpjr/newreligions/index.html.

39   Christmas Humphreys, *Buddhism: An Introduction and Guide* (London: Penguin Books, 1990), 174-75.

40   Mamory Billy Ogata, "What We Can Learn from Japan's New Religious Movements," *Evangelical Missions Quarterly* 4 (October 1991): 365.

41   Henry Van Stralen, *Modern Japanese Religions* (New York: T. P. Press, 1963), 98.

42   "Soka Gakkai International," *Religious Movements*, 2001 [article online]; retrieved on January 25, 2006, from http://religiousmovements.lib.virginia.edu/ nrms/nich.html.

43   Tetsunao Yamamori, *Church Growth in Japan* (Pasadena, CA: William Carey Library, 1974), 145.

44   Walter Martin, *The New Cults* (Ventura, CA: Regal Books, 1980), 325.

45   H. Neil McFarland, *The Rush Hour of the Gods* (New York: Macmillan, 1967), 208.

46   Noah Brannen, "Soka Gakkai's Theory of Value: An Analysis," *Contemporary Religions in Japan*, 5 (June 1964): 143-54.

47   Hesselgrave mentions that the most important reasons for joining Soka Gakkai stated by the members are 1) physical and emotional healing, 2) ethical and spiritual reform (including betterment of home relationships), 3) economic and practical success in finding work, a job promotion or business success, more money, etc. Hesselgrave, "Soka Gakkai," 144.

48   Ian Reader, Esben Andreasen, and Finn Stefansson, *Japanese Religions: Past and Present* (Honolulu: University of Hawaii Press, 1993), 33. Similar conclusions are expressed by Ruiko Kameyama, "Japanese Sense of Religiousness," *Compass Online*, 1999-2000 [article online], retrieved on February 10, 2006, from http://www.tsujiru.net/compass/ compass_1999/reg/kameyama_ruiko.htm.

49   Matthews, *World Religions*, 240.

50   Otto Johnson, ed. *Information Please Almanac–Atlas & Yearbook: 1996*, 49th ed. (Boston and New York: Houghton Mifflin, 1996), 213.

51   Adapted from Mark Reasoner, *How to Share the Good News with Your Japanese Friend* (Colorado Springs, CO: International Students, 1992), 27-32.

52   Clark, "Shinto," 207.

CHAPTER 16

Christian Witness to the Chinese and Other East Asians

1. *Cultural Background*

a. The family is the foundation of Chinese culture and community. The Chinese are a nation of families. Chinese family values have remained throughout the ages. "Through all the agonies and triumphs of Chinese history, the family has remained the strongest cord in the civilization."[1]

b. Most Chinese function best in family units. The Chinese do not easily form themselves into units other than family units, nor do they normally function effectively outside the family unit.[2] Men with leadership ability in the Chinese community do not tend to form corporate structures outside the family.[3]

c. Psychologically, the Chinese man is secure in his primary relationship with the family, and so has little need to seek satisfaction in wider alliances and associations. The family includes the extended family and, to some extent, the clan. His concern for a higher goal and status in life is limited by the extent to which they affect the security of his relationships. He maintains his primary relationships with his family as the permanent core of all other relationships.[4]

> The family is, of course, important in Western religion, with its sacrament of marriage, its commandment to honor the parents, and its duty to raise the children in the true faith. But the religious character of the Chinese family goes far beyond these aspects. This character, developing out of the so-called ancestor worship, makes religion more a family matter than an individual choice. Family religion is basic, while individual and communal religion are secondary.[5]

d. Chinese people tend to have closed social groups, where outsiders and their ideas are not welcome. For centuries the Chinese had an intellectual aversion to foreign ideas. Anything not Confucian was immediately suspect. To give honor and respect to true learning, other religions had to be rejected. These maxims were taught in China for a long time, and candidates for government positions were expected to know them well.[6]

2. *Chinese Attitudes Towards Christianity*

a. Most Chinese elders regard Christianity as a foreign religion. Their attitude is: "We worship our gods, and the foreigners have Jesus Christ. There should be no interference." Christianity is just one religion, and all religions are the same. They cannot differentiate between Christianity and other religions. They see Christianity's claim as the only or best way to a relationship with God as rather presumptuous.[7]

b. Due to unfortunate events such as the "gunboat diplomacy," the Opium War (1839-42), and some unequal treaties that arose after the arrival of missionaries to China,[8] Christianity became associated with Western imperialism.[9]

c. Socially and culturally, the Chinese felt that Christianity could not fit in well with Chinese society. This impression came about because when early Western missionaries brought the Christian gospel to China they also brought their culture, dress code, arts, and Western way of life. Many early missionaries also reacted against Chinese culture, branding all forms as pagan and demonic.[10]

d. The Chinese felt a sense of social and cultural pride. China had five thousand years of rich cultural heritage, superior to the West.[11] Because religion and culture are so closely intertwined, the Chinese were not open to Christianity or to anything they considered as foreign and anti-Chinese.

e. Christianity is seen as being against filial piety (love and respect for one's parents and ancestors). For example, the funeral of a loved one is a sacred moment for paying respects, yet some Christians do not participate in it. To Chinese elders that is unforgivable. The old people are afraid that if their children become Christians, nobody will burn money or give food to them after they die.[12] Christians are derogatorily described in Taiwan as "people without people mourning."[13]

f. Many Chinese are willing to listen to the Gospel but find it difficult to make a firm decision. This can be verified from one of the teachings of Confucius which teaches that while we should respect spiritual things, we should keep them at a distance.[14]

g. A Chinese may think that baptism is a break with the Chinese culture and heritage, since many Christians have implied that the Chinese is "pagan" and that the Western culture is "Christian." Christianity to them is synonymous with the Western culture.

h. However, the most phenomenal growth of Christianity among the Chinese is taking place not among those living in close contact with Western ideas, but in mainland China.[15] The numbers for Protestant Christians in mainland China vary between 15 and 58 million. In 2000 the Chinese government admitted there were about 35 million Christians.[16] Most of its growth is related to the phenomenon of house churches.

3. *A Chinese Phenomenon: House Churches*

a. Historical background

1) House churches are not new in China or in the church worldwide. Even from apostolic times, the Gospel has spread not only through preaching in public places, but also through meetings in believers' homes. Throughout the Christian era, house churches flourished in periods of both revival and persecution.

2) Before the 1949 Communist Revolution in China, many believers started meeting in homes. House churches in this period were related to traditional denominations, as well as to indigenous movements such as "The

Jesus Family," "The True Jesus Church," "The Independent Church," and "The Little Flock."

3) Following the 1949 Communist Revolution, the "Three Self Patriotic Movement" (TSPM) was responsible for organizing the institutional church. Indigenous self-propagating churches were suppressed by the TSPM, and meetings in homes were declared illegal. In spite of that, many Christians, discouraged by the growing politization of TSPM churches, risked their liberty by meeting secretly in homes.

4) Then in 1966 all churches were closed, and only small groups that met very covertly survived. At first it was a phenomenon of the coastal provinces where Protestant missionary activity had a longer history, but somehow the idea has spread throughout China. Today house churches can be found in almost all major villages. Practically all Protestants use this approach.

5) In China there are "open churches" and "closed churches." "Open churches" are congregations that meet in buildings provided by the TSPM. The congregation must send tithe money to the TSPM to support their pastor. Both Christians who worship on the first and the seventh day of the week share the same pastor and building. I attended church services in open churches with an attendance of two thousand and three thousand in Beijing and Shanghai, respectively. "Closed churches" consider that sending tithe to an organization related to the government is not right, so they meet illegally in houses.

6) A student of mine from mainland China shared this testimony:

> My mother organized training sessions in our house, which has four rooms. A new group of about eight brothers and sisters would come every two weeks and slept wherever they could in my house. She trained them, reviewed with them the Bible doctrines, and taught them how to nurture a congregation and how to preach. The people that would come to the training session were peasants and farmers. They would come, stay for two weeks, and leave. Then another group would come, stay for two weeks, leave, and so forth. My mother is still offering these training sessions in my house. . . . We have a river nearby, very beautiful and very clean, and many of our believers have been baptized there. But it was not safe, so my mother built a baptistry inside our house. Baptismal candidates come to our house and our pastor and my mother baptize them. This year my mother has baptized 496 people in my house.[17]

I went to China and visited this student's mother and attended several of her underground congregations. By then she had already baptized more than five thousand!

b. Main factors for the rapid growth of house churches:

    1) The breakdown and closure of the institutional church.

    2) The irrepressible desire in the hearts of believers for Christian fellowship.

    3) The desire to have their church free from political overtones or government control.

    4) The new opportunities for evangelism when cultural policies were reversed and Christian meetings were no longer illegal.

    5) Christian broadcasting has been used to bring many to a faith in Christ.[18]

c. Characteristics of Chinese House Churches[19]

    1) They are indigenous. They do not have formal ties with the Church outside China. Any form of connection with the West is risky. Chinese traits are seen in Christian paintings, music, and styles of worship.

    2) They are stripped of nonessentials. They have had to exist without buildings, set times of worship, or a paid ministry.

    3) They emphasize the lordship of Christ. Because Jesus is the head of His body, the Church cannot accept control by any outside organization. The state must not require Christians to act against their consciences or the principles of the Word of God.

    4) They have confidence in God's care. Christians rejoice to see God's protection in times of crisis. They have miracle stories that confirm their faith.

    5) They love the Word of God. They have made great sacrifices in order to obtain copies of the Bible. Nowdays it is easy, as the government itself prints the Bible for distribution.

    6) They are praying churches. Their existence has depended entirely on God's power.

    7) They are caring and sharing churches. They rightly feel that they reflect primitive Christianity. The love they show for one another creates a

tremendous force of spontaneous evangelism, even without the usual efforts of organized campaigns.

8) They are rooted in family units. This is a normal thing for the Chinese culture and was a necessity in times of persecution.

9) They depend on lay leadership. Because so many Chinese pastors were put into prison or work camps, ministry is made up of people from various walks of life. Young pastors, trained at TSPM seminaries, are being appointed and ordained by the state-sponsored organization to serve in open churches, but conservative members feel that they cannot trust them much. In house churches formed by peasants in the countryside, many pastors are illiterate. In some areas, most house churches are led by courageous women.

10) They are in need of biblical teaching. Some have been led astray by extreme teaching of one kind or another, so it is possible to find True churches, True-true churches, and many other small factions.

11) They have been purified by suffering. Nominal Christians could not have survived the severe tests of the Cultural Revolution (1966-1976).

12) They are zealous in evangelism. The main method of witness in China today is through the personal lifestyle and behavior of Christians, accompanied by their proclamation of the gospel, often at great personal risk.

4. *Christian Witness*

a. Understanding their culture. As with any other religion, we need to understand the Confucian ethics and historical development, and should carefully study evangelistic strategies that will work for the Chinese.[20]

b. For the Chinese, the best method in witnessing is to do it among the members of the family. Since in Confucian teaching, three of the five basic relationships have to do with family ties (father/son, elder brother/younger brother, husband/wife), the best method in witnessing to a Chinese is in the setting of his own family. For the Chinese, religion is more a family matter than an individual choice. While doing public evangelism in Taiwan and in Hong Kong, I noticed that while many parents were willing to allow their children to become Christians, non-Christian grandparents begged them not to do it, and this was very important for the entire family. Family religion is basic, while individual and communal religion are secondary.[21] Social solidarity demands that whole families and groups of families be won for Christ if viable churches are to be planted and are to make an adequate impact on the community.[22] The conversion of individuals to Christianity poses enormous problems; this obstacle would be greatly minimized if the church functioned along family lines.[23] The Gospel flows along the web of family relationships.[24] This concept is also valid for the Chinese living abroad. Chinese who wonder what their families will think if they decide to follow Christ need to be encouraged that, in the long run, their family life will be better because of their relationship with Christ. Believers should introduce their Chinese friends to other Christians. By modeling what it is like to participate in a Christian home, a believer can fill a Chinese friend with hope for change in his or her family.

c. Christians with Confucian parents should be willing to witness to them through warm personal relationships. They should be willing to supply the material needs of their elderly parents, to show love according to Chinese patterns, and pay respect (*xiao jin*) and obedience (*xiao shun*) as a way of showing filial piety.[25]

d. In Taiwan, where the majority of people are Chinese, friendship evangelism through house churches or home cell Bible studies is the most effective method of evangelism. "In fact, all evangelistic techniques used in Taiwan have to be related and built upon the concept of friendship evangelism. Friends winning their friends is a key for church growth in Taiwan."[26]

e. The interest for English among the Chinese provides the way for the development of English schools that could be used as evangelistic centers. During the 1980s China ended its post-1949 isolation with an "open door" policy. As the country soon discovered, English is the key to making the "open door" a functioning passageway for dialogue with and benefit from the rest of the world. This concept is also valid for the Chinese living abroad. An estimated one out of four Chinese in mainland China now study English in some way; English is on the curriculum from the very earliest school years.[27]

f. The church should make the children and students their target for outreach through Christian schools. There are several reasons. First, because of the increasing population, there is a severe shortage of schools.[28] Second, schools have proved to be the most important source of baptisms among the Chinese. Many Chinese send their children to Christian schools because they acknowledge the quality of their education. This creates a unique opportunity for evangelism.[29]

g. In house churches, Chinese believers practice contextualization. This term refers to the process of making the biblical text and its context meaningful and applicable to the thought patterns and situations of a given people.[30] If the Christian message is addressed at the cultural and worldview level of the Chinese, it is more likely that the Confucian/Taoist/Buddhist Chinese will become more responsive and winnable to Christ.

h. Human beings, including the Chinese, "show an overwhelming predisposition to band together with 'their own kind.'"[31] According to the strategy of "homogeneous unities," Chinese in the Diaspora (living outside China) should strive for having their own ethnic churches. Non-Chinese congregations may offer support to individuals who are willing to create a Chinese Sabbath School or small group. Church growth expert Donald McGavran affirms that people "like to become Christians without crossing racial, linguistic or class barriers."[32]

i. Homes are a natural place for friendships and relationships to develop. While an unbeliever may be hesitant to attend a formal church service, he is usually quite willing to visit the home of a Christian friend to have a Bible study, prayer, fellowship, and maybe some refreshments.

5. *Strategic Approaches to Evangelism Among East Asians*

a. A basic difference between witnessing and evangelism is that, while witnessing is sharing a personal experience with Jesus Christ, evangelism is sharing His message. Evangelism is the presentation of biblical doctrines in the power of the Holy Spirit in such a way that people will be persuaded to accept Jesus as Savior, be baptized, and serve Him in the fellowship of the church. Many East Asian pastors have a limited understanding of evangelism. Some believe that a Christmas program or a community services project should be enough, while others view evangelism as preaching one sermon on John 3:16.

b. An adequate period of cultivation should precede any organized series of evangelistic meetings. Sometimes this is also called "ground preparation." It may be done through simple friendship, small groups, seminars, etc. The form and content of the strategy should address the culture and felt needs of the audience, such as the study of the Bible in English, health strategies like herbal medicine, and small groups.

c. Neighbors, relatives, and friends may be invited to participate in a series of studies either in a home or in a neutral hall (not a church). The first four or five subjects may be of a non-doctrinal content. The purpose should be to help non-Christians to appreciate the value of Christian teachings. The subjects, properly advertised, may attract many interested in the topics. Once the group has developed fellowship and established confidence in the Bible, they will proceed with a set of five to seven transitory lessons before entering into the distinctive Christian teachings.

d. Churches are threatening places for non-Christians who have a defensive attitude. Experience teaches that a series offered in a neutral place such as a hotel or a gymnasium will facilitate the attendance of non-Christians.

e. Non-Asians doing evangelism among Asians should contextualize the presentations with graphics and stories with which the audience can identify. Specifically, avoid Western motifs, illustrations, and images. A non-East Asian evangelist should ask many questions and study much about local history and culture before developing a sound evangelistic for Hong Kong, Taiwan, Japan, or Mongolia.

f. Further contextualization in public evangelism may require a change in the sequence of topics, added emphasis on certain issues, a carefully design sequence of presentations, as well as use of appropriate music and audiovisuals. In an era when technology is accessible to most people, evangelists should do their best to present the Gospel in ways that are familiar to the audience. If evangelists are not able to illustrate a sermon with technology, they should illustrate it with stories (remember that Jesus never preached without using illustrations, according to Matt 13:34). Using existing cultural forms and means does not guarantee that the message will be accepted, but at least it will ensure that the message will be more easily understood.

g. For most East Asians, their ancestors and elderly are a major concern. Christianity in Taiwan is known as the religion that does not remember the parents when they die. Address the issue by studying with the audience what the Bible says about the state of the dead, honoring to the parents, worship to God, etc. Suggest that young East Asians show their parents even more love and respect than before (Christianity should not destroy their Chinese culture). Also suggest that they assure their parents and grandparents that they will honor and remember them always. They can also tell their parents that on the anniversary of their death they could offer a memorial service at the church (anthropologists call this a "functional substitute"). They will tend to their graves. They can also hang a picture of their parents in a special place in the house.

h. The central importance of the family is no doubt a prominent characteristic of East Asians. They may find the biblical concept of family as relevant to their culture. A strategy based on the family should be a natural way to penetrate East Asian cultures. For an evangelistic strategy aimed to reach out to Asians in the Diaspora, the first step is to work with Asian Christians living in the area.

Notes

1   Kevin Sinclair and Iris Wong Po-yee, *Culture Shock! China* (Singapore: Times Books International, 1990), 202.

2   John H. Rantung, "How to Witness to Indonesian-Chinese-Mahayanist Buddhists," paper for the course MSSN670 Religions of the East, Adventist International Institute of Advanced Studies, October 1994, 8.

3   This is amply demonstrated in the world of industry. There are many Chinese millionaires throughout Asia, but there are not large corporations such as General Motors or Sony among the Chinese. In other words, most of the wealthy Chinese head their own family businesses. Corporate success is rare outside the family. In this regard, they are virtually opposite from the Japanese, who seem to function most effectively in large corporate structures. Paul E. Kauffman, *China, the Emerging Challenge: A Christian Perspective* (Grand Rapids: Baker, 1982), 260-61.

4   Mery Chung, "Proposed Worldview Transformation Among the Overseas Chinese in Los Angeles," paper for the class M735 Worldview and Worldview Change, Fuller Theological Seminary, March 1979, 10; quoted by Rantung, "How to Witness to Indonesian-Chinese-Mahayanist Buddhists," 8.

5   Lawrence G. Thomson, *Chinese Religions: An Introduction*, 3rd ed. (Belmont, CA: Wadsworth, 1979), 34.

6   Paul A. Cohen, *China and Christianity: The Missionary Movement and the Growth of Chinese Antiforeignism* (Cambridge, MA: Harvard University Press, 1963), 11.

7   See Lee Chong Kau, *How to Speak to Our Elders About Christ* (Singapore: Overseas Missionary Fellowship, 1972), 9-11.

8   Albert Feuerwerker, "China: History" in *Encyclopedia Americana*, 1979 ed.

9   Cohen, *China and Christianity*, 4.

10 Lee Chong Kau, *How to Speak to Our Elders About Christ*, 9.

11 In an extended description of the Chinese, a missionary anthropologist stated that the Chinese feel that "China is the oldest country in the world and the Chinese is superior, but there are many Chinese who are ignorant and inferior." George J. Jennings, *All Things, All Men, All Means: to Save Some* (LeMars, IA: Middle East Missions Research, 1984), 161.

12 Gregory P. Hunt, "Chinese Worldview and Strategy for Evangelism in Taiwan," in *Chinese Around the World* 115 (September 1992): 5.

13 Daniel Hung, "Mission Blockade: Ancestor Worship," *Evangelical Missions Quarterly Online*, January 1983 [article online]; retrieved on April 20, 2006, from https://bgc.gospelcom.net/emqonline/emq_article_read.php?ArticleID=2753.

14 Pao-chen Lee, *Read About China* (Taipei: Lucky Book, 1958), 104.

15 An April 1990 source in Beijing reported that whereas new membership of the Chinese Communist Party (CCP) had decreased by 45% in 1987-89 compared to 1984-86, over the same period numbers joining Three Self Patriotic Movement (TSPM) churches had risen by 170%. In Tanjin the figures, respectively, were -80% (CCP) and +150% (Christians). In Chengdu, new Party members had decreased by 14%, while new church members had increased by a staggering 500 percent. Tonny Lambert, "Students in China Coming to Christ in Large Numbers," *Evangelical Missions Quarterly* 29 (January 1993): 60-62. For an expanded view, see Tonny Lambert, *The Resurrection of the Chinese Church* (London: Hoddler & Stoughton, 1991).

16 Paul Davenport and Alex Buchan, "New Government Statistics on China's Christians," *Compass Direct News Service*, 1999-2005 [article online]; retrieved on January 26, 2006, from http://www.worthynews.com/news-features/compass-china-survey.html.

17 From the unedited version of a Sabbath School mission story as told to Melissa Martin, "A Seminary in my House," Mission Story for January 13, 1996, *Mission Teen*, 42 (Jan-March 1996), 7-8.

18 David H. Adeney, *China: The Church's Long March*, Foreword by James Hudson Taylor III (Singapore: Overseas Missionary Fellowship, 1985), 145-46.

19 Ibid., 146-65.

20 John H. Rantung, "Witnessing to Confucianist Chinese in Indonesia," TMs, Missions Department, Adventist International Institute of Advanced Studies, Silang, Cavite, Philippines, 1994.

21   Lawrence G. Thompson, *Chinese Religions: An Introduction*, 3rd ed. (Belmont, CA: Wadsworth, 1979), 34.

22   "Lausanne Occasional Paper 15: Christian Witness to Buddhists," *Lausanne Committee for World Evangelization*, 2004 [document online from the 2004 Forum for World Evangelization]; retrieved on December 6, 2005, from http://www.lausanne.org/ Brix?pageID=14724.

23   Paul E. Kaufman, *China, the Emerging Challenge: A Christian Perspective* (Grand Rapids: Baker, 1982), 264.

24   Chua Wee Hian, "Evangelization of Whole Families," in *Perspectives on the World Christian Movement: A Reader*, ed. Ralph D. Winter and Steven C. Hawthorne (Pasadena, CA: William Carey Library, 2000), 514.

25   See Lee Chong Kau, "Parent-Child Sensitivities," chap. in *How to Speak to Our Elders About Christ* (Singapore: Overseas Missionary Fellowship, 1972), 19-24.

26   Gregory P. Hunt, "Study of the Effectiveness of Evangelistic Techniques with Chinese Christians," M.A. Thesis, Liberty University, May 1987, 49; quoted by Gregory P. Hunt, "Chinese Worldview and Strategy for Evangelism in Taiwan," *Chinese Around the World* 115 (September 1992): 9.

27   Bradley Baurain, "Teaching English Feeds a Worldwide Craving," *Evangelical Missions Quarterly* 28 (April 1992): 165.

28   Rantung, "Witnessing to Confucianist Chinese," 42.

29   Myron Widmer researched the evangelistic success (24 students and 2 teachers baptized) of an Adventist school for the Chinese in Macao where 99% is non-Christian. The principal said, "We have a higher purpose. Our school is solely for soul-saving." Myron Widmer, "Miracles in Macao," *Adventist Review*, January 18, 1996, 14.

30   Carlos G. Martin, "What Constitutes Acceptable Contextualization," *Asia Adventist Seminary Studies* Vol. 1, No. 1 (1998): 19-25.

31   Charles H. Kraft, "An Anthropological Apologetic for the Homogeneous Principle of Missiology," *Occasional Bulletin of Missionary Research* 2 (October 1978): 121. A full discussion of this issue is offered by C. Peter Wagner, *Our Kind of People* (Atlanta: John Knox Press, 1979).

32   Donald A. McGavran, *Understanding Church Growth*, fully revised (Grand Rapids: Eerdmans, 1990), 223.

PART V

RELIGIONS OF THE MIDDLE EAST

CHAPTER 17

Judaism

1. *Introduction*

a. According to the *Halacha*, the traditional law of Judaism, a Jew is the child of a Jewish mother or a convert to Judaism. However, there is a distinction between the Jewish people and the religion of Judaism. Not all Jewish people consider themselves to be religious. Many profess to be atheists, agnostics, or secular.[1]

b. The oldest of the four monotheistic religions, Judaism is the parent of both Islam and Christianity. While most Christians have no problem understanding that their religion developed from Judaism, the various "Christian" approaches to Judaism have ranged from "Christ-killers" to a view where all Jews will eventually be saved because of God's promises to Abraham. The New Testament explains that Jesus came to His own people but they did not receive Him (John 1:11). Then God established the Christian church as His new Israel to share the gospel with the world (Matt 23:37-38). Although Israel as a nation rejected His love and corporately is no longer His formal chosen people, the Bible predicts scores of Jews will one day accept God's last-day message (Rom 11:23-24). Those who accept Christ and His truth become Jews according to the promise given to Abraham (Gal 3:27-29).[2]

2. *Population*

a. There are two major Jewish groups: 1) Ashkenazic Jews are the Jews of France, Germany, and Eastern Europe and their descendants. 2) Sephardic Jews are the Jews of Spain, Portugal, North Africa, and the Middle East and their descendants. The word "Ashkenazic" comes from *Askenaz*, the Hebrew word for "German," while the word "Sephardic" is derived from the Hebrew word for "Spain."[3]

b. Most estimates suggest that there are about thirteen million to fourteen million Jews in the world. The majority of Jews live in the *diaspora* (Gk., "dispersion"). The term "Diaspora" refers to Jews living outside Israel. About five million Jews live in the United States and about five million in Israel.

There are less than two million Jews in Europe, 400,000 in Latin America and 350,000 in Canada. In Africa, there are less than 100,000 Jews, about 90% of whom live in the country of South Africa. There are about 100,000 Jews in Australia and New Zealand combined. There are about 50,000 Jews in Asia (not including Israel).[4]

c. Top ten largest national Jewish populations[5]

Rank	Country	Jews	% Jewish	% of Total
1	United States	5,914,682	2.00	40.50
2	Israel	5,021,506	80.00	34.40
3	Russia	717,101	0.50	4.91
4	France	606,561	1.00	4.16
5	Argentina	395,379	1.00	2.71
6	Canada	393,660	1.20	2.70
7	United Kingdom	302,207	0.50	2.07
8	Ukraine	142,276	0.30	0.97
9	Germany	107,160	0.13	0.73
10	Brazil	95,125	0.05	0.65

d. Factors for a reduced number of Jews include the decimation of Jewish communities during the Holocaust, when an estimated one-third of the total Jewish population was annihilated by Nazis, a declining birthrate in most Jewish communities, and a process of assimilation into non-Jewish societies in significant numbers.[6]

d. Cities with the largest Jewish population in the Diaspora:[7]

New York, USA	1,750,000	Boston, USA	208,000
Miami, USA	535,000	London, UK	200,000
Los Angeles, USA	490,000	Moscow, Russia	200,000
Paris, France	350,000	Buenos Aires, Argentina	180,000
Philadelphia, USA	254,000	Toronto, Canada	175,000
Chicago, USA	248,000	Washington DC, USA	165,000
San Francisco, USA	210,000	Kiev, Ukraine	110,000

3. *Summary of Jewish History*

a. Traditionally, Jews trace their history back to Adam and Eve. They set 3760 B.C. as the date for Creation.[8] In the "Jewish calendar" the year A.D. 2000 is A.M. 5760 (A.M. stands for *anno mundi*, or years of the world since Creation).[9]

b. The Jewish people are descendants of the ancient Hebrews. The name "Hebrew" is generally traced to Eber or Heber, their traditional ancestor (Gen. 10:21). Eber was a descendant of Shem, a son of Noah. From Shem comes the word "Semitic," which refers to a group of people that includes both Jews and Arabs.

b. Patriarchal era. Abraham, called from Ur of the Chaldees in about the year 2,000 B.C. Abraham's son, Isaac, had two sons: Esau and Jacob. Jacob had twelve sons (and one daughter), who originated the "twelve tribes of Israel" (Luke 22:30). Jacob's name was changed to "Israel" (Gen 32:22-32), meaning "God contends." The descendants of Jacob from then on were known as "the children of Israel" (Hos 3:5).

c. Egyptian bondage and Exodus. During the Egyptian New Empire, also called the Second Teban Empire, the Hebrews were enslaved in Egypt for 430 years (approximately 1875 B.C. to 1445 B.C.). Moses led the children of Israel out of Egypt and they wandered in the desert for 40 years, until about 1405 B.C.

d. Judges. There were 15 judges: the first was Othoniel and the last was Samuel. This period spans from Joshua's death (1385 B.C.) to the coronation of Saul, the first king of Israel (1051 B.C.).

e. The Kingdom united. This was Israel's most glorious period. King David prepared for the building of the Temple and his son, Solomon, accomplished it.

f. The Kingdom divided. After Solomon's death, the kingdom was divided: Ten tribes followed Jeroboam and formed the kingdom of Israel in the North and two remained loyal to Rehoboam and formed the kingdom of Judah (2 Chron 10) in the South. The kingdom of Israel suffered progressive apostasy under 20 kings (from Jeroboam to Oseah) until Samaria fell to the Assyrians in 722 B.C. The kingdom of Judah had 21 kings between Rehoboam and Sedekiah, when Nebuchadnezzar burned the temple and the Jews were taken to Babylon (586 B.C.).

g. Captivity. This covers 70 years (Jer 25:11) from 605 B.C., the year of the first of Nebuchadnezzar's raids, to 535 B.C., the return under Cyrus. The kingdom of Israel disappeared under the Assyrian captivity. During this time there were three decrees for the restoration of the walls and the Temple of Jerusalem (Ezra 6:14). A small group from the kingdom of Judah returned under the decree of Cyrus (2 Chron 36:23). Darius (Ezra 6:3-12) and Artaxerxes (Ezra 7:12-26) also decreed their return and the reconstruction of Jerusalem that took place under the leadership of Ezra and Nehemiah. Artaxerxes' decree (457 B.C.) was the one that enabled Nehemiah to do this work.[10] None of the ten tribes from the kingdom of Israel returned from the Assyrian captivity. The majority of those who returned from the Babylonian captivity were from the kingdom of Judah. Jews are the descendants of Judah, and their religion is known as "Judaism."

h. Resurgence and decadence. After the Medo-Persian rule (539-331 B.C.), the Jews fell under the rule of the Greeks (331-128 B.C). The Jews became independent under the leadership of the Maccabeans by the middle of the second century B.C. Under Roman rule (from 63 B.C. to A.D. 200), the Jewish nation became more and more unsettled until in A.D. 70 the destruction of the Temple changed the Jewish religion. "The loss of a central shrine changed the nature of the religion and ushered in rabbinic Judaism."[11] After a rebellion under Bar Kobcha (A.D. 132-35), Emperor Hadrian built a pagan temple on the original Temple site. He renamed Jerusalem *Aeila Capitolina* and forbade Jews access to enter or even to look at the sacred city. He also changed the name of the nation to Palestine in honor of the Philistines, the ancient foes of Israel.[12]

i. Middle Ages. Persecution continued in many lands. However, under the Muslim domination, the conditions of life for many Jews improved. In Europe the popes forbade usury (money-lending) but permitted it to the out-of-the-fold Jews, and in time they became the European moneylenders and bankers.[13]

j. Zionism. A political movement dating from the late nineteenth century, it is concerned with the return of the Jews to the land of Israel. This movement crosses Jewish divisions and seeks the restoration of Palestine as a Jewish state. It found a clear expression at the World Zionist Congress held in Basilea in 1897.

k. The Holocaust. During World War II, 1939-45, about six million Jews were exterminated, including 1,500,000 children—an entire generation. Two-thirds of Ashkenazic Jews were killed, or one-third of the world population of Jews. Without an understanding of the Holocaust, one cannot truly comprehend the psyche of the Jewish people today.[14]

> Anti-Semitism (alternatively spelled antisemitism) is hostility toward or prejudice against Jews as a religious, ethnic, or racial group, which can range from individual hatred to institutionalized, violent persecution. The highly explicit ideology of Adolf Hitler's Nazism was the most extreme example of this phenomenon, leading to a genocide of the European Jewry.[15]

c. In 1947 a plan creating a Jewish state was adopted by the General Assembly of the United Nations. The purpose was to offer a haven for the persecuted and homeless Jews. The State of Israel was formally recognized on May 14, 1948, when British rule ended and proclaimed the State of Israel, under the leadership of David Ben Gurion.[16] The city of Jerusalem, however, was divided in two—between the Palestinians and the Jews. During the "Six-Day War" in 1967, the Israelis captured all of Jerusalem—the first time they had held it as a free people since 586 B.C. The problem is that both Jews and Palestinians claim the same territory. Without an understanding of the historical development of the problems in the Middle East, it is far more difficult for Christian missionaries to address the various cultural groups struggling in this area.[17]

4. *Four Major Sects in Judaism During New Testament Times*

a. The Pharisees were the popular orthodox majority party. They were committed to a rigid adherence to the law in its entirety. They were so devoted to the oral law of the great *rabbis* ("teachers") that in time they came to regard the oral tradition with equal authority to that of the written law of Moses.

b. The Sadducees were the great rivals of the Pharisees. They were not large in numbers but, for the most part, they were wealthy, aristocratic, and influential. They were the materialists, the liberals, the secularists of the day. They denied the existence of angels, the resurrection, and a future life. They also denied the value of tradition.

c. The Essenes were mystics. They lived in monastic, small, and exclusive communities. Membership was granted after passing through severe initiation. They wore white clothes to symbolize purity. They lived in the desert of Judah near the Dead Sea from about 150 B.C. to their destruction by the Roman soldiers in A.D. 68. Part of their literature, the so-called Dead Sea Scrolls, has been found in 11 caves at Khirbet Qumran since 1947.[18]

d. The Zealots were political in their interests and in their program. They sought to incite the people of the Iudaea Province to rebel against the Roman Empire and expel it from the country by force of arms. Religiously they seemed to side with the Pharisees, but politically they refused to have anyone rule over them but God.[19] Today, "zealotry" denotes zeal in excess, usually on behalf of God.

5. *Three Major Groups in Judaism Today*

a. Orthodox Judaism. This was the only kind of Judaism until the eighteenth century. Orthodox Jews hold that every word of the Pentateuch (the first five books of the Bible, written by Moses), as well as the interpretations in the oral law, came from God. They strictly observe all traditions and use only Hebrew in worship. They do not travel or even carry money on the seventh-day Sabbath. In all cases, the sexes are segregated. Jesus is considered to be an imposter.[20] Hasidic Jews, usually called "Hassidim,"[21] are an ultra-Orthodox movement characterized by strict observance of the Law of Moses, mystical teachings, and are socially separatist. The men always wear a black hat or cap, demonstrating respect to God. Caftan beards and dangling earlocks are also worn, giving the Hasidim a distinctive look. There are several Hasidic groups in existence; each group finds its identity in a leader, called the *rebbe*, who is the dynastic head of that particular group.[22]

b. Reform Judaism. This movement began in Germany. Led by men like Abraham Geiger (1810-74), a reform was sought to free Jews from tradition and bring them to the modern world. In this liberal view the *Torah* is no longer received as revelation but is replaced by scientific thinking. Each congregation can modify, accept, or reject any tradition. Dietary laws are optional. They observe the Jewish holidays but often do not wear hats, phylacteries, or prayer shawls. Most Sabbath services are in the vernacular (local language), not Hebrew. Women are active in the worship services. Since the 1970s, the Hebrew Union College ordains women as rabbis.[23]

c. Conservative Judaism. Many European Jews were uncomfortable with Reformed liberals and ushered in the Conservative Jewish movement at the end of the nineteenth century. Among Conservatives, law and tradition are seen as authoritative, but there is a latitude in interpretation so as not to divide. They view other religions as the way Gentiles are saved. Like the Orthodox, they also observe all dietary and Sabbath laws. Sexes are not segregated. Sabbath services are in both the vernacular and in Hebrew.[24]

d. Secular Jews do not practice Judaism. In fact, many Jews are anti-religious militants committed to Marxist ideology; they hold an atheistic viewpoint, but consider themselves to be Jews by birth and descent. Others identify themselves with militant Zionism.[25]

6. *The Teachings of Judaism*

a. Rabbi Moses Ben Maimon (1135-1204), or Maimonides, wrote the most famous of all summaries of Judaism. The "thirteen principles of Maimonides" are now in the form of a hymn, known as the *Yigdal*, customarily used to concluded many Jewish religious services. However, assent to a creed is not demanded in Judaism, and not all Jews agree with Maimonides' summary of the faith.[26]

b. Basic to all Judaistic teaching is the full personality of God, His freedom from any limitations or imperfection, His spiritual nature, and His continuing power in the universe.[27] Not only was the Israelite religion the first to develop the concept of a single personal God who created the world, but it was also the first to embrace ethical monotheism: an offense against morality is an offense against God.[28] Deuteronomy 6:4 articulates the *Shema* ("Hear"), or summary of the Jewish religion: "Hear O Israel, the Lord our God, the Lord is One." The *Shema* is repeated in all Sabbath and festival services.

c. At the heart of Jewish religion lies the concept of a covenant between God and His people. A covenant is an agreement between two parties in which one lays down the obligations, and the second accepts the conditions. Judaism can be said to be uniquely a religion of Covenant.[29]

d. The Messiah is another central theme. He is personal and will redeem man on earth. The Orthodox Jews still expect the Messiah, but actually believe he will fully redeem Israel.[30] The conservative and liberal branches of Judaism look for a kingdom and messianic era when, with the cooperation of all men and God's help, a kingdom of truth, justice, and peace will form.[31] They accept converts but do not seek them.

7. *The Jewish Scriptures*

a. The basis of Judaism is the Hebrew Bible. These scriptures are divided into three sections: the *Torah* ("Law"), the *Nevi'im* ("Prophets"), and the *Ketubim* (Writings"). The three together are known as the *Tenach* or *Tanakh*,[32] an acronym of the first three letters of the books (TeNaCh).[33]

b. The *Torah*, or Law, consists of the Pentateuch–the first five books of the Bible. The Law includes the Ten Commandments, 613 commandments, 2487 positive injunctions, and 365 prohibitions.[34]

c. The Prophets contain the records of the writings of the prophets during the periods of the united monarchy, the divided monarchy, and the exiles. They also include the historical books, which recount the story of Israel from their entrance into Canaan until after the Babylonian Captivity.

d. The Writings contain the ancient Hebrew poetry and philosophy. They are divided into three sections: The first includes Job, Psalms, and Proverbs. The second section contains the "Five Scrolls" of Ecclesiastes, Ruth, Song of Songs, Esther, and Lamentations. The third section is made up of the remaining books: Judges, Samuel, Kings, Chronicles, Nehemiah, and Ezra.[35]

e. Judaism did not cease to develop with the completion of the Old Testament. Rabbis and scholars studied and interpreted the scriptures in order to adapt thyem to daily life; this is known as "Rabbinic Judaism." These interpretations became known as the oral law (*Talmud*), as contrasted with the written law (Pentateuch). The oral law is as binding as the written. In the second century B.C., Rabbi Hanassi compiled the oral laws into *Mishnah* (first writings after the Old Testament, written in Hebrew). Later interpretations are in the *Gemara* ("supplement," written in Aramaic). These made up *Talmud*, which serves as a guide to civil laws, religious laws, and teachings.[36] The five books of the *Torah* consist of about 350 pages, but the *Talmud* takes up 523 books printed in 22 volumes.[37]

f. Many Jews of the Diaspora ("dispersion") had forgotten Hebrew, their native tongue, as Greek became increasingly the *lingua franca* of the ancient world. Jews from Palestine were settled in Alexandria, Egypt, and commissioned to translate the Jewish scriptures into Greek that the Hellenic ("Hellene" is an ancient name for Greece) Jews could read for themselves. Tradition says that the work was produced by 72 Jewish scholars and is known as the *Septuagint* ("The Seventy"), generally abbreviated "LXX." The work was finished between 285 and 130 B.C. This is the version quoted throughout the New Testament.[38]

8. *Customs and Practices*

a. Modern Hebrew is the official national language of the Jewish people in Israel and the religious language of the Jews of the Diaspora. However, the influence of other tongues and cultures is observable in their use of Yiddish, Ladino, and other languages. *Yiddish* ("Jewish") is the language of Ashkenazic Jews, and is spoken by about four million Jews all over the world, especially in Argentina, Canada, France, Israel, Mexico, Romania, and the U.S. Its vocabulary is basically German, but it has been enlarged by borrowings from Hebrew, Slavic, the Romance languages, and English. Ladino is the language of Sheparadic Jews, mixing medieval Spanish and Hebrew.[39]

b. Jews indicate their obedience by meticulous attention to dietary regulations known as *kashrut* ("fit," "proper," or "correct"). *Kosher* describes food that meets those standards. The animals from which meat is taken must be slaughtered in prescribed ways, usually by an official (*shochet*). Milk and meat must not be eaten at the same meal–they should even be prepared separately. A strict *kosher* household will have two sets of utensils: one is for meat and the other is for milk.[40]

c. Boys are circumcised eight days after they are born. This surgical operation in the name of the faith cuts off the foreskin of the penis. The accompanying ceremony, called *brit milah* ("Covenant of Circumcision"), is universally followed. Even secular Jews who observe no other part of Judaism almost always observe these laws. The commandment to circumcise is given at Genesis 17:10-14 and Leviticus 12:3. The covenant was originally made with Abraham.[41]

d. Boys become *bar mitzvah* ("son of the Law") or full, responsible members of the community at the age of thirteen. The ceremony, also referred to as *Bar Mitzvah*, generally consists of a synagogue service followed by an extended and elaborate reception with a full meal. In addition, Conservative and Liberal Jews also have a *Bat Mitzvah* ("daughter of the Law") ceremony, whereby a young woman is considered an adult. Often young women are considered adults at the age of 12 without any ritual.[42]

e. The Orthodox Jews require a *ketabah,* or marriage contract, which is the groom's obligation to the bride. The couple is married under the *happa,* or canopy, symbolizing the bride and groom and their future home. They sip wine from a single glass, which the groom breaks as a reminder of the destruction of the Temple, though some believe the ceremony symbolizes the idea that even happy times should be balanced by serious reflection. Like other Jewish ceremonies, there must be at least ten male Jews present in order for the ceremony to be valid.[43]

f. During *Shabbat,* or Sabbath, Jews will generally abstain from work, from driving, and from lighting a fire. Many who do not follow the traditional observance will at least prepare a special family meal for the beginning of the *Shabbat* on Friday evening. The *Shabbat* begins when three stars can be seen in the sky. By sunset on Friday, the woman of the house indicates the beginning of the *Shabbat* by lighting two candles. According to Jewish tradition, *Shabbat Shalom* ("Sabbath peace" or "peaceful Sabbath") is an appropriate greeting at any time on Sabbath, although it is most commonly used at the end of a Sabbath service. *Shabbat* ends at nightfall, when three stars are visible, approximately forty minutes after sunset.[44]

g. Deuteronomy 6:4-9 is known as the *Shema,* the first word of the sentence. It reads, *"Sh'ma Yisrael Adonai Elohaynu Adonai Echad"* ("Hear, Israel, the Lord is our God, the Lord is One"). Based on the admonition, "You shall bind them [these words] on your arms and they shall be an ornament between your eyes," Orthodox men bind a *tefillin* around the left arm and another on the forehead at the week-day morning service. *Tefillin* ("prayer boxes," the "phylacteries" of Matthew 23:5) are small black boxes containing the *Shema* that must be wrapped around the arm and forehead according to a certain pattern.[45]

h. Following the instruction "You shall write them on the doorposts of your house and upon your gates," Orthodox Jews fasten a *mezuzah* ("doorpost") on the exterior of the front door and on all interior doors, except for the bathroom. It is a wooden, metal, or glass case, about eight centimeters long, which contains the first two paragraphs of the *Shema.* Though a traditional practice, many Jews have adopted it as a way of affirming their identity, not necessarily related to a religious belief.[46]

i. The synagogue is the Jewish house of worship. During and after the exile, the Jewish synagogue developed as a place of prayer, singing, reading, discussion, and teaching, but not as a place of sacrifice. Ten male Jews are required to establish a synagogue.[47] They do not use the term "churches"; Jews have "congregations." The spiritual leader, teacher, and interpreter of scripture in a synagogue is the rabbi. He is chosen by the congregation he serves. There is no single religious head of Judaism. There are no priests in modern Judaism. In the *Shabbat* meetings, on Friday night and Saturday mornings, a cantor (*chazzan*) leads the congregation in chanting portions of prayers, usually in Hebrew.[48]

9. *Selected Feasts of Judaism*

a. The Jewish calendar is tied to the moon's cycles instead of the sun's. The Jewish calendar loses about eleven days relative to the solar calendar every year, but makes up for it by adding a month every two or three years. As a result, the holidays don't always fall on the same day, but they always fall within the same month or two. The Chinese calendar (which is also lunar) works the same way, which is why Chinese New Year occurs on different days but is always in late January or early February. The Muslim calendar is lunar but does not add months, which is why Ramadan circles the calendar.[49]

b. Three of the most popular festivals are known as "pilgrim" or "foot" festivals because in ancient times pilgrims used to travel to the Jerusalem Temple to celebrate Passover, Pentecost, and Tabernacles. There are two Jewish festivals that are serious occasions–The New Year and the Day of Atonement. There are also two popular minor festivals–Purim and the Festival of Lights; the latter is not based on the Bible.[50]

c. *Pesach,* or Passover, is a holiday that commemorates the Exodus from Egypt. Almost all Jews observe Passover, even if they only go to their parents house for a ritual dinner. Most Jews avoid bread and grain products to one extent or another throughout this holiday, in memory of the fact that their ancestors left Egypt in a hurry and did not have time to wait for their bread to rise.

d. *Shabuoth,* or Pentecost, commemorates the giving of the Torah at Mt. Sinai, and it also celebrates the first fruits of the harvest. In the United States it takes place between Memorial Day and Independence Day, and lasts for one or two days, depending on the branch of Judaism.

e. *Sukkoth* is the festival of Tabernacles, or booths, that commemorates the biblical period of wandering in the desert, and is commemorated by building a temporary shelter, called a *sukkah*, in the yard and eating meals in it. Some spend considerable time in the *sukkah*, even sleeping there. *Sukkoth* begins on the fifth day after Yom Kippur, in late September or October, and lasts for seven days. This is also a holiday of thanksgiving that celebrates the fruit harvest.

f. *Rosh Hashanah* is the Jewish New Year, the day when the year number on the Jewish calendar increases. *Rosh Hashanah* is a happy, festive holiday, but somewhat more solemn than the American New Year. Like New Year, it is a time to look back at the past year and make resolutions for the following year. It is also a wake-up call, a time to begin mental preparations for the upcoming day of atonement, *Yom Kippur*. *Rosh Hashanah* starts at sunset the night before the day shown on the calendar. Jews will be offended if important events, meetings, or tests are scheduled on *Rosh Hashanah*, just as many Christians would feel bad if someone scheduled such activities on Christmas or Easter.

g. *Yom Kippur* is the Jewish Day of Atonement, a day of fasting and repentance to reconcile with the Creator for the mistakes made in the last year. It occurs on the ninth day after the first day of *Rosh Hashanah*. *Rosh Hashanah* occurs on the first day of the lunar month of Tishri, in the course of September and October; *Yom Kippur* occurs on the tenth. So *Yom Kippur* is usually in late September or early October. This is the busiest day of the year for synagogues.

h. *Purim* celebrates the rescue of the Jews from the threat of extermination under Ahsuerus, king of Persia, as recounted in the Book of Esther. The story is read publicly morning and evening; the audience makes noises whenever the name of the villain, Haman, is read out.

i. *Hanukkah* or *Chanukkah* is the festival of lights. It commemorates the rededication of the Temple in Jerusalem in 165 B.C. after a successful revolt against the Selucid Greeks. As part of the rededication, the victorious Jews needed to light the Temple's *menorah* (candelabrum), but they had only enough oil to last one day and it would take eight days to prepare more oil. Miraculously, the one-day supply of oil lasted for eight days. The miracle of the oil is commemorated with this eight-day candle-lighting holiday. *Hanukkah* begins between Thanksgiving and Christmas. About half the time it overlaps with Christmas, but their celebrations are completely different. Almost all Jews light candles with their families for at least some nights of the holiday, so people like to be at home during this holiday.

10. *Christian Witness*

a. "Never initiate a religious conversation with a Jewish friend (he will think you are trying to convert him) and, unless he brings up the subject, never talk about religion in front of his family and friends."[51]

b. Develop a caring friendship.[52] Express appreciation for Jewish culture and history. Whatever the person's spiritual inclinations, you should show an interest in Jews and Jewish culture. Show sympathy for the sufferings of Jews.

c. Share your conviction that the ancient Hebrew prophets were inspired by God.

d. Share with your Jewish friend that you believe God has made all nations of "one blood." Both Christians and Jews are descendants from Abraham.

e. Express the thought openly that Christians see themselves as spiritual Jews.

f. One way to demonstrate that Jesus was the promised Messiah is using broad prophecies at first and then narrowing the field to include increasingly specific and detailed prophecies. The Messiah must be a human being, a Jew from the tribe of Judah and from the family of David, born in Bethlehem, despised and rejected by the Jewish people, die as a result of a judicial proceeding, be guiltless, and start His ministry in A.D. 27. Obviously, as the prophecies become increasingly detailed, the field of qualified "candidates" becomes increasingly narrow.[53]

g. Share culturally relevant Bible studies. When you actually enter into religious discussion with your Jewish friends, ask questions such as the following:

1) In your opinion, why has the Jewish race suffered so much down through the centuries? Why did God allow the Egyptian bondage, the Babylonian captivity, the destruction of Jerusalem, and the Holocaust? (See Deuteronomy 28; Jeremiah 17).

2) Who was Isaiah the prophet talking about in Isaiah 53? Read the entire chapter aloud with your friend.

3) Review Old Testament prophecies relating to the Messiah in Dan 9:23-27; Mic 5:2; Isa 9:6; 7:14; Ps 22; and Gen 49:10.

4) Invite your Jewish friend to systematically study the ancient prophecies of Daniel with you.

5) Share your testimony describing the peace, forgiveness, freedom from guilt, and assurance of salvation that Jesus gives you personally.[54]

h. Words and terms to avoid:[55]

1) Christian jargon in general: "The precious blood of our Lord Jesus Christ," "saved," "born again." To say "a Jewish man" is better than to say "a Jew." "A Jewish woman" is better to say than "a Jewess." "Jewish" should only be used to indicate people, land, religion, or language. Terms like "Jewish money" or "Jewish control of media" reflect anti-Semitic attitudes.

2) "The cross" symbolizes persecution for many Jews. It is better to speak about "the death of Christ." "Convert" also implies leaving behind one's Jewishness. It is better to speak of "becoming a believer (or follower) of Jesus."

3) Some suggest replacing the name "Jesus" with the Hebrew equivalent of "*Y'shua*," but many will never know that you are referring to the historical Jesus unless you also use "Jesus."

4) Also it is preferable to speak of "the Messiah Jesus" rather than "Jesus Christ." Many Jews do not realize that "Christ" means "Messiah" and think that "Christ" was his last name.

i. Jews are proud of their identity as Jews, even though they may not be active in Judaism. For many Jews, their Jewish identity is more cultural than it is religious, but this doesn't mean that their Jewishness is unimportant to them. Therefore in witnessing to Jewish people about Jesus, it is important to stress that they do not need to give up their identity as Jews in order to embrace Jesus as Messiah.[56]

j. Many Christians are reconsidering the concept of working with "Messianic Synagogues."

> The truth is, every church must be culturally relevant to and negotiable with the community it serves . . . . What the Jewish community needs to be saved are thousands of growing synagogues with home Torah studies, *yajmakahs*, Jewish music, ceremonies, holidays, traditions, testimonies, special events, and everything revolving around and pointing toward a very Jewish *Yeshua* [Jesus] who is Lord of all, Jews and Gentiles as well. Such synagogues can throw their doors open wide with the confidence that God will fill them with Jewish souls

and also with people who are of non-Jewish descent but are nevertheless true, born-again, spiritual Jews. These truly born-again believers in *Yeshua*, unlike many anti-Semitic nominal 'Christians,' love the Jews in all their Jewishness.[57]

k. Current strategies to evangelize Jewish people include cyber-evangelism, city-wide evangelistic campaigns, radio and television ministries, outreach events during the Jewish holy days, direct mail to Jewish homes, specialized approaches to reach specific Jewish groups such as "Generation J," Jewish "New Agers," "JuBus" (Jewish Buddhists), "HinJus" (Jewish Hindus), the intermarried, and post-modern Jewish people.[58]

11. *Glossary of Jewish Terms*

a. *Cabbala* ("revelation"). Cabbalism was an exotic blend of superstition, false hermeneutics, myth, astrology, occultism, numerology, and spiritualism. Cabbalists claimed that the Cabbala was given at the same time as the Torah, but only for chosen mystics. The publication of the *Book of Formation* in the ninth century fanned superstitious ideas that already existed in New Testament times, that supernatural powers were supposed to reside in the letters of the Hebrew alphabet.

b. *Diaspora* ("dispersion"). The exile of Jews from the Land of Israel; Jews who live somewhere other than Israel. The dispersion of the Jews after the Babylonian Captivity.

c. *Gemarah*. The commentary based upon the *Mishnah*.

d. *Hanukkah*. The feast of dedication celebrating the Maccabean victory in 167 B.C.

e. Messiah. The anointed descendant of King David prophesied in scripture to come at the end of time. In Judaism this Messiah is not the same as Jesus Christ.

f. Messianic Jews. Jews who believe, and have accepted, *Yeshua* (the Hebrew name for Jesus) of Nazareth as the promised Messiah of the Jewish Scriptures. These Jews believe in maintaining a Jewish lifestyle of faith while celebrating many customs that are in line with Holy Scripture. They normally worship God through the Jewish *Shabbat*, festivals, and holy days, rather than the Christian holy days most churches observe.

g. *Mishnah.* Oral law in general to be distinguished from scripture.

h. Passover (*Pesach,* meaning "pass over," "to spare"). An annual feast commemorating the deliverance of the firstborn in Egypt when the angel of death took all those who did not have blood on the doorpost.

i. Pharisee (from *perush*, meaning "separatist"). A sect in ancient Judaism that believed that, in addition to the conventional written Torah, there was an oral Torah revealed at Sinai and preserved through a succession of sages.

j. Pentateuch. The first five books of the Old Testament, written by Moses.

k. Pentecost. The feast of weeks observed fifty days after the Passover. Also called *Shabuoth.*

l. *Purim.* A feast commemorating Esther's intervention on behalf of the Jews when they were in Persia.

m. *Rabbi* ("my lord"). A master of the Torah; title for a teacher.

n. *Rosh Hashanah.* The Jewish New Year.

o. *Seder.* The festival held in Jewish homes on the first night of the Passover commemorating the Exodus from Egypt.

p. Septuagint. Translation of the Old Testament into the Greek language, made between 285 and 130 B.C. This is the version quoted throughout the New Testament.

q. *Shofar.* The ram's horn that is blown during services on Rosh Hashanah.

r. *Sukkoth.* The feast of tabernacles celebrating the harvest.

s. *Talmud.* The Jewish library of oral law and tradition consisting of *Mishnah* and *Gemara.*

t. *Torah.* Refers to the first five books of the Old Testament (The Law). It also can refer to the entire corpus of the Jewish law.

u. *YHWH.* The *Tetragrammaton* (Greek, "word with four letters") is the usual reference to the Hebrew name for the God of Israel. In Judaism, the *Tetragrammaton* is the ineffable name of God and is therefore not to be read

aloud. In the reading aloud of the scripture or in prayer, it is replaced with
*Adona*i (Lord). Many sacred name ministries who believe that YHWH consists
of four vowels pronounce these four vowels as "ee-ah-oo-eh" and believe that it
indicates that God's name was either "Yahweh" or "Yahuweh." A common way
to convey the name in English is "Jehovah."

Notes

1   J. Immanuel Schochet, "Who Is a Jew? 30 Questions and Answers About this
Controversial and Divisive Issue," *Who Is a Jew?*, 5749 Jewish calendar [book
online]; retrieved on January 22, 2006, from http://www.whoisajew.com/.

2   Mark Finley, *Studying Together* (Fallbrook, CA: Hart Research Center, 1995), 147.

3   Tracey R. Rich, "Ashkenazic and Sephardic Jews," *Judaism 101*, 2002
[encyclopedia online]; retrieved on January 22, 2006, from
http://www.jewfaq.org/populatn.htm.

4   Tracey R. Rich, "Jewish Population," *Judaism 101*, 2002 [encyclopedia online];
retrieved on January 22, 2006, from http://www.jewfaq.org/populatn.htm.

5   "The Jewish Population of the World," *Jewish Virtual Library*, The American-
Israeli Cooperative Enterprise, 2005 [article online]; retrieved November 30, 2005,
from http://www.jewishvirtuallibrary.org/jsource/Judaism/jewpop.html.

6   "Lausanne Occasional Paper 7: The Thailand Report on Jewish People," *Lausanne
Committee for World Evangelization* (Wheaton, IL: Lausanne Committee for World
Evangelization, 1980) [document online]; retrieved on March 6, 2006, from
http://www.lausanne.org/Brix?pageID=14607.

7   "The Largest Jewish Communities," *Adherents*, 2005 [article online]; retrieved on
November 15, 2005, from http://www.adherents.com/largecom/
com_judaism.html#cities.

8   Bishop James Ussher (1581-1656) made it Sunday, October 23, 4004 B.C.; his dates
were included in many editions of the King James Version of the Bible. Doug
Linder, "Bishop James Ussher Sets the Date for Creation," *University of Missouri-
Kansas City School of Law*, 2004 [article online]; retrieved on February 18, 2006,
from http://www.law.umkc.edu/faculty/projects/ftrials/scopes/ussher.html.

9   Norman Solomon, *Judaism: A Very Short Introduction* (New York: Oxford
University Press, 2000), 19.

10 Uriah Smith, *The Prophecies of Daniel and the Revelation* (Washington, DC: Review & Herald,1944), 208-11.

11 Naomi Pasachoff and Robert J. Littman, *A Concise History of the Jewish People* (Lanham, MD: Rowman & Littlefield, 2005), 86.

12 David A. Rausch and Carl Hermann Voss, *World Religions: Our Quest for Meaning* (Valley Forge, PA: Trinity Press International, 1993), 140-41.

13 Geoffery Cowling, "Story of a Nation," in *Eerdmans' Handbook to the World Religions*, ed. Pierce R Beaver et al. (Grand Rapids: Eerdmans, 1982), 284-86.

14 United States Holocaust Memorial Museum, "The Holocaust," *Holocaust Encyclopedia* [encyclopedia online]; retrieved on March 10, 2006, from http://www.ushmm.org/wlc/en/.

15 "Anti-Semitism," *Wikipedia, the Free Encyclopedia*, 2006 [article online]; retrieved on June 20, 2006, from http://en.wikipedia.org/wiki/Anti-Semitism.

16 John L. Esposito, Darrell J. Fasching, and Todd Lewis, *World Religions Today*, 2nd ed. (New York: Oxford University Press, 2006), 111-15.

17 See Colin Chapman, *Whose Promised Land?* (Belleville, MI: Lion Publishing, 1983), 27-98. Also, Jonathan Dimbleby, *The Palestinians* (New York: Quartet Books, 1979), 86.

18 Siegfried H. Horn, *Biblical Archaeology: A Generation of Discoveries* (Washington, DC: Biblical Archaeology Society, 1985), 23-29.

19 "The Sects of Judaism," *Seventh-day Adventist Bible Commentary*, rev. ed., ed. Francis D. Nichol (Washington, DC: Review & Herald, 1976-80), 5:51-55.

20 Marvin Wilson, "Branches in Judaism," in *Eerdmans' Handbook to the World's Religions*, ed. Pierce R Beaver et al. (Grand Rapids: Eerdmans, 1982), 292.

21 H. Rabinowicz, *A Guide to Hassidim* (New York: Thomas Yoseloff, 1960), 114-23.

22 Richard Robinson, "Judaism and the Jewish People," in *The Compact Guide to World Religions*, ed. Dean C. Halverson (Minneapolis, MN: Bethany, 1996), 124.

23 Wilson, "Branches in Judaism," 293-94.

24 Jacob Neusner, *Judaism: An Introduction* (London: Penguin Books, 2002), 250-55.

25   Theodore Herzl's publication of *Der Judenstaat* ("The Jewish State") in 1896 gave birth to political Zionism. He believed that anti-Semitism was inevitable as long as the majority of Jewish people lived outside their homeland. Rausch and Voss, *World Religions*, 141.

26   Emil L. Fackenheim, *What is Judaism?* (New York: Collier Books, 1988), 21-23.

27   H. D. Leuner, "Judaism," in *The World's Religions*, ed. Sir Norman Anderson (Grand Rapids: Eerdmans, 1989), 58.

28   T. Patrick Burke, *The Major Religions: An Introduction with Texts*, 2nd ed. (Malden, MA: Blackwell Publishing, 2004), 220.

29   Robert Banks, "The Covenant," in *Eerdmans' Handbook to the World's Religions*, ed. Pierce R. Beaver et al. (Grand Rapids: Eerdmans, 1982), 278-79.

30   Wilson, "Branches of Judaism," 293.

31   Leuner, "Judaism," 63.

32   "The Holy Scriptures: The Tanakh," *Jewish Virtual Library*, 2006 [online library]; available on June 20, 2006, at http://www.jewishvirtuallibrary.org/jsource/Bible/jpstoc.html.

33   Fackenheim, *What is Judaism?*, 63.

34   Ibid., 64-65.

35   Ibid., 64.

36   Robert Banks, "Torah and Mishnah," in *Eerdmans' Handbook to the World's Religions*, ed. Pierce R. Beaver et al. (Grand Rapids: Eerdmans, 1982), 289-90.

37   John Phillips, *Exploring the World of the Jew* (Neptune, NJ: Loizeaux Brothers, 1993), 55.

38   "The Languages, Manuscripts, and Canon of the Old Testament," *Seventh-day Adventist Bible Commentary*, rev. ed., ed. Francis D. Nichol (Washington, DC: Review & Herald, 1976-80), 1:25-45.

39   Tracey R. Rich, "Yiddish," *Judaism 101*, 2004 [encyclopedia online]; retrieved on March 2, 2006, from http://www.jewfaq.org/yiddish.htm.

40   Solomon, *Judaism: A Very Short Introduction*, 89-91.

41   Tracey R. Rich, "Birth and the First Month of Life," *Judaism 101*, 1997-2005 [encyclopedia online]; retrieved on March 7, 2006, from http://www.jewfaq.org/ birth.htm.

42   Tracey R. Rich, "Bar Mitzvah, Bat Mitzvah and Confirmation," *Judaism 101*, 1996-2005 [encyclopedia online]; retrieved on March 5, 2006, from http://www.jewfaq.org/ barmitz.htm.

43   Leuner, "Judaism," 76-77.

44   Tracey R. Rich, "Shabbat," *Judaism 101*, 2002 [encyclopedia online]; retrieved on January 22, 2006, from http://www.jewfaq.org/shabbat.htm.

45   Solomon, *Judaism: A Very Short Introduction*, 86.

46   David Harley, "Life in a Jewish Family," in *Eerdmans' Handbook to the World's Religions*, ed. Pierce R. Beaver et al. (Grand Rapids: Eerdmans, 1982), 304.

47   Phillips, *Exploring the World of the Jew*, 61.

48   David Harley, "Chosen People: Judaism," in *Eerdmans' Handbook to the World's Religions*, ed. Pierce R. Beaver et al. (Grand Rapids: Eerdmans, 1982), 274.

49   Tracey R. Rich, "A Gentile's Guide to the Jewish Holidays," *Judaism 101*, 2004 [article online]; retrieved on March 6, 2006, from http://www.jewfaq.org/ holidayg.htm.

50   Solomon, *Judaism: A Very Short Introduction*, 54-67.

51   Clifford Goldstein, "How to Approach Our Jewish Friends with the Gospel," *Dialogue* 2 (1990): 14.

52   Many materials in this section were taken from Finley, *Studying Together*, 149-50.

53   Ron Rhodes, "Jesus is the Messiah," *Reasoning from the Scriptures Ministries* [article online]; retrieved on June 20, 2006, from http://home.earthlink.net/ ~ronrhodes/Jews.html.

54   Dean C. Halverson provides "selected Messianic prophecies fulfilled in Christ" and ways to use the New Testament in *Compact Guide to World Religions* (Minneapolis, MN: Bethany, 1996), 138-39.

55   Goldstein, "How to Approach our Jewish Friends," 14.   Robinson, "Judaism and the Jewish People," 132-33.

56   David Brickner, "Pointers on Witnessing to Jews," *Jews for Jesus*, 2006 [article online]; retrieved on March 11, 2006, from http://files.jewsforjesus.org/pdf/other/pointers.pdf.

57   Phillip E. Goble, *Everything You Need to Grow a Messianic Synagogue* (Pasadena, CA: William Carey Library, 1974), 11.

58   "Jewish Evangelism: A Call to the Church," Lausanne Occasional Paper No. 60, *Lausanne Committee for World Evangelization*, 2004 [document online]; retrieved on March 8, 2006, from http://community.gospelcom.net/lcwe/assets/LOP60_IG31.pdf.

CHAPTER 18

Zoroastrianism

1. *Introduction*

a. This religion is known by several names, including Parsism, Mazdaism, Zoroastrism, Zarathustrism, and Zoroastrianism. "Parsism" derives from "Persia," the faith's ancestral homeland. A Parsee is a person who follows the teachings of Parsism. Mazdaism derives from Ahura-Mazda, the name of this religion's god. The other names derive from its founder, Zarathustra.

b. World religions usually number their adherents in the millions. However, the total membership of Zoroastrianism amounts to only about 140,000.[1] Three basic reasons for their decline are a low birthrate among members, a rising death rate as the community rapidly ages, and a prohibition to accepting converts to the faith.[2]

c. Most Zoroastrians live in India and Pakistan (over 110,000), where they are called *Parsees* ("Persians"). There are about twenty thousand Zoroastrians in Iran, where they are called *Gabras* ("infidels"),[3] and smaller communities in North America, Britain, East Africa, New Zealand, and Hong Kong.[4] UNESCO stated that the total number of Zoroastrians in India has dropped 33% in 50 years to only 76,000 in 1991, leaving behind empty villages and deserted homes.[5]

2. *Historical Development*

a. Zarathustra Spitama was born around 650 B.C. in Persia (present-day Iran). *Zoroaster* is a Greek corruption of Zarathustra. *Spitama* indicates that he was probably born into a warrior clan linked to the royal family of Ancient Persia. *Zarathustra* may mean "possessor of camels," possibly indicative of a nomadic lifestyle.[6] The date and place of his birth are unknown, but Parsees celebrate his birthday on March 25.[7]

b. Trained as a priest, at age 20 Zarathustra left his home and the wife that had been chosen for him in a search for answers to life's deepest questions.[8] At the age of 30 he received enlightenment. As the account goes, Zarathustra received a vision on the banks of the Daity River when a large figure appeared to him. This personage identified himself as *Voho Manah* ("good thought"). This figure took Zarathustra into the presence of the wise lord *Ahura-Mazda*, who instructed Zarathustra in the true religion.[9]

c. Zarathustra spent the next ten years proclaiming his newly discovered truth, but with little success. The movement began to grow after Zarathustra converted a prince named Vishtaspa, who helped propagate the faith. During the following years the faith spread rapidly. Zoroastrian tradition records two holy wars which were fought over the faith, the second of which took the life of Zarathustra at the age of seventy-seven.[10]

d. In the Old Testament, the Parsee kings Cyrus the Great (576-529 B.C.), Darius I (522-486 B.C.), Xerxes (Ahasuerus, 486-465 B.C.), and Artaxerxes I (465-423 B.C.) are depicted in positive terms. In the book of Daniel the Parsee kings Cyrus and Darius promoted Daniel to the highest position in the land. In the book of Esther, Zoroastrian king Xerxes saved the Jewish nation from annihilation. In 2 Chronicles 36, Zoroastrian king Cyrus liberated the Jewish people and sent them to rebuild the temple of God. In Ezra and Nehemiah, Zoroastrian kings Cyrus, Darius, and Artaxerxes not only sent the Jewish people to rebuild the Lord's temple, but also gave money. The only Gentile in the Old Testament that the Lord ever called His anointed and His Shepherd was the Zoroastrian king Cyrus (Isa 44:28; 45:1).

e. Zoroastrianism was severely threatened by the 331 B.C. invasion of Alexander the Great but was later reestablished in a shrunken Iranian empire by the Parthians, who ruled for almost five hundred years to A.D. 224. Under the Sassanids of the third to mid-seventh centuries, Zoroastrianism became the state religion. Another major threat came from the spread of Islam after the death of

Muhammad in A.D. 632. A number of Zoroastrians avoided conversion to Islam by migrating to western India.[11]

3. *Scriptures*

The sacred scripture of Zoroastrians is known as the *Avesta*, originally written in an old Iranian language called *Avestan*. Of the original work, only a small fraction has survived. The total size is about one-tenth of the Bible. The *Avesta* contains hymns, prayers, and ritual instruction. The *Avesta* is divided into four major sections:[12]

a. The *Yasna* is the oldest and most important portion. Within the *Yasna* there is a group of five hymns known as the *Gathas*, which are assumed to be the closest account we have of the very words of Zarathustra. They stress the lordship of *Ahura-Mazda*.

b. The *Visparad* has 20 chapters or hymns with invocations, praises, and sacrifices to all the divine lords of Zoroastrianism.

c. The *Yashts* contains hymns to 21deities, angels, and heroic humans. Among the most important are hymns to Mithra, god of light (worshiped as the god of the sun on the first day of the week, as a later development in the Roman empire).[13]

d. The *Videvdat* (also known as *Vendidad*), written much later, contains the law against the demons, along with other codes and regulations.

4. *Teachings*

a. According to Zarathustra, there is one true deity to be worshiped. His name is *Ahura-Mazda* ("wise lord"). Scholars understand Zarathustra's belief in one god, however, as a "qualified monotheism" rather than an absolute monotheism because this religion worships many other gods.[14] First, Ahura Mazda created His "Beneficent Spirit" or Creative aspect, Spentas Mainyu. Through this second being Ahura Mazda created other good deities. Among these deities are the six "Holy Immortals," who bridge the gap of holiness between God and human beings.[15] They are at once an aspect of God, his emanation, and independent divinity. In turn, they created other lesser immortals, the *yazatas* (beings "worthy of worship"), who strive under Ahura Mazda to further good and defeat evil.[16]

b. The existence of evil led Zarathustra to the concept of dualism. In the Zoroastrian universe there are two primordial, opposing principles: *Asha* ("Truth") and *Druj* ("Lie"). Embodied by the deities that embraced them, they clash in an eternal struggle.[17] Although Ahura-Mazda is the supreme deity, he is opposed by another powerful force known as Angra Mainyu or Ahriman ("destructive spirit"). These two are co-equal and co-eternal. From the beginning of existence these two antagonistic spirits have been at odds with each other.

> Truly, there are two primal Spirits, twins renowned to be in conflict. In thought and word, in act, they are two: the better and the bad. And those who act well have chosen rightly between these two, not so the evildoers. And when these two Spirits first came together they created life and not-life, and how at the end Worst Existence shall be for the wicked, but the House of Best Purpose shall be for the just man. Of these two Spirits, the Wicked One chose achieving the worst things. The Most Holy Spirit, who is clad in the hardest stone, chose right, and so do those who shall satisfy Ahura Mazda continually with rightful acts (*Yashna* 30:3-5).[18]

c. Contending for *Druj* or evil is Angra Mainyu (also known as Ahirman and Shaitin[19]–transliterated "Satan" in Aramaic), whose very nature is evil and destructive.[20] Following Ahura Mazda's acts of creation, Angra Mainyu countered them by bringing into being evil spirits, including the *daevas*, ancient amoral gods of war; and with them he attacked the good creations. These spirits strive instinctively to the same end as their creators. Man, however, must act on deliberate choices. At death each individual will be judged. If his good thoughts, words, and deeds outweigh his bad, his soul crosses the broad Chinvat Bridge and ascends to heaven. If not, the bridge contracts and he falls into hell, with its punishments.[21] "There is no eternal hell in Zoroastrianism, for good is ultimately victorious. With the help of all individuals who choose goodness over evil, the world will gradually reach a state of perfection. . . ."[22]

5. *Basic Observances*

a. Zoroastrians, or Parsees, hold fire in high esteem. Some even attach as much importance to fire as the "Creator God" himself. Fire is usually referred to as the "son of God" and is considered to be the visible representation of the invisible god. Zoroastrian temples are devoted to fire and are known as "fire-temples." In these temples there is a central room housing a large vessel with a lit fire, fueled by wood and fragrances. Parsees traditionally pray to this fire, often bowing low or bowing on their faces before it. Some devotees feel the duty to pray five times daily in the presence of fire. Their reverence for fire also extends even into everyday life. At home a blessing is generally murmured whenever a light is lit. A flame is never blown out, but allowed to die. Care is taken not to spill anything on fire, and if this does happen, a penance must be performed.[23]

b. A Zoroastrian generally prays standing up. While uttering the appointed prayers, the worshiper unties and reties the *kusti*. This is the sacred cord, which should be worn constantly. It goes three times round the waist and is knotted over a sacred shirt.[24]

c. They abhor pollution of earth or water and maintain the strictest cleanliness in their persons and homes. Because unbelievers are necessarily unclean, they cannot enter fire-temples or be present at Zoroastrian acts of worship.

d. Ceremonies at death are very important. The body is given into the charge of professionals, who, because of their profession, are regarded as unclean persons and live lives apart from other Parsees. The body is carried to one of their special circular buildings open at the top (*dakhma*), known as "the towers of silence," where the polluting flesh is devoured by vultures and the bones are bleached by sun and wind. Corpses cannot be cremated because that would contaminate the sacred fire, and cannot be buried because that would contaminate God's pure earth. Death is considered to be the work of Angra Mainyu, the embodiment of all that is evil.[25]

e. A *magus* was a member of the Magi tribe of priestly specialists from ancient Media. They were responsible for religious and funerary practices that included magic and astrology. Later they accepted the Zoroastrian religion, but not without reshaping the original message of its founder.[26] In time, Zoroastrian priests were called *magi*. This is the source for the English word "magic." Zoroastrian priests wear white, the color of purity.

6. *Christian Witness*

a. The Zoroastrian view of God is dualistic. Ahura Mazda has many of the attributes of Jehovah; however, the good god of Zoroastrianism falls short in at least two ways: first, Angra Mainyu, the spirit of evil, appears to be as powerful as Ahura Mazda. This dualism indicates that Ahura Mazda is not really sovereign and omnipotent. Second, Ahura Mazda is not a personal god like the God of the Bible. Worship is centered around ritual forms, not a personal relationship.

b. Salvation is achieved by works, not by faith. If a man's good works outweigh his bad works, he is allowed into heaven. However, the problem of man's sinfulness is never resolved, and heaven will be populated by sinners. Clearly, Ahura Mazda does not possess the burning righteousness of the God of the Bible.

c. The practice of Zoroastrianism involves occultism and superstitions, something explicitly condemned in the Scripture. This is especially true concerning the near worship of the sacred fire. The practice of drinking *haoma*, a hallucinogenic, has become a central rite in Zoroastrian worship.[27]

d. There are only about thirty Parsees who have become born-again Christians, yet there are still possibilities for mission work.[28] Parsees are known for having high rates of cancer, serious eye diseases, and other health problems. UNESCO conducts research and provides treatment to Parsees in India.[29] Similar work by faith-based relief agencies would at least establish a presence among Parsee communities and build meaningful connections with the people. The similarities between Zoroastrian literature and the Bible as well as frequent mention of Zoroastrian Persian kings in the Old Testament make reading the Scriptures attractive to Parsees and opens another door to evangelism.[30]

7. *Glossary of Zoroastrian Terms*

a. Ahura Mazda. The supreme deity, creator of the world, the personification of good.

b. Angra Mainyu or Ahriman. The evil creator, archenemy of Ahura Mazda.

c. *Avesta.* The sacred scriptures of Zoroastrianism.

d. Fire temple. The place where fire worship is carried on. An important practice in present-day Zoroastrianism.

e. Towers of silence. Place where the Zoroastrians dispose of their dead by leaving the bodies partially uncovered to be eaten by vultures. This practice keeps the soil and water from being contaminated with dead flesh.

f. *Yasna.* The most important portion of the *Avesta.*

g. *Zend-Avesta*. A third century A.D. commentary on the Zoroastrian scriptures (Avesta) is known as the *Zend*. The combining of the two is called the *Zend-Avesta*.

Notes

1   B. A. Robinson,, "Zoroastrianism," *Ontario Consultants on Religious Tolerance*, 2005 [article online]; retrieved on March 8, 2006, from http://www.religioustolerance.org/ zoroastr.htm.

2   Masee Rahman, "A Race Nearly Finished," *Time* Asia Edition, March 16, 1998, 25. One of the few surviving *magi* explains: "It's quality, not quantity that matters. What we've doing we've been doing for millennia."

3   "Major Branches of Religions Ranked by Number of Adherents," *Adherents.com*, 2006 [article online]; retrieved on February 20, 2006, from http://www.adherents.com/ adh_branches.html.

4   "Zoroastrian," *Adherents.com*, 2006 [encyclopedia online]; retrieved on March 8, 2006, from http://adherents.com/Na/Na_675.html.

5   "Demographics," UNESCO Assisted Parsi Zoroastrian Project, 2004 [article online]; retrieved on March 9, 2006, from http://www.unescoparzor.com/ project/demographics.htm.

6   Lewis Hopfe, "Zoroastrism," *Religions of the World*, 6th ed., ed. Lavinia R. Hopfe, Jr. (New York: Macmillan, 1994), 246.

7   Kaezad Dadachanjee, "The Parsee: Liberating an Unreached People by Prayer and Fasting," *International Journal of Frontier Missions* Vol. 15:4, Oct-Dec 1998 [article online]; retrieved on March 10, 2006, from http://www.ijfm.org/ PDFs_IJFM/15_4_PDFs/ 03%20The%20Parsee.pdf.

8   Warren Matthews, *World Religions*, 4th ed. (Belmont, CA: Wadsworth Thomas, 2004), 261.

9   Hopfe, "Zoroastrianism," 248-49.

10   Mary Pat Fisher, *Living Religions*, 6th ed. (Upper Saddle River, NJ: Pearson Prentice Hall, 2005), 223.

11   "History of Zoroastrianism," *British Broadcasting Corporation*, 2006 [article online]; retrieved on March 9, 2006, from http://www.bbc.co.uk/print/religion/religions/ zoroastrian/history/index.shtml.

12 Robert E. Van Voorst, *Anthology of World Scriptures*, 5th ed. (Belmont, CA: Thomson Wadsworth, 2006), 188.

13 "Mithraism," *Wikipedia: The Free Encyclopedia*, 2006 [article online]; retrieved on February 15, 2006, from http://en.wikipedia.org/wiki/ Mithraism#Parallels to _Christianity.

14 William Malandra, ed., *An Introduction to Ancient Iranian Religion: Readings from the Avesta and the Achaemenid Inscriptions*, Minnesota Publications in the Humanities (Minneapolis, MN: University of Minnesota Press, 1983), 6.

15 Matthews, *World Religions*, 262.

16 Mary Boyce, *Zoroastrians: Their Religious Beliefs and Practices* (London: Routledge and Gegan Paul, 1979), 21.

17 Gherardo Gnoli, "Zoroastrianism," in *Religions of Antiquity; Religion, History and Culture*, ed. Robert M. Seltzer (New York: Macmillan, 1989), 131.

18 Mary Boyce, trans., "Zarathustra's dualism," *Livius*, 1999-2006 [article online]; retrieved on March 8, 2006, from http://www.livius.org/au-az/avesta/avesta01.html. Another translation available at Van Voorst, *Anthology of World Scriptures*, 193.

19 "The Ancient Middle East," *Geocities* [article online]; retrieved on March 8, 2006, from http://www.geocities.com/Heartland/Estates/6913/mideast.htm.

20 John Hinnells, "The Cosmic Battle: Zoroastrianism," in *Eerdmans' Handbook to the World's Religions* (Grand Rapids: Eerdmans, 1994), 81.

21 Theodore M. Ludwig, *The Sacred Paths: Understanding the Religions of the World*, 4th ed. (Upper Saddle River, NJ: Pearson Prentice Hall, 2006), 335.

22 Fisher, *Living Religions*, 224-25.

23 Dadachanjee, "The Parsee."

24 Fisher, *Living Religions*, 225.

25 "The Towers of Silence," *British Broadcasting Corporation*, 2006 [article online]; retrieved on March 11, 2006, from http://www.bbc.co.uk/religion/religions/ features/parsis/.

26 Ibid.

27   Josh McDowell and Don Stewart, *Handbook of Today's Religions* (Nashville: Thomas Nelson, 1983), 361.

28   Dadachanjee, "The Parsee."

29   "Medical," *UNESCO Assisted Parsi Zoroastrian Project*, 2004 [article online]; retrieved on March 9, 2006, from http://www.unescoparzor.com/project/medical.htm.

30   Dadachanjee, "The Parsee."

CHAPTER 19

Islam

1. *Introduction*

a. In the early twenty-first century about 1.3 billion people (or one in five people in the world) are Muslims. Islam is the second largest religion in the world, trailing only Christianity. Muslims (followers of Islam) are spread primarily over the areas of North Africa, the Middle East, South Central Asia, and Indonesia. Non-Arab Muslims outnumber Arab Muslims by a ratio of almost three to one. The four nations with the largest number of Muslims (2005) are all outside the Middle East:[1]

Indonesia	182,503,000
Pakistan	142,272,000
India	138,188,000
Bangladesh	127,628,000

b. About 99.5% or more of the native populations and nearly all of the foreign workers are Muslim in the following countries: Bahrain, Comoros, Kuwait, Maldives, Mauritania, Mayotte, Morocco, Oman, Qatar, Somalia, Saudi Arabia, Tunisia, United Arab Emirates, Western Sahara, and Yemen.[2]

c. The challenges that the Islamic world presents to the Christian mission demand a basic understanding of Muslim history, beliefs, and practices.

2. *Historical Development*

a. In A.D. 570 Muhammad was born into the Arabian Quraysh tribe, an influential tribe that controlled the city of Mecca. Mecca was important economically because it served as a convenient resting place for trading caravans. It was also important religiously because the *Ka'bah* was located there. The *Ka'bah* was a cubical structure that at the time of Muhammad contained 360 deities. Each Arabian tribe handpicked its own deity and came to Mecca each year to pay homage to its god.[3] Muslims believe that the *Ka'bah* is the first temple to the one God, built by Abraham and Ishmael but later becoming misused by infidels.[4]

b. At the age of 25, he became employed by Khadija, a wealthy widow merchant 15 years older than he. In 595 Muhammad married Khadija in a Christian ceremony performed by Khadija's cousin, Waraqa bin Nawfal.[5]

c. It was the custom of those who were spiritually minded to retreat to a place of solitude once a year. Muhammad observed this practice for several years in a cave at Mount Hira.[6] In the year 610, at age 40, Muhammad reportedly received his first revelation from the angel Gabriel (*Surah* 961-3), marking the beginning of a series of revelations that were eventually compiled into Islam's sacred scripture, the *Qur'an*, which means "recitations." Because Mohammed could not read or write, the *Qur'an* is his reciting of revelations given to him.[7] Muhammad is said to have doubted the origin of these new revelations at first. He thought perhaps he had been possessed by *jinn*, or demons. His wife Khadija, however, reassured him and encouraged him to teach that which had been revealed to him.[8]

d. Muhammad met with only limited success in the 12 years that he preached in Mecca. As he began to preach more publicly, the leaders of his own tribe pressured him to keep quiet about his message of strict monotheism.[9] They viewed Muhammad as a threat to the source of their livelihood, since they benefitted economically from pilgrimages to the *Ka'bah*. Muhammad, however, refused to stop. Three years of preaching yielded fewer than forty converts. However, a decade later there were several hundred families acclaiming him as God's spokesman.[10]

e. In 620 Muhammad told his followers that on a "Night Journey" he had been carried miraculously by Gabriel and a winged horse from Mecca to Jerusalem: "Glory be to He Who carried His servant by night, from the Holy Mosque to the Furthest Mosque" (*Surah* 17:1).[11] According to the "Hadith of the Night Journey and Ascension," there he was welcomed by Moses, Aaron, Enoch, Jesus, John the Baptist and Abraham before ascending through the seven heavens. On that night Muhammad received instructions concerning praying five times a day.[12] Following his divine meeting, Muhammad was flown back to Mecca, arriving there before dawn.[13] Today the building that was built around the rock from which Muhammad is said to have ascended to heaven is known as the Dome of the Rock.[14] The Dome is the third holiest shrine in Islam. It was built on the same rock where Abraham almost sacrificed his son (Ishmael, according to Islam[15]) and where Solomon built the Temple.[16]

f. In 622 the people of Yathrib, a city about 250 miles north of Mecca, invited Muhammad to bring his religious message to their region. They felt that his call to monotheism and his emphasis on tolerance would have a stabilizing influence among the diverse pagan and Jewish faith groups in the city. Persecution increased against the followers of this new religion in Mecca, and eventually around seventy Muslim families were forced to flee to Yathrib.[17] Muhammad followed them shortly thereafter. This event is known as the *Hegira*, which means "a series of migrations." Muslims now look to the year of his flight to Yathrib as the beginning of the Muslim calendar (A.D. 2007 corresponds to A.H. 1428). At that time Yathrib was ruled by a Jewish elite, but soon Muhammad became the city's religious, political, and military leader.[18] At first he attempted to persuade the Jews in Yathrib to attest to his claims. Muhammad required that his followers keep *kosher*, observe the fast of Yom Kippur, become circumcised, and pray facing north toward Jerusalem.[19] When the Jews rejected him and his teachings, Muhammad replaced the Day of Atonement with the Ramadan month of fasting and changed the prayer direction to Mecca.[20] Yathrib was later renamed *Madinat an Nabi* ("City of the Prophet"), in honor of Muhammad, but it is more commonly known as Medina.[21] Over time, Muhammad persecuted the Jews and either drove them out of Medina or killed them. He massacred some eight hundred men by beheading them and enslaved their women and children.[22]

g. While in Medina, there was a substantial change in the tenor of Muhammad's revelations from Allah. His teachings changed from the poetic and apocalyptic to the practical and pragmatic: theological teachings were inseparably mixed with political and military matters.[23] Muhammad began to replace customary law with divine law. He was fully convinced that his decisions were the verdict of Allah himself.[24] Another significant change was his attitude toward non-believers; he became much more antagonistic, even toward the "people of the Book," i.e. Christians and Jews.[25]

h. From 595 to 619 Muhammad had only one wife, Khadijah. After her death he married Aisha, the daughter of Abu Bakr, who later became the first caliph. Aisha was only six years old at the time of the betrothal (a mutual promise to marry). Muhammad married Aisha, after the *Hegira*, when she was nine years old and he was fifty-three.[26] Later he was to marry more wives, for a total of 11 (nine or ten living at the time of his death).[27]

i. After several successful sieges and military victories against Mecca, and after making treaties with the Quraysh tribe, Muhammad and his army took control of Mecca in 630. Without pressing his victory, Muhammad accepted the mass conversion of the city.[28] Upon entering the city, he personally destroyed the idols in the *Ka'bah*; he then returned to Medina. Within a year of Mecca's submission to Muhammad, all the tribes of the Arabian peninsula were united following the prophet. He died suddenly at age 63 on June 8, 632.[29] His tomb is in the Mosque of the Prophet in Medina.[30]

j. Immediately after Muhammad's death Muslims began a wave of religious expansion by means of *jihad*, or holy war. They captured Damascus, 635; Antioch, 636; Jerusalem, 638; Caesarea, 640; Alexandria, 642; Carthage, 697; and Spain, 715. The Muslim armies were finally stopped by Charles Martel in Tours, France, 732.[31] At the same time, Arabs advanced eastward, and by 699 they already occupied Afghanistan. Islam entered Punjab in India and advanced far into Central Asia. Islam was introduced in Indonesia along the coast by Muslim traders from India.[32]

k. Pope Urban II launched the Crusades in 1095. The Crusades could be described as a "Christian *jihad*." Jerusalem was captured in 1099, followed by a massacre of 70,000 Muslims. However, Muslims soon recaptured Jerusalem. There were seven crusades against Muslims between 1095 and 1272.[33] They caused major damage to the Christian cause.

l. There was a second tide of Muslim expansion over Europe during the fifteen century, when Ottoman Turks invaded Greece and the Balkans. Constantinople, the imperial capital, fell in 1453. Muslims were stopped in Vienna, Austria, in 1683.[34] After a period of decline due to European colonialism,[35] Islam is now experiencing a new wave of expansion. The revival is due to the impact of petrodollars, the presence of young Islamic nations as a result of wars of independence, and immigration into western countries.

3. *The Qur'an*

a. Allah sent revelation through Gabriel to Muhammad over a period of 25 years. Compiled, these revelations have become the *Qur'an*. According to Muslims, the *Qur'an* was dictated; thus it is considered to be the inerrant word of Allah, and is only completely accurate as such in the Arabic language.[36] The *Qur'an* itself, however, was not written by Muhammad. The *Qur'an* suggests that Muhammad was illiterate (*Surah* 7:157). His followers memorized the words that Muhammad said while in trance and recorded his words on bark, bones, leaves, and scraps of parchment.[37] The fourth Caliph, 'Ali ibn Abi Talib, compiled the *Qur'an* based on oral accounts of what Muhammad said when he was originally proclaiming the messages he had received.[38] Tradition says that the task was completed around 650.[39]

b. The *Qur'an* is comprised of 114 *surahs*, or chapters. The *surahs* are arranged in the *Qur'an* by length—longer chapters in front, shorter in back.[40] Each *surah* is known by a name rather than a number; these are usually taken from a key word in the *surah*. For instance, "Night," "The Cow," and "Unity" are names of *surahs*[41] The *Qur'an* is about four-fifths the length of the New Testament. It makes reference to many Bible stories, such as those of Moses and Abraham, but it does not offer a sustained narrative. It has a lot to say about morals and conduct, but it does not have a moral code, as the Bible offers in Exodus 20.[42]

c. The *Qur'an* is part of the everyday life of all devout Muslims. When a baby is born, the father will repeat words from the *Qur'an* in his ear. Verses are read at marriage ceremonies. At funerals, sections of the *Qur'an* are recited.[43] "Its language sets the standards for determining grammatical rules in Arabic. Its guidelines are used as the basic laws in Muslim societies. Artists paint its verses on buildings with an elaborate calligraphy. Ordinary people pattern their speech and their behavior after it."[44]

4. *The Sects of Islam*

a. It is said that there are 73 sects of Islam.[45] The two major sects of Islam, Sunni and Shi'a, were originally divided over a dispute as to who should serve as the first *Caliph*, or successor, to Muhammad. Since Muhammad failed to appoint one before his death, Sunni Muslims insisted that Muhammad's successor should be elected. Shi'a Muslims (also known as "Shi'ites") thought he should come through Muhammad's bloodline, which would have meant Ali—Muhammad's cousin and son-in-law (married to Muhammad's daughter,

Fatima) would be the first Caliph. The killing of Ali's son, Husayn, in 680 was a major event in the development of Shi'ism.[46] *Sunnah* means "well-trodden path," or "tradition," so *Sunnis* are "traditionalists." *Shi'ites,* or *Shi'a,* means "partisans" of Ali.[47] Additionally, they differ in these areas:

1) Extension: Sunnis comprise 80% of all Muslims (about 940 million in 2000), while Shi'ites comprise 16% (about 120 million) and are found mostly in Iran, Iraq, and Yemen.[48]

2) Prayers: Sunnis say their prayers five times a day; Shi'ites pray three times daily, having combined some of the prayer times.

3) Source of authority: Sunnis emphasize the authority of the written traditions, which include not only the *Qur'an* but also the *Sunnah* (Muhammad's non-Qur'anic actions), *Hadith* (Muhammad's non-Qur'anic sayings), and the principles that the *ulama* (religious scholars) arrived at by consensus based on traditions.[49] Shi'ites believe that God spoke through an *Imam,* the Muslim equivalent of the Catholic pope. In the ninth century, however, the twelfth *Imam* became hidden,[50] and the source of authority was passed on to the *ulama.* They considered themselves collectively to be the general representatives of the twelfth *Imam,* called the *Mahdi.* Shi'ites are still waiting for the return of the twelveth *Imam.* This belief is similar to the way Christians look for the return of Christ.

4) The relationship between state and religion: Sunnis believe there should be a separation between civil and religious authorities. Shi'ites maintain that the religious authorities should also exercise political power.

5) Identification of holy cities: Both sects recognize Mecca and Medina, but Shi'ites add Najaf and Karbala.

b. Sufism is the esoteric, ascetic, and mystical third wing of Islam. The goal of the Sufi's quest is union with the Divine, where the believer must renounce worldly attachments, see only God in all things, and attain assimilation of the self into the vast Being of God. They long for the One.[51] Most Sufis reach religious ecstasy by repeating the name Allah over and over again and use jerking of their heads and bodies; Turkish *dervishes* attain it in a "whirling dance."[52] Sufism is essentially pantheistic.[53] "Muslim mystics do not abandon Islam's theological foundations. Most of them cling to Islam's five pillars, but apply them through the sieve of mystical experiences."[54] The mystics' spiritual leaders are commonly called "*sheikhs.*" About 70 percent of all Muslims are being influenced by Sufism in one form or another. Consequently, "there are more than 600 million Muslims who teach and practice forms of Islam [that] place unorthodox experience over orthodox theology."[55]

c. There are also several minor Muslim sects. As is true with all major religions, there are adherents within all branches of Islam who consider some of or all of the other branches to not actually be part of their religion. Some of the Islamic sects are:

1) The Wahhabis: located primarily in Saudi Arabia. Its founder, Muhammad ibn Abd al-Wahhab (1703-92), believed Islam should return to its seventeenth-century form.[56] This radical reform movement controls the *Hijaz*, the region that contains Mecca and Medina, and the great wealth generated by the Saudi Arabian oil fields. The Wahhabis, therefore, enjoy a great deal of prestige within the Islamic community. Wahhabism has fostered a great number of terrorist organizations throughout the world.[57]

2) The Druze: located primarily in Lebanon, Syria, and northern Israel. In contrast to other Muslims, Jews, and Christians, Druze elevate Jethro, the father-in-law of Moses, to the status of major prophet. They also believe in the wisdom of classical Greek philosophers such as Plato. They do not emphasize individual prayer. They are not required to follow the Muslim duties of prayer and fasting, nor do they have to make a pilgrimage to Mecca.[58]

3) The Ahmadiyyas: located primarily in Pakistan. Ahmadiyya Islam was founded in 1889 by Mirza Ghulam Ahmad (c. 1839-1908) in Qadian, Punjab, India. Ahmad claimed to be the appearance of the Promised Messiah (or, according to some sources, a reappearance of the Prophet Muhammad) as well as an incarnation of the Hindu god Krishna. Ghulam Ahmad taught that Jesus feigned his crucifixion and resurrection, then lived to be 120 years old in India. This contradicts the orthodox Muslim doctrine that Jesus was taken up into heaven before his death. By 2000 there were about one hundred seventy million Ahmadiyya Muslims in the world.[59]

4) The Nation of Islam: based in the U.S. and previously known as "Black Muslims." Wallace Fard Mohammed formed the Nation of Islam in Detroit in 1930. Sometime after 1935, Elijah Mohammed assumed leadership of the movement. Elijah taught that a mad black scientist had created whites, who would rule the earth for six thousand years–that period ended in 1914. In the 1950s and 1960s, Malcolm X began moving away from Elijah Mohammed's positions and teachings. He challenged the leadership of Elijah Mohammed and was eventually assassinated by Black Muslims in 1965. The Nation of Islam grew rapidly in the 1960s and 1970s. When Elijah Mohammed died in 1975, his

son, Wallace D. Mohammed, took over and relaxed the strict discipline of the movement, which caused the movement to lose momentum. Louis Farrakhan (born 1933) resurrected the Nation of Islam in 1978 and reclaimed the heritage and principles of black separatism.[60]

5. *The Six Articles of Faith*

Aamanto billaahi wa malaa-ikatihi was kotobihi was rosolihi wal yaomil aakhir wal qadha-I wal qadri khairibi was sharrihi minallaahi ta'aala.

I believe in Allah and His angels, and His books, and His messengers, and the Day of Judgment, and His power over good and evil.[61]

a. The Oneness of Allah. The central doctrine of Islam is that God is one and that no partner is to be associated with him. To associate a partner with God is to commit the sin of *ishrak*, or blasphemy, for which the *Qur'an* offers no forgiveness (*Surah* 4:48, 116; 31:13). Thus, Muslims reject Christian claims about the divinity of Jesus and the doctrine of the Trinity. They use rosary beads to remind themselves of Allah, to aid in prayer as a talisman to indicate the rightness or wrongness of an action, and even as a magical agency for healing. It has 99 beads or three sets of 33, each representing one of the beautiful names of Allah.[62]

b. Angels. In the gap between the God of the *Qur'an* and humankind exists a hierarchy of angels. Each person has two angels assigned to him or her, one to record the person's good deeds and the other to record the bad deeds. At the bottom of the hierarchy are the *jinn*, from which we get the English word "genie." Muslims believe that the host of *jinn* were created from fire (*Surah* 55:14), are usually bad, and are able to possess people.[63] There are four archangels. The archangel Jibreel (Gabriel) is the highest ranking, succeeded by the rest of the angels. Jibreel is the transmitter of the revelations of Allah, Mikaeel is the guardian of the physical world, Israfeel is the caretaker of books of records, and Israeel is the angel of death.[64]

c. Holy Books. Four of the high-ranking prophets were given books of divine revelation. Moses was given the *Tawrat* (*Torah*), David was given the *Zabur* (Psalms), Jesus was given the *Injil* (Gospel), and Muhammad was given the *Qur'an*. Of those four books, Muslims contend that only the *Qur'an* has been preserved in an uncorrupted state.[65]

d. Prophets. According to the *Qur'an*, God has sent a prophet to every nation to preach the message of the one God. In all, 124,000 prophets have been sent, according to tradition.[66] Of these, 313 are called apostles, 8 are *rasuls* (those having a separate people for whom they are responsible), 6 are lawgivers, and 6 have special qualities. There are 28 prophets mentioned by name in the *Qur'an*.[67] Six are the most important:[68]

Adam	the chosen of God
Noah (*Nooh*)	the preacher of God
Abraham (*Ibrahim*)	the friend of God
Moses (*Moosa*)	the speaker of God
Jesus (*Isa*)	the word of God
Muhammad	the apostle of God

Although Muslims reject the divinity of Jesus and His death on the cross, they believe that He was a prophet of Allah and affirm the virgin birth as well as the miracles He performed. Each of the prophets was given a particular age, but Muhammad is the only prophet who is for all time. He is considered to be the "Seal of the Prophets."[69]

e. Predestination. For Muslims, one can enter into Allah's favor through repentance alone. No atonement for sin is necessary. This makes Islam a fundamentally works-oriented religion.[70] Muslim believe in the decrees of God–everything is foreordained by the unchangeable will of Allah. Allah is even the author of evil (*Surah* 45:7). Muslims are fatalists; their fatalism has contributed to the lethargy and lack of progress which until recently has characterized Muslim societies for centuries.[71]

f. Day of Judgment. Those whose bad deeds outweigh their good deeds will be damned in a fiery torment, but those whose good deeds outweigh the bad will be rewarded with paradise. Since this is a subjective matter, a Muslim has no assurance that he or she will be accepted by God. There will be a day of resurrection and separation. Both the *Qur'an* and subsequent Muslim literature contain the most graphic descriptions of the terrors of hell and the pleasures of paradise.[72]

6. "The Five Pillars," or the Obligations of Islam

Without distinction of sects, all Muslims are committed to the following practices:[73]

a. To recite the *shehadah*: *"Ashadu anna la ilaha illa 'l-Lah, wa anna Muhammadan rasulu 'l-Lah"* ("I bear witness that there is no God but Allah and that Muhammad is his messenger"). The word *shehadah* means "to bear witness." Saying the *shehadah* with sincerity is all it takes to become a Muslim.[74] The average Muslim will repeat the *shehadah* twenty times a day, as it is foremost among religious duties.[75]

b. To pray (*salat*). Prayers are not considered to be an informal, relational dialogue and communion with God as in Christianity. Prayer consists of repetition in Arabic of selected portions of the *Qur'an* which have been committed to memory, and prescribed stances, genuflexions, and prostrations. Prayers differ slightly between the schools of Islam. After ceremonial washing, or ablutions, the worshiper turns and faces Mecca to offer prayer.[76] Sunnis pray five times a day: at dawn, noon, late afternoon, sunset, and one hour after dark, while Shi'ites pray three times a day. The noon service on Friday is the only time when Muslims are expected to gather at the mosque.

c. To fast (*sawm*). In commemoration of Muhammad's receiving the *Qur'an* during the ninth lunar month of *Ramadan*, Muslims are expected to fast during the daylight hours that month. The *Qur'an* indicates that the fast should begin when the light from the rising sun is sufficient to distinguish between a black thread and a white thread (*Surah* 2:187). During the fast they must abstain from eating, drinking, smoking, and sexual relations. After sundown, Muslims are allowed to partake of all those things until sunrise. The fundamental intention of the fasting is to focus one's attention on Allah. During *Ramadan* there is time for reflection, reconciliation is encouraged, and community solidarity is stressed.[77]

d. To give alms (*zakat*). Muslims are expected to give one-fortieth (2.5 percent) of their income to the poor and needy–this varies from country to country. The believer gains merit and often gives alms in relation to a return from a trip, during feasts, or at a new birth. In most cases the money is collected and distributed by the state.[78] The *zakat* provides a way of purification of the soul and means to atone for sins caused by self-interest or irresponsible stewardship of possessions.[79] The *Qur'an* directs that "people of the Book" who live in Islamic countries may be allowed to practice their faith as long as they submit to Muslim rule and pay a tribute tax. However, *zakat* and tribute tax are not to be confused.[80]

e. To make the pilgrimage (*hajj*). Every Muslim must make the trip to Mecca at least once during his or her lifetime, provided he or she is able with respect to health and finances. Each pilgrim must wear the white garments called *ihram*, which eliminate all class or status distinctions during the *hajj*. The process of visiting several sacred sites usually takes more than a week, and sometimes even a month. It can be grueling at times, as pilgrims stand and pray for an entire day under the sun in a certain open field. At Mecca, events in Muhammad's life are reenacted, there are animal sacrifices, and the pilgrims walk seven times around the *Ka'bah* which houses the Black Stone (possibly a meteorite). Pilgrims drink from the sacred well and commemorate the flight of Hagar and her son Ishmael.[81]

7. *Muslim Practices*

a. The mosque is the place of worship for the Muslim and also a center for Muslim cultural life. Ideally, prayers should be offered at the mosque five times a day; if it is not convenient, Muslims create a sacred space around them by praying on a mat. All Muslims are required to attend a special service in the mosque on Friday at 11:00 a.m. Some historians claim that Friday was chosen in opposition to the Jewish Sabbath as a reaction against the Medinese Jews who rejected Muhammad and his message.[82] Women are allowed to attend, but they must sit separately from men—usually in the back or in a side room.[83]

b. Marriages are usually arranged. After Muhammad's first wife died, he married Aisha when she was six years old, and consummated his marriage when she was nine and he was fifty-three.[84]

c. Perhaps one of the most controversial issues facing Muslim women today is the wearing of the veil, or *hijab*. The *Qur'an* only says that women should "draw their cloaks closely around them when they go outside their home" (*Surah* 33:59). Some oppose the full covering of women, while others support the enforcement of its use out of modesty.[85]

d. According to *Surah* 4:34, under certain circumstances the husband may strike his wife. Muslim scholars have set limitations on how he may do so, including that he must hit her in a way that is "non-violent" and must not break bones, leave bruises, or cause blood to flow.[86]

e. Islam is the only world religion that specifically approves polygamy. According to the *Qur'an*, Allah revealed to Muhammad that men are allowed to take up to four wives (*Surah* 4:3); however, Muhammad was the only human that he allowed to have an unlimited number of wives (*Surah* 33:50-53). Muhammad had nine or ten wives at the time of his death.[87]

f. Circumcision is obligatory for all Muslim boys. The age varies from region to region; in some cases it is performed between the ages of ten and twelve. Circumcision is traditionally accompanied by some kind of celebration, including music and feasting. It is not mentioned in the *Qur'an*, but recommended in the *Hadith* (collection of Muhammad's sayings). Female circumcision, in the form of cutting away all or part of the clitoris, is also widely practiced on girls, although not as an Islamic obligation.[88]

g. The most important festivals celebrated by Muslims include *Id al-Fitr*, "The Feast of Fast Breaking," at the end of Ramadan and *Id ul-Adha*, "The Feast of the Sacrifice," on the tenth day of the last Muslim month to commemorate Abraham's willingness to sacrifice his son Ishmael by sacrificing a goat. Shi'ites add *Muharram* on the tenth day of the first month of the Muslim year to commemorate the martyrdom of Hazrat Imam Hussain, Muhammad's grandson, at Karbala, Iraq.[89]

h. As a Muslim approaches death, he is encouraged to repeat the *Shehadah*. The dead person's feet must be turned to Mecca. Coffins are seldom used. The dead are buried in a white shroud. The burial takes place on the same day of death, lest the angels that enquire about his earthly deeds be kept waiting.[90]

i. The crescent moon and star is an internationally-recognized symbol of the faith of Islam. The symbol is featured on the flags of several Muslim countries, and is even part of the official emblem for the International Federation of Red Cross and Red Crescent Societies. The origin of the crescent has been traced to pre-Islamic times. Many evidences indicate that *al-ilah* ("the god") was the generic name for the pagan moon god, Hubal, in Arabia.[91]

j. A *muezzin* is a believer who calls from a minaret (a tower used for the call to prayer). His call is:

> God is most great. God is most great.
> I testify that there is no god but God.
> I testify that Muhammad is the Prophet of God.
> Arise and pray;
> God is most great. God is most great,
> There is no god but God.

8. *Islam and Violence*

a. In the aftermath of September 11, 2001, and given the fact that Osama bin Laden, the al-Qaeda organization, and the 9/11 terrorists call themselves

Muslims, questions have arisen about the relationship of Islam to politics, violence, and terror. The world has become familiar with the Arabic word *jihad.*

> *Jihad,* in Islam, [is] the struggle to please God. *Jihad* is the duty of all mainstream Muslims, who belong to the branch known as Sunni Islam. There are four ways they may fulfill a *jihad*: by the heart, by the tongue, by the hand, and by the sword. The first refers to the inner, spiritual battle of the heart against vice, passion, and ignorance. The second is speaking the truth and spreading the word of Islam with one's tongue. The third way involves choosing to do what is right and to combat injustice and wrongdoing. The fourth way refers to defending Islam and waging war against its enemies with the sword.[92]

b. The following are only some of the verses in the *Qur'an* that can and have been used in the history of Islam in support of violence in the name of God. "Fight and slay the pagans wherever ye find them, and seize them, beleaguer them, and lie in wait for them in every stratagem (of war)" (*Surah* 9:5). "Fight them, and God will punish them by your hands, cover them with shame" (9:14). "Fight those who believe not in God nor the Last Day nor hold that forbidden which hath been forbidden by God and his apostle nor acknowledge the Religion of Truth (even if they are) of the people of the Book, until they pay the Jizya [religious tax] with willing submission, and feel themselves subdued" (9:29). Unlike the divine commands to destroy infidels found in the Old Testament that were specific to a time, place, and people group, Orthodox Muslims believe that the Qur'anic commands are universal and thus applicable for all times and places.

c. Some Muslims argue that "actual armed *jihad* is permissible under two conditions alone: one is for self-defense, and the other is for fighting against oppression."[93] However, many Orthodox Muslims believe that if nations' leaders do not acknowledge the rule of Islam, then those rulers are "oppressors" and thus a legitimate target for war. So, extremist Muslims find scriptural basis for their actions.[94] *Jihad* in the form of extremism, as well as wars of conquest in the past and wars of independence in the present, are Muslim ways of being missionary and fulfilling Allah's will.[95]

9. *Glossary of Muslim Terms*

a. A.H. ("After Hejira"). Islamic dating of years, beginning with Muhammad's flight to Medina in 622. The year 2000 A.D. corresponds with the year A.H. 1420.

b. *Allah*. The Arabic word for "God." Allah is not God's name. Allah is the one true God.

c. *Basmala*. The *Bismi'llah* saying, "in the Name of Allah," that invokes a blessing upon an action or undertaking of a Muslim.

d. Caliph, *Khalif*, "deputy, successor." A political leader of the Muslim community. The most important of these were the four Rightly-Guided Caliphs who ruled after the death of Muhammad.

e. Five Pillars. The five primary duties of every Muslim: profession of faith (*shahada*), ritual prayer (*salat*), fasting during Ramadan (*sawm*), pilgrimage to Mecca (*hajj*), and charity (*zakat*). Fulfillment of these duties brings rewards on earth and in the afterlife.

f. *Hajj*, "pilgrimage." Pilgrimage to Mecca required of every able Muslim at least once during his or her life. One of the Five Pillars of Islam.

g. *Hejira*. The Prophet's flight to Medina in 622, marking the beginning of the Muslim calendar.

h. Feast of the Sacrifice, *Id al-Adha*. Holiday marking the end of the *hajj*.

i. Feast of the Breaking of the Fast, *'Id al-Fitr*. Holiday celebrated at the end of the month of Ramadan.

j. *Ihram*. White cloth wound around the body during the *hajj*.

k. Ishmael. Son of Jewish patriarch, Abraham, and the maidservant, Hagar (Genesis 16). According to both Jewish and Islamic tradition, he is the ancestor of the Arabs.

l. *Islam*, "to surrender." To surrender to the will of God; the name of the religion founded by Muhammad.

m. *Jihad*, "striving." Holy war; the defense of Islam against its enemies. Sufism focuses on the "greater" *jihad* against sin in oneself.

n. *Jinn* (from *junna*, "to be mad, furious, possessed"; singular *jinni* or genie). Shape-shifting fiery spirits, especially associated with the desert. Belief in *jinn* predates Islam, where they were widely believed to be the inspiration of poets and seers. In Islam, they are spiritual beings inferior to angels and devils. who will face salvation or damnation along with humans.

o. *Ka'bah*. Cube-shaped monument in Mecca containing a sacred black stone. All Muslims pray facing the direction of the *Ka'bah*.

p. Pbuh - "Peace be upon him." Used after the name of the Prophet Muhammad (pbuh) to indicate one's respect (also used after the names of other prophets). ·

q. People of the Book. Muhammad's designation for Jews and Christians, and sometimes Zoroastrians and Hindus. Because their religions featured scriptures and some aspect of divine revelation, they were not required to convert. However, they were required to pay a special tax (the *jizya*) for the privilege.

r. *Qur'an*, "recitation." The sacred text of Islam, revealed to Muhammad over a 20-year period by the Angel Gabriel.

s. Ramadan. The ninth month in the Islamic calendar, for the duration of which Muslims fast during the daylight hours to commemorate the giving of the *Qur'an*. It is a time for spiritual reflection, prayer, doing good deeds, charity, and spending time with loved ones. The Islamic years consists of 354 days. As a result, Ramadan occurs about eleven days earlier each year, and it rotates through the seasons in a cycle totaling about thirty-three years. For example, the following dates are set for the beginning of Ramadan: September 24, 2006; September 13, 2007; September 2, 2008; August 22, 2009. *Eid ul-Fitr* ("feast of the breaking of the fast") is a time for festivities and merriment at the end of the month.

t. *Salat* (also *salaat, salaah, salah*), "prayer." Ritual prayer performed three times (Shi'ites) or five times (Sunnis) per day facing the direction of Mecca. One of the Five Pillars of Islam.

u. *Shehada*, "testimony" or "witness." The profession of faith that "There is no god but God, and Muhammad is the prophet of God," which is the only requirement for joining the Muslim community. As one of the Five Pillars of Islam, it must be spoken aloud with full understanding and faith at least once in one's lifetime. It is also included in the call to prayer, most ritual prayers, and is recited at death.

v. *Sharia*. Islamic law, both political and religious.

w. *Sunnah*, "tradition." Record of the words and deeds of the Prophet. While not the Word of God on a level with the *Qur'an*, the *Sunnah* is regarded as inspired and authoritative.

x. *Surah*. A chapter of the *Qur'an*.

Notes

1   "Islam," *Adherents.com*, 2006 [article online]; retrieved on March 7, 2006, from http://www.adherents.com.

2   "Muslims: The Facts," *New Internationalist*, 2002 [article online]; retrieved on March 2, 2006, from http://www.newint.org/issue345/facts.htm.

3   "Kaaba," *Wikipedia, the Free Encyclopedia*, 2006 [article online]; retrieved on March 6, 2006, from http://en.wikipedia.org/wiki/Kaaba.

4   Mohammed Ovey, *Muslim-Christian Relations: Past, Present, and Future* (Maryknoll, NY: Orbis Books, 1999), 31.

5   "Muhammad," *Good News for the Crescent World* [article online]; retrieved on March 4, 2006, from http://gnfcw.org/.

6   T. J. Winter and John A. Williams, *Understanding Islam and the Muslims* (Louisville, KY: Fons Vitae, 2002), 7.

7   "Islam," *Refuge Outreach*, 2005 [article online]; retrieved on March 7, 2006, from http://www.refuge-outreach.org/religions/islam.htm.

8   Huston Smith, *Islam: A Concise Introduction* (New York: HarperSan Francisco, 2001), 12.

9   James A. Beverly, *Understanding Islam* (Nashville: Tomas Nelson, 2001).

10 Smith, *Islam: A Concise Introduction*, 14-16.

11 It should be noted, however, that by 620 the Jerusalem Temple was completely destroyed, that in all Palestine there was no mosque, and that the first mosque in Jerusalem was built in 691. Some interpret this as a proof that Muslims added stories to the Qur'anic text. Sam Shamoun, "Muhammad's Alleged Night Journey to the Jerusalem Temple," *Answering Islam*, 1999-2006 [article online]; retrieved on March 9, 2006, from http://www.answering-islam.org/Shamoun/ nightjourney.htm.

12 "Hadith of the Night Journey and Ascension," *Noble Sanctuary* [document online]; retrieved on March 7, 2006, from http://www.noblesanctuary.com/miraj.html.

13 The ascension lasted between three and four hours. Hajjah Amina Adil, *Muhammad: The Messenger of Islam* (Washington, DC: Islamic Supreme Council of America, 2002), 265-66. This book dedicates 120 pages describing what happened during the Journey.

14 To the eyes of pious Muslims, the rock still has the visible mark of Muhammad's footprint. Daniel Brown, *A New Introduction to Islam* (Malden, MA: Blackwell Publishing, 2004), 44.

15 Muhammad Ghoniem and M. S. M. Saifullah, "The Sacrifice of Abraham: Isaac or Ishmael," *Islamic Awareness* [article online]; retrieved on March 16, 2006, from http://www.islamic-awareness.org/Quran/Contrad/MusTrad/sacrifice.html. It should be noticed that *Surah* 37:99-109 does not specify who was the son.

16 Walid Khalidi, "The Dome of the Rock," *Saudi Aramco World*, 1996 [article online]; retrieved on March 8, 2006, from http://www.saudiaramcoworld.com/issue/ 199605/the.dome.of.the.rock.htm.

17 Smith, *Islam: A Concise Introduction*, 18.

18 Ignaz Goldziher, *Introduction to Islamic Theology and Law* (Princeton, NJ: Princeton University Press, 1981), 8.

19 Joseph E. Katz, "The Prophet Muhammad, a Jewish Pseudo-Messiah," *Eretz Yisroel*, 2001 [article online]; retrieved on March 12, 2006, from http://www.eretzyisroel.org/ ~jkatz/theprophet.html.

20 William M. Miller, *A Christian Response to Islam* (Phillipsburg, NJ: Presbyterian & Reformed, 1976), 27.

21 "Islam," *Refuge Outreach*.

22 "What Really Happened with the Banu Qurayza?" *Answering Islam*, 2006 [article online]; retrieved on March 12, 2006, from http://answering-islam.org.uk/ Muhammad/Jews/ BQurayza/banu3.html.

23 Bernard Lewis, *The Crisis of Islam: Holy War and Unholy Terror* (New York: Modern Library, Random House, 2003), 10-11.

24 E. Bethmann, *Bridge to Islam* (Nashville: Southern Publishing Assn., 1950), 3.

25 Passages from the Meccan period urged his followers to live peacefully with people of other beliefs, especially other monotheists (*Surahs* 2:256; 15:94; 16-125-28). Passages from the Medinese period demand that Muslims fight against anyone who might "threaten the faith" (*Surahs* 3:23; 4:95; 8:72; 9:5, 81, 88; 47:33-35).

26 Phil Parshall and Julie Parshall, *Lifting the Veil: The World of Muslim Women* (Waynesboro, GA: Authentic Media, 2002), 30.

27 "Muhammad's marriages," *Wikipedia, the Free Encyclopedia*, 2006 [article online]; retrieved on March 10, 2006, from http://en.wikipedia.org/wiki/ Muhammad%27s_marriages.

28 Smith, *Islam: A Concise Introduction*, 21.

29 J. Bloom and B. Sheila, *Islam: A Thousand Years of Faith and Power* (London: Yale University Press, 2002), 30-31.

30 "Medina: General Information," *Believe* [article online]; retrieved on March 15, 2006, from http://mb-soft.com/believe/txh/medina.htm.

31 Interestingly, with the exception of Spain, all of the nations that became Islamic during this time still maintain a Muslim majority today.

32 Denise Carmody and T. L. Brink, *Ways to the Center: An Introduction to World Religions*, 6th ed. (Belmont, CA: Thomson Wadsworth, 2006), 304-8.

33 "Crusade," *Wikipedia, the Free Encyclopedia*, 2006 [article online]; retrieved on March 8, 2006, from http://en.wikipedia.org/wiki/Crusades.

34 Roger Schmidt, Gene C. Sager, Gerald T. Carney, Albert C. Muller, Kenneth J. Zanca, Julius J. Jackson, Jr., C. Wayne Mayhall, and Jeffrey C. Burke, *Patterns of Religion*, 2nd ed. (Belmont, CA: Wadsworth, 2005), 418.

35 William A. Young, *The World's Religions: Worldviews and Contemporary Issues* (Upper Saddle River, NJ: Pearson Prentice Hall, 2005), 221.

36 Goldziher, *Introduction to Islamic Theology and Law*, 105.

37 Smith, *Islam: A Concise Introduction*, 26.

38   Steven Emerson, *American Jihad: The Terrorists Living Among Us* (New York: The Free Press, 2002), 222.

39   Michael Cook, *The Koran: A Very Short Introduction* (New York: Oxford University Press, 2000), 6.

40   With the exception of the short first *surah*, the Qur'an begins with the longest *surah* and ends with the shortest one. Thus *Surah* Two has 286 verses, *Surah* Three has 200, down to *Surah* One Hundred Fourteen, which has only six.

41   Young, *The World's Religions: Worldviews and Contemporary Issues*, 218-19.

42   Cook, *The Koran: A Very Short Introduction*, 6.

43   Seyyed Hossein Nasr, *The Heart of Islam* (New York: HarperCollins, 2002), 22-26.

44   Young, *The World's Religions: Worldviews and Contemporary Issues*, 219.

45   Bill Musk, *The Unseen Face of Islam: Sharing the Gospel with Ordinary Muslims*, Foreword by Lord Coogan (Speldhurst, England: Evangelical Missionary Alliance, 1984), 281.

46   Goldziher, *Introduction to Islamic Theology and Law*, 174-76.

47   "Comparison of Islamic Sects," *Religion Facts*, 2004-2006 [article online]; retrieved on March 8, 2006, from www.religionfacts.com/bahai/symbols.htm.

48   Dore Gold, *Hatred's Kingdom* (Washington, DC: Regnery, 2003), 20.

49   Goldziher, *Introduction to Islamic Theology and Law*, 37.

50   The different branches of Shi'ism are identified in terms of which successor became hidden. There are "Sevener" Shi'ites, who believe that their seventh *imam* became hidden, and "Twelver" Shi'ites, whose twelfth successor received that distinction. Goldziher, *Introduction to Islamic Theology and Law*, 192-93.

51   Mary Pat Fisher, *Living Religions*, 6th ed. (Upper Saddle River, NJ: Pearson Prentice Hall, 2005), 388-92.

52   "Dervish," *Wikipedia, the Free Encyclopedia*, 2006 [article online]; retrieved on March 16, 2006, from http://en.wikipedia.org/wiki/Dervish.

53   "In his spiritual journey, the Sufi passes through three distinct conceptions of the Absolute Being. At first the simple creed, 'There is no god but Allah,' implies three things: there is no agent but Allah, there is no object of worship save Allah, and there is no existence save Allah. In the second phase the creed takes the form, 'There is no god but Thou.' In the final stage the creed becomes 'There is no god but I.' This is the final goal of the Sufi's journey along the Path." L. Bevan Jones, *The People of the Mosque* (Calcutta: YMCA Publishing House, 1939), 156.

54 Ken Peters, "Touching the Mystical Heart of Islam," *Evangelical Missions Quarterly*, October 1989 [online edition]; retrieved on June 24, 2006, from https://bgc.gospelcom.net/emqonline/emq_article_read.php?ArticleID=3263.

55 Ibid.

56 John L. Esposito, *Islam: The Straight Path*, rev. 3rd ed. (New York: Oxford University Press, 2005), 118-19.

57 Stephen Schwartz goes as far as to say, "Not all Muslims are suicide bombers, but all Muslim suicide bombers are Wahhabis," with a few exceptions. "Ground Zero and the Saudi Connection," *Spectator* [article online]; retrieved on March 2, 2006, from http://cresentlife.com/heal%2othe%2oworld/ground_zero_and_the_saudi_connection.htm. Although this statement may not be absolutely correct, it is a useful generalization in that it illustrates the dominant role of Wahhabism in the formation of Islamic terrorist organizations. They even hate their own leaders, whom they believe to have abandoned the tenets of their faith. Michael Scott Doran, "The Saudi Paradox," *Foreign Affairs*, January/February 2004, Vol. 83, No. 1 [article online]; retrieved on March 5, 2006, from http://www.foreignaffairs.org/20040101faessay93105/michael-scottt-doran/the-saudi-paradox.html.

58 "Druze," *Wikipedia, the Free Encyclopedia*, 2006 [article online]; retrieved on March 5, 2006, from http://en.wikipedia.org/wiki/Druze.

59 "Islamic Denominations and Sects," *Religion Facts*, 2004-2006 [article online]; retrieved on March 8, 2006, from http://www.religionfacts.com/islam/sects.htm.

60 Steven Tsoukalas, *The Nation of Islam* (Phillipsburg, NJ: P. & R. Publishing, 2001); Edward E. Curtis, *Islam in Black America* (New York: State University of New York Press, 2002); Mother Tynetta Muhammad, "A Brief History of the Origin of the Nation of Islam in America: A Nation of Peace," *Nation of Islam*, 1996 [article online]; retrieved on March 7, 2006, from http:/www.noi.org/history-of-noi.html.

61 Moh'd Ali Laguindab, *Handbook on Salah: Prayers in Islam* (Marawi City, Philippines: Djamla, 1996), 4-14.

62 J. Christy Wilson, *Introducing Islam* (New York: Friendship Press, n.d.), 21.

63 Musk, *The Unseen Face of Islam: Sharing the Gospel with Ordinary Muslims*, 38.

64 Laguindab, *Handbook of Salah: Prayers in Islam*, 6.

65 Ahmad S. Dallal, "Islam," *Microsoft Encarta Encyclopedia 2000* [digital media] (Redmond, WA: Microsoft Corporation, 1999). Christy Wilson, "The Qur'an," in *Eerdmans' Handbook to the World's Religions* (Grand Rapids: Eerdmans, 1994), 319.

66 Some count 248,000, and still others are unsure as to how many prophets have been sent to men. Sir Norman Anderson, "Islam," in *The World's Religions*, ed. Sir Norman Anderson (Grand Rapids: Eerdmans, 1989), 116-17.

67 Phil Parshall, *Muslim Evangelism: Contemporary Approaches to Contextualization* (Waynesboro, GA: Gabriel Publishing, 2003), 150.

68 Laguindab, *Handbook of Salah: Prayers in Islam*, 9.

69 Dallal, "Islam."

70 Iskander Jadeed, "Sin and Atonement in Islam and Christianity," *The Good Way* [article online]; retrieved on March 145, 2006, from http://www.the-good-way.com/eng/ article/a09.htm.

71 Anderson, "Islam," 118.

72 Smith, *The World's Religions*, 241. Even though the *Qur'an* speaks of women in Paradise (*Surah* 9:72), there is very little written about their state of being. The *Qur'an* speaks a lot about *houris*: fair-skinned, newly created virgins, with wide, lovely eyes (*Surah* 56:22-23; 56:35-37; 52:17-20; 44:51-54), waiting for all faithful Muslim men, closely guarded in pavilions, reclining on green cushions and fair carpets (55:71-76). A Hadith makes the number of wives seventy-two. Seventy females are *houris*, and two are human females. Ibn-Kathir commenting on *Surah* 56:35-37; quoted by M. Rafiqul-Haqq and P. Newton, "The Place of Women in Pure Islam," *Newton*, 1996 [article online]; retrieved on March 15, 2006, from http://debate.domini.org/newton/womeng.html.

73 Laguindab, *A Handbook of Salah*, 15-20.

74 George W. Braswell, *Understanding World Religions*, rev. ed. (Nashville: Broadman and Holman, 1994), 106.

75 Wilson, *Introducing Islam*, 34.

76 Anderson, *"Islam,"* 118; Braswell, *Understanding World Religions*, 106-7; David Kerr, "The Worship of Islam," in *Eerdmans' Handbook to the World's Religions* (Grand Rapids: Eerdmans, 1994), 317-18.

77 Kerr, "The Worship of Islam," 36.

78   Dallal, "Islam."

79   Ibid., 318.

80   Thomas W. Lippman, *Understanding Islam* [digital audio book] (Ashland, OR: Blackstone Audiobooks, 1991).

81   Wilson, *Introducing Islam*, 37; Kerr, "The Worship of Islam," 319-20.

82   Goldziher, *Introduction to Islamic Theology and Law*, 15.

83   Maulana Muhammad Ali, *The Religion of Islam* (Chelsea, MI: Book Crafters, 1990), 291.

84   Phil Parshall and Julie Parshall, *Lifting the Veil: The World of Muslim Women* (Waynesboro, GA: Authentic Media, 2002), 30.

85   Anthony Giddens, "Beneath the Hijab: A Woman," *New Perspectives Quarterly* 21 (Feb 2004): 9-11; Muslim Women's League, "An Islamic Perspective on Women's Dress," 1997 [article online]; retrieved on March 5, 2006, from http://www.mwlusa.org/publications/ positionpapers/hijab.html.

86   Kecia Ali, "Qur'an 4.34," *The Feminist Sexual Ethics Project*, 2003 [article online]; retrieved on March 7, 2006, from http://www.brandeis.edu/projects/fse/Pages/adifficultverse2.html#anchor_daraba.

87   Parshall and Parshall, *Lifting the Veil: The World of Muslim Women*, 25.

88   Ibid., 119-29.

89   Kees Couprie, "Islamic Holidays," 2001 [article online]; retrieved on March 1, 2006, from http://home.casema.nl/couprie/calmath/events/islamic.html.

90   Parshall, *Muslim Evangelism: Contemporary Approaches to Contextualization*, 229.

91   Robert Morey, *The Islamic Invasion* (Eugene, OR: Harvest Home Publishers, 1992); Brother Andrew, "Hubal and Allah the Moon God?" *The Interactive Bible*, 2006 [article online]; retrieved on March 10, 2006, from http://www.bible.ca/islam/islam-moon-god.htm; Dee Finney, "Religions and Cultures of Moon Worship," *Great Dreams*, 2003 [article online]; retrieved on March 8, 2006, from http://www.greatdreams.com/moon/ moon_worship.htm.

92   "Jihad," *Microsoft Encarta*, 2005 [article online]; retrieved on March 4, 2006, from http://encarta.msn.com/encyclopedia_761582255/Jihad.html.

93 Diana Eck, *A New Religious America* (New York: HarperSan Francisco, 2001), 238.

94 John Kelsay, *Islam and War* (Louisville, KY: Westminster/John Knox Press, 1993), 35.

95 Braswell, *Understanding World Religions*, 123.

CHAPTER 20

Christian Witness to Muslims

1. *Introduction*

a. Over 80% of all Muslims have never heard the gospel, but regard the Bible as a holy book and Jesus as a holy man.[1] Of the 236 countries in the world recognized by the United Nations, 51 have a Muslim population of 50% or more.

b. "Islam is the fastest growing religion in the United States, with a 60-fold increase since 1970."[2] The Council on American-Islamic Relations and three other US Muslim groups claim that by 2004 there were 7.0 million Muslims in the U.S.A., about 2.3% of the national population.[3] "Roughly one-fifth of the more than 530,000 international students in the United States come from 40 Islamic countries."[4] As Muslims spread throughout the world, most committed Christians will find an opportunity to talk with a Muslim about religion.

2. *Islam and Christianity Contrasted*

Words often evoke contradictory images or impressions, as they are heard by people from around the world. It is critical for a Christian to understand the meanings and even subtle differences in order to effectively communicate the gospel to Muslims.[5]

Words	Muslim	Evangelical Christianity
God	Distant Merciful Vengeful Almighty	Personal Loving Judgmental Holy
Christ	Prophet	God
Bible	Revelation from God Changed, corrupted	Revelation from God Authoritative
Trinity	Father, Mother, Son	Father, Son, Holy Spirit
Sin	Shame, embarrassment	Guilt
Salvation	Requirement: faith and works	Requirement: faith
Faith	Faith in God, devotion directed to Muhammad	Love to God, expressed in commitment to Jesus

Table 20.1

3. *Evangelistic Approaches to Muslims*

a. General Principles in reaching a Muslim[6]

1) We must remember that a Muslim is a monotheist, a believer in the one true God, and that he is willing to obey Him.

2) In the heart of every true Muslim is a fear of God.

3) Most Muslims have a certain sense of sin.

4) In light of the foregoing reasons, we must try to forget that he is a Muslim and remember that he is a human being, as well as a sinner, like ourselves.

5) It is also extremely important to remember that the message we bring is judged by the character of the messenger.

6) We must make use of the truth that he knows to lead him on to accept the whole truth of the Word of God.

7) As with (most) everyone, Muslims respond to love.

b. The following are guidelines for witnessing:[7]

1) Get ready to witness to them. Study their culture and the way they think. Try to get acquainted with Muslim neighbors, and try to understand their point of view.

2) Learn their language. Many Muslims today can be reached without any knowledge of Arabic. However, a worker considering full-time service among Muslims must master the Arabic language. Often, Muslims show hostility toward foreigners. But when they find that he speaks their language fluently, their attitudes change and conversation is started. "Enough Arabic to know the religious terms is important in reaching Muslims abroad. They have their own religious vocabulary, and the Christian missionary must know and use it."[8]

3) Be open for opportunities to witness.

4) Pray with and for them.

5) Love them sincerely and be gentle; they will sense this. Understand that the objective is to win the person, not the discussion. The goal is not just to defend Christianity, but to present Christ.

6) Consult the Bible often to explain and support what you believe. This will expose your Muslim friends to the Bible's ring of authority and authenticity.

7) Meet with them individually. Witnessing to Muslims is best done one-on-one. When you meet with Muslims in a group, they tend to be defensive of their religion and will not open up.

8) Stress common beliefs. We may agree with them on every point where we can consistently do so and do our best to be in harmony with them as far as possible.[9] Muslims and Christians believe in an almighty, all-knowing, loving God. Both religious systems believe in the final judgment; they accept the fact that human beings are morally responsible for their actions. Both faiths believe in a final resurrection from the dead at the Messiah's return. Believers give great emphasis to assisting and helping the poor. Prayer is a priority for both faiths. They place emphasis on obedience to God. Both faiths believe in a great controversy between good and evil angels.[10]

9) Use Jesus' parables and stories about Him. Muslims are more influenced by stories and parables than they are by logical arguments.

10) Read at least a few portions, if not all, of the *Qur'an* so that you will become familiar with the Muslim concept of God.

11) Be patient and persistent. Muslims are notoriously slow in turning to Jesus Christ for salvation. Listen patiently to what they say; you will understand them better. Your turn to speak will come. Muslims must hear many times before they will believe.

12) Handle the Bible respectfully. Christians must remember to treat the Bible with the same reverence as Muslims treat the *Qur'an*. They will never hold the *Qur'an* lower than the waistline because it is precious and holy to them. Muslims also keep the *Qur'an* on the highest shelf in the house, for nothing should be placed above or on the *Qur'an*. For this reason, when they see tracts or Scriptures which contain the name of God trampled underfoot, they tend to despise them.[11]

13) Explain the Gospel very simply, in everyday terms. Do not forget to define such words as "sin," "prayer," "Son of God," and "faith." These words often have a different meaning to the Muslim.

14) Point to Jesus as often as you can without being offensive. Stress His uniqueness that is also found in the *Qur'an*: His miraculous birth (*Surah* 3:47; 19:16-22), His sinless life (19:19), His extraordinary teachings, and His miracles (3: 49-51; 5:109-110). The *Qur'an* ascribes to Jesus unique names: "the Word of God" (4:45), "a spirit of God" (4:171), and "Messiah" (4:45). The *Qur'an* also speaks of His death (3:55; 5:17; 19:33), resurrection (19:33), and ascension (3:55); it refers to the fact that Jesus is alive in heaven (3:45) as intercessor (39:445) and that He is returning (43:61).

15) Share how you found peace and assurance of salvation through Christ.

16) Stress the fact that God is absolutely holy and that He demands righteousness, whereas man is unrighteous and is enslaved by his sinful nature. The sinner's condition does not need to be made better by education: rather, he needs to be "born again" in order to become a new person.

17) Answer objections with gentleness and kindness; at the same time ask: How do you know that the Gospel is not true? Have you read it? Have you ever studied the Bible for yourself, or are you just repeating, without thinking, what others have said about it? How can you know if God has pardoned you? Do you have the assurance of salvation? Do you have eternal life?

18) A message may be quickly forgotten, but the Scriptures speak continuously. Almost every believer from a Muslim background testifies to the importance that the Scriptures have played in bringing him to the faith. The Gospel according to Luke can be especially helpful for the Muslim to start with. Matthew is also valuable, but some Muslims may find it difficult because it is very Jewish. Mark introduces a stumbling block in the very first sentence by speaking of Jesus as "the Son of God." The Gospel according to John may be more helpful at a later time.[12]

19) Invite your Islamic friends to your home for a vegetarian meal.

20) Share your concern for genuine Christianity. Acknowledge the apostasy in Christianity and the need for reform.

21) Studies on Biblical prophecy help to confirm the authenticity of the Scriptures.

22) Since the Muslim family unit is extremely strong with the father's highly respected leadership role, be sure to respect the father as the family leader.

c. The following are examples of what not to do while witnessing:

1) Do not be critical of Islam, the *Qur'an*, or Muhammad. In fact, try to avoid such subjects altogether. Instead, accentuate the Good News of the Gospel. "Hold to the affirmative."[13]

2) Do not take your Muslim friend to church until you know he or she is ready. There is much happening at a church service that the typical Muslim

would find dishonoring to God. If you do bring a Muslim to church, discuss
with him or her what to expect. It is best to begin by taking your Muslim friend
to an informal Bible study.

3) Do not argue with your Muslim friend. It should be understood that
a Muslim cannot lose an argument, because he or she would then lose respect.
Try to sensitively provoke your friend's thinking instead. Do not look for
disputes and controversy–they only generate anger. However, do not avoid them
if it is necessary. One must show that the Bible has an answer that is logical and
true.

4) Do not be misled by their belief in Jesus or the Bible. Normally,
their belief has a Muslim context and not a Biblical one. Although some
religious expressions are used in common, the Christian should never assume
that such religious expressions as the atonement, Calvary, the Cross, the new
birth, regeneration, the Son of God, sin, and faith mean the same to the Muslim
as they do to the Christian.

5) Do not be fooled by the claim that they know all about Christianity.
Muslims do not want to admit their ignorance about true Christianity.

6) Do not speak right away about Jesus' being the Son of God; they will
not accept this.

7) Do not use an underlined Bible nor one with pictures, since these
things are considered irreverent and offensive.

4. *Visiting a Mosque*

a. The word "mosque" is an Anglicized version of the Arabic word
"*masjid*," meaning "a place of prostration." When you visit a mosque, keep in
mind what you would expect if a group of Muslims were to visit your church:
they would be expected to listen rather than to preach to you. If you are
planning to go as a group, it would be appropriate to make contact either with
the *imam* or some other leader of the Muslim community. The *imam* has a
position roughly similar (but not identical) to that of the pastor in a Christian
church.[14]

b. Women visiting a mosque during a Friday service at 11:00 am should
wear a scarf to cover their heads. On any other occasion they may be expected
to wear a long skirt and have their arms covered. Possibly women may have a

separate entrance to the mosque. Both men and women should be prepared to take their shoes off before going to the main room of the mosque.

c. Muslims may want to explain their faith to Christian visitors. As there may be opportunities to ask questions, visitors may think in advance of some questions they may want to ask. They should be prepared to stay at least an hour and not be in a hurry to leave.

d. Visiting Christians may be able to see the place where those who come to the mosque carry out *wudu*: the ritual washing of the hands, arms, face, nose, and feet before prayer. The hosts may be willing to demonstrate how they say their prayers and what the ritual means to them.

e. In the prayer hall, visitors will see the *mihrab*, a concavity in the wall that marks the direction of Mecca, which indicates the direction that Muslims face to pray. The *mimbar* is the pulpit with steps, usually made of wood, from which the *imam* gives a sermon at the Friday prayers. There is often Arabic writing on the walls, such as the name of God, the name of Muhammad, the *Fathia* (the first *surah* of the *Qur'an*). In most mosques in America the call to prayer is heard only inside the mosque. There may be a separate prayer room for women.

5. *Obstacles to Muslim Conversion*

a. In order to be effective, a Christian witness must be aware of the theological differences between Christianity and Islam. All the differences are important, but a Christian should especially be aware of three great dogmatic offenses:

1) God has a son who is equal to Him in power and glory. Muslims speak of the sin of *ishrak*–associating a partner with God (*Surah* 25:2-3). The sonship of God is abhorred by Muslims as an unthinkable, sensual degradation of Allah (18:4-5; 19:88-92). "It is not befitting to (the majesty of) Allah that He should beget a son" (19:34-35). Most Muslims think that the Trinity consists of God, Mary, and Jesus (5:116). Muslims conclude that Christians believe that either God had sexual intercourse with Mary and they had a son, Jesus; or the Holy Spirit in the form of a man (Gabriel) married Mary and by intercourse produced Jesus. Naturally, all of this appears as sheer blasphemy to the Muslim.[15] The *Qur'an* explicitly denies the divinity of Jesus, rejects the doctrine of Trinity, affirms that Jesus was no more than a messenger of Allah, and that Allah is too exalted to have a son (4:169, 171; 5:17, 72-73, 75).

2) Christ was crucified. Allah needs no sacrifice and no mediator to reconcile the world to himself, for he forgives whomever and whenever he wants. Concerning the death of Jesus, the statements of the *Qur'an* seem contradictory. *Surah* 3:55; 5:17; and 19:33 all mention the death of Jesus, but *Surah* 4:157 obscures the picture: "And for their saying we have killed the Messiah, Jesus, Son of Mary, and the messenger of God: they killed him not nor did they crucify him but they thought they did." Some think that it was inconceivable to Muhammad that a prophet of God could suffer such an ignominious death as crucifixion.[16] However, this passage simply denies that the Jews caused Jesus to be crucified. Jesus is presumed to be in heaven and to have access to the throne of God. He is expected to return to this world shortly before the Day of Judgment (43:61).

> Presenting Christ as a victor over Satan is a way to open doors without getting the usual Islamic objections. . . . Our goal from this angle is to present Jesus as the One who is more powerful than evil. . . . Presenting the death, burial, and resurrection of Jesus as a purposeful act designed to overcome evil takes away the shame so often associated with this fact in Jesus' life. His death and resurrection becomes linked to a celestial battle to overcome evil.[17]

3) The Bible has been corrupted. This is known as the doctrine of *tahrif*, or alteration. Whatever is not in accord with the *Qur'an* is regarded as corrupted and untrue. However, the *Qur'an* bears witness to the Bible's accuracy (*Surah* 3:3; 10:94). Muslims are required to believe in the Bible (3:84).[18] Muhammad himself spoke of the Bible as being trustworthy (3:94; 4:49-50; 5:68). *Surah* 3:94 records: "O people of the Book, ye have no ground to stand on, until ye observe the *Taurat* [Jewish Torah, the Law] and the *Injil* [Gospels] and that which hath been sent down to you from your Lord." Almost all Muslims believe the Bible has been abrogated by the *Qur'an*. There is, however, not a single word in the *Qur'an* to support this opinion. Concerning the charges of corruption, Muslims point to the following passages: "A party of them [Jews] heard the Word of Allah, and perverted it knowingly after they understood it" (2:75), and "Woe to those who write the Book with their own hands, and then say: 'This is from Allah,' to traffic with it for a miserable price!" (2:78-79). It should be noticed that these passages speak of misinterpreting Scripture and against false teachings, but they do not speak of altering the actual biblical manuscripts themselves.[19]

b. In addition to the three major obstacles to conversion mentioned above, there are differences in Christian and Muslim views on other important areas. One is their understanding of God. Man was created not in the image of God, but more as His slave. Prostration in Islam with the back of the worshiper bent, represents an interpretation of the word *Islam*. It signifies surrender, submission, and devotion to Allah. Allah is a distant, mighty dictator-god who is worshiped and feared. Every assertion of the nearness of God and His fatherly care is regarded as strange, ridiculous, and even blasphemous. The *Qur'an* and the Bible offer contrasting descriptions of God's nature and character:[20]

1) The God of the *Qur'an* is a singular unity, but the God of the Bible is a compound unity who is one in essence and three in person (Matt 28:19; John 10:30; Acts 5:3-4).

2) The God of the *Qur'an* is not a father, and he has begotten no sons (*Surahs* 19:90-92; 112:3), but the God of the Bible is a Trinity who has eternally existed as Father, Son, and Holy Spirit (Matt 28:19; Luke 3:21-22; John 5:18).

3) Through the *Qur'an*, Muslims believe God broke into history through a word that is written, but through Jesus Christ, God broke into history through the Word who is a Person (John 1:1, 14; Col 1:15-20; Heb 1:2-3; 1 John 4:9-10; compare with *Surah* 4:45).

4) The God of the *Qur'an* "loves not the prodigals" (*Surahs* 6:142; 7:31), but Jesus tells the story of a father, a metaphor for God the Father, who longs for the return of his prodigal son (Luke 15:11-24).

5) "Allah loves not the wrongdoers" (*Surah* 3:139), and neither does he love "him who is treacherous, sinful" (*Surah* 4:107), but "God demonstrates his own love for us in this: while we were still sinners, Christ died for us" (Rom 5:8).

6) "Allah desires to afflict them for some of their sins" (*Surah* 5:49; also see *Surahs* 4:168-69; 7:179; 9:2); but the God of the Bible does not "take any pleasure in the death of the wicked" (Eze 18:23) and is "not wanting anyone to perish, but everyone to come to repentance" (2 Pet 3:9).

7) The God of the *Qur'an* provided a messenger, Muhammad, who warned of Allah's impending judgment (*Surahs* 1:119; 5:19; 7:184, 188; 15:89) and who declared that "no bearer of a burden can bear the burden of another" (*Surahs* 17:15; 35:18). However, the God of the Bible provided a sinless Savior, Jesus, who took our sins upon Himself and bore God's wrath in our stead (Matt 20:28; 26:28; Luke 22:37; John 3:26; 10:9-11; 2 Cor 5:21; Gal 3:13; 1 Thess 5:9-10).

c. Their understanding of revelation. They believe that Allah dictated his revelations to Muhammad word by word. In addition, the *Qur'an* was written in a kind of rhyme that is memorable and catchy in the Arabic language.[21]

Sometimes, for the sake of rhyme, Muhammad inserted words where they did not fit according to the context or changed syllables to secure the rhythm of the intonation. The Gospel was not written in the form of a poem but in prose, and demands thinking and understanding. The Muslim does not hear that tuneful rhythm in the Gospel, and the reading process itself seldom creates in him a willful decision or reflection.

d. Their understanding of conversion. No Arab country, except Lebanon, allows the conversion of a Muslim to Christianity. The religious freedom spoken of in the constitution of some Muslim countries relates to the fact that the Christian minority is allowed to remain Christian or become Muslim, but not the reverse. There is virtually no way for an Arab Muslim to legally change his religious affiliation unless he emigrates and accepts a new nationality. The parents of a convert regard their child as dead or ensure that he emigrates and thus disappears from view. The *Qur'an* literally demands the killing of a convert (*Surah* 4:89-90).

6. *Contextualization Among Muslims*

a. "Contextualization attempts to communicate the Gospel in word and deed to establish the church in ways that make sense to people within their local cultural context, presenting Christianity in such a way that it meets people's deepest needs and penetrates their worldview, thus allowing them to follow Christ and remain within their own culture."[22]

b. Christians with a high view of Scripture would agree that any attempt at accommodation should not alter the content of the gospel.[23] Missionaries must agree with people as much as possible, on every point on which they can consistently do so,[24] and must also learn to adapt their approaches to the condition of the people—"to meet people where they are."[25] However, any attempt at contextualization must not compromise the integrity of biblical doctrines.[26]

c. The "C-Scale" or "Contextualization Spectrum" measures on a scale from 1 through 6 the level of contextualization among "Christ-centered Communities" found in the Muslim context.[27] A major contention is concerning the validity of a C-5 approach. Christians with a high view of scriptures believe that C-5 falls within the area of syncretism.[28]

C-1   Traditional church using outside language.

C-2   Traditional church using inside language.

C-3   Churches using inside language and religiously neutral inside cultural forms such as music, artwork, and ethnic dress.

C-4   Contextualized Christ-centered communities using inside language and biblically permissible cultural and Islamic forms that may include praying with one's arms raised, touching the forehead on the ground while praying, and separating men from women. C-4 missionaries may start with C-5 strategies, but little by little they bring believers to "the whole counsel of God." C-4 believers are aware of the fact that they have become Christians.

C-5   Communities of believers who refer to themselves as Muslims but are followers of Isa, the Messiah. C-5 believers still live within the community of Islam legally, culturally, and religiously. Most believe that the *Qur'an* is inspired, and Muhammad is still considered to have been a true prophet. C-5 missionaries teach that Muhammad's teachings were misunderstood and that a remnant must be formed within Islam that will restore the original truths.

C-6   Secret/underground believers that are believed to be Muslims by the Muslim community, and they themselves say that they are Muslims. Certainly, this model is far from God's ideal.

d. C-5 is valid only as a strategy, not as an end. Eventually Muslim seekers must arrive at a point when, individually or as a community, they will become aware of their own identity as Christians and become C-4 believers. Only will then will they be ready for baptism.[29]

7. *Missionary Strategies to Approach Muslims*

a. The vast majority of the barriers and stumbling blocks are social and cultural rather than religious. For this reason, many have begun to ask if it is possible for believers from a Muslim background to come together and form churches of their own.[30]

b. Tentmakers (Acts 18:1-4) are Christians who use their training and expertise to support themselves in a cross-cultural setting for the purpose of sharing the gospel, making disciples, and planting churches. The concept of "tentmakers" is becoming more and more popular in missiological circles.[31] "For the most part, these [missionaries] will be independently operating, self-supporting, and cross-trained in a nonmissions area. In most cases [they] . . . need to be silent about their missionary vocation."[32]

c. The penetration of non-entered areas by means of radio.[33] It is certainly no easy task to produce meaningful, culturally relevant programs that will catch the attention of Islamic people; however, this can be developed as a viable strategy.

d. The caring of interested listeners or students of the Bible Correspondence School. Because of circumstances, national pastors are not the best individuals to visit people that are interested. Tourist-style visitors might be a better option. They could be sent out from, and report to, an office in a neutral area. This network should be anonymous and totally unconnected with local structures.

e. Public evangelism in Muslim countries should use Christian terminology to invite Christians of all confessions to assemble and listen to Christian lectures. This procedure may be used to reach some marginal Muslims. Some may even come to listen to "Christians criticizing other Christians." Muslim-related titles should never be used.

f. Schools are one of the most effective ways to win souls in many Muslim countries.[34] Teachers have a "captive audience," and "chapel" services provide a good opportunity for evangelism. Teachers need to understand the primary tenets of Muslim faith and be trained to approach, answer their questions, stimulate interest, and address concerns in such a way that they will appreciate Christian perspectives. The most important element is that the teachers and administrators must be missionary minded.

g. English-as-a-second-language schools are an important evangelistic tool. In some countries the younger generation is very interested in learning English. I have been invited to preach a direct evangelistic sermon to the class members, most of them Muslims.

h. Since the medical and temperance work is often permitted to enter the most strict Islamic countries, different forms of medical work should be explored to establish Christian presence, such us maternity clinics, dental clinics, public health, and preventive medicine. Again, all staff should be missionary-minded in order to use as many open doors as possible to do more than just medical work.[35] Relief work is sometimes the only entering wedge in Muslim regions.[36]

i. Muslim women are especially open to the Gospel, but any approach must come from another woman. Women-only health, cooking, and exercise classes are ways of offering them an opportunity to interact with Christians.[37]

j. In some Muslim countries, missionaries have followed a C-5 radical program that creates "followers of Isa" within the Islamic culture and religion.[38] Proponents of this approach maintain that "Muslims should not have to stop being Muslims."[39] This strategy has been criticized because it affects the integrity of the doctrines of the church, inspiration, revelation, and baptism.[40]

k. A Muslim may be hard to win, but he is easier to approach than the average Westerner, who may not be interested in talking about religion. The Muslim is often bigoted, prejudiced, and fanatical, but has a fear of God and is interested in talking about religion. Muslims are approachable. It is not impossible to win their confidence, and when contact is really established, they are often gripped with the Christian message.

Notes

1   Bryant L. Myers, *The Changing Shape of World Mission* (Monrovia, CA: MARC, 1996), 43.

2   Susanne Washburn, "The American Muslim Experience," *National Catholic Reporter*, February 10, 2006 [online edition]; retrieved on February 27, 2006, from http://ncronline.org/NCR_Online/archives2/2006a/021006/ss021006g.php.

3   "Islam in the United States," *Wikipedia, the Free Encyclopedia*, 2006 [article online]; retrieved on March 1, 2006, from http://en.wikipedia.org/wiki/Islam_in_the_United_States.

4   Dean C. Halverson, "Islam," in *The Compact Guide to World Religions*, ed. Dean C. Halverson (Minneapolis, MN: Bethany, 1996), 103. These figures have changed since September, 2001. For instance, during the 1970s there were 200,000 Iranian students in the United States; that figure was down to around 2,000 by 2005. Lionel Beehner, "Q&A: Soft Diplomacy in Iran," *The New York Times*, February 21, 2006 [online edition]; retrieved on February 23, 2006, from http://www.nytimes.com/cfr/international/ slot2_022106.html.

5   Phil Parshall, *Muslim Evangelism* (Waynesboro, GA: Gabriel Publishing, 2001), 93-99.

6 Summarized from C. R. Marsh, *Share Your Faith with a Muslim* (Chicago: Moody Press, 1975), 8-13.

7 Adapted from Halverson, "Islam," 108-10, and Mark Finley, *Studying Together: A Ready-Reference Bible Handbook* (Fallbrook, CA: Hart, 1991), 138-39.

8 Marsh, *Share Your Faith with a Muslim*, 6.

9 Ellen G. White, *The Review and Herald*, June 13, 1912, par. 4.

10 Mark Finley, *Studying Together* (Fallbrook, CA: Hart Research Center, 1995), 138.

11 Marsh, *Share Your Faith with a Muslim*, 94.

12 Consultation on World Evangelization, *Lausanne Occasional Paper No. 4, The Glen Eyrie Report–Muslim Evangelization* (Wheaton, IL: Consultation on World Evangelization, 1978), 20.

13 Ellen G. White, *Testimonies to the Church* (Boise, ID: Pacific Press, 1948), 9:147.

14 Colin Chapman, *Cross and Crescent: Responding to the Challenge of Islam* (Downers Grove, IL: InterVarsity Press, 2003), 49-53.

15 Abdl-Al-Masih, *Why Is It Difficult for a Muslim to Become Christian?* (Villach, Austria: Light of Life, n.d.), 5-7.

16 Hamilton A. R. Gibb and J. H. Kramers, *Shorter Encyclopedia of Islam* (Ithaca, NY: Cornell University Press, 1965), 173.

17 Roy Oksnevad, "Christ the Victor," in *The Gospel for Islam: Reaching Muslims in North America*, ed. Roy Oksnevad and Dotsey Welliver (Wheaton, IL: Evangelism and Missions Information Service, 2001), 99.

18 J. Dudley Woodberry, "The Christian Response to Islam," in *Christian Witness in Pluralistic Contexts in the Twenty-First Century*, ed. Enoch Wan, Evangelical Missiological Society Series, Number 11 (Pasadena, CA: William Carey Library, 2004), 39.

19 Halverson, "Islam," 111.

20 Ibid., 110-11.

21 M. S. M. Saifullah, 'Abd ar-Rahman Robert Squires, and Muhammad Ghoniem, "What Is the Challenge of the *Qur'an* with Respect to Arabic Prose and Poetry?" *Islamic Awareness*, 1999 [article online]; retrieved on March 14, 2006, from http://www.islamic-awareness.org/ Quran/Miracle/ijaz.html.

22   Darrel L. Whiteman, "Contextualization: The Theory, the Gap, the Challenge," *Candler School of Theology: Emory University*, 2001 [article online]; retrieved on May 10, 2006, from http://www.pitts.emory.edu/globaltexts/Archive/Whiteman%20on%20Contextualization.htm.

23   Donald A. McGavran, *The Clash between Christianity and Cultures* (Washington, DC: Canon Press, 1974), 52-54.

24   Ellen G. White, *The Review and Herald*, June 13, 1912, par. 4.

25   Ellen G. White, *Evangelism* (Washington, DC: Review & Herald, 1974), 484, 485.

26   Carlos G. Martin, "What Constitutes Acceptable Contextualization," *Asia Adventist Seminary Studies* Vol. 1, No. 1 (1998): 19-25.

27   John Travis, "The C-1 to C-6 Spectrum," *Evangelical Missions Quarterly* Vol. 34, No. 4 (October 1998): 407-8.

28   "Syncretism is the reshaping of Christian beliefs and practices through cultural accommodation so that they consciously or unconsciously blend with those of the dominant culture. It is the blending of Christian beliefs and practices with those of the dominant culture so that Christianity loses its distinctive nature and speaks with a voice reflective of its culture." Gailyn Van Rheenen, "Worldview and Syncretism," *Missiology.org*, 2003 [lecture online]; retrieved on May 10, 2006, from http://www.missiology.org/mongolianlectures/ worldviewandsyncretism.htm.

29   Carlos G. Martin, "C-5 Muslims, C-5 Missionaries, or C-5 Strategies?" *Journal of the Adventist Theological Society*, Vol. 17, No. 2 (Autumn 2006): 122-34.

30   See models for contextualization in Phil Parshall, *New Paths in Muslim Evangelization* (Grand Rapids: Eerdmans, 1980), 157-80.

31   J. Herbert Kane, "Recent Developments," chap. in *Understanding Christian Missions*, 4th ed. (Grand Rapids: Baker, 1986), 384-99.

32   Tetsunao Yamamori, *God's New Envoys: A Bold Strategy for Penetrating "Closed Countries"* (Portland, OR: Multnomah Press, 1987), 58.

33   Bert R. Smith, "Radio Evangelism in the Middle East: Analysis and Strategy," in *The Three Angels and the Crescent: A Reader*, ed. Jonquil Hole and Borge Schantz (Bracknell, Berkshire, England: SDA Global Centre for Islamic Studies, Newbold College, 1993), 231-43.

34 Hans Christian Oster, "Education as an Opening Wedge," in *The Three Angels and the Crescent: A Reader*, ed. Jonquil Hole and Borge Schantz (Bracknell, Berkshire, England: SDA Global Centre for Islamic Studies, 1993), 217-29.

35 G. Gordon Hadley, "The Medical Work in Relation to Islam," in *The Three Angels and the Crescent: A Reader*, ed. Jonquil Hole and Borge Schantz (Bracknell, Berkshire, England: SDA Global Centre for Islamic Studies, 1993), 197-207.

36 Yamamori speaks of the "four R's" of evangelical relief and development: Relief, Recovery, Redevelopment, and Reconciliation in *God's New Envoys*, 58.

37 Valerie Bernard-Channer, "Women in Islam," in *The Three Angels and the Crescent: A Reader*, ed. Jonquil Hole and Borge Schantz (Bracknell, Berkshire, England: SDA Global Centre for Islamic Studies, 1993), 69-93.

38 Jerald Whitehouse, "Contextual Adventist Mission to Islam: A Working Model," in *The Three Angels and the Crescent: A Reader*, ed. Jonquil Hole and Borge Schantz (Bracknell, Berkshire, England: SDA Global Centre for Islamic Studies, 1993), 245-60.

39 Coleen Moore Tinker quotes Jerald Whitehouse in "Muslim Relations Revolutionized," *Adventist Today*, November/December 1997, Vol. 9, No. 6 [article online]; retrieved on March 10, 2006, from http://www.atoday.com/magazine/ archive/1997/novdec1997/news/Muslim.shtml.

40 Carlos G. Martin, "Questions on C-5," *Journal of Adventist Missions*, Vol. 1, No. 2 (Fall 2005): 34-41.

CHAPTER 21

Baha'ism

1. *Introduction*

a. The Bahá'í Faith is a monotheistic religion with a worldwide population of some five million people. They come from more than two thousand different tribal, racial, and ethnic groups and live in 235 countries and dependent territories. They have magnificent houses of worship in all continents. The *Britannica Book of the Year* (1992) referred to the Bahá'í Faith as the second-most geographically widespread religion in the world, after Christianity. It originated in Iran in 1844.[1]

b. At the core of Baha'i belief is the idea that the one God who created the universe has been the author of one unified religion. This one religion, its followers claim, was revealed by God in stages throughout history through different prophets, whose appearance at different times and different cultures has been misinterpreted as opposing rival religious civilizations. It claims to be the religion of unity and peace and the fulfillment of all previous religions.[2] "To be a Baha'i simply means to love all the world, to love humanity and try to serve it, to work for universal peace and universal brotherhood.[3]

c. The following statement shows how Baha'is see themselves:

The Baha'i Faith is an independent world religion, divine in origin, all-embracing in scope, broad in its outlook, scientific in its method, humanitarian in its principles and dynamic in the influence it exerts on the hearts and minds of men. It upholds the unity of God, recognizes the unity of His prophets and inculcates the principle of oneness and the wholeness of the entire human race.[4]

2. *Development of Baha'ism*

a. Islam experienced splits and splinters from its earliest days. After the death of Muhammad, no clear successor was left. Although Abu Bakr became a Caliph (a successor of Muhammad as temporal and spiritual head of Islam), this was by no means a unanimous decision. Those who wanted Ali, Muhammad's son-in-law, formed the Shi'ites. They became further divided into the Sevener and the Twelver sects due to a controversy over the number of Imams, or successors to Muhammad, each group accepts. The Sevener sect accepts seven Imams while the Twelver sect accepts twelve. The Baha'i religion developed from the Twelver Shi'i sect, which believes that the twelfth Imam (Muhammad al-Mahdi) disappeared in the year A.D. 873, or A.H. 260, and that he will reappear at the end of time.[5]

b. This eschatological hope gave rise to another sect, the Shaykhis. This sect was founded by Shaykh Ahmad al-Ahsa'i in the 1820s.[6] Among their doctrines is the belief that "there must always exist among men on earth some person who is in direct supernatural communication with the Hidden Imam, and acts as the channel of grace between believers and the Hidden Imam . . . ."[7] At the death of their leader, two factions split the Shaykhs. One followed Hajji Karim Khan and used the name "Shaykhi" to refer to themselves. The other group followed Sayyid 'Ali Muhammad. This group came to be called Babis.[8]

c. Sayyid 'Ali Muhammad (1817-50) proclaimed himself to be the *Bab* ("The Gate," the intermediary between the Hidden Twelfth Imam and the Shi'i faithful) on May 23, 1844,[9] in Karbala, Iraq. He understood his calling to be that of a forerunner to a greater person, the herald of the promised one of all religions, for whom he prepared the way. However, he changed his original position to that of a major Manifestation of Deity.[10] The *Bab* was persecuted, and finally the government of Persia (the state religion was Twelver Shi'ism) executed him in 1850. During the next two decades over twenty thousand Babis (followers of the Bab) were brutally killed.[11]

d. Mizra' Husayn- 'Ali (1817-92) was born into a wealthy family in Teheran, Iran. He became a follower of the *Bab* about 1847. As the Persian government confiscated his properties, he fled to Iraq. In 1852, when a Babi attempted to assassinate the Shah (monarch of Iran), he was imprisoned in Baghdad. While in prison and on the eve of his deportation to Constantinople on April 21, 1863, he adopted the title *Bahá'u'lláh* ("The glory of God") and declared that he was the Promised One of all religions, the promised manifestation of God. Baha'u'llah claimed to be the twelfth Imam, the fulfillment of the eschatological hope of Shi'ism. He sent letters to the kings and rulers of the earth in his days, including Napoleon III of France, Kaiser William I of Germany, Nicolaevitch Alexander II of Russia, Pope Pius IX, and Queen Victoria of the British Empire, inviting them to accept him as the Promised One.[12] The authorities of the Ottoman Empire exiled the group of Baha'is (new name given to the followers of Baha'u'llah) to Constantinople (now Istanbul), then to Adrianople (now Edirne) in Turkey from 1863 to 1868. In 1868 the group was exiled permanently to the prison-city of Akka or Acre, Palestine (near present-day Haifa, Israel). From there, Baha'u'llah proclaimed his message of peace for the world if all religions would come to him. Throughout his years of imprisonment, he wrote nearly fifteen thousand documents, which together with the writings of the Bab and 'Abdu'l-Baha, represent the extensive Scriptures of the Baha'i Faith. The Scriptures of Baha'ism are unique in that for the first time in history, the Holy Writings of a world religion were authentically available in the handwriting of its founders. Baha'u'llah died of natural causes on May 29, 1892.[13]

e. Abbas Effendi (1844-1921), Baha'u'llah''s eldest son, became the head of the Baha'i Faith from 1892 to 1921. He adopted the title *'Abdu'l-Baha* ("servant of God"). He made a trip to Europe and the United States in 1911-1912. 'Abdu'l-Baha institutionalized the Baha'i Administrative Order by organizing "Houses of Justice" and "Spiritual Assemblies." He passed away on November 18, 1921, and was buried on Mount Carmel in the same shrine as the *Bab*.[14]

f. 'Abdu'l-Baha's son, Shoghi Effendi, served as the head of the Baha'i Faith from 1921 to 1957. After Shoghi Effendi's death, the administration and interpretation of the Baha'i Faith was placed in the Universal House of Justice, the highest elected council which is located in Haifa, Israel.[15]

h. It was publicly introduced to Americans during the World Parliament of Religions in Chicago in 1893.[16] By 2001 there were over seven million Baha'is worldwide, with nearly half of the world membership in Iran and India, and over 750,000 in the United States.[17]

3. *Baha'i Principles*

The principles of the Baha'i Faith were established by Baha'u'llah and promulgated by his son 'Abdu'l-Baha.[18]

    a. The oneness of mankind. "There is only one human race and the differences of race, language, color, country, etc., are merely variations in the human family. All men are brothers and, once this is accepted, such things as wars, race, class, and political differences can no longer be justified."[19]

    b. Universal peace upheld by a world government. The Universal House of Justice will become the Supreme Court of the World. Not only the personal lives of believers but also the political affairs of the world will be ordered according to the laws of Baha'u'llah.

    c. God is the same in all religions. All the gods worshiped by humans are the same God. There is only one universal God. Nevertheless, the Baha'i understanding also includes the "manifestations of God" (Baha'is generally use this term rather than "prophets"). God speaks through manifestations. These manifestations include: Confucius, Krishna, Gautama the Buddha, Abraham, Zoroaster, Jesus, Muhammad, the Bab, and most recently, Baha'u'llah.[20] While the manifestations are not God, they have powers and abilities that other humans do not.[21] Baha'is flatly deny the Christian doctrine of the incarnation.[22]

    d. The unity of all religions. Baha'u'llah is to Baha'is as Christ in his Second Coming is for the Christians, the Messiah for the Jews, the fifth Buddha for the Buddhists, the Twelfth Caliph for the Muslims, and the reincarnation of Krishna for the Hindus.[23] The Baha'is teach that eventually all "sectarian" churches will be abandoned and replaced by a spiritual center in each community. These spiritual centers are to be teachers of universal education and will involve the spiritual and moral training of mankind.

    e. Elimination of prejudice of all kinds. The purpose of the Faith is to unify all humanity into one family (considered the culmination of social evolution on this planet), which can be done only by eliminating racism in all of its forms. It also demands the equality of men and women.

    f. Universal compulsory education. Eventually this education will supposedly lead to a universal auxiliary language and solution of all economic and moral problems.[24]

g. A universal auxiliary language. A world language will be either made or chosen from the existing languages and will be taught at the schools of all countries. There is a natural bond between the promoters of Esperanto, "the most widely spoken constructed international language,"[25] and the Baha'i Faith.[26]

h. Progressive Revelation. The "Messengers of all religions" were sent by one and the same God. Their message is meant for a specific time and place, but the spiritual truths of all religions are the same. All religions are only evolutionary stages in God's plan to educate and unify the whole planet. Religious knowledge is revealed incrementally according to humanity's collective ability. Baha'u'llah was not the last manifestation, but the latest. A full one thousand years will pass before the next manifestation will appear.[27]

4. *Baha'i Practices and Organization*

a. The *Kitab-i-Aqdas* ("The Most Holy Book") is the main scripture written by Baha'u'llah. It is a collection of detailed laws, prohibitions, and ordinances (recommended but not obligatory).[28]

b. The Bab, Baha'u'llah, and 'Abdu'l-Baha wrote hundreds of prayers. The prayers found in Baha'i prayer books are addressed to any of the "Manifestations of God." Some prayers have been set to music and are sometimes sung at Baha'i gatherings. There are obligatory daily prayers for which they must face the Baha'i World Center in Haifa, Israel.[29]

c. The Baha'i year is divided into 19 months each with 19 days, for a total of 361 days. They insert four "intercalary days" in ordinary years, and five in a loop year between the eighteenth and nineteenth months.[30] On the first day of each month, Baha'is gather for the Nineteen-Day Feast, which is the central worship experience in the Faith, and which only committed Baha'is are allowed to attend. They have several holy days commemorating special occasions in Baha'i history, and intercalary days (February 26-March 1, added to their calendar year to keep it concurrent with solar years), to which Baha'is are encouraged to bring friends who are "seekers."[31]

d. The Baha'i "Administrative Order" is a combination of top-down authority and bottom-up democratic empowerment. The structure is organized in three levels: local spiritual assemblies, national spiritual assemblies, and a Universal House of Justice (UHJ), all of them composed by nine individuals. Local and national spiritual assemblies are elected annually, the latter by delegates from local assemblies. Once every five years, delegates gather to elect the nine members of the UHJ. Baha'is believe that infallible authority and guidance flow from the Universal House of Justice. Global civilization will eventually be guided by the UHJ until the appearance of the next Manifestation of God.[32]

e. Magnificent "Houses of Worship" have been built on all five continents. They have nine doors and a central dome symbolizing the diversity and oneness of humanity. Local communities do not have separate buildings in which they worship. Prayer, scripture readings, meditations, and lectures are prominent functions in the assemblies. The scriptures of the major religions are used in the worship services, as well as *a capella* music. Baha'is also observe a fast from March 2-20 each year, in which no food or drink is consumed during daylight hours. There are no clergy in the Baha'i community.[33]

5. *Christian Witness*

a. The Baha'i's faith holds up ethical ideals, which on the surface seem to be in keeping with Christian doctrine. A closer examination, however, reveals that these teachings fall far short of Christianity.

b. They claim they are tolerant of other faiths and allow for free investigation of truth. However, the Baha'i beliefs and writings do not bear this out. In Baha'ism only the Baha'i writings and Baha'u'lla can interpret the meanings of biblical scriptures. Their interpretation of scripture must be accepted over the individual's interpretation or the interpretation of other biblical scholars, historians, or Bible-believing Christians. They claim to welcome and accept all religions, but these religions are then reinterpreted to conform to the teachings of the Baha'i faith.

c. Baha'ism is a system that advocates peace and unity, but is marked by a long history of schism and organizational fracture. Baha'is so desire the unity of religions that they completely overlook the vast differences between the religions of the world.

d. The Baha'i view of God is burdened with a concept of progressive revelation to the point that God is made to contradict earlier revelations.

e. Christians must define terms when discussing religious truths. All Baha'is acknowledge Christ Jesus as the "Word made flesh" and "as the Son of God." In their words, "Baha'u'llah . . . fully confirms the teachings of Christ and no person is permitted to become a Baha'i without first acknowledging

Christ Jesus as the Word made flesh . . . and as the Son of God. Thousands of
Jews and Muhammedans have accepted Christ through the Baha'i teachings.
Baha'is believe that Baha'u'llah is the spirit of truth foretold by Jesus . . . (John
16:12)."[34] However, Baha'is do not believe that Christ is or was divine. The
title "Son of God" to them simply means that Christ was a great educator for this
particular age. That many Jews and Muslims have come to "accept Christ" must
be evaluated in the light of their own terminology. For a committed Christian it
means to accept Jesus Christ as being fully God and to give one's life in obedient
surrender to Him as Savior and Master. The words are the same, but the
commitment and degree of divinity ascribed involved is worlds apart. Their
interpretation of the Bible ignores context, language, intent, and historical
setting.

    f. "Baha'is have little to say of sin and salvation and more to say about
enlightenment and progress."[35] Baha'ism lacks an understanding of sin and fails
to address the issues raised by sin. They believe that salvation is right morals or
right knowledge and correct self-action, rather than forgiveness, wholeness, and
a faithfulness of mankind brought about by God through reconciliation in Jesus
Christ.

Notes

1   "Terraces of the Shrine of the Bab," *Baha'i International Community*, 2005 [article
online]; retrieved on March 13, 2006, from http://terraces.bahai.org/bahai.en.html.

2   Werner Schilling, "Unity and Peace: The Baha'i Faith," in *Eerdmans' Handbook to
the World Religions*, ed. Pierce R. Beaver et al. (Grand Rapids: Eerdmans, 1982),
268.

3   J. E. Esslemont, *Baha'u'llah and the New Era* (Wilmette, IL: Baha'i Publishing
Trust, 1950), 90.

4   From a pamphlet received at the "Baha'i House of Worship" of Nahapur, New
Delhi, India, 1998.

5   Peter Smith, *A Short History of the Baha'i Faith* (Rockport, MA: Oneworld, 1997),
14-16.

6   Ibid., 17.

7   William M. Miller, *The Baha'i Faith: Its History and Teachings* (Pasadena, CA:
William Carey Library, 1974), 9.

8   Smith, *A Short History of the Baha'i Faith*, 25-26.

9   Baha'is use the prophecy of Daniel 8:14, related to the "2300 days," to prove the prophetic origin of their faith. David Friedman, "Bahá'í response to Francis Beckwith's article 'Bahá'í-Christian Dialogue: Some Key Issues Considered,'" *Baha'i Library* [article online]; retrieved on June 28, 2006, from http://bahai-library.com/essays/beckwith.response.html.

10   Miller, *The Baha'i Faith: Its History and Teachings*, 15.

11   Smith, *A Short History of the Baha'i Faith*, 19-47.

12   Joseph Sheppherd, *The Elements of the Baha'i Faith* (Rockport, MA: Element, 1997), 38-47.

13   Mike McMullen, "The Baha'i Faith in the World and in America," in *World Religions in America,* ed. Jacob Neusner, 3rd ed. (Louisville, KY: Westminster John Knox Press, 2003), 260-64.

14   Smith, *A Short History of the Baha'i Faith*, 74-87.

15   Ibid., 101-15.

16   George W. Braswell, *Understanding Sectarian Groups in America* (Nashville: Broadman & Holman, 1994), 296.

17   "Baha'i Faith, World, Iran, India, United Sates, 2001," *Adherents*, 2006 [article online]; retrieved on March 12, 2006, from http://www.adherents.com/Na/Na_63.html.

18   "Principles of the Baha'i Faith," *The Baha'i Faith*, 2006 [article online]; retrieved on March 16, 2006, from http://www.bahai.com/Bahaullah/principles.htm#About.

19   "The Baha'i Faith," *Update* 9 (September 1983): 4.

20   Smith, *A Short History of the Baha'i Faith*, 66-67.

21   M. Thomas Starkes, "American Baha'is and the Baptist Witness," *Home Mission* 46 (March 1975): 57-61.

22   Francis Beckwith, *Baha'i* (Minneapolis, MN: Bethany, 1985), 13.

23   Schilling, "Unity and Peace: The Baha'i Faith," 268.

24   Starkes, "American Baha'is and the Baptist Witness," 61.

25   "Esperanto," *Wikipedia, the Free Encyclopedia*, 2006 [article online]; retrieved on March 16, 2006, from http://en.wikipedia.org/wiki/Esperanto.

26   "The Baha'i Faith and Esperanto," *Bahaa Esperanto-Ligo* [article online]; retrieved on March 16, 2006, from http://www.bahai.de/bahaaeligo/angla/englisch.htm.

27   McCullen, "The Baha'i Faith," 261-62.

28   Smith, *A Short History of the Baha'i Faith*, 71-73.

29   McCullen, "The Baha'i Faith," 264.

30   Sheppherd, *The Elements of the Baha'i Faith*, 105-6.

31   McCullen, "The Baha'i Faith," 265-67.

32   The number "nine" appears regularly in Baha'i symbols. They explain: "Nine is the highest digit, hence symbolizes comprehensiveness, culmination; also, the reason it is used . . . is because 9 has the exact numerical value of Baha' (in the numerology connected with the Arabic alphabet) and Baha' is the name of the Revealer of our Faith, Baha'u'llah." Helen Hornby, *Lights of Guidance: A Baha'i Reference Guide* (New Delhi: Baha'i Publishing Trust, 1983), 416. Also, see in McCullen, "The Baha'i Faith," 267-68.

33   Mary Pat Fisher, *Living Religions*, 6th ed. (Upper Saddle River, NJ: Pearson Prentice Hall, 2005), 465.

34   Elizabeth H. Cheney, *Prophecy Fulfilled* (Wilmette, IL: Baha'i Publishing Trust, 1944), 16.

35   Braswell, *Understanding Sectarian Groups in America*, 307.

PART VI

CHRISTIANITY

CHAPTER 22

Christianity

1. *Introduction*

a. With over two billion adherents, Christianity is the largest religion of the world.[1] In comparison to the world's population, Christianity has decreased from 34.5% in 1900 to 33% in 2000.[2] Nevertheless, Christianity is the best-distributed religion on the planet. Only Christians are found in all 238 countries, and they are found in at least 11,500 of earth's 12,600 ethnic language groups. Christians are a majority on five of the six continents (Asia is the exception).[3]

b. Christianity is a religion centered around the person of Jesus Christ. The New Testament of the Christian scriptures was written in Greek, and the name "Jesus" is a transliteration of the Hebrew name *Joshua* ("God is salvation"). The name Jesus became related to the title "Christ," which comes from the Greek word *Christos*, meaning "anointed" or "anointed one." "Christ" means the same as the Hebrew word *Messiah* (John 1:41).

c. Judaism and Christianity share the same roots and many beliefs and practices. Christians believe that the Jews were God's chosen people until their leaders rejected Jesus as their Messiah. After that rejection, a new covenant was made that included all who accepted Jesus as the Messiah, or Christ.

2. *Early Christianity (A.D. 30-100)*

a. Jesus was born in 4 B.C.[4] in Bethlehem of Judea but was raised in Nazareth, in Galilee. He was a carpenter, but after His baptism at the age of 30, he became an itinerant preacher for 3.5 years. During His ministry Jesus gathered together a band of followers, mostly from Galilee. In addition to preaching repentance, love, and the coming kingdom of God, He performed miracles (Matt 9:35) that confirmed His call, established His authority, demonstrated His power, and exemplified His message. He was executed by crucifixion in A.D. 31. Hundreds of witnesses saw Him resurrected (1 Cor 15:3-8) during the forty days before He ascended to Heaven (Acts 1:9-11). He promised to come again (John 14:1-3). On the Jewish feast of Pentecost His disciples began to preach the message of Jesus (Acts 2).

b. What Christians believe about Jesus' life and teachings is based largely on the first four books of the New Testament, which are called the *gospels* ("good news"). They were written about forty to sixty years after Jesus' death. The first three gospels (Matthew, Mark, and Luke) are so similar that they are called "synoptic," due to the fact that they can be "seen together" as presenting similar views and facts about Jesus. The Gospel of John was the last to be written, at the end of the first century. However, the oldest writings of the New Testament were letters of the apostle Paul. In addition to what Christians said about Jesus, there are references to the "historical Jesus" in Jewish and Roman sources.[5]

c. Christianity did not emerge as a new religion. Rather, early Christians regarded themselves as a sect within Judaism (Acts 24:5). They continued to pray in the Temple (2:46; 3:1; 5:42), keep the Sabbath day (13:42, 44; 16:13; 18:4), practice circumcision (15:1; 16:3), and observe Jewish customs (18:18; 21:23-26) and festivals (20:6, 16). In addition to whatever it meant to be Jewish, they met in one another's homes (2:46) to celebrate *agapes* ("love feasts," Jude 12) and to remember Jesus' death. Tension between "traditional Jews" and "Jewish Christians" mounted until a persecution erupted. Many Christians fled to regions outside Jerusalem, thus giving rise to early missionary activity (Acts 8:1-4). The early followers of Jesus called their religious faith simply "the Way" (19:9, 23; 24:14, 22). The word "Christian" first came into use in the city of Antioch (11:26) about ten years after Jesus' death and resurrection.

d. At Antioch, a center of Christianity outside Israel, it was agreed that the gospel should be preached to Gentiles (non-Jews). Saul (later known as "Paul") was one of the first missionaries (Acts 13:1-3). Greek converts were soon outnumbering Jewish Christians. A council, convened at Jerusalem in A.D. 51, removed the need for circumcision (Acts 15), and Christianity acquired a universal character. By the end of the first century, Christianity had spread throughout the Roman Empire, and five bishops had become prominent: one in the West (Rome) and four in the East (Jerusalem, Antioch, Alexandria, and Constantinople).

3. *The Second Century to the Middle Ages (A.D. 100-538)*

a. During this period, writings that were deemed to have been written by an apostle or close associate and were accepted by the Church at large as authoritative became part of the canon (collection of sacred writings).[6] Many books were rejected,[7] such as the "Gospel according to Thomas," the "Gospel of Mary Magdalene," the "Gospel of Peter," and the "Acts of Paul." They became known as "apocryphal" (non-inspired).

b. Early Christians faced fierce persecution for several reasons. They were charged with atheism because they did not respect the Roman emperor as a god and refused to burn incense in his honor. They had no altars, images, or temples where they worshiped. Emperor Trajan blamed Christians for the fact that sacrifices to the traditional gods had been abandoned.[8] Emperors criticized Christians for not being willing to defend the empire by serving in the army. Christians were even accused of cannibalism and human sacrifice (a misunderstanding of the Christian communion service). Persecution became the lot of Jesus' followers. In 202, Septimus Severus issued an edict forbidding Christians to make more converts. In 250 Decius demanded that all Roman citizens should publicly burn incense to signify loyalty to him. In 255 Valerian forbade Christians to worship. In 303 Diocletian ordered the destruction of Christian scriptures, required that all citizens participate in public sacrifices to the traditional Roman gods, and ordered the execution of many Christians.[9]

c. Emperor Constantine (ca. 285 - 337) was a key figure in this period. He was the first Christian emperor of the Roman world. In 312, before a battle, he saw the shape of a cross in front of the sun and heard a voice saying, "in this sign you will conquer." It is said that after this event Constantine was immediately converted to Christianity; however, he never resigned his position as *Pontifex Maximus* (supreme pagan pontiff or priest) of the cult of *Sol Invictus* ("the Invincible Sun"–Mithra) of the pagan state. In 313, Constantine issued the Edict of Milan, which recognized the right of persons to worship as they chose. On March 7, 321, he decreed: "On the venerable Day of the Sun [Sunday] let the magistrates and people residing in cities rest, and let all workshops be closed."[10] Constantine moved the capital city of the empire to the ancient Greek city of

Byzantium and renamed it Constantinopolis (City of Constantine). In 325, he summoned the bishops of the East and West to Nicaea to discuss the nature of Christ. He was baptized on his deathbed in 337.

d. Many Christological controversies (disputes about the divine/human nature of Jesus) precipitated ecumenical (churchwide) councils. These assemblies of bishops took their names from the places where they were convened–two in the fourth century: Nicaea in 325 (which resulted in the condemnation of Arianism that negated the divinity of Jesus) and Constantinople in 381. In the fifth century there were two schisms over Christology. The first happened after the Council of Ephesus in 431. This Council declared that Jesus was one Divine Person from the womb, and therefore Mary is the Mother of God. It resulted in the condemnation of Nestorianism, with Syrian and Palestinian bishops leaving the council. About thirty years later a man named Apollinarius started teaching that Christ was not only one person but only had one Divine Nature and will. This was rejected at the Council of Chalceadon in 451. Those that went into schism were called Monophysites. This resulted in the loss of the Egyptian, Ethiopian, and Nubian churches, and later of the Armenian church.[11]

e. During this period some Christians turned away from the world to live in solitary communion with God as ascetics. By the fourth century, Christian monks were living simply in caves in the Egyptian dessert–these solitary monks were called "hermits" or "anchorites." By the fifth century, however, the monastic life shifted from solitary life to communal living–they were now known as "coenobites." Monasteries were set up to help monks persevere in their calling. The Rule of St. Benedict (ca. 530) became a model for all later monastic orders in the West with its three vows: poverty, chastity, and obedience to the abbot; their monasteries combined work and prayer.[12]

f. The Church in the West, centered in Rome, adopted Latin as its official language. The Church in the East, centered in Constantinople, used the Greek tongue. Due to the service of many able men, location, political factors, and the tradition that it was established by Peter, the Church at Rome became dominant.[13]

4. *The Middle Ages (A.D. 538-1517)*

a. From 538 to 1517 the Roman Church dominated the Western world. The Roman Catholic Church controlled religion, philosophy, morals, politics, art, and education. This drove the Western world into the Dark Ages. In spite of many centuries of persecution, faithful Christians "who followed closely and adhered steadfastly to the beliefs and practices delivered by the apostles to the saints" launched a great missionary work that took the gospel beyond the sphere of influence of the popular church.[14]

b. After the Council of Chalcedon, relations between East and West deteriorated as opposing preferences and practices became the catalyst for permanent division. Rome claimed universal jurisdiction over the Church while the West preferred a collegiate authority involving bishops from the major Christian centers. During the iconoclast controversy over the use of images in 787 at Nicaea II, the Eastern churches opted for the veneration of icons rather than statues. The rivalry between Pope Leo IX (1002-1054) and the Patriarch of Constantinople, Michael Cerularius (d. 1054), led to a permanent division as they exchanged excommunication in 1054.[15]

c. During the Middle Ages the papacy exercised enormous secular power. Those who disagreed could be threatened with excommunication. Pope Gregory VII (ca. 1020-1085) set forth unprecedented claims for the papacy. The pope, he asserted, was divinely appointed and therefore could be ruled by no human. The pope had the right to depose emperors.[16]

d. Building on this increased realm of authoritative rule, in reaction to Islamic expansion, in 1095 Pope Urban II (1042-1099) launched the Holy Wars to recover the Holy Land from Muslim control. The Crusades (from 1095 to about 1290) were more failures than successes. The Holy Land was returned to Christian control for only a brief time. Crusaders even ravaged the city of Constantinople, widening the distance between the East and the West. However, through the Crusades the West came in touch with the Arab culture and Greek language. The works of Aristotle and others became available to the returning Crusaders, thus creating the background for the cultural explosion of the Renaissance.[17]

e. During the twelfth and thirteenth centuries many new monastic orders appeared as a reaction against decadent society. A major influence was a community in Clunny, France; its monks specialized in liturgical elaborations. The Cistercians, Gregorians, and Carthusians returned to St. Benedict's Rule of combining work and prayer. In contrast with monks and nuns' living secluded lives, mendicant friars worked among the people. The Dominicans and the Franciscans were the first mendicant orders to be created. In 1215, Dominic de Guzman established the Dominican Order, primarily to teach the faith and refute heresies. The Franciscan Order, created by Francis of Assisi (1182-1226), aspired to emulate the life and suffering of Christ. The Augustinians, or Hermits of St. Augustine, were founded in 1256 to focus on education.[18] The Society of Jesus, whose members are known as Jesuits, was founded by Ignatius Loyola in 1540 to serve the pope (in the aftermath of the Protestant Reformation, 1517).[19] Monastic and mendicant orders were under the discipline of an abbot, while secular priests (served "in the world") under the authority of a bishop.

f. The thirteenth century saw the power of the papacy fueling the Inquisition, an ecclesiastical court set up in 1229 to investigate and suppress heresy. It was a common practice to torture and burn heretics to deter others from dangerous views. In 1542 the Congregation of the Holy Office was assigned to the Dominican Order.[20]

g. The fourteenth century was a period of unprecedented degradation among the clergy. Due to political strife, the seat of the papacy was moved from Rome to Avignon, France. From 1378-1417 there were three simultaneous popes, each claiming to be the true pope, anathematizing and excommunicating one another: Urban VII, an Italian; Clement VII, a Frenchman; and Alexander V, elected by the Council of Pisa.[21]

5. *The Protestant Reformation*

a. There were several factors leading to the development of the Protestant Reformation: the rise of literacy brought about by the Renaissance ("Rebirth"), the invention of the printing press, a decline in the prestige of the pope among the kings, the corrupt lives and arrogance of the clergy, and the people's desire to reform the Church.

b. On October 31, 1517, Martin Luther, a German Augustinian monk, nailed the Ninety-five Theses to the door of his church at Wittenberg to protest the selling of indulgences. He did it on the eve of All Saints Day (Halloween), when most of his parishioners would come to church. He was excommunicated in 1520, but his friends saved him by hiding him in a castle. In 1529, at the Diet of Speyer, the Emperor Charles V attempted to repress Luther's movement by force, but some of the German state princes stood up in protest. Thus, because of their protest, the movement began to be known as the "Protestants."[22] What had originally been intended to bring reform to Catholicism from within was now an ousted reformation, forced to split from the original body.

c. The four most important traditions to emerge directly from the Reformation were the Lutheran tradition, the Reformed/Calvinist/Presbyterian tradition, the Anabaptist tradition, and the Anglican tradition. Subsequent

Protestant traditions generally trace their roots back to these initial four schools of the Reformation.

c. Major differences between Roman Catholics and Protestants include:[23]

1) Authority and interpretation of Scriptures: Protestants believe that the individual's conscience and reason, under the guidance of the Holy Spirit, are the keys to understanding Scripture. Catholics assert the authority of church tradition and the infallibility of the pope about essentials of the faith.

2) Salvation: Protestants believe that salvation is achieved only by God's grace, through repentance and faith. Roman Catholics support the doctrine of salvation by both faith and good works. Protestants believe that only trust in Jesus as Lord and Savior saves a person. Roman Catholics regard Mary as co-redemptrix with Jesus.

3) Church authority: Protestants affirm the "priesthood of all believers," which stresses that ministry is the work of the church and the individual's direct relationship to God. Roman Catholics stand on the mediation of God's grace through the officials of the Church. In Protestantism, church authority is within the believer, the local church, and the denomination, while in Roman Catholicism, authority is vested in the hierarchy of the church. In Protestantism, officials can be married, while in Roman Catholicism, they are expected to remain celibate.

4) Ordinances: Protestants insist that the only ordinances are those instituted by Jesus and regard them as commemorative and symbolic. Roman Catholics consider the sacrament as mystical vehicles of God's grace.

5) Biblical canon: Most Protestants accept only the 66 books of the Old and New Testaments. Roman Catholics and Anglicans add the deuterocanonics (books of a second level or second canon).

d. Protestants have formed "denominations." Protestant denominations may be loose ideological groups that overlap in many ways. "A denomination, in the Christian sense of the word, is an identifiable religious body, organization under a common name, structure, and/or doctrine."[24] According to the *World Christian Encyclopedia*, at the beginning of the twenty-first century there were "over 33,000 denominations in 238 countries." In the United States alone there were 5,100 Independent, 660 Protestant, 400 Marginal, and one Anglican, for a total of 6,161 denominations: Every year there is a worldwide net increase of around 270 to 300 denominations.[25]

6. *Modern Developments*

a. During the sixteenth and seventeenth centuries, Roman Catholics sent Franciscans and Jesuits to Asia, Africa, and the Americas. The "Father of Protestant Missions," William Carey, was sent to India in 1792. Within a generation after William Carey, many Bible societies were established and missionary societies were created to send missionaries all around the world.[26] Historian Kenneth S. Latourette describes the nineteenth century as "the great century"of Christian missions.[27] Two hundred years later, by 2005, there were 443,000 missionaries in the mission field.[28]

b. In the nineteenth century, the "social gospel" movement brought Protestant churches to the forefront of efforts for social and moral reform. In 1911 "fundamentalists" in the United States held as their uncompromising tenets the total inerrancy of the Bible, Christ's literal virgin birth, substitutionary atonement, bodily resurrection, and anticipated second coming.[29] "Modernist" theologians led an effort to analyze the Bible as literature; liberal Protestants tend to emphasize ecumenism and downplay conversion to Christianity. Beginning in the 1930s, the heirs of the fundamentalism, now called "evangelicals," have become a vigorous movement in many Protestant churches.[30]

c. Among Christians of all classes and nations, there is a renewal movement that overlaps somewhat with the evangelical surge, known as the charismatic movement. It emphasizes an emotional spiritual experience, manifestations of spiritual gifts, specially the gift of tongues and healing. Members of this Pentecostal-charismatic movement have grown from 1.3% of Christians in 1900 to 20% in 2000. They numbered 426.7 million in mid-2005, second only to Catholicism as a bloc.[31]

d. The Roman Catholic Church called the Vatican Council I (1869-70) to approve papal infallibility: the pope can never err when he speaks *ex cathedra* (from the seat of his authority) on matters of faith and morals.[32] In 1962 Pope John XXIII convened the Vatican Council II for the express purposes of updating and energizing the Church; changes included the approval of offering mass in local languages rather than in Latin, simplification of rites, and the use of local tunes and instruments during worship. They emphasized ecumenism and opened lines of dialogue with Jews, Muslims, and other world religions.[33] Pope John Paul II is remembered by his conservative stances and extensive traveling. On April 19, 2005, Cardinal Joseph Ratzinger was elected as the new pope, choosing the name of Benedict XVI. Once the archbishop of Munich, Germany, and for many years prefect of the Sacred Congregation for the Doctrine of Faith (the successor to the Holy Office, or Inquisition), Ratzinger had been one of the most powerful men in the Vatican and was widely acknowledged as a leading theologian.

e. The ecumenical movement has had an influence on mainline churches, beginning as early as 1910 with the Edinburgh Missionary Conference. Its origins lay in the recognition of the need for cooperation on the mission field in Africa, Asia, and Oceania. Since 1948 the World Council of Churches has been influential. The movement aims for rapprochement among all branches of Christianity and presses for the restoration of unity among all Christians. There are also ecumenical bodies at regional, national, and local levels around the globe.[34]

Notes

1   "Major Religions of the World Ranked by Number of Adherents," *Adherents.com*, 2006 [article online]; retrieved on March 30, 2006, from http://www.adherents.com/ Religions_By_Adherents.html#Christianity.

2   David Barrett, George Kurian, Todd Johnson, "The Status of Christianity and Religions in the Modern World," *World Christian Encyclopedia*, 2nd ed., Vol. 1 (New York: Oxford University Press, 2001), 5.

3   Michael Jaffarian, "The Demographics of World Religions Entering the 21st Century," in *Between Past and Future: Evangelical Missions Entering the 21st Century*, J. Bonk, ed. (Pasadena, CA: William Carey Library, 2003), 261-62.

4   "Christ was born between three and four years before the beginning of the Christian Era, that is, before the year called A.D. 1. The mistake of dating the Christian Era somewhat over three years this side of the birth of Christ, instead of dating it from the year of His birth, as it was designed to be, arose on this wise. One of the most important of ancient eras was reckoned from the building of the city of Rome–*ab urbe condita*–expressed by the abbreviation A.U.C., or more briefly, U.C. In the year which is now numbered A.D. 532, Dionysius Exiguus, a Scythian by birth, and a Roman abbot, who flourished in the reign of Justinian, invented the Christian Era. According to the best evidence at his command, he placed the birth of Christ U.C. 753. But Christ was born before the death of Herod; and it was afterward ascertained on the clearest evidence that the death of Herod occurred in April, U.C. 750. Allowing a few months for the events recorded in Christ's life before the time of Herod's death, his birth is carried back to the latter part of U.C. 749, a little more than three years before A.D. 1. Christ was therefore thirty years of age [at the time

of His baptism] in A.D. 27." Uriah Smith, *The Prophecies of Daniel and Revelation* (Washington, DC: Review & Herald, 1944), 213, footnote.

5 References from historians Tacitus, Suetonius, and Pliny the Younger in Henry Bettenson, ed., *Documents of the Christian Church*, 2nd ed. (New York: Oxford University Press, 1967), 1-4. References from Jewish sources in Josephus, Antiq. xviii, iii. William Whiston, trans., *The Works of Josephus*, complete and unabridged (Peabody, MA: Hendrikson, 1985), 379.

6 F. F. Bruce, *The Canon of Scripture* (Downers Grove, IL: InterVarsity Press, 1988), 17.

7 "The New Testament canon during the 2nd century did not develop so much through a process of collecting apostolic writings as through a process of rejecting those whose apostolic origin was not established." "The Language, Manuscripts, and Canon of the New Testament," *Seventh-day Adventist Bible Commentary*, rev. ed., ed. Francis D. Nichol (Washington, DC: Review and Herald, 1976-80), 5:128.

8 Bettenson, *Documents of the Christian Church*, 4.

9 Ibid., 7-14.

10 "Codex Justinianus," lib. 3, tit. 12, 3; trans. in Philip Schaff, *History of the Christian Church*, Vol. 3, 5th ed. (New York: Scribner, 1902), 380, note 1.

11 Harold O. J. Brown, *Heresies: The Image of Christ in the Mirror of Heresy and Orthodoxy from the Apostles to the Present* (Garden City, NY: Doubleday, 1984), 116-80.

12 Mary Pat Fisher, *Living Religions*, 6th ed. (Upper Saddle River, NJ: Prentice-Hall, 2005), 309, 310.

13 Albert Henry Newman, *A Manual of Church History*, Vol. 1, 24th ed. (Valley Forge, PA: Judson Press, 1953), 396-406.

14 Benjamin George Wilkinson, *Truth Triumphant: The Church in the Wilderness* (Mountain View, CA: Pacific Press, 1944), 9.

15 Carl A. Volz, *The Medieval Church from the Dawn of the Middle Ages to the Eve of the Reformation* (Nashville: Abingdon, 1997), 21-27, 65-68.

16 Thomas Oestreich, "Pope St. Gregory VII," *Catholic Encyclopedia*, online edition, 2003; retrieved on March 12, 2006, from http://www.newadvent.org/cathen/06791c.htm.

17   Kenneth Scott Latourette, *The Thousand Years of Uncertainty*, Vol. 2 of *A History of the Expansion of Christianity* (Grand Rapids: Zondervan, 1970), 308–42.

18   Robert A. Baker, *A Summary of Christian History* (Nashville: Broadman, 1959), 139-42.

19   Ibid., 251-54.

20   "Inquisition," *Wikipedia, the Free Encyclopedia*, 2006 [article online]; retrieved on March 17, 2006, from http://en.wikipedia.org/wiki/Inquisition.

21   Henry S. Lucas, *The Renaissance and the Reformation* (New York: Harper & Brothers, 1934), 63-75.

22   William R. Estep, *Renaissance and Reformation* (Grand Rapids: Eerdmans, 1986), 112-60.

23   B. A. Robinson, "Comparing the Beliefs of Roman Catholics and Conservative Protestants," *Ontario Consultants on Religious Tolerance*, 2005 [article online]; retrieved on March 25, 2006, from http://www.religioustolerance.org/chr_capr.htm.

24   "Christian Denomination," *Wikipedia, the Free Encyclopedia*, 2006 [article online]; retrieved on April 1, 2006, from http://en.wikipedia.org/wiki/Christianity_Denominations.

25   David Barrett, George Kurian, Todd Johnson, "Denominations," Table 1-5, *World Christian Encyclopedia*, Vol. 1, 2nd ed. (New York: Oxford University Press, 2001), 16.

26   Between 1804 and 1840 some 63 different Bible societies in America, Europe, and Asia were formed. At least 15 missionary societies were established in America between 1796 and 1837. LeRoy Edwin Froom, *Movement of Destiny* (Washington, DC: Review & Herald, 1978), 50-59.

27   Kenneth Scott Latourette, *The Great Century: Europe and the United States* Vol. 4 of *A History of the Expansion of Christianity* (Grand Rapids: Zondervan, 1970).

28   Center for the Study of Global Christianity, "All Humanity in Mission Perspective in Mid-2005," *Gordon-Conwell Theological Seminary*, 2005 [article online]; retrieved on March 27, 2006, from http://www.gordonconwell.edu/ockenga/globalchristianity/index.php.

29   George M. Mardsen, *Fundamentalism and American Culture: The Shaping of Twentieth-Century Evangelicalism, 1870-1925* (New York: Oxford University Press, 1982).

30 Louis Gasper, *The Fundamentalist Movement: 1930-1956* (Grand Rapids: Baker, 1963).

31 Luis Bush, "Where Are We Now?" *Mission Frontiers*, June 2000 [article online]; retrieved on April 15, 2006, from http://www.missionfrintiers.org/2000/03/200003.htm.

32 "Vatican Council," *Catholic Encyclopedia* [article online]; available on March 30, 2006, at http://www.newadvent.org/cathen/15303a.htm.

33 "Documents of Vatican II," *Roman Catholic Net*; available on March 30, 2006, at http://www.rc.net/rcchurch/vatican2/.

34 Robert McAfee Brown, *The Ecumenical Revolution* (Garden City, NY: Doubleday, 1967), 18.

CHAPTER 23

Catholicism

1. *Introduction*

a. With more than one billion communicants, the Roman Catholic Church is the most powerful religious force in the world. This Christian body alone outnumbers all the Buddhists of the world combined (Mahayana, Theravada, Vajrayana) and all Hindus combined. However, the Roman Catholic Church is not the only church that claims the name "Catholic." There are more than twenty Catholic bodies. Characteristic marks among the several Catholic churches include allegiance to creeds, belief in apostolic succession, observation of seven sacraments, and use of a liturgical language.

b. Catholic (from Greek *catholikos*; *kata*, "according to," and *holos*, "the whole," meaning "universal") is a religious term with a number of meanings:[1]

1) It can refer to the notion that all Christians are part of one Church, regardless of denominational divisions. It is used in this sense in the Nicene Creed ("one holy catholic and apostolic church"), written during the fourth century A.D.

2) It can refer to the members, beliefs, and practices of the Roman Catholic Church in all of its more than twenty rites. For instance, the Eastern Rite churches (also called Uniate churches) recognize the authority of the pope, but they keep their own traditional liturgies.

3) It can be used to refer to those Christian churches who maintain a belief that they should possess an episcopate (bishops) that can be traced directly to the apostles (apostolic succession). Among those who regard themselves as ''Catholic'' but not ''Roman Catholic'' are the various Orthodox churches, Anglicans, the Old Catholic Church, and the Ancient Catholic Church.

2. *Roman Catholic Church*

a. The Vatican-based Catholic Church, comprising both the Western and the Eastern Rites, claims to be the "One, Holy, Catholic and Apostolic Church."[2] However, many American Catholics prefer not to use "Roman" as part of the name for their church.

b. According to *The Official Catholic Directory*, by 2005 there were 67,259,768 Roman Catholics in the United States (23% of the U.S. population), and 1,070,315,000 Roman Catholics worldwide.[3] The Roman Catholic Church is the largest denomination in the country. By 2005, the second largest was the Southern Baptist Convention, with over sixteen million members, and the third was the United Methodist Church, with over eight million.

c. The Roman Catholic clergy is organized in a strict, sometimes overlapping hierarchy:[4]

1) Pope: Head of the church, based at the Vatican. The Vatican State is also the Holy See (Latin: *Sancta Sedes*, lit. "holy seat") of the Roman Catholic Church. It is less than one square mile. It was established as an independent state on February 11, 1929. The Roman Catholic Church holds that the pope is infallible in defining matters of faith and morals. The title "pope" stems from the Greek word *papas*, which means "father."

2) Cardinal: Appointed by the pope, 178 cardinals worldwide, including 13 in the U.S., make up the College of Cardinals. As a body, it advises the pope and, upon his death, elects a new pope. Because of the scarlet color of their vestments, cardinals are the namesakes of the bird of the same name.

3) Archbishop: An archbishop is a bishop of a main or metropolitan diocese, also called an archdiocese. A cardinal can concurrently hold the title. The U.S. has 45 archbishops.

4) Bishop : He is a teacher of church doctrine, a priest of sacred worship, and a minister of church government. The word "bishop" comes from

Old English *biscop*, a variant of Latin *episcopus*, meaning "supervisor, overseer." A bishop oversees a diocese. The U.S. has 290 active bishops. A bishop, like a priest, is ordained to this office.

5) Priest: An ordained minister who can administer most of the sacraments, including the Eucharist, baptism, and marriage. He can be with a particular religious order or committed to serving a congregation.

6) Deacon: A transitional deacon is a seminarian studying for the priesthood. A permanent deacon can be married and assists a priest by performing some of the sacraments.

d. The Eastern Rite Catholic churches are Eastern or Oriental in rite and canonical tradition. Sometimes called *Uniate* ("united with Rome") churches, they are in communion with and under the authority of the Bishop of Rome, but they are autonomous or self-governing. They accept the full dogma of the Roman Catholic Church as expounded by the 21 councils they recognize as ecumenical. The following are the principal Eastern Rite Catholic churches and communities:[5]

1) Byzantine Rite: The Ukrainian Catholic Church (the largest Eastern Catholic church), the Ruthenian Catholic church, the Melkite Church, the Romanian Catholic Church, the Greek Catholics of Greece, the Slovakian Diocese of Presov, the Diocese of Hajdudorog, and the Italo-Greeks.

2) East Syrian Rite: The Chaldean Church and the Syro-Malabar Church in South India.

3) West Syrian Rite: The Maronite Church, the Syrian Catholic Church Church, and the Syro-Malankara Church in South India.

4) Other Rites: The Armenian Catholic Church, the Coptic Catholic Church, and the Ethiopian Catholic Church.

3. *Orthodox Churches*

a. The English word "orthodox" is the equivalent of the Greek *orthodoxia*, which is etymologically derived from two Greek words, *orthos* ("right") and *doxa* ("opinion" or "glory"). The meaning of this combination is "right-belief," as opposed to heresy or heterodoxy.[6]

b. The Orthodox family includes three major groupings of churches:
1) Eastern Orthodox churches that, along with the Roman Catholic Church,
recognize seven councils held between the fourth and eight centuries; 2) the
Church of the East, or Nestorian Church, that accepts only the authority of the
Council of Nicaea; 3) Oriental Orthodox is the family of churches united by
acceptance of three ecumenical councils and by the rejection of the ecumenical
authority of the Council of Chalcedon.

c. By the third century A.D. there were five bishops: one in the West
(Rome) and four in the East of the Roman Empire (Jerusalem, Alexandria,
Constantinople, and Antioch). The Eastern church claims itself to be "orthodox"
and condemns the Western church as heterodox because (among other things) it
includes the *filioque* clause (the Holy Spirit "proceeds from the Father *and the
Son*") in its creed. Although both East and West always claimed both names,
gradually "Catholic" became the most common name for the church in the West,
and "Orthodox" for the churches in the East.[7] Political, cultural, and doctrinal
differences separated the Eastern Orthodox churches from the Roman churches
in 1054. Eastern Orthodox churches do not consider themselves to be separate
denominations, but one faith with independent administrations. The major
Eastern bodies are the Greek and Russian Orthodox Churches. The Patriarch of
Constantinople is the Ecumenical Patriarch who serves as a bond to the Eastern
Orthodox churches in general, even though he does not have governmental
authority. By the beginning of the twenty-first century there more than
225,000,000 communicants in Eastern Orthodox churches. Today there are

1) Fifteen autocephalous (self-governing) Orthodox churches, mainly
found among Greek, Slavic, and Middle Eastern peoples: The American
Orthodox Catholic Church, the Orthodox of Albania, Alexandria, Antioch,
Bulgaria, Constantinople, Cyprus, Czech and Slovak Republics, Georgia,
Greece, Jerusalem, Poland, Romania, Russia, and Serbia.

2) Four autonomous (self-ruling) Orthodox churches: the Church of
Sinai, the Church of Finland, the Church of Japan, and the Church of Ukraine
(the last three are mostly composed of Russian expatriates).

d. The Church of the East, also known as the Nestorian Church, is but a
remnant of its former greatness, as it once extended from Beijing and Central
Asia to the Middle East. It accepts only the Council of Nicaea as having
ecumenical authority. The Church of the East recognizes Christ's two natures
but does not believe that they were equal; it insists that Mary bore only the
human nature of Christ—she did not bear God (Mary is not the "Mother of God").

e. Oriental Orthodox is the family of churches united by acceptance of three ecumenical councils and by the rejection of the ecumenical authority of the Council of Chalcedon.[8] They were condemned at the Council Chalcedon in A.D. 451. The Council approved the doctrine of the two equal natures of Christ but the Oriental Orthodox held that Christ is of one person (*mono*) and of one nature (*physis*). They are known as "monophysites." By the beginning of the twenty-first century they numbered over 36,000,000.

The Oriental Orthodox bodies are:

1) The Armenian Apostolic Church (established in Armenia as a bishopric in 260, it customarily celebrates Holy Communion only on Sunday, using pure wine [without water] and unleavened bread).

2) The Coptic Churches of Egypt and Ethiopia. Formerly one of the largest Christian groups in the world, this group diminished through persecution. Today, found mainly in Egypt, its numbers are increasing. The Ethiopian Church differs from the Coptic on several points, as it 1) accepts Apocrypha as Scripture; 2) venerates the Sabbath along with Sunday; 3) recognizes Old Testament figures as saints; and 4) observes many Old Testament regulations on food and purification.

3) Syrian Orthodox Churches. Under the leadership of Jacob Baradeus (his followers were often called Jacobites), who was a monophysite, the Syrian churches spread throughout the Mediterranean region and beyond.

4) The Mar Thoma Church of South India is a special case because it is a reformed Oriental church which is in full communion with the Anglican Church.

f. With the Roman Catholic Church, Orthodox churches recognize the Bible *and* Tradition as authority, and accept seven sacraments. They hold a sacramental view of salvation. Orthodox churches differ from Roman Catholics in that they practice baptism by triple immersion of children, offer communion with leavened bread, offer the laymen both the bread and the wine, ordain married priests (even though bishops remain unmarried), use icons but not images, do not believe in purgatory, and do not recognize the authority of the bishop in Rome.

4. *Sacramental View of Salvation*

a. It affirms that God's grace is given or mediated to transform a person's inward spiritual life through outward, tangible signs instituted by Christ. Sacraments produce or convey sanctifying grace automatically, but must be received or taken with the belief that they are effective. A person is infused with spiritual power which enables him to obey God's commandments, avoid sin, do good works, and meet the divine standard of righteousness. One becomes acceptable to God by *doing* what God wants, while relying on His supernatural help or power. Therefore, people are saved by God's grace and their good works (merits) through faith and the receiving of the sacraments. The only way a person lives as a member of Christ's body and receives the supernatural empowering of the Holy Spirit is through participation in these acts or rituals. At the Council of Florence (1439) the tradition of sacraments was formally accepted.[9]

b. The seven sacraments (Eastern and Oriental Orthodox call them "mysteries"):[10]

1) Baptism washes away the guilt of actual and original sin. Through sprinkling,[11] the person becomes a Christian and is qualified to partake of the other sacraments. Orthodox churches practice triple full immersion of children and converts in the name of the Holy Trinity.

2) Confirmation strengthens the person so that he or she can perform the duties of the Christian life. The gift of the Holy Spirit is bestowed when the bishop lays his hand on the person's forehead and makes the sign of the cross with his thumb moistened with oil. The Eastern Church does this at baptism, while the Roman Church confers it on children at age 12, after instruction in the catechism.

3) The eucharist (from Greek, *eucharistia*, "thanksgiving"), or mass, replenishes and nourishes the person with sanctifying grace for daily living. Christ's sacrifice on the cross for sins is reproduced at the altar. The bread and wine change into the real body and blood of Christ. The miracle of transubstantiation occurs when the priest says the words of consecration, "This is my body." The Orthodox Church gives both elements to the lay-persons, while the Roman Church usually gives only the bread at communion.

4) Penance, or reconciliation, conveys forgiveness of sins committed after baptism. The priest pronounces absolution, or God's pardon of eternal punishment, but requires the person to show true sorrow by performing "acts of

satisfaction" which remove the tangible or temporal penalties (fines) which the Church attaches to specific offenses. Any unpaid fines are removed in purgatory after death.

5) Ordination empowers men to exercise the role and authority of priests (presbyters) and bishops through performing the sacraments. Celibacy is required in the Roman Church. The Orthodox Church allows men already married to become priests, but bishops must be unmarried.

6) Matrimony through the mutual pledges made under the priest's direction consecrates the marriage union between a man and a woman. It is God's gift for moral life and the raising of children.

7) Anointing of the sick, or extreme unction, gives health to and fortifies the soul and the body, especially at the time of death. The organs of the senses are anointed with olive oil, and indulgence is thereby given for unconfessed sins of the body.

5. *Tradition*

a. Tradition is the oral transmission of the doctrine revealed by Jesus Christ or the apostles, independent of what is found in the Scriptures. Tradition is "the sum of revealed doctrine which has not been committed to sacred Scripture (though it may have appeared in uninspired writing) but which has been handed down by a series of legitimate shepherds of the Church from age to age."[12]

b. The biblical foundation for tradition is built on the fact that John 20:30-31 says that there were "many other things which are not written in this book" (also 21:25). Acts 20:35 records words of Jesus which are not registered in any of the four Gospels. For Roman Catholicism, tradition has the same authority as the Scripture.

> Sacred Tradition and sacred Scripture, then, are bound closely together, and communicate one with the other. For both of them, flowing out from the same divine well-spring come together in some fashion to form one thing, and move towards the same goal. Sacred Scripture is the speech of God as it is put down in writing under the breath of the Holy Spirit. And Tradition transmits in its entirety the Word of God which has been entrusted to the apostles by Christ the Lord and the Holy Spirit. . . . Hence, both Scripture and Tradition must be accepted and honored with equal feelings of devotion and reverence.[13]

c. Jesus denounced teachings based on tradition: "You have made the commandment of God of no effect by your tradition. . . . Teaching as doctrines the commandments of men" (Matt 15:5-9), "making the word of God no effect through your tradition which you have handed down" (Mark 7:13). Paul warned that "the time will come when they will not endure sound doctrine, . . . they will turn ears away from truth, and be turned aside to fables" (2 Tim 4:3-4) and admonished, "Beware lest anyone cheat you through philosophy and empty deceit, according to the tradition of men" (Col 2:8).

e. Examples of traditions added to the Scripture throughout history[14]

Year (A.D.)

160	First prayers for the dead
260	First monastic communities
320	Beginning of use of candles
321	Emperor Constantine decrees Sun-day observance
364	Sunday observance decreed by Council of Laodicea
451	Veneration to the "Mother of God"
593	Gregory the Great teaches doctrine of purgatory
600	Latin as the language for worship
610	Boniface III begins the use of the title "Pope"
709	Kissing the pope's feet and ring
786	Veneration of cross, images, and relics
850	Holy water, mixed with a pinch of salt and blessed by a priest
995	Canonization of saints, first by John XV
998	Mass as a sacrifice
1090	The rosary, introduced by Peter the Hermit
1079	Celibacy of priests/monks ordered by Gregory VII
1184	The Inquisition, instituted by the Council of Verona
1190	Sale of indulgences
1215	Transubstantiation, proclaimed by Pope Innocent III
1215	Auricular confession of sins to a priest, in Lateran Council
1220	Adoration of the wafer (host), decreed by Pope Honorius III
1287	The scapular, invented by Simon Stock, an English monk
1414	Cup forbidden to the people at communion, Constance
1545	Tradition and Bible have equal authority, Council of Trent
1545	Apocryphal books added to the Bible, Trent

6. *The Catholic Bible*

a. The Catholic Church accepts some books as "deuterocanonical," meaning "second canon."[15] Protestants affirm that they are *apocrypha*, not inspired.[16] The deuterocanonics are: III Ezra, IV Ezra, Tobit, Judith, Wisdom, Ecclesiasticus, Baruch, I and II Maccabees, additions to the book of Esther, additions to the book of Daniel, and additions to 2 Chronicles. They were written between 200 and 100 B.C. Jerome (d. 420) did not accept them when he wrote the official translation of the Latin Bible, the Vulgata Latina. In the Council of Trent, April 8, 1546, the deuterocanonics were officially recognized by the Roman Catholic Church.

b. Those who reject the deuterocanonical book argue that 1) they were never considered inspired by the Jews, who had been trusted with the Scriptures (Rom 3:2); 2) they are never quoted in the New Testament, even though there are 280 quotations from all the books of the Old Testament; 3) they are not included in any list of the early fathers of the Church until after Jerome (fifth century); 4) the very writers did not pretend to be inspired (1 Mac 4:46; 9:27; 14:41); 5) they teach doctrines which are not in harmony with the Scriptures, such as purgatory and prayers for the dead (2 Mac 12:38-46), reincarnation (Wisdom 8:19-20), and intercession of the saints (2 Mac 15:12-16); and 6) they contain superstitions (Tobit 6:5-17) and historical mistakes (Judit 1:15), in addition to doctrinal errors.

7. *Mary*

a. Official statements concerning Mary are found in the documents of Council Vatican II. "Mary has by grace been exalted above all angels and men to a place second only to her Son, as the most holy mother of God she was involved in the mysteries of Christ: She is rightly honored by a special cult in the Church."[17] She is described as "Advocate, Mediatrix, and Co-redemptrix."[18]

b. At the Niceaen [Nicene] Council, 325, Mary was given the title of *Theotokos*, Mother of God. This term is used in the "Hail Mary." The Dogma of the Immaculate Conception [that she was born without the stain of original sin], proclaimed by Pious IX in the Bull *Ineffabilis Deus* of 1854, also defined that Mary never committed a sin. The Dogma of the Assumption of Mary [that her body was taken to heaven after her death], defined by Pious XII in the Bull *Manifficentissimus Deus* on November 1, 1950. She is called *Regina Coeli* ("Queen of Heaven").[19] Mary has allegedly appeared throughout history in more than one hundred different places (Guadalupe, Mexico, 1531; Lourdes, France,

1858; Fatima, Portugal, 1917; Bearaing and Banneux, Belgium, 1933; Garabandal, Spain, 1960; Zeitun, Egypt, 1963; Akita, Japan, 1974; Cuapa, Nicaragua, 1980; Medjugorje, Bosnia-Herzegorvina, 1981; Kibeho, Rwanda, 1991-95; Conyers, Georgia, USA, 1987-98).[20]

c. The cult of Mary is called Mariolatry. Mariology is the body of belief and the systematic study of the Virgin Mary. Catholics divide worship into three categories: 1) *Latria*: "That supreme homage and religious worship which is due to God alone. . . . Relative *latria* is paid to images of the Sacred Heart, to crucifixes, and to such other religious objects that are exclusively connected with a divine person;"[21] 2) *Dulia*: "The reverence and homage paid to saints and angels on account of their supernatural excellence and union with God;"[22] and 3) *Hyperdulia*: "The special homage paid to Mary on account of her supreme dignity as Mother of God, and her consequent unique holiness and nearness to God."[23]

d. The "Ave Maria," better known as the "Hail Mary," did not come into use, according to the *Catholic Dictionary*, until "the end of the twelfth century." Words were added to the prayer by the Franciscans about the middle of the fifteenth century. The whole Ave Maria as it now stands was decreed by Pope Pius V in 1568.[24]

e. Even though Catholics claim that their devotion to Mary does not overshadow their devotion to her Son, in the city of Rome there are 15 churches dedicated to Christ and 121 dedicated to Mary; there are 22 liturgical festivities dedicated to Christ and 41 dedicated to Mary; and in the Rosary there are 155 "Hail Marys" (or prayers to Mary), 15 "Lord's Prayers," and 3 "Gloria Patri."

f. The Protestant phrase that describes Jesus as "only and all-sufficient Savior" refers to the fact that, even though Catholics may not explicitly say it, Catholic theology assumes that Jesus and what He did on the cross was not enough. Catholicism teaches that Jesus' sacrifice must be repeated (Mass is the bloodless repetition of His sacrifice), that we need saints to intercede for us before Him, and that He needs Mary's help as co-redemptrix, advocate, and mediatrix before the Father. According to the Bible, Jesus' sacrifice was enough (Heb 9:12, 28; 10:10). Mary cannot be a mediatrix because there is only One qualified to serve as a Mediator between God and Man (1 Tim 2:5-6; John 14:6); cannot be co-redemptrix because our Redeemer offers His own blood in our behalf (Heb 4:14-16); nor can she be our advocate (1 John 2:1-2).

8. *The Mass*

a. The Mass is the bloodless repetition of the sacrifice of Jesus Christ. The essential words for consecration are *Hoc est corpus meus*, "This is my body." Catholics believe in the doctrine of transubstantiation, the change of the substance of bread and wine into that of the body and blood of Christ.[25] Because they are the presence of Christ himself, Catholics worship and adore the elements–the congregation kneels down when the priest utters the words of consecration.

b. Development of the doctrine: In 394 Mass became a daily service. By 700 they started the use of a round wafer, in imitation of Egyptian practices. In 831 a Benedictine monk, Radaberto Pascacio, was the first in speaking of "real presence." In 1215 the Fourth Lateran Council, under Pope Innocent III, established transubstantiation as a dogma. At the Council of Florence, in 1439, the cup was withdrawn from the laity. As a part of the counter-Reformation, the Council of Trent in 1551, under Paul III, confirmed the dogma of transubstantiation.

c. Colors for different liturgical occasions[26]

1) White	Sundays in Christmas and selected festivals
2) Red	Pentecost, Martyrs, and Holy Week
3) Purple	All Saints Day and Lent
4) Green	Sunday after Epiphany and Pentecost
5) Black	Black Friday and Mass for the dead
6) Blue	Immaculate Conception
7) Pink	Third Sunday of Advent and fourth of Lent

d. Biblical references related to the Lord's Supper indicate that the bread must be broken (1 Cor 11:24), but the Catholic wafer is not broken. All must drink from the cup (Matt 26:27), but the Catholic laity normally do not partake of it. After the Communion service the bread is still bread (1 Cor 12:26), but in Catholic theology it is now the actual body of Christ. A service is *in memoriam* (1 Cor 11:24-25) when the person is not present. During the Reformation, Zwinglii taught that the expression "This is my body" in 1 Cor 11:24 means "This represents my body."

e. The Bible clearly teaches that "without shedding of blood there is no remission of sin" (Heb 9:22), which precludes a "bloodless sacrifice." But what is even more important is the fact that, in contrast with the concept that Mass is the repetition of the sacrifice of Christ, the Bible teaches that "Christ was offered once" (Heb 9:28) and that He did it "once for all" (Heb 10:10). Paul stressed that "Christ dies no more" (Rom 6:9-10). Jesus is "alive forevermore" (Rev 1:18).

9. *Veneration to Saints and Images*

a. Canonization is the act by which the pope decrees that a deceased person has been admitted among the saints and that he or she may be venerated. It must be preceded by Beatification: the process by which a most searching scrutiny is made on the life, writings, and miracles. When the pope unveils a picture of the *beatus* in St. Peter's Church at Rome, he or she may henceforth be referred to as the Blessed so-and-so.[27] Canonization can take place only 50 years after his or her death, and miracles must have occurred. The first canonization was for Bishop Ulrich of Augsburg in the year 993 by Pope John XV.[28]

b. Where the Roman Catholic Church predominates, generally each country, city, parish, town, and believer has their own patron saint.[29] A few samples from the Sanctorale are Clare (eye disorders), Dimas (thieves), Erasmus (colic), Gabriel the Archangel (philatelists), Genesius (printers), James the Greater (rheumatoid sufferers), Joseph (Russia), and Our Lady of Lourdes (Tennessee).[30]

> There are more than 10,000 Roman Catholic saints and beatified people. Among the Eastern Orthodox and Oriental Orthodox Communions, the numbers may be even higher, since there is no fixed process of 'canonization' and each individual jurisdiction within the two Orthodox communions independently maintains parallel lists of saints that have only partial overlap.[31]

c. Some saints are occasionally "discontinued." In 1969, 101 saints were decanonized by Pope Paul VI, but their festivities are still popular. Among the decanonized saints are St. Valentine (February 14, patron of those in love),[32] St. Nicholas (December 6, patron of Bakers and Pawnbrokers, and of Russia–who became the basis for Santa Claus),[33] St. Brigid (January 21),[34] St. Ursula (October 21), and St. Christopher (July 25).[35]

d. One of the Ten Commandments forbids bowing before images (Exo 20:3-6), and many other biblical references express similar concerns (Isa 44:13-17, Deut 4:15-19, and Ps 115:4-8). The Bible says that the saints have not yet reached the promise of a reward (Heb 11:39), including David (Acts 2:29, 34) and Paul (2 Tim 4:6-8). There is only one mediator between God and men (1 Tim 2:5), the Lord Jesus (John 14:6; Acts 4:12).

10. *The Pope*

a. The Bishop of Rome, known as the Pope, is the head of the Roman Catholic Church. The Catholic clergy is organized in a strict, sometimes overlapping hierarchy. It includes deacons, priests, bishops, archbishops, cardinals, and the Pope. The official documents of the Church state:

> The Roman Pontiff, by reason of his office as Vicar of Christ, namely, and as a pastor of the entire Church, has full, supreme and universal power over the whole Church, a power which he can always exercise unhindered. The order of bishops is the successor to the college of the apostles in their role as teachers and pastors, and in it the apostolic college is perpetuated. Together with their head, the Supreme Pontiff, and never apart from him, they have supreme and full authority over the universal Church; but this power cannot be exercised without the agreement of the Roman Pontiff. The Lord made Peter alone the rock foundation and the holder of the keys of the Church . . . .[36]

b. The person holding the office of the pope also has the titles:

Holy Father
His Holiness
Bishop of Rome
Vicar of Jesus Christ
Successor of St. Peter
Supreme Pontiff of the Universal Church
Primate of Italy
Patriarch of the West
Servant of the Servants of God
Sovereign of the State of Vatican City
Prince of the Apostles

b. Biblical records do not support the concept of "papal supremacy." When Peter talks about himself, he is "an apostle of Jesus Christ" (1 Pet 1:1) and "an elder" among others (1 Pet 5:1). When he speaks of the Rock, he always points to Jesus (1 Pet 2:4-8, Acts 4:10-12).

c. For Roman Catholics, the passage of Matt 16:17-19 is of crucial importance: Peter received the keys of the kingdom, only through his succession can the church administer the forgiveness of sin, and he is the rock upon which Jesus built His Church.[37] However, an examination of the passage reveals something different.

1) "Upon this rock I will build my church" was a reference to what Peter had just said, "You are the Christ!" Peter is not the rock. "Petra" means a loose stone, in contrast with a rock that may serve as a foundation for a structure. Many Bible passages identify Jesus as the rock, the cornerstone, and the foundation (1 Pet 2:3-6; 1 Cor 3:10-11; Eph 2.10-22; Acts 4:10-12; 1 Cor 10:3-4). Jesus Christ is the head of the Church (Eph 4:11-16; 5:23). Four verses later, Jesus calls Peter "Satan" and a "stumbling stone" (Matt 16:23).

2) Concerning the expression, "You will receive the keys of the kingdom," it is important to know that others had the keys (Luke 11:52). Since Peter was the first who identified Jesus as the Messiah or Christ, Jesus gave him the privilege of being the first to announce it (Matt 16:20). Peter was the first who preached a sermon to Jews (Acts 2), was involved in the first baptism of Samaritans (Acts 8), and opened the doors to the Gentiles (Acts 10). Jesus has the keys now (Rev 1:18; 3:7).

3) The assertion "Whatever you bind on earth will be bound in heaven" was for the entire church (Matt 18:15-18; John 20:13).

d) Nowhere in the Bible is Peter shown as having supremacy. There were three discussions about supremacy, but Jesus never used them to give Peter any particular privilege (Matt 18:1-4; Matt 20:20-27; Luke 22:24-26). Peter helped choose a successor (Acts 1:24-26). The apostles sent Peter and John to Samaria (Acts 8:14). Peter commanded Cornelius, "Do not kneel down before me" (Acts 11:2) and instructed Simon, "Pray to God for forgiveness" (Acts 8:20-22). Church members argued with Peter (Acts 11:2), and the apostle Paul even reprimanded Peter in public (Gal 2:13, 14). Peter is presented as being on the same level as other apostles (Gal 2:9), in the council of Jerusalem a collective decision was made by the apostles and elders (Acts 15:22-24), and Paul introduced himself as not being less than the other apostles (2 Cor 2:11). The Holy Spirit, not a human being, is the only infallible guide of the Church (2 Pet 1:19-21; John 14:15-17; 1:25-26; 16:5-7; 16:13-14; 1 John 2:20, 26-27).

e. The Roman Catholic Church claims uninterrupted apostolic succession, so it alone can administer the sacraments and ordain ministers. However, history shows that when many Roman bishops died, the position was vacant for extended periods of time. For instance, when John III died (573), a new bishop was elected ten months later; the same happened with Pelagius II (d. 590), seven months; Gregory I (d. 604), five months; Fabianus (d. 650), eleven months; Boniface II (d. 532), six months; Martin I (d. 653), one year and two months; Paul I (d. 767), one year and one month; Nicholas I (d. 877), eight years and seven months; Clement (d. 1268), two years and five months; Nicholas IV (d.1292), two years and three months later.

11. *Witnessing to Roman Catholics*

a. Be a good listener. Never act shocked at assertions which you might consider flagrant and preposterous. Remember, the Catholic was taught from infancy the tenets of his church, and they are woven into his very being.[38]

b. Be patient. The Catholic's lack of education about the Bible and initial inability to grasp the principles of truth will need patience on your part.

c. Never argue. The longer you hold out on a controversial question, the more stubborn his heart will become. Never say, "I am going to prove that you are wrong." Change the subject to one which is less polemic. The "milk of the word" should be given before administering the "strong meat."

d. Affirm their confidence in the Bible. The first and most important step in instructing the Catholic is to direct his mind to the Bible as the only rule of faith. Insist that the true religion is not to do what a priest, a teacher, or a pastor says, but to do what God says. Once he is convinced that the Holy Scriptures are inspired by God, it will not be very difficult to convince him of the various points of your faith.

e. Be aware of Catholic terminology. The Bible should be referred to as "the Holy Scriptures." Jesus should be referred to as "our Blessed Lord" and "our Savior." The Lord's Supper is known to the Roman Catholic as the "Sacrament of the Holy Eucharist," or "Holy Communion." Mary could be referred to as "the blessed Virgin," without detracting any Biblical teaching.[39]

f. Treat the Bible with much reverence. When studying or conversing on sacred things with a Catholic, you should exhibit profound solemnity, both in language and demeanor. The Bible should be handled with reverential awe.

g. Seek a common ground before studying controversial issues. Events which tie in with prophecies of the Second Coming are good subjects to use to awaken an interest in the Holy Scriptures. Catholics are also fascinated with such subjects as Daniel 2 and Christ's life predicted in advance. Easter/Holy Week is the most important evangelistic season in some Roman Catholic countries, due to the interest that the crucifixion, burial, and resurrection awakens in the Catholic mind.

h. Know the Roman Catholic teachings. If the Bible instructor is prepared to state facts as to how the various Catholic doctrines came in and related historical facts, this knowledge on his part will spark confidence in the mind of the Catholic.

i. Pray with them. Catholics will greatly appreciate your praying warm, fervent, heartfelt prayers in their behalf.

12. *Glossary of Catholic Terms*

a. Advent. The four-week season before Christmas. During Advent Catholics should pray and fast to prepare to celebrate the advent of Jesus.

b. Archbishop. In Catholicism, this is a title given automatically to bishops who govern archdioceses.

c. Beatification. The last step toward canonization of a saint.

d. Canon law. The codified body of general laws governing the Church.

e. Clergy. Collective term referring to male persons who administer the rites of the Church through holy orders.

f. Encyclical. A pastoral letter written by the pope for the entire Roman Catholic Church.

g. Epiphany. The feast that celebrates the "shining forth" or revelation of God to humankind in human form, in the person of Jesus. It runs from the birth of Jesus, the visit of the wise men and all of Jesus' childhood events, up to his baptism.

h. Eucharist. The sacrament of the Lord's Supper.

i. Hierarchy. The ordered body of clergy, divided into bishops, priests, and deacons. In Catholic practice, the term refers to the bishops of the world or of a particular region.

j. Holy See. The diocese of the pope, Rome.

k. Host. The bread under whose appearance Christ is and remains present in a unique manner after the consecration of the mass.

l. Immaculate Conception. A feast on December 8 that celebrates the fact that Mary was preserved by God from the stain of original sin at the time of her own conception.

m. Lent. A season of fasting and penitence in preparation for Easter. It covers the forty days before Easter, not including Sundays. Mardi Gras is the last day before the beginning of Lent. The Wednesday on which Lent begins is known as Ash Wednesday.

n. Liturgy. An organized routine, or ceremony, by tradition usually in a religion. For example, the Catholic mass is a liturgy.

o. Patron saints. Special protectors or guardians over areas of life.

p. Pontiff. An alternative form of reference to the pope. Pontifical has to do with the pope.

q. Purgatory. The state or condition in which those who have died in the state of grace, but with some attachment to sin, suffer for a time before they are admitted to the glory and happiness of heaven.

r. Relics. The physical remains and effects of saints, which are considered worthy of veneration inasmuch as they represent people who are with God.

s. Rosary. A prayer of meditation primarily on events in the lives of Mary and Jesus, repeating the Lord's Prayer, the Hail Mary and the *Gloria Patri*. Generally, the rosary is said on a physical circlet of beads.

t. Sacrament. A formal religious act conferring a specific grace on those who receive it. Grace is received through participation in the sacraments. There are seven sacraments.

u. Saint. A person officially recognized, especially by canonization, as being entitled to public veneration and capable of interceding for people on earth.

v. Sanctorale. The section of the liturgical book (Breviary or Missal) containing the proper offices of the saints and the calendar for their feasts.

w. Scapular. A devotional artifact in the form of a cloth pendant that confers a benefit to the wearer.

x. Transubstantiation. The scholastic term used to designate the unique change of the eucharistic bread and wine into the body and blood of Christ. "Transubstantiation" indicates that through the consecration of the bread and the wine there occurs the change of the entire substance of the bread into the substance of the body of Christ, and of the entire substance of the wine into the blood of Christ--even though the appearances or "species" of bread and wine remain.

Notes

1   "Catholic," *Wikipedia, the Free Encyclopedia*, 2006 [article online]; retrieved on April 1, 2006, from http://www.objectsspace.com/encyclopedia/index.php/Catholic.

2   Austin Flannery, ed., "Dogmatic Constitution of the Church," *Vatican Council II: The Conciliar and Post Conciliar Documents*, rev. ed (Northport, NY: Costello, 1988), 381.

3   "The Catholic Church in the United States at a Glance," *United States Conference of Catholic Bishops*, 2006 [article online]; retrieved on April 1, 2006, from http://www.usccb.org/comm/statisti.shtml. Figures from *The Official Catholic Directory 2005* (New Providence, NJ: P. J. Kennedy & Sons, 2005).

4   "Roman Catholic Church Hierarchy," *Infoplease*, 2006 [encyclopedia online]; retrieved on April 15, 2006, from http://www.infoplease.com/ipa/A0922582.htm.

5   Epke VanderBerg, "The Christian Family Tree," *United Religions Intitiaive*, 2004 [article online]; retrieved on March 20, 2006, from http://www.uri.org/Christian_Family_Tree.html.

6   "Lausanne Occasional Paper 19: Christian Witness to Nominal Christians Among the Orthodox," *The Lausanne Committee for World Evangelization* [online document from the 1980 Pataya Consultation]; retrieved on April 1, 2006, from http://www.lausanne.org/Brix?pageID=14728.

7   Adrian Fortescue, "Orthodox Church," *Catholic Encyclopedia*, 2005 [article online]; retrieved on April 1, 2006, from http://www.newadvent.org/cathen/11329a.htm.

8   "Eastern Orthodoxy and Oriental Orthodoxy," *Orthodox Tradition*, Vol. 13, No. 1 (1996): 20-22.

9   Bengt Hagglund, *History of Theology*, trans. Gene J. Lund (Saint Louis, MO: Concordia, 1968), 195.

10   "Catholic Sacraments," *Wikipedia, the Free Encyclopedia*, 2006 [article online]; retrieved on April 2, 2006, from http://en.wikipedia.org/wiki/Catholic_sacraments.

11   The Roman Catholic Church admits that "to baptize (Greek *baptizein*) means to 'plunge' or 'immerse'; the 'plunge' into the water symbolizes the catechumen's burial into Christ's death, from which he rises up by resurrection with him, as 'a new creature.'" "Catechism of the Catholic Church," *Vatican*, 2006 [document online]; retrieved on April 10, 2006, from http://www.vatican.va/archive/ ccc_css/archive/catechism/p2s2c1a1.htm. Officially, the Church offers immersion and aspersions or sprinkling, but in practice it is limited to aspersion.

12   *A Catholic Dictionary*, ed. Donald Attwatter, s.v. "Tradition."

13   Austin Flannery, ed., "Dogmatic Constitution on Divine Revelation [Dei Verbum]," *Vatican Council II: The Conciliar and Post Conciliar Documents*, rev. ed. (Northport, NY: Costello, 1988), 755.

14   Jack L. Arnold, "The Roman Catholic Church of the Middle Ages," *Third Millennium Magazine Online*, March 1 to March 7, 1999; retrieved on March 12, 2006, from http://www.thirdmill.org/newfiles/jac_arnold/CH.Arnold.RMT.1.html.

15   George J. Reid, "Canon of the Old Testament," *Catholic Encyclopedia*, 2005 [online encyclopedia]; retrieved on April 1, 2006, from http://www.newadvent.org/ cathen/03267a.htm.

16   Charles Cutler Torrey, *The Apocryphal Literature: A Brief Introduction* (Hamden, CT: Archon Books, 1963).

17   Flannery, "Dogmatic Constitution of the Church," *Vatican Council II: The Conciliar and Post Conciliar Documents*, rev. ed. (Northport, NY: Costello, 1988), 421.

18   Ricardo Cardinal J. Vidal, "Pope John Paul II Calls Mary Our Advocate, Mediatrix, and Coredemptrix," *The Lady of All Nations*, 2001 [document online]; retrieved on April 3, 2006, from http://www.mariansolidarity.com/ladyofallnations/ dopp01c.html.

19   "Christian Beliefs about Mary," *Religion Facts*, 2004-2006 [article online]; retrieved on April 3, 2006, from http://www.religionfacts.com/christianity/ beliefs/mary.htm.

20   Elliot Miller and Kenneth R. Samples, *The Cult of the Virgin: Catholic Mariology and the Apparitions of Mary* (Grand Rapids: Baker, 1992), 88-99. "Major Apparitions of Jesus and Mary," *Apparitions*, 2004 [article online]; retrieved on April 3, 2006, from http://www.apparitions.org/.

21   *A Catholic Dictionary*, s.v. "Latria."

22   Ibid., s.v. "Dulia."

23   Ibid., s.v. "Hyperdulia."

24   Herbert Thurston, "Hail Mary," *Catholic Encyclopedia*, 2006 [online encyclopedia]; retrieved on April 1, 2006, from http://www.newadvent.org/cathen/07110b.htm.

25   "The Real Presence of Christ in the Eucharist," *Catholic Encyclopedia*, 2005 [online encyclopedia; retrieved on April 15, 2006, from http://www.newadvent.org/cathen/ 05573a.htm.

26   Jay A. Finelli, "Liturgical Vestements, Colors and Seasons," *Father Finelli's Medugorje Page*, 2005 [article online]; retrieved on April 3, 2006, from http://www.medugorje.com/catholic/lit_color.html.

27   *A Catholic Dictionary*, s.v. "Beatification."

28   Julie Zimmerman, "Test Your Knowledge on How Saints Are Made," *American Catholic*, 2002 [article online] retrieved on April 15, 2006, from http://www.americancatholic.org/   e-News/FriarJack/fj072302.asp#F2.

29   A complete list is found on "Patron saints," *Catholic Online*, 2005; available at http://www.catholic.org/saints/patron.php?letter=A.

30   A traditional practice was to name children after a saint honored on their birth date. For instance, those who were born on November 9 would be given one of these names: Agrippinus, Alexander, Benignus, Vitonus, Ursinus, Theodore Tyro, Orestes, or Pabo. "Feastday List," *Catholic Online*, 2005; retrieved on January 18, 2006, from http://www.catholic.org/saints/f_day/nov.php.

31   "List of saints," *Wikipedia, the Free Encyclopedia*, 2006 [article online]; retrieved on April 6, 2006, from http://en.wikipedia.org/wiki/List_of_saints.

32   "Saint Valentine," *The Free Encyclopedia*, 2006 [article online]; retrieved on April 1, 2006, from http://en.wikipedia.org/wiki/Saint_Valentine.

33 B. K. Swartz, "The Origin of American Christmas Myth and Customs" [article online]; retrieved on April 1, 2006, from http://www.bsu.edu/web/01bkswartz/xmaspub.html.

34 "St Bridgid's Cross," *Cross and Crucifix*, 2006 [article online]; retrieved on April 1, 2006, from http://www.crosscrucifix.com/brigid2.htm.

35 "All About Saints," *Catholic Online*, 2006 [article online]; retrieved on April 1, 2006, from http://www.catholic.org/saints/faq.php.

36 Flannery, "Dogmatic Constitution of the Church," 375.

37 G. H. Joyce, "The Pope," *Catholic Encyclopedia*, 2006 [article online]; retrieved on April 2, 2006, from http://www.newadvent.org/cathen/12260a.htm.

38 Adapted from Mary Walsh, *Bible Lessons for Catholics* (New York: Teach Services, 2005), 2-4.

39 Walter Schubert, "Evangelization of Apostolic Roman Catholics," Bible Conference (Takoma Park, MD: September 12, 1952), 4.

CHAPTER 24

Protestantism

1. *Introduction*

a. The nature of this book makes it impossible to consider each Protestant denomination in particular and the ways to deal with their specific deviations. This chapter will offer an overview of Protestant denominations and general suggestions to work with them.

b. The earliest use of the term "Protestant" was in connection with a group of German nobles, theologians, and delegations present at the Holy Roman Imperial Diet ("general assembly") of Speyer in 1529. They protested the revocation of the suspension, granted at the Diet of Speyer in 1526, of the Edict of Worms of 1521, which had outlawed Martin Luther and his followers. In reaction to Catholic threats, the Lutheran minority drafted a statement of "protest" and thus became "protesters" or "protestants."[1] The term "Protestant" in general makes reference to those who are not Catholics.

2. *Precursors of the Reformation*

a. The Protestant Reformation began in 1517 and spanned the sixteenth century. The causal factors involved in the Reformation were complex and interdependent. These reform groups and precursors were largely suppressed.[2]

b. Peter Waldo began to preach by 1160 and gathered a number of followers who came to be called "the poor men of Lyon." His followers, the Waldensians, promoted true poverty, public preaching, and the literal interpretation of the scriptures. Declared heretical, the movement was brutally persecuted by the Roman Catholic Church during the twelfth and thirteenth centuries, and it was almost totally destroyed.

c. John Wycliffe (1329-84) is known as "the morning star of the Reformation,"[3] because he was a man ahead of his time. Wycliffe criticized abuses and false teachings in the Church. In 1382, he translated an English Bible–the first European translation done in over one thousand years. The Lollards were itinerant preachers that followed Wycliffe.[4] Forty-four years after he died, the pope ordered his bones exhumed and burned.

d. John Huss (1369-1415) was a religious thinker and reformer living in Bohemia (now know as the Czech Republic). He initiated a religious movement based on the ideas of John Wycliffe. His followers became known as Hussites. The Catholic Church considered his teachings heretical. Consequently, Huss was excommunicated in 1411, condemned by the Council of Constance, and burned at the stake in 1415.[5]

e. Jerome of Prague (1379-1416) was one of the chief followers and most devoted friends of John Huss. He spread Wycliffe's theological writings in Bohemia. He was condemned by the Council of Constance and burned at the stake in 1416.

f. William Tyndale (1493-1536) was educated at Oxford and Cambridge. He was forced to flee to Cologne, Worms, and Antwerp. Tyndale translated the Old Testament into English. He was arrested, strangled, and burned at the stake near Brussels before he was able to finish the translation of the New Testament. Tyndale's Bible translation was the foundation for the 1611 King James Bible.

3. *Protestant Reformers*

The Protestant Reformers are those theologians, churchmen, and statesmen whose careers, works, and actions brought about the Protestant Reformation of the sixteenth century.

a. Martin Luther (1483-1546) was an Augustinian monk, a priest, and a professor. In 1517 he openly questioned the sale of indulgences (remission of the punishment for sin by the clergy in return for services or payments) by several agents of Pope Leo X for collecting money for the completion of St. Peter's Church in Rome. In 1520 Luther was excommunicated by Pope Leo X. However, there were several people in Germany, such as princes and noblemen, priests and monks who supported Luther; thus he succeeded in defying the emperor and the pope. Luther was asked to come before Emperor Charles V at the Diet of Worms in 1520-21, where he refused to take back anything he had said, maintaining that his statements were not contradictory to the Bible.[6] Luther was protected by Duke Frederick of Saxony, and he spent the following 25 years laboring for the Church in Germany. Luther rejected the Roman Catholic idea of transubstantiation (at the moment of consecration of the bread and wine, they become the actual body and blood of Christ) but held to consubstantiation (Christ is spiritually present in the elements). Luther had been criticized for not going far enough in his reform. He retained the crucifix, candles, infant baptism, Sunday keeping, and other elements of Roman Catholicism.

b. Philip Melancthon (1497-1560) was a brilliant linguist and a professor of Greek at the University of Wittenberg. He became a loyal supporter of Luther. He outlined the Augsburg Confession, which was presented to Emperor Charles V at the Diet of Augsburg in 1530.

c. Ulrich Zwinglii (1484-1531) led a revolt against the Catholic Church in Switzerland. Since at Marburg (1529) he did not agree with Luther on sacraments (he maintained that the bread and wine were only symbols), his movement was referred to as the Reformed Church, as distinguished from Luther's Protestant Church.[7]

d. John Calvin (1509-64) was a French Reformer who took refuge in Geneva, Switzerland, because he was regarded as a heretic in France. His doctrines were clearly and concisely set down in a book called *Institutes of the Christian Religion*. John Knox (1514? -1572) introduced Calvinism in Scotland, where it was called Presbyterianism because the management of the Church was in the hands of Presbyters, or elders. The Pilgrims of New England, as well as the Puritans, were Calvinists.[8]

e. King Henry VIII (1491-1547) broke with Rome because the pope did not agree with his decision to divorce his wife, Catherine of Aragon, so that he could marry Anne Boleyn. Thus in 1534 the King persuaded Parliament to pass the Act of Supremacy, which replaced the pope with the king as head of the Church in England. Changes were made in the sacraments and also in the prayer books, which were translated from Latin to English. England allied once again with Rome under Queen "Bloody" Mary (1553-58), but the Anglican Church was firmly established during the long reign of Queen Elizabeth I (1558-1603).[9]

f. Thus many Protestant bodies such as Lutheranism, Anglicanism, and Calvinism (Presbyterians and Congregationalists) arose in the sixteenth century. Followers of Menno Simons (1496-1561), called Mennonites,[10] sprang up in Switzerland and Holland, while the Quakers and the Baptists (who favored baptism by immersion of believers) became well known in England after 1600. The German Pietist movement, together with the influence of the Puritan Reformation in England in the seventeenth century, were important influences upon John Wesley and the development of Methodism. Many denominations emerged as a result and in the aftermath of the Second Great Revival in America (1792-1830).

4. *Protestant Groups*

The following is only one way to put many denominations together according to general characteristics. In some cases, a denomination could be part of more than one family.[11]

a. Lutheran Family: Even though October 31, 1517, is often thought to be the start of the Lutheran Church, a more persuasive argument may be made for the year 1530, in which the Augsburg Confession was published. This confession became the standard that congregations used to justify their independent existence. Some of the twelve major Lutheran bodies are Apostolic Lutheran Church of America, Evangelical Lutheran Church in America, Lutheran Church-Missouri Synod, and American Association of Lutheran Churches.

b. Reformed-Presbyterian Family: The force behind this family was John Calvin, who established the Reformed church in Geneva, Switzerland, in the 1540s. Calvin derived his Reformed theology from the major premise of God's sovereignty in creation and salvation. He taught that God predestined only some to salvation and that atonement is limited to those whom God has elected. Today, a strict or lenient interpretation of predestination separates many Reformed churches. On the European continent, the churches were known as Reformed; in the British Isles they came to be known as Presbyterian. Most of the Calvinist Churches are members of The World Alliance of Reformed Churches. In the United States, the largest bodies of this family are the Presbyterian Church (U.S.A.), Presbyterian Church in America, and the Congregationalists.

c. Pietist-Methodist Family: Three groups of churches fall under this category: the Moravian Church, the Swedish Evangelical churches, and the

Methodist (Wesleyan) churches. As a movement of pietism, these churches reacted to Protestantism as practiced in the late 17th century. They wanted to move away from the rigidity and systematic doctrine of the scholastic Lutheran and Calvinist theologians. They wanted a shift from scholasticism to spiritual experience, yet they did not wish to leave their established churches. There are about 125 Methodist denominations around the globe and 23 separate Methodist bodies in the United States–the United Methodist Church being the largest. The Salvation Army can also be included in this family.

d. Holiness Family: Through the influence of John Wesley's teaching of perfection, the holiness movement uses Matthew 5:48 as its theme: "Be ye perfect as my Father is perfect." It is distinct from modern Wesleyism and other Protestant churches by how it understands the framework of holiness and perfection. These believers have traditionally separated themselves from Christians who did not strive high enough for perfection. Examples of these are Church of God, the Holiness Church, and the Pentecostal Holiness Church.

e. Pentecostal Family: Today's Pentecostal family is usually traced back to the "Azuza Street Revival" and to the work of Rev. Charles Parham and his experience at Bethel Bible College in 1901. What makes this family distinct from other Protestant churches is not their doctrinal differences–it is their form of religious experience and their practice of speaking in tongues, called glossolalia. They believe that speaking in tongues is a sign of baptism by the Holy Spirit. Speaking in tongues is often is accompanied by other forms of spiritual gifts such as healing, prophecy, wisdom, and discernment of spirits. Pentecostals seek the experience, interpret events from within it, and work to have others share in it. Those who do not manifest the experience are often thought to be less than full of the Spirit. The largest Pentecostal denominations in the United States are the Assemblies of God, the Church of God in Christ, Church of God (Cleveland), and the United Pentecostal Church.

f. European Free-Church Family: While Luther and Calvin advocated a fairly close relationship with the state, sixteenth-century radical reformers from within the Roman Catholic Church advocated a complete break with the state church. From this group evolved the Mennonites, the Amish, the Brethren, the Quakers, and the Free Church of Brethren. Because many of them shunned allegiance to the government, they suffered persecution. Many members of these groups, particularly the Quakers and Mennonites, are pacifists in their response to war.

g. Baptist Family: As a free association of adult believers, Baptists make up the second largest religious family on the American landscape. Though they may also be related to the continental free-church family, American Baptists seem more related to British Puritanism. Although they are a free association, they have organized themselves into various groupings, depending upon emphases of creed and the necessity for control. At times, the differences in theological perspectives were due to the American phenomenon of regionalism (e.g., Southern and Northern Baptist conventions). In the United States the two largest Baptist organizations are the Southern Baptist Churches (SBC) and the American Baptist Churches (ABC)–with the former being the more conservative branch. There are now more than fifty Baptist groups in the United States alone.

h. Restoration Family: During the early 1800s in the United States, Restorationism sought to renew the whole Christian church on the pattern set forth in the New Testament. They rejected the creeds developed over time in Catholicism and Protestantism, which allegedly kept Christianity divided. Churches that grew out of the Restoration Movement include the Church of Christ, the Independent Christian Churches/Churches of Christ (often designated "Instrumental" for their acceptance of musical instruments within worship), and the Disciples of Christ.

i. Independent Fundamentalist Family: Following the lead of Englishman John Nelson Darby (1800-1882), Independent Fundamental churches distinguish themselves from Baptists by their belief in dispensationalism (even though the Southern Baptist Convention is the largest fundamentalist body in the U.S.). Fundamentalists believe the Bible is the history of God's actions with people in different periods. This dispensational framework has resulted in much speculation about prophecy of the "Last Days." The Fundamentalist family frequently uses the Scoffield Reference Bible as a major source for doctrine. Bob Jones University, Dallas Theological Seminary, the Christian and Missionary Alliance, and Grace Gospel Fellowship are representatives.

j. Adventist Family: The feature that distinguishes the Adventist family from other Christian groups is their belief in the expectation, or imminent return, of Christ. At that time Christ will replace the old order of the world with an order of joy and goodness in connection to a millennial period. Even though a belief in the imminent return has long roots, it was heightened with the work of William Miller, a Baptist farmer from New York. He believed that biblical chronology could be deciphered, a belief that prompted him to predict Christ's return between March 21, 1843, and October 22, 1844.[12] Some of the more well-known families that have evolved from the millennial expectation are the Seventh-day Adventists, Church of Jesus Christ of the Latter-Day Saints, the Jehovah's Witnesses, the British Israel Movement, and the Worldwide Church of God.

5. *Cardinal Principles of Protestantism*

a. Supremacy of Jesus Christ. A personal relationship with Christ is the very heart of the evangelical faith. Salvation is only in Christ: *Sola Christus.*

b. Justification by faith. Salvation is received only by accepting by faith *(sola fide)* God's gift of forgiveness: *Sola gratia.*

c. Authority and supremacy of the Bible: *"Sola Scriptura."* Tradition must be evaluated by the Bible and rejected if not in harmony.

d. The priesthood of all believers. All believers have direct access to God. There is no difference between priests and laymen. All are responsible before God for the edification of the church.

6. *Pentecostal and Charismatic Influences on Protestantism*

a. The impact of Pentecostals and Charismatics can be observed in various ways. The majority of about fifty mega-churches in the world, each with over fifty thousand members, belong to the Pentecostal-Charismatic movement. Pentecostals and Charismatics have made serious penetration into the media world through radio, television, movies, literature, and magazines. Financial giving in these churches is far above the global average (although giving to world missions is weak). And over one-third of the world's "full-time" Christian workers are Pentecostals, Charismatics, or neo-Charismatics. "They are also in the forefront of the concern for world evangelization and together constitute the fastest growing segment of the church today."[13]

b. Peter Wagner describes "three waves" of supernatural manifestations among evangelicals in this century:[14]

1) The "first wave" was known as the Pentecostal movement. The movement began at the dawn of the twentieth century with the "Azuza Street Revival" and with the events at Bethel Bible College. It was taught that speaking in tongues was an indispensable condition for salvation. Followers created their own denominations.

2) The "second wave" was the Charismatic movement that appeared in the middle of the twentieth century.[15] Both the Pentecostal and the Charismatic movements emphasized the gift of tongues as a sign of authentication from the Holy Spirit. Speaking in tongues was still necessary, but it was not required for

believers to leave their denominations. In contrast with the Pentecostal movement, the Charismatic movement took place inside established Christian bodies. Over 23% of all Christians today are Pentecostals or Charismatics.

3) Those evangelicals who accept the tenets of "Power Evangelism" are now called the "third wave." Wagner affirms that "one can be filled with the Holy Spirit and minister through spiritual gifts in power and be a channel for healing the sick and casting out demons, all without speaking in tongues."[16] The new emphasis is power prayer and power gifts. Evangelicals in the "third wave" do not stress the gift of tongues as much as the other two,[17] even though it is welcomed when manifested. The "third wave" is remarkable in its blending of evangelical commitments and charismatic practices,[18] and the subsequent blurring of distinction between charismatic and non-charismatic evangelicals.[19]

Notes

1   Henry Lucas, *The Renaissance and the Reformation* (New York: Harper and Brothers, 1934), 466-7.

2   Albert Henry Newman, *A Manual of Church History*, Vol. 1, 24th ed. (Valley Forge, PA: Judson Press, 1953), 570-600.

3   Ellen G. White, *The Great Controversy* (Mountain View, CA: Pacific Press, 1950), 80.

4   "The Lollards," *Open Directory Project*, 2002; available at http://dmoz.org/Society/ Religion_and_Spirituality/Christianity/Denominations/Catholicism/History/By_Reg ion/ Europe/United_Kingdom/England/Middle_Ages/The_Lollards/.

5   William R. Estep, *Renaissance and Reformation* (Grand Rapids: Eerdmans, 1986), 69-77.

6   "My conscience is captive to the Word of God, I cannot and will not recant anything, for to go against conscience is neither right nor safe. God help me. Amen." Quoted in Roland H. Bainton, *The Reformation of the Sixteenth Century* (Boston: Beacon, 1952), 61.

7   Robert V. Schnucker, "Huldreich Zwinglii," in *Eerdmans' Handbook of Christianity*, ed. Tim Dowley (Grand Rapids: Eerdmans, 1977), 262.

8   A. Lindt, "John Calvin," in *Eerdmans' Handbook of Christianity*, ed. Tim Dowley (Grand Rapids: Eerdmans, 1977), 380.

9   David L. Edwards, *Christian England*, Vol. 2 of *From the Reformation to the Eighteenth Century* (Grand Rapids: Eerdmans, 1983).

10   William R. Estep, *The Anabaptist Story* (Grand Rapids: Eerdmans, 1963), 108-28.

11   Major resources for this summary were J. Gordon Melton, *The Encyclopedia of American Religions* (New York: Triumph Books, 1989); and Epke VanderBerg, "The Christian Family Tree," *United Religions Initiative*, 2004 [article online]; retrieved on April 1, 2006, from http://www.uri.org/Christian_Family_Tree.html.

12   William Miller, *Evidence from Scripture and History of the Second Coming of Christ About the Year 1843* (Boston: Joshua V. Himes, 1842).

13   Hwa Yung, "Endued with Power: The Pentecostal-charismatic Renewal and the Asian Church in the Twenty-first Century," *Asian Journal of Pentecostal Studies* Vol. 6, No. 1 (2003): 63-82.

14   C. Peter Wagner, *The Third Wave of the Holy Spirit: Encountering the Power of Signs and Wonders*, with Foreword by John Wimber (Ann Arbor, MI: Vine, 1988).

15   One commentator suggested that this second wave is just a "restrained, white, middle class reinvention of original working-class, black style, 'holy roller,' Pentecostalism." J. I. Packer, "Piety on Fire," *Christianity Today* 33, No. 8 (May 12, 1989): 20.

16   C. Peter Wagner, *How to Have a Healing Ministry Without Making Your Church Sick* (Ventura, CA: Regal, 1988), 26.

17   While Third Wavers accept speaking in tongues, it is viewed as only one of many gifts of the Spirit, not the "badge of spirituality" that all Christians must have. Vinson Synan, *The Spirit Said "Grow": The Astounding Worldwide Expansion of Pentecostal and Charismatic Churches*, with Foreword by C. Peter Wagner, Innovations in Mission Series, ed. Bryant L. Meyers, (Monrovia, CA: MARC, 1992), 57-62. Pentecostals are less than happy with this de-emphasis on speaking in tongues. James A. Beverly, "Toronto's Mixed Blessing," *Christianity Today* 39 (September 11, 1995): 24.

18   Ken L. Sarles, "An Appraisal of the Signs and Wonders Movement," *Bibliotheca Sacra* 145 (January-March 1988): 57.

19   Gerhard F. Hasel, "The 'Third Wave's Roots of Celebrationism," *Adventists Affirm* 2 (Fall 1991): 36-40.

CHAPTER 25

Sects and Cults

1. *Introduction*

a. Christianity is truly a world religion. "Religion" is a belief system that provides answers to the ultimate questions about the world, humanity, and God, as well as the practices (rituals) and moral codes (ethics) that result from that belief.[1] Within a religion there may be denominations or subgroups. A "denomination" is an established religious group, which has usually been in existence for many years and has geographically widespread membership.[2] Sects are offshoots from a religion or a denomination. Cults are new religious movements that sometimes emerge as sects, but with specific characteristics.

b. It is difficult to find a single accurate term to refer to many religious groups which have developed outside traditional religions and denominations. George Braswell relates that the terms "cults," "sects," "deviations," "new consciousness groups," and other terms have attempted to categorize the movements.[3] Many Christians, seeking to effectively witness and minister to persons in these groups, use terms other than "cult" or "sect" because of their negative connotation. They prefer terms such as "alternative religions," "non-traditional religions," "new religions," "unconventional religions," "emergent religions," "non-normative religions," "marginal religious movements" and, most frequently, "new religious movements."[4] Popular and often sensationalist descriptions of cults and sects tend to stress the bizarre or play up such adjectives as "strange," "curious," and "unconventional."[5]

c. Statistics indicate that It is not inappropriate to speak of a "cult explosion." "Conservatively estimated, there are 3,000-5,000 cults in America affecting nearly as many lives as alcohol or drug addiction, yet receiving far less attention than other social problems."[6]

2. *Heresy*

a. A dictionary definition: "A religious belief opposed to the orthodox doctrines of a church; especially, such a belief specifically denounced by the church and regarded as likely to cause schism."[7] The word comes from the Greek *hairesis* ("choice"), which is translated as "sect" in Acts 24:14 (NAS, RSV); "heresies" (KJV), "factions" (NAS, RSV, NKJV), "parties" (Williams), "divisions" (Beck), "differences" in 1 Cor 11:19 (NIV); "party-spirit" (RSV, Williams) in Gal 5:20; and "teachings" (Beck) in 2 Pet 2:1.

b. From a Christian perspective, it could be said that heresies are "doctrines and/or practices that contradict those of the Scriptures as interpreted by traditional Christianity."[8] However, what is "traditional Christianity"? For Roman Catholics that signifies one thing, and for a member of a mainline Protestant denomination, that may mean another thing. For some church members even altering the order of the worship service may be considered a heresy! "What really matters is not a label of 'conventional' or 'unconventional' religion, but God's objective truth."[9]

c. Jesus warned against false teachers that would try "to deceive the elect" (Matt 24:24). In a similar manner, Peter foretold, "There will be false teachers among you, who will secretly bring in destructive heresies, even denying the Lord who bought them, and bring on themselves swift destruction" (2 Pet 2:1-22). Sometimes these "ungodly men" . . . "creep in unnoticed," "turn the grace of our God into licentiousness, and deny the only Lord God and our Lord Jesus Christ" (Jude 4). "For such men are false apostles, deceitful workers, disguising themselves as apostles of Christ and no wonder for even Satan disguises himself as an angel of light. Therefore it is not surprising if his servants also disguise themselves as servants of righteousness; whose end shall be according to their deeds" (2 Cor 11:13-15 NASB).

3. *Sects*

a. The word "sect" comes from Latin *sequi*, "to follow." The term "sect" was used to translate the Greek *hairesis*, "choice." It has regularly been applied to groups that break away from existing religious bodies. A sect is a small religious group that is an offshoot of an established religion or denomination. It holds most beliefs in common with its religion of origin, but has a number of concepts that make it different from that religion.

b. From a sociological perspective, a sect may be a faction, a fellowship of nonconformists, a group of dissidents, or schismatics. They break off from the "conventional consensus and espouse very different views of the real, the possible, and the moral."[10] They usually exhibit great alienation from other dominant social structures and the prevailing culture.

c. From an anthropological perspective, some see the birth of new religious movements as deliberate efforts by members of a society to construct a more satisfying society. Sometimes these movements not only take place in the religious sphere, but in that of the entire cultural system.[11] Wallace has interpreted the emergence of new denominations and sects as revitalization movements in which an attempt is made, sometimes successfully, to change the society. He believes that all religions stem from revitalization movements.[12] According to Wallace, there are five overlapping stages in the birth of a new religion: 1) steady state; 2) increased individual stress; 3) cultural distortion; 4) revitalization; and 5) new steady state.[13]

d. From a religious perspective, "sects are movements of religious protest,"[14] deviations from the established religion. Most religious movements were born as "sects." Buddhism was an offshoot of Hinduism. Baha'ism was born within Shi'a Islam. To first-century Judaism the Christian Church was a sect that deviated from prevailing orthodoxy and was described as "the sect of the Nazarenes" (Acts 24:5). At first, Seventh-day Adventists were considered to be a sect and a cult. However, since the days when Walter Martin explained in detail why they should be considered as evangelical Christians,[15] that has changed. Today Seventh-day Adventists are considered by many as a respectable denomination.

e. From a Christian perspective in particular, a sect is a deviation or a group that calls itself Christian, that uses the Bible and Christian terms, but deviates in its theology from basic biblical doctrine as accepted by historic Christianity.[16] Roman Catholics often refer to "the Protestant sect," meaning all Protestants, using the word in its etymological sense. Roman Catholic writers and others often use the term as equivalent to "denomination," in distinction from "Church." "Evangelicals generally use sect when referring to those Christian denominations not regarded as evangelical."[17]

4. *Cults*

a. The term "cult" is more difficult to define than "sect." First of all, it should be noted that the word derives from the Latin *cultus*, "worship." In this sense, the cultic art is an act of worship, involving external rites and ceremonies, as well as attitudes of reverential homage. The word "cult" has also been applied "to a disparate collection of groups and movements and consequently has become unsuitable as a precise legal or social scientific category."[18]

b. It is possible to establish a difference between sects and cults. A cult has been defined as a religious group which looks for its basic and peculiar authority outside the Christian tradition. A sect, on the other hand, is closer to traditional Christianity than a cult.[19] Rosado defines a sect as "a religious group that claims to be the true expression of a traditional religious faith, and whose beliefs and behaviors challenge the norms of society."[20] A cult, in contrast, is a small, recently created, religious movement that represents a radical break from existing religious traditions. A cult in this sense may simply be a new religious movement on its way to becoming a denomination.[21] A cult may have all the elements suggested in the definition of "sect," plus the fact that the person usually falls under the absolute control of an organization, charismatic leader, or an authoritarian figure to the point that the person loses his or her own free will.[22]

c. According to cult watchers, the following characteristics, when found in a particular group, are sufficient to call the group a cult:[23]

1) A charismatic leader (male or female) who directs the group and seeks to draw all attention to himself rather than to God. The leader's interpretations of the "truth" are accepted by the members without question. "The members' self identity and life goals are redefined and have meaning only in relation to the leader and the group."[24]

2) Deceitful practices and a hidden agenda are identifiable in the recruitment process. Usually the name of the group is not disclosed in the beginning, and the prospective recruit is given a rosy picture of idealistic young people working together for a better world. No mention is made of turning over one's possessions or of maintaining total obedience to the leader through the subordinates.

3) The initiation or conversion process is very rapid, and there is no opportunity for the recruit to evaluate what is happening and to discover if it is really what he expected. Most cult groups will not permit recruits to visit their

parents or friends, and they will keep the recruit in the company of a committed member during the entire indoctrination time.

4) There is usually great difficulty in leaving the group.

5) There is a great secrecy concerning the disposition of the money collected by the membership. Also, there is a lack of visible signs that these funds are used as the donor intended. Evidence suggests that the typical cult leader lives in great splendor, often having several residences and means of transportation, while the general members live in inconsequential surroundings.

6) Celibacy is a requirement or an encouraged ideal in a number of the new-age cults. "Communities often ban sexual relations at times in their history when it is especially important that energy and attention be devoted to group tasks."[25] The Bible warns: "Now the Spirit expressly says that in latter times some will depart from the faith, giving heed to deceiving spirits and doctrines of demons . . . forbidding to marry" (1 Tim 4:1-3).

d. According to the Evangelical Christian and Counter-cult Movement, a cult is any religious group which accepts most, but not all, of the historical Christian doctrines (such as the Bible, the Trinity, virginal birth, and salvation by faith in Jesus).[26]

e. Doomsday/Destructive/Apocalyptic cults are religiously based, very high intensity, controlling groups that have caused or are liable to cause loss of life among their membership or the general public. Examples are Aum Shinrikyo, Heaven's Gate, Branch Davidians, Order of the Solar Temple, Rajneeshees, Jim Jones, and the Manson Family.[27]

5. *The Issues of Seduction and Brainwashing*

a. One major contention against cults is their deceptive recruiting methods. However, not all cultic organizations do such. The Oakland family of the Unification Church, in California, used the term "heavenly deception" to draw followers. The "Children of God" went to extremes, using religious prostitution–they called it "flirty fishing."[28]

b. Brainwashing became part of the popular vocabulary during the Korean War, when American prisoners of war were subjected to psychological and physical methods of mind manipulation.[29] The term "brainwashing" was first used to explain religious conversion by the British psychiatrist William Sargant, who wrote the book *Battle for the Mind*.[30] This book is the main source of the term as used today.

    c. The word "brainwashing" appears regularly in scholarly literature, along with more academic-sounding equivalent terms like "thought control," "mind control," and "coercive persuasion."[31] Another related term is "snapping," which makes personality changes possible.[32]

> Once tentative interest has been manifested by the potential convert, intense group pressure and group activity are initiated. Lectures, sermons, Bible studies, and indoctrination sessions—sometimes tape-recorded—are part of a constant round of activity designed to surround the new recruit with only cult associations and separated from any input or feedback from the "outside" —while at the same time placed in a position where questioning is discouraged and dissent is not tolerated—the individual is deprived of any opportunity to exercise self-expression and independent thought. He is surrounded by a group of singing, chanting, or meditating peers whose verbal interaction is sprinkled with . . . "thought-termination cliches."[33]

Former members of extremist cults generally report having experienced some kind of sensory deprivation—usually food and sleep. The cultist is also stripped of his past. Renunciation and rejection of his prior associations and relationships are mandatory. All connections with family, friends, and the home community are severed.[34] What some have described as "brainwashing," others have argued was not. They "reject the brainwashing thesis not only because it represents an attack upon religious conversion generally but also because there is considerable evidence that people join new religions of their own will."[35]

    d. Those who assume that members of cults are in fact brainwashed sometimes attempt to undo the brainwashing by means of a process called "deprogramming." Deprogrammers claim to "rescue" people from cults by using a variety of techniques to coerce them into renouncing their former allegiances. Deprogramming is a mechanical method of reversing what a person has experienced, through deception, hypnosis/drugs, or a lowering of normal resistant rationality by special techniques of deprivation. Deprogramming rests on the assumption that members of the new religions have been unwittingly "programmed,"[36] which is not true in most cases. Anti-cultists perceive the apparent religious commitment of converts to marginal religions as actually representing "mind suppression,"[37] "psychological kidnaping,"[38] a "mental manipulation"[39] process involving "isolation, repetition of chants, monotonous music, intimate touching, lack of sleep, physical duress, and fatigue."[40] Because of its use of coercion and violence, deprogramming is a violation of religious liberty and, as such, has been condemned by responsible Christians.[41] Coercion and violence are not the way that God has commissioned Christians to convert sinners, those who err, or those who abandon their faith. Furthermore, deprogramming robs people of their sense of responsibility. Instead of encouraging people to accept the fact that they made a mistake, it encourages people to deny their actions and blame others. Thus, deprogramming is not only psychologically destructive but profoundly un-Christian.[42] At present there is a less controversial methodology being used that is known as "exit counseling." In some ways it is similar to deprogramming, but it usually lacks the coercive dimension.[43]

6. *Witnessing to Persons in Cults/Sects*

a. Acquire a clear understanding of basic Christian doctrine, especially the doctrine of Christ. Be able to support your faith with specific biblical texts.[44]

b. Become familiar with general sect characteristics and their "pet" verses.[45] Study carefully one or two cults/sects.

c. Be willing to listen to a person in a cult/sect. Seek to understand why someone joined the group. Attitudes usually speak louder than words.

d. Be bold. Take and keep the initiative.

e. Establish the authority of the Bible early in your encounter.

f. Clearly define your terms. Don't assume that the other person knows what you mean. Cults often redefine familiar Christian terms. Call for normative Christian definitions of God, man, salvation, and Christ. Watch for Eastern religious concepts: man having the divine spark within them, etc. No genuine witness occurs unless the meanings of commonly used terms are understood.

g. Discuss basics of the Christian faith, especially how to become a Christian. Do not try to explain every Christian doctrine. Many will jump to a completely different subject when they feel cornered.

h. Present a strong, positive Christian testimony. Include these points: what it means to accept Christ as a personal Savior and Lord, the joy of the Christian life, and the certainty of salvation through faith in Jesus (1 John 5:13).

I. Remember that the primary reasons that people are attracted to cults are social in nature. A group of believers may have the right message, but if it does not have the right Christian atmosphere, a former cultist seeking for the truth may find it difficult to join this congregation.

j. Cultists often think that only their group is serious about spiritual things. They need to see in you something vital, real, and life-transforming. "A Christlike life is the most powerful that can be advanced in favor of Christianity."[46]

k. Another option is awaiting voluntary withdrawal and being prepared to receive those who have entered cults and are ready for voluntary or self-initiated withdrawal. It has been noted that "identification with another belief system or organization for most persons comes after major dissonance has set in, and the possibilities for leaving become viable."[47] This approach rests in the fact that there is a cycle in the experience of those who join cults: evidently they will pass through a period of concentrating efforts to adapt, understand, and live according to the newly adopted religion; but eventually they will become disenchanted. Many secular organizations have developed ways to rehabilitate those leaving the cults,[48] but rehabilitation is not enough. We have an urgent responsibility to help them find Jesus as their Savior. The suggestion at this point is that Christians have to maintain a steady watch, waiting for the best opportunity to help[49] and present the gospel to those who will abandon the movement.

Notes

1   Marc Gellman and Thomas Hartman, *Religion for Dummies* (New York: Eiley Publishing, 2002), 10.

2   "Religious Denomination," *Wikipedia, the Free Encyclopedia*, 2006 [article online], retrieved on April 4, 2006, from http://en.wikipedia.org/wiki/ Religious_denomination. "Denominations" in Islam are usually called "sects."

3   George W. Braswell, *Understanding Sectarian Groups in America* (Nashville: Broadman Press, 1986), 11.

4   Ronald Enroth et al., *A Guide to Cults and New Religions* (Downers Grove, IL: InterVarsity Press, 1983), 11.

5   Leon McBeth, *Strange New Religions* (Nashville: Broadman Press, 1977), 3.

6   John Morehead, "What Is a Cult?" *Apologetics Index*, 2006 [article online]; retrieved on April 3, 2006, from http://www.apologeticsindex.org/c09a04.html.

7   *Webster's New World Dictionary of the American Language*, 1960 ed., s.v. "Heresy."

8   James W. Sire, *Scripture Twisting* (Downers Grove, IL: InterVarsity Press, 1980), 20. From this perspective, Buddhists or Hindus are not heretics. "Buddhists don't just deviate from Christianity, they differ. They don't disbelieve a few essential doctrines or hold a few heretical notions, they don't believe anything we do." Ronald M. Enroth and J. Gordon Melton, *Why Cults Succeed Where the Church Fails* (Elgin, IL: Brethren Press, 1985), 4, 83.

9   Ronald Enroth, "Cult/Countercult," *Eternity*, November 1977, 35.

10   John Lofland, *Doomsday Cult* (Englewood Cliffs, NJ: Prentice-Hall, 1966), 1.

11   "Such a drastic solution arises when a group's anxiety and frustration have reached such a degree that the only way to reduce the stress is to overturn the entire social system and replace it with a new one." William A. Haviland, *Cultural Anthropology* (New York: Holt, Rinehart, & Winston, 1975), 365.

12   See Anthony F. C. Wallace, *Religion: An Anthropological View* (New York: Random House, 1966).

13   Adapted from Paul G. Hiebert, *Cultural Anthropology* (Philadelphia: Lippincott, 1976), 388-94. Scholars have found that once a new religion is established, it will succeed if it fulfills a series of conditions. See Rodney Stark, "How New Religions Succeed: A Theoretical Model," in *The Future of New Religious Movements*, ed. David G. Bromley and Phillip E. Hammond (Macon, GA: Mercer University Press, 1987), 11-29.

14   Bryan Wilson, *Religious Sects*, World University Library Series (Englewood Cliffs, NJ: McGraw-Hill, 1970), 2.

15   Walter R. Martin, *The Truth about Seventh-day Adventism* (Grand Rapids: Zondervan, 1960).

16   Walter Martin provides a definition for "cult" that I would offer for "sect": "A group of people polarized around someone's interpretation of the Bible and . . . characterized by major deviations from Orthodox Christianity relative to the cardinal doctrines of the Christian faith, particularly the fact that God became a man in Jesus Christ." Walter Martin, *The Rise of Cults*, 12.

17   John H. Gerstner, *The Theology of the Major Sects* (Grand Rapids: Baker, 1976), 9.

18 Thomas Robbins, "Religious Movements, the State, and the Law: Reconceptualizing 'The Cult Problem,'" *New York University Review of Law and Social Change* Vol. 9, No. 1 (1980-81): 33.

19 William W. Sweet, *American Culture and Religion*, 92; quoted by Russell P. Spittler, *Cults and Isms* (Grand Rapids: Baker, 1962), 12, 13.

20 Caleb Rosado, "Lessons from Waco–Understanding the Chaos of Cults and Sects," *Ministry*, July 1993, 7.

21 "Definitions of Terms: Cults, Sects and Denominations," *Ontario Consultants on Religious Tolerance*, 2006 [article online]; retrieved on April 3, 2006, from http://www.religioustolerance.org/cults.htm.

22 "A cult . . . is defined by the power relationships within it. Members give up their personal power to a leader who purports to have special, magical knowledge denied to the rest of the world." Victoria Loe, "Upheaval Feeds Cults, Experts Say," *The Dallas Morning News*, March 7, 1993, 37A.

23 These characteristics were collected by the Interfaith Coalition of Concerns about Cults (ICCC), a cult- watching organization founded by four major faith groups in New York City. Quoted in James J. LeBar, *Cults, Sects, and the New Age* (Huntington, IN: Our Sunday Visitor, 1989), 14-15.

24 Enroth et al., *A Guide to Cults & New Religions*, 18.

25 Rosabet Moss Kanter, *Commitment and Community* (Cambridge, CA: Harvard University Press, 1972), 78.

26 "Definition of Terms," *Ontario Consultants*.

27 "Doomsday/ Destructive Cults," *About*, 2006 [article online]; retrieved on April 3, 2006, from http://altreligion.about.com/cs/cults/bl_doomsday.htm.

28 Craig Branch, "The Children of God/The Family," *The Watchman Expositor*, 2000 [article online]; retrieved on April 2, 2006, from http://www.watchman.org/profile/fampro.htm.

29 See Robert J. Lifton, *Thought Reform and the Psychology of Totalism* (New York: W. W. Norton, 1960). This book is an analysis of brainwashing techniques used against Chinese intellectuals and Western prisoners in mainland China.

30 William Sargant, *Battle for the Mind* (London: Pan Books, 1959).

31 Ronald Enroth, *Youth, Brainwashing, and the Extremist Cults* (Grand Rapids: Zondervan, 1977), 157.

32 Irving Hexam and Karla Poewe, *Understanding Cults and New Religions* (Grand Rapids: Eerdmans, 1987), 9.

33 Enroth, *Youth, Brainwashing, and the Extremist Cults*, 159, 160.

34 Francine Jeanne Daner, *The American Children of Krsna* (New York: Holt, Rinehart and Winston, 1976), 73-74.

35 Hexam and Poewe, *Understanding Cults and New Religions*, 9-10. Similar contentions are offered by J. Gordon Melton and Robert L. Moore, *The Cult Experience: Responding to the New Religious Pluralism* (New York: The Pilgrim Press, 1982).

36 Stuart A. Wright, *Leaving Cults: The Dynamics of Defection* (Washington, DC: Society for the Scientific Study of Religions, Monograph Series, 1987), 2.

37 Jack Sparks, *The Mindbenders: A Look at Current Cults* (Nashville: Thomas Nelson, 1977), 104.

38 Anson D. Shupe, Roger Spielman, and Sam Stigall, "Deprogramming: The New Exorcism," in *Conversion Careers: In and Out of the New Religions*, ed. James T. Richardson (Beverly Hills, CA: Sage Publications, 1977), 149.

39 M. Conlan, "Officials Ask Probe of Cult Brainwashing," *Fort Worth Star Telegram* February 2, 1977, A9; M. Montagno, "Is Deprogramming Legal?," *Newsweek* (February 1977), 44; Steven J. Gelberg, ed. *Hare Krishna, Hare Krishna: Five Distinguished Scholars on the Krishna Movement in the West* (New York: Grove Press, 1987), 47-56, 88-95.

40 Flo Conway and Jim Siegelman, *Snapping: America's Epidemic of Sudden Personality Change* (New York: Delta Publications, 1979), back cover of the paperback edition. This book is to date the most influential exposition of the hypothesis that cults use brainwashing which can only be reversed by deprogramming. See a balanced treatment of accusations against Hare Krishnas being deprived of sleep, balanced food, and social contact with the "outside" world, in Angela Burr, "Brainwashing: Fact or Fiction–Conversion or Subversion?" in *I Am Not My Body: A Study of the International Hare Krishna Sect* (New Delhi: Vikas Publishing House, 1984, 257-75; also J. Gordon Melton and Robert L. Moore, "Deprogramming and the Anti-cult Movement," in *The Cult Experience: Responding to the New Religious Pluralism* (New York: The Pilgrim Press, 1982), 72-80.

41 See complete text of the "Resolution on Deprogramming," adopted by the Governing Board of the National Council of Churches, February 28,1984, in Melton, *The Cult Experience*, 153-54.

42 Hexam and Poewe, *Understanding Cults*, 11.

43 Enroth and Melton, *Why Cults Succeed*, 40.

44 From "Cult/Sect Overview," Interfaith Witness Department, Home Mission Board of the Southern Baptist Convention, Atlanta, Georgia, 1987; Gary Leazer, "Witnessing to Sectarians," pamphlet distributed by Interfaith Witness Department, Home Mission Board of the Southern Baptist Convention, Atlanta, GA, n.d.

45 Normal L. Geisler and Ron Rhodes, *When Cultists Ask: A Popular Handbook on Cultic Misinterpretations* (Grand Rapids: Baker Books, 1997), 18.

46 Ellen G. White, *Testimonies to the Church* (Boise, ID: Pacific Press, 1948), 9:21.

47 Wright, *Leaving Cults*, 50. Wright points out a list of influences or factors which motivate devotees for this voluntary withdrawal.

48 Lowell D. Striker, "An Alternative," chap. in *Mind Bending: Brainwashing, Cults and Deprogramming in the 80's* (Garden City, NY: Doubleday, 1984), 170-98.

49 An evangelical option for helping them is presented by Melton and Moore, "Coping: Guidelines for Helpers and Families," chap. in *The Cult Experience*, 112-23.

CHAPTER 26

The Secular Mind

1. *Introduction*

a. If one combines the numbers for nonreligious, agnostics, and atheists, the total number of secularists is around 16 percent of the world's population.[1] Protestant churches in the United States have experienced a loss of nearly 4.5 million members over the last 50 years (-9.5 percent). Meanwhile, the population increased 11.4 percent, a gain of over 24 million people (we are not even keeping up with biological growth!). Not one county in the U.S. has a greater church population today than 50 years ago. Average church attendance has gone down from 50 to 40 percent or less since 1980. The U.S. is the third largest mission field in the world.[2]

b. The process of secularization is felt all around the globe. All religions and worldviews are experiencing secularization and losing their earlier influence with large populations. For instance, the Japanese culture's historic relation to Shinto has experienced substantial secularization since World War II. Most traditional religions lose control of their people when they move to the cities. Iran and Afghanistan's Islamic revolutions represent Shi'ite Islam's attempt to stand against the tide of secularization eroding Islamic cultures. In China, the secularization of Communism's influence has produced a spiritual void among the population.[3] Each experience of secularization in the examples listed above is distinct, but common features include the impact of science, nationalism, humanism, urbanization, and the de facto Westernization of much of the earth.[4]

2. *Definition of Related Terms*

a. An atheist is one who says there is sufficient evidence to show that God does not exist.

b. An agnostic is one who says there is insufficient evidence to know whether or not God exists.

c. The functional atheist is one who is apathetic concerning God's existence.

d. An ignostic is one who does not know what Christians are talking about, even though he/she may live in a "Christian" country.

e. A nominal Christian is one who is somewhat active in church, but his/her life is not significantly influenced by the Christian faith.

f. For the purposes of this study, the term "secular person" will be used to include all five listed above. Secularization is a process in which, even though a person or society may not have consciously rejected religion or God, there is an erosion of belief in the supernatural. It has been described as "the decline of religion," "conformity with the world," "disengagement of society from religion," "the gradual loss of a sense of the sacred," and the "transposition" of religion with a secular substitute.[5]

g. Secularism refers to a consciously-adopted philosophy. "It has been defined as a system which rejects all forms of religious faith, and accepts only the facts and influences derived from the present life."[6]

h. "A secularist may be described as a 'missionary' for secularism. He is in contrast, however, to the typical secular person who finds religion to be irrelevant to his life, but is not hostile toward it."[7]

i. When we speak of the secular mind, there is a danger that we think in terms of a highly educated, scientific person. This is a grave mistake. When we are talking about the secular mind, we are speaking of the majority of people who are concerned only about the things of this world and the day-to-day problems that accompany their ordinary existence. Mark Finley describes four types of secularists:[8]

1) The secular materialist, characterized by the young business executive, for whom the *summum bonum* of life is his job. Material values are paramount in his life, and possessions are his chief passion.

2) The secular religious dropout was brought up in a religious home, but he no longer attends religious services. He has his own value system. He is concerned with social and philosophical issues, but is also attracted to the party life of drinking and smoking.

3) The secular hard-hat is a tough man who works from early morning to late at night. His chief happiness in life comes from the sports pages and television. His attitude toward religion is, "Don't bother me about that stuff. I'm a working man, a good moral man, and I do my best." He does not think about philosophical issues, and he is not obsessed with possessions.

4) The secular philosopher is introspective and thoughtful. He has intellectually rejected Christianity as a viable option. He has accepted a naturalistic worldview.

3. *The Rise of Secularism*[9]

a. The Renaissance (ca. A.D. 1400 to 1600). The invention of the printing press with movable types in the early 1400s by Johann Gutenberg provided people with more accessibility to writings. This led some to a deeper religiosity (Reformation), while others were led to humanistic matters (Renaissance). Toward the end of the Renaissance, the modern method of empirical (based on experiment and observation) science began to develop. Ideas of men such as Galileo Galilei (1564-1642) challenged the authority of the church, which had developed assumptions not based on actual observations of the universe. As a result of this controversy between the church and Galileo, the schism between reason and faith had begun. The philosopher René Descartes (1595-1650) arrived to the conclusion that nothing could be known for certain. His method of questioning everything in order to establish one unquestionable fact led the doubter to believe that he could be certain only of his own existence.

b. The Enlightenment (ca. 1600 to 1800). During this period people began to elevate science to the level of being the ultimate test and truth. The discoveries of the laws of science by men like Francis Bacon (1561-1626) and Isaac Newton (1642-1727) gave support to the analogy that the universe was like a machine. Such an analogy tended to dismiss the need for a God as sustainer of the universe. Most people during this period, including scientists, believed in the existence of a rational and personal Creator. At that time there was no alternative theory to that of creation that could adequately explain the existence of an orderly universe.

c. The Modern Age (ca. 1800 to 2000). In 1859 Charles Darwin (1809-82) published *On the Origin of the Species*. In this book Darwin theorized that life forms had resulted from natural, random processes and not from the design of an intelligent Creator. Many scientists became fascinated with the theory of evolution and began to apply it to every field of study, including history (Karl Marx) and psychology (Sigmund Freud). For many, the belief in God became an unnecessary hypothesis. If mankind was to find solutions for its problems and hope for its future, people must look to themselves, not to God.

d. Transition to Postmodernism (1945 to 1990). Experience demonstrated that human reason, as the instrument of progress, has failed. The Second World War demonstrated that the age of reason and enlightenment had produced very little in the way of human evolution. In the years following the war, this disillusionment was compounded by the rise of the Communist ideology, the Vietnam fiasco, weapons of mass destruction, youth rebellions, assassinations, political corruption, racial wars, and gas shortages. Some say that the modern age ended with the Second World War, while others point to the baby-boomer youth rebellions, the dawning of the Age of Aquarius, or the pulling down of the Berlin Wall.[10]

d. The Postmodern Era (ca. 1990 to present day). Postmodernism is a term used to designate a multitude of trends–in the arts, philosophy, religion, technology, and many other areas–that come after, react to, and deviate from the many twentieth-century movements that constituted modernism. Although a difficult term to pin down, "postmodern" generally refers to the criticism of absolute truths.[11] Unlike the modern rationalist, the postmodernist will not challenge the truth of the Gospel of Jesus Christ. He will merely say, "Yes, but it is your truth." The issue is no longer truth versus error, or right versus wrong, as was the case in the modern age. The concept of error or wrong has been removed from the postmodern vocabulary with one exception: It is an error to say that someone is in error. Heresy no longer exists.[12]

4. *The Beliefs of Secularism*[13]

a. The denial of God. The denial of the existence of the supernatural is the most fundamental tenet of secularism. According to secularism, belief in God is nothing more than a projection of man's own thoughts and desires.

b. The denial of miracles. If God and the supernatural do not exist, it is logical to conclude that miracles are not possible. This attitude includes the denial of revelation and inspiration, and of miracles such as Christ's virginal birth, resurrection, and ascension.

c. The fact of evolution. The theory of evolution sufficiently explains the existence and complexity of the universe. Personality and mind are also products of evolutionary processes through the interaction of chemical and biological elements.

d. The potential of humanity. Humans can find the answers to their problems within themselves, reason, and science. Religion is restrictive and escapist. Humanity will be able to face the issues squarely only when freed from the shackles of religion.

e. The centrality of science. The scientific method of inquiry is the only reliable avenue by which to discover truth and knowledge. There is an irreconcilable antagonism between reason and faith, empirical observation and revealed authority.

f. The stress on relativity. There is no absolute moral reference point beyond humanity. Humanity is good by nature, and all that is needed to realize that innate goodness is education, not religious transformation.

5. *Characteristics of Secular People*[14]

a. They are essentially ignorant of religious tenets. Among Christians, many are biblically illiterate and uninformed of basic Christianity (e.g., they may not know the difference between the Old and New Testaments).

b. They are seeking life before death. They fear extinction more than they fear hell or seek heaven. While seeking to salvage this life, they struggle to make sense of their life, to find meaning and purpose, and to make a contribution during their lifetime. Others are simply moved to enjoy the pleasures of this life, without a care for the consequences in this life or beyond.

c. They are conscious of doubt more than guilt. Until fairly recent times, a non-Christian audience in the Western world was highly conscious of personal guilt and sought forgiveness. New generations have been trained to think largely in terms of doubt and have developed a resistant frame of mind.

d. They have a negative image of the church. They doubt the relevance and credibility of the church and its advocates. They believe that the church does not relate to their situation in life.

e. They have multiple alienations. They do not know their neighbors, they do not have time to spend with their families, they do not believe in politicians and are disappointed with economic systems. They lack a sense of belonging. Alienated people are characteristically lonely.

f. They are untrusting. People enter the world needing love and affirmation from the earliest days (latch-key kids). Lack of meaningful relations, and feelings of being manipulated and exploited move people to be on guard.

g. They experience forces in history as "out of control." They face the future with great anxiety. History is an endless series of large-scale surprises, from the dismantling of the Soviet Union to volatile stock markets, and from urban violence to the AIDS epidemic. Many people feel that "no one is in charge."

h. They experience forces in their personality as "out of control." They can be seen from family crises to self-destructive addictions such as work, making money, sex, gambling, and chemicals. They feel they cannot control their own inner forces and fall into problems they cannot manage.

6. *Approaches to Secular People*

a. These ideas are developed in answer to the characteristics of the secular population as described earlier in this book.

b. The atheist says that he does not believe in God, and the agnostic says he cannot know whether there is a God or not. It may be a false concept of God that they are rejecting, and they may respond favorably when this misconception is cleared up. Often they are troubled about the problem of human suffering and find difficulty in reconciling this with the concept of a loving God. Determine what kind of God the person rejected. Do not assume that all secularists have rejected the personal God of the Bible. Others may come from cultures influenced by various non-Christian religions and might not have considered the possibility that there is no personal God. Ask questions to discern their concept of God.

c. Provide ministries of instruction. Secular people are largely ignorant of basic Christianity. The Christian communicator must be prepared to explain, over and over, what Christianity is, stands for, and offers. Many Christian witnesses fail by presupposing the basics, which most secular people do not understand.

d. Invite people to dedicate their lives. It is a serious mistake to assume that just because people come to church they are Christians. One of the reasons for a decline of Christianity is that modern preachers characteristically omit inviting people to decisively and radically commit their lives to Christ. The average minister is trying to help people continue something they have not yet begun. Altar calls and public invitations are important evangelistic and ministerial tools.

e. Help secular people find meaning. If secular people are obsessed with this life and are not concerned about eternity, then the church should help people make sense of their lives and find meaning and purpose.

f. Engage secular people in dialogue. If conscious doubt, not conscious guilt, is characteristic of a secular population, authoritative preaching is not the best approach to the unchurched masses. The speakers who get a hearing today engage in animated conversation. The evangelist is primarily listening, probing, sharing answers, and confessing faith, but he is also identifying with those who are struggling.

g. Address secular people's doubts and questions. Since they do not rely on the church's capacity to know and teach the ultimate truth, the church should offer relevant answers to their questions.

h. Provide opportunities to meet credible Christians. The church can organize social occasions in which seekers can meet credible Christians, study their faces, ask questions, and be in their company. Informal testimonies and small groups are powerful witnessing tools. Secular people can understand Christianity when they see a faith that works–touching the issues of racial injustice, poverty, hopelessness, addiction, exploitation, and abuse.

i. Provide opportunities for people to overcome alienation. Retreats in natural settings, small groups, and involvement in Christian social causes are tools in overcoming different forms of alienation. Secular people can understand the language of authentic friendship. We need to provide ministries that will touch them at the point of friendship.

j. Engage in ministries of affirmation. Because many secular people do not trust in others, they want to know in advance that they will not be rejected, insulted, humiliated, or set up.

k. Offer people hope in the Kingdom of God. If they perceive that history is out of control and fear the future, then the Christian hope needs to be clearly defined.

l. Reach across social networks. Secular people can be better reached by credible Christians in their kinship and friendship networks than by Christian strangers.

m. Offer culturally appropriate forms of ministry. Secular people are reached more effectively through the people, language, liturgy, music, architecture, needs, struggles, issues, leaders, and leadership styles that are indigenous to their culture. When secular people experience "church" as culturally alien to them, they assume that the Christian God is not for people like them.

n. Narrative evangelism, or story telling, has a universal appeal. Abstract sermons will not attract the secular mind.[15] Modern generations, who are used to the audio-visual impact of media, will appreciate dynamic services more than straightforward sermons.

o. Experience and involvement are crucial for people who used to be active participants in the secular world. For instance, get nonbelievers involved in Christian music and drama.[16]

p. Multiply "units" of the church. Newly planted churches find it easier to translate the Gospel into languages that secular people can understand.[17]

q. Offer ministries that meet perceived needs. This will demonstrate Christianity's "relevance." Christian witnesses must learn to touch people at the point of their needs and learn to adapt their labor to the condition of the people–to meet men where they are.

r. Your personal testimony may help others if you can present a positive account of how God has answered your questions and doubts. Talk about the change that this has made in your life. Positive affirmation will accomplish far more than argument. You should be ready to discuss arguments concerning the existence of God. It is very possible that the atheists and agnostics you are in contact with have never really heard a correct presentation of the Gospel. When you gain their confidence, give them a Gospel presentation. Remember that even in the case of the agnostic or the atheist, it is true that the "wonderful love of Christ will melt and subdue hearts."[18]

s. The nominal Christian is probably more than likely disposed toward both the Bible and Christ. He may or may not feel his need of a deeper spiritual experience. You may want to lead this person directly to Christ by a presentation of the gospel. With his background, he may be ready to make a wholehearted commitment of his life to Christ. If you are able to lead him to a total surrender of his life to Christ, you should enroll him in a systematic Bible study program so that he may grow in his Christian experience.

7. *Evangelizing Secular People*

a. Offer evidences for God's existence[19]

1) Anselm, the founder of medieval scholasticism, provided the ontological (relating to essence or the nature of being) argument: God is, by definition, the unsurpassable One, and since a necessary being surpasses one who is not necessary, God must necessarily exist.

2) The cosmological (relating to the physical universe) argument finds its classical expression in Thomas Aquinas' Five Ways: 1) Since motion exists, there must be a Prime Mover; 2) since everything needs a cause, there must be a First Cause; 3) since that which does not exist begins to exist only through something already existing, a Necessary Being; 4) since there are degrees of value, there must be an Absolute Value; and 5) since there is an evident purpose in nature, there must be a Divine Designer.

3) Immanuel Kant (1724-1804) provided a moral argument: Since all men are inescapably confronted by the rational imperative of morality, there must be Someone who will make possible its perfect fulfillment. The best explanation for why we have moral sensibilities is that our Source must be both moral and personal, because impersonal natural forces do not have moral sensibilities. In other words, since there is a moral law binding on all of us, there must be a Moral Lawgiver.[20]

4) The second law of thermodynamics says that while the total amount of energy remains constant (the first law), the availability of usable energy is constantly decreasing (the second law). The inevitable cooling of a cup of hot tea is an example of the constraints imposed by the second law.

If the universe has always existed, then an infinite amount of time has already passed before reaching this present moment. But it cannot be true that an infinite amount of time has passed to get to this point because, according to the second law, the universe, which contains a finite amount of energy, would then be in a state of equilibrium—a cold and lifeless state of absolute rest.[21]

b. Contradictions and problems within secularism[22]

"There is no absolute truth"	Such a statement itself claims to be an absolute truth.
"Life is meaningless"	The person who makes such a statement contradicts himself because he is claiming to make a meaningful statement.
"Science is the only avenue to truth"	Such a statement cannot itself be proven to be true by its own avenue to truth—the scientific method.
"All morality is relative"	How can we tell if a person who makes such a statement is telling the truth, since he might consider it convenient to lie? Also, such a person often does not hesitate to make moral judgments concerning social issues, or questions why God permitted evil.
"There is no ultimate purpose"	If there is no ultimacy to any purpose, then even the individual purposes are meaningless.
"The theory of evolution contends that complexity (life) arises out of simplicity (nonlife)"	The law of entropy, which is an indisputable law of nature, says that complex things disintegrate to a state of simplicity.
"Humanity is, by nature, good"	Such a statement lacks meaning since there is no moral reference point in secularism by which to measure goodness. Also, if humanity is indeed by nature good, then why doesn't goodness come more naturally to people?

"What is needed today is rational and logical thinking"	How can our thoughts be trusted to reflect reality if they are nothing more than the product of chemical and biological elements?

Table 26.1

Notes

1   "Major Religions of the World Ranked by Number of Adherents," *Adherents.com*, 2006 [article online]; retrieved on April 10, 2006, from http://www.adherents.com/ Religions_By_Adherents.html#Nonreligious.

2   Jeff Glass, "Reaching Postmodern People," *Congregational Life Ministries*, 2003 [article online]; retrieved on April 10, 2006, from http://www.brethren.org/ genbd/clm/ EvangelismPartTwo.html.

3   Even though, since the establishment of the People's Republic, religion in all its forms has been systematically discouraged, sociologists are intensely interested in observing a revival of religion in China. Donald E. MacInnis, *Religion in China Today: Policy and Practice* (Maryknoll, NY: Orbis, 1989), provides an encouraging report on this subject.

4   George G. Hunter III, *How to Reach Secular People* (Nashville: Abingdon, 1992), 2.

5   See Larry Shiner, "The Concept of Secularization in Empirical Research," *Journal of the Scientific Study of Religion* 6 (1967): 207-20; also Gottfried Oosterwal, "The Process of Secularization," in *Meeting the Secular Mind: Some Adventist Perspectives*, ed. Humberto M. Rassi and Fritz Guy (Berrien Springs, MI: Andrews University Press, 1985), 42.

6   Lausanne Committee for World Evangelization, "Christian Witness to Secularized People–Thailand Report No. 8," *Lausanne Occasional Papers, in How Shall They Hear?*, Let the Earth Hear His Voice Series (Wheaton, IL: Lausanne Committee for World Evangelization, 1980), 6.

7   Jon K. Paulien, "The Gospel in a Secular World," in *Meeting the Secular Mind: Some Adventist Perspectives*, ed. Humberto M. Rassi and Fritz Guy (Berrien Springs, MI: Andrews University Press, 1985), 18, 19. Emphasis is mine.

8   Mark A. Finley, "Target and Tactics," in *Meeting the Secular Mind: Some Adventist Perspectives*, ed. Humberto M. Rassi and Fritz Guy (Berrien Springs, MI: Andrews University Press, 1985), 18, 19.

9   Dean C. Halverson, "Secularism," in *The Compact Guide to World Religions*, ed. Dean C. Halverson (Minneapolis, MN: Bethany, 1996), 183-85; Oosterwal, "The Process of Secularization," 49-52.

10   Don Matzat, "Evangelism in a Postmodern Age," *Issues Etc.*, 1998 [article online]; retrieved on July 1, 2005, from http://www.issuesetc.org/resource/ archives/conessay.htm.

11   "Postmodernism," *Wikipedia, the Free Encyclopedia*, 2006 [article online]; retrieved on April 9, 2006, from http://en.wikipedia.org/wiki/Postmodernism.

12   James Montgomery Boice and Benjamin E Sasse, *Here We Stand* (Grand Rapids: Baker Book House, 1996), 61.

13   Halverson, "Secularism," 185-86.

14   Hunter, *How to Reach Secular People*, 43-54. These characteristics of Western secularized people may be applied to non-Christians living in secularized environments.

15   Kevin Ford, *Jesus for a New Generation* (London: Hodder & Stoughton, 1996), 178, 179.

16   Hunter, *How to Reach Secular People*, 55.

17   Ed Stetzer, *Planting a New Church in a Postmodern Age* (Nashville: Broadman & Holman, 2003), 130-34.

18   Ellen G. White, *The Desire of Ages* (Mountain View, CA: Pacific Press, 1940), 826.

19   Information for the ontological, cosmological, and moral arguments from Yandall Wooden, *With All Your Mind: A Christian Philosophy* (Nashville: Abingdon, 1980), 38-46.

20   Norman Geisler and Ron Brooks, *When Skeptics Ask: A Handbook on Christian Evidences* (Wheaton, IL: Victor Books, 1990).

21   Halverson, 188.

22   Ibid., 191.

PART VII

TRADITIONAL AND ALTERNATIVE RELIGIONS

CHAPTER 27

Traditional Folk Religions

1. *Introduction*

a. This unit will consider some religious forms that are somehow different from the ones considered before. It is difficult, if not impossible, to find a definition and to use terms which will satisfy everyone. African scholar John Mbiti finds fault with just about all of the terms used to identify African religion–polytheism, ancestor worship, primitivism, totemism, fetishism, and naturism.[1] And he is probably justified with most of his criticisms.

b. Some terms do not seem acceptable.[2] Some use "tribal religion" to describe the practices not related to world religions. However, its practitioners may be found in Los Angeles, New York, or Sao Paulo. Also, its expressions have many non-tribal aspects. Religious expressions that do not fall within the category of world religions may appear in unexpected places. For instance, Donald Reagan, former White House chief of staff under Ronald Reagan, wrote:

> Virtually every major move or decision the Reagans made during my time as White House chief of staff was cleared in advance with a woman in San Francisco who drew horoscopes to make certain that the planets were in a favorable alignment for the enterprise.[3]

c. The terms "primitive religions" and "primal religions" are not appropriate since traditional religions are neither chronologically nor conceptually primitive, but frequently quite sophisticated. As a matter of fact, these religious expressions may prove more complex than some of the world religions. From another perspective, they transmit the idea of being backward, illiterate, savage, and archaic, terms that especially do not satisfy insiders. These terms are related to evolutionistic ideas which suggest that these "rudimentary" beliefs and practices were the first religion of man.[4]

d. Terms used by many modern anthropologists include ethnoespiritism,[5] traditional folk religion,[6] or simply traditional religions.[7] We define "traditional religion" as the body of belief and ritual designed to help humankind cope with the realities of life as seen in many forms in cultures that do not follow any one of the major world religions. However, high religious perspectives of the major world religions and traditional folk religions may coexist in the same mind.

e. For the purposes of this book, the terms "low religions," "traditional religions," "traditional folk religions," "primitive religions," "tribal religions," "primal religions," "ethnoespiritism," and "animism" will be interchangeable.

2. *Animism*

a. One of the oldest terms to describe beliefs and practices not related to world religions is "animism." Sir Edward Burnett Tylor (1832-1917) invented the term while researching the origin of religious beliefs. He noted many examples of beliefs in supernatural beings and powers. For instance, the Dayaks of Borneo believe rice has a soul, and they hold feasts to contain the soul (*anima*) securely in order to prevent crop failure. The Koryaks of Asia, after killing a bear, would flay the animal, dress one of their people in the skin, and dance around chanting to convince the spirits (*animas*) that they were not really responsible for killing the bear but that the Russians killed it.[8]

b. Animism has been defined as the belief that impersonal spiritual forces and personal spiritual beings "have power over human affairs and, consequently, that human beings must discover what beings and forces are influencing them in order to determine future action and, frequently, to manipulate their power."[9] In short, animism is the manipulation of supernatural power. In contrast to animism, Christians believe that humans should never attempt to manipulate God. They should rely on God and trust Him to care for them through the ups and downs of life. Rather than manipulation, Christians seek out a personal relationship with God because they believe Him to be loving and good.

c. Animist beliefs and practices vary all over the world. However, the common denominator tying them all together is the belief that the world is filled with personal and impersonal spiritual forces that have power over people's activities. Typically, animists believe that there are literally scores of these spiritual forces inhabiting rocks, trees, mountains, people, heaven, etc. These spirits may include gods, ancestors, ghosts, totemic spirits (birds, insects, and animals from whom the people believe they have originated or have been given life), spirits of nature, angels, demons, and Satan.[10]

> Animism is typical of those who see themselves as being a part of nature rather than superior to it. This takes in most hunters and gatherers and some food-producing peoples. Among them, gods and goddesses are relatively unimportant, but the woods are full of all sorts of spirits. Gods and goddesses, if they exist at all, may be seen as having created the world, and perhaps making it fit to live in. But it is spirits to whom one turns for curing, who help or hinder the shaman, and whom the ordinary hunter may meet in the woods.[11]

d. Animism has not died; in many cases it has extended itself. It is reshaping itself into new, contemporary forms. About 40% of the world's population base their lives on animistic thinking.[12] "Among the 88 percent of those classified as unreached peoples, it is estimated that 135 million are tribal animists and 1.9 billion are involved in a world religion based in animism."[13] There are more animists than what appears on the surface. Some studies have shown that the number of witches in France exceeds the Protestant population.[14]

g. Animists fall into the category of low religions, but in all high religions there are segments of people that should be considered in a special category related to low religions. For instance, Buddhists of Burma manipulate *nats*, or spirits;[15] the typical Hindu believes that *rakasas* (evil spirits) and ancestors affect his life;[16] Folk Muslims manipulate the spiritual power of *baraka* (magical force);[17] Roman Catholics venerate relics and ascribe special powers to holy water;[18] and Shintoists and Confucianists worship ancestors.

e. In order to understand how to communicate the principles of the Gospel in animistic contexts, missionaries must understand basic distinctions between what some scholars call "high religions" and "low religions."[19] A basic difference is that high religions teach the worship of God, while low religions seek to manipulate the supernatural. Differentiating between these categories helps the missionary understand how Christianity might be accepted on one level, while at the same time animism continues on another.

HIGH RELIGIONS World Religions	LOW RELIGIONS Folk Traditional Religions
Examples: Hinduism, Buddhism, Taoism, Confucianism, Zoroastrianism, Islam, etc.	Examples: Shamanism, fortune telling, African traditional religions, animism.
1) They are concerned with cosmic questions of life, such as "Where did we come from?" (Origins), "How have we become what we are?" "Where are we heading?" (Destiny), "What is the ultimate purpose of human existence?"	1) They are concerned with immediate issues of everyday life such as crises of disease, a barren woman, death, and drought. The questions may be, "Who has caused this affliction to come upon me?"
2) They have written texts: The Bible, Qur'an, Rig Veda, Tao-te King, Tripitaka.	2) They have few authoritative texts. Their beliefs are transmitted from person to person through "oral tradition." Their beliefs are affected over time by change.
3) They are institutionalized. They have leadership roles, bureaucratic organizations, creedal formulations, and locations for institutional activity (temples, schools, offices).	3) They are informally organized. Leaders creatively deal with new circumstances. Buildings are not significantly important.
4) They provide ethical and moral directives.	4) They are amoral and have no ethical standards. Their morality is that of the local culture.
5) They were founded on historical figures such as Jesus, Muhammad, and Buddha.	5) They do not have major historical figures.
6) They tend to have a universal character and are not limited by geographical boundaries. They may exhibit a missionary nature, hold to one true creed, and hold exclusiveness in belief.	6) Sometimes they exist as secondary manifestations of high religions (for instance, Popular Catholicism, Folk Islam, and Taiwanese Folk Religion).

Table 27.1

3. *Common Features of the Various Traditional Belief Systems*

a. Hierarchy of spiritual beings. To the animist, the spirit world is very real. He believes in a variety of spirits, all the way from the spirits that inhabit the stones and the trees to the Great Spirit of the sky. Every known tribe recognizes the existence of a Supreme Being, a Creator, with varying mythological views of his character and the story of creation. But this "Supreme God" of the animist is deemed to be far off, aloof, and uninvolved in the daily affairs of men. He is content to play the part of a disinterested observer. Furthermore, He is considered to be benevolent and thus harmless, so the animist feels he does not need to pay attention to Him.[20] Closer at hand are the innumerable multitude of spirits which populate the realm of nature. A few of these are good spirits, such as tribal ghosts that watch over the welfare of the people but for the most part they are malevolent. They dwell in all sorts of places, such as trees, rivers, rocks, caves, mountain passes, river crossings, animals, and so on. Animists are chiefly concerned about this vast array of spirits. When adequately appeased, the personalized supernaturals may help in life–or at least not cause harm. When not properly appeased, these beings can bring sickness, loss, and even death.[21]

b. Existence of an impersonal and mysterious life force which pervades everything. Anthropologist Marett called this concept "animatism."[22] While supernatural power is often thought of as being vested in supernatural beings, it does not have to be. Many believe in impersonal powers. The Melanesians, for example, think of *mana* as a force inherent in all objects. The Melanesian word *mana* has been adopted by scholars to describe this sacred power. *Mana* may concentrate on certain things such as stones, plants, trees, animals, and people with varying degrees of intensity. A warrior's success in fighting is not attributed to his own strength but to the *mana* contained in an amulet which hangs around his neck.[23] Traditional religions explain social position, abilities, or successful achievement by the concept of *mana*. Victories and defeats may be explained by the presence or absence of *mana*. Certain rocks may possess *mana* and thereby be expected to bring great harvest when planted in the garden. A person's success or position in the community depends largely on the amount of *mana* he possesses, so its acquisition and manipulation are of extreme importance to him. *Mana* can be gained by wearing certain charms, by performing certain rites, or by eating the flesh or drinking the blood of an animal (such as a lion). The practice of cannibalism found its origin in this same idea. The warrior believed that by eating the flesh of his enemy, the victim's strength would be added to his own. The belief in *mana* can be seen in Western culture with the idea of a "rabbit's foot"–a good luck charm, the special object that brings good fortune.[24]

c. Belief in magic. The belief in spirits and spiritual forces leads to the development of magic and the religious expert. Magic is based on the belief that supernatural powers can be compelled to act in certain ways for good or evil purposes by using certain specified formulas. Magic is the use of rituals and objects to manipulate supernatural power in order to achieve one's desired goals. White magic is used by a group or society to achieve good goals such as rain, victory in battle, etc. About 90% of all magic is white magic. Black magic is usually used by an individual to harm or destroy someone else in the society.[25]

d. The presence of the shaman. He is a religious specialist, an important and powerful personage in animistic societies. He is able to discern and influence offended spirits, cure sickness, direct communal sacrifices, and escort the souls of the dead to the other world. The shaman is supposed to have the ability to leave his body in an altered state of consciousness, sometimes described as a "a magical flight," and observe events in distant places.[26] This "journey" is usually induced by rhythmic drumming or other types of percussion sound, or in some cases by the use of psychoactive drugs.[27]

4. *Example from Africa: African Traditional Religions*

a. The major world religions frequently must serve many forms of social structure, but tribal religions often explain the existence of single tribal groups. Many African traditional religions (ATR) are tribal religions which show a one-to-one association with a particular social group.

> Traditional Religion places the community of the living and the dead at the centre of its world-view. Everything, as it were, exists for the benefit of man in the community. Man will submit to the unseen supernatural forces that he cannot control and he will manipulate, sometimes by magic or juju, those that he can. In other words, the traditionalist adheres to his religion in order to maintain a cosmological balance and enjoy the maximum benefits. Man, however, is not only an individual; rather, he belongs to the community of both the living and the dead. And such elements of "salvation" or "a fulfilled existence" include: acceptance in the community, wholesomeness, health, productivity, fertility, full or old age, and perpetual remembrance after death.[28]

b. While tremendously complex and different, ATR conform to the general nature of traditional religions around the world. Most ATR conceive a high, creator God,[29] who is detached from human activity.[30] At the same time, most ATR also hold to a basically polytheistic faith that has either a pantheon of gods or large numbers of spirit ancestors, or other deities that stand between humankind and the ultimate deity.[31] Other elements of faith in ATR include belief in "cultic prohibitions" (called taboos) and moral violations, which can cause disruption of human relationships. ATR offer sacrifices performed for various purposes, such as warding off evil, securing ancestors' support, appeasing divinities and supernatural beings, and expressing gratitude for plentiful harvest, deliverance from accidents, or life experiences. They believe in the continued existence of the dead in the invisible world, where they could be of help and assistance to the living. Some tribes believe in full reincarnation, while others believe in partial reincarnation. They believe in judgment from God and/or from dead elders, who may offer rewards for good deeds or retributions for evil or wicked deeds, essentially in this world and, on rare occasions, after death.[32] Medicine, divination, rituals, and festivals are also important parts of most African religious expressions.[33]

c. The breakdown of tribalism brought about by the efforts of European missionaries in the nineteenth century made it very difficult for the African animist to maintain selfhood and cultural integrity and identity.[34] ATR have suffered much at the hand of Westerners who have seriously distorted the facts about the religions of the African continent.[35] The twentieth century witnessed a phenomenal growth of new religious structures grouped under such terms as the African Church Independency movement. Many independent churches have a syncretistic nature, with many pre-Christian elements remaining in their life and worship. The indigenous movement attempts to produce an indigenous Christianity on African soil.[36]

d. There are specific areas where the Gospel meets the spiritual needs of the followers of ATR:[37]

1) Fear. Due to the unpredictability of the spirits and the ability of people to curse their enemies, many people in African Traditional Religions live in fear. When someone in the village has died, the spirits are much more active and closer to humans. In the modern world, when many of the traditional ways of dealing with the spirits do not seem to work, fear is heightened. The Gospel offers freedom from fear (2 Tim 1:7). "If God is for us, who can be against us? . . . in all things we are more than conquerors" (Rom 8:31-39).

2) Cyclical worldview. Life in Africa is often painful. Drought, floods, disease, and poverty often bring heartache and disappointment. Followers of African Traditional Religions know that death is always near and that they will go to the realm of the dead for a short while, only to be reborn into the land of the living to suffer again. This circular worldview breeds hopelessness. The Gospel offers to break the cycle of suffering (Heb 9:27, 28) and provides hope for the future.

3) Limited power. African Traditional Religionists are very aware of the power of the principalities and powers in the unseen realm. They only have limited power to protect themselves from the spirits and those who would wield the might of these spirits against them. They also feel primarily powerless to change their lot in life. The gospel offers protection (Eph 6:10-20) and power to overcome evil (Phil 4:13).

5. *Example from America: Native-American Religions*

a. It is customary to view the religious history of North America as originating with the first European settlers and the transplantation of Christianity into the New World. This perspective ignores the vast timespan during which the continent was inhabited only by the indigenous traditions. Today there are 530 Native American tribes in the United Sates.[38] Only three have been selected for a brief description of their worldviews:

1) In the past the Cheyenne covered a territory that extended from Montana to Kansas and Colorado, including nearly eight states. "The Cheyenne world view is action oriented. The Cheyenne are not given to philosophical speculation; they do not draw fine elaborations of the metaphysical characteristics of spirits and deities. . . ." There is an all-knowing high god, and many spirits and ghosts. At death the soul dwells in benign proximity to the Great Wise One.[39]

2) The Navajo, currently located in Arizona and New Mexico, are the largest Indian tribe in North America. "The Navajo has for centuries lived with the idea that he, by some careless act, some small failure to observe proper behavior, could upset the balance of the world and create disaster. Thus his religion, if we may call it that, is a matter of constantly observing the laws of the universe rather than the commands of God. He has little real theology but much wisdom that can be applied to everyday life." Many of their myths have similarities to myth elements of other Native peoples and even peoples of Asia, including a story of Creation and of a Flood. Mother Earth is forever growing old and withered, only to emerge again in the spring as a young and beautiful woman. There are dozens of "Holy People" associated with specific natural features of the land, and with aspects of the weather, vegetation, mineral deposits, and certain animals.[40]

3) The Sioux are located in the Great Plains (the broad expanse of prairie and steppe which lies east of the Rocky Mountains). On December 29, 1890, the government sent a regiment of soldiers to crush the Ghost Dance

among the Lakota at a settlement called Wounded Knee. Indian prophets in the 1880s had taught Indians a circle dance that he said was the prelude for the restoration of traditional Native American cultures and the destruction of their white oppressors. About three hundred men, women, and children were slaughtered by soldiers.[41] The Sioux have a central deity, Wakan Tanka, to whom they pray. The feathers of the highest flying bird, the eagle, symbolize Wakan Tanka. At the same time, this deity represents 16 important supernatural beings and powers. "Rather than a single being, Wakan Tanka embodies the totality of existence. The Sioux believe that they must live in balance with all living things.[42] The earth is understood as their "mother." However, Wakan is not confined to "deities"; everything has a *wakan*, or spirit. Sometimes holiness is spoken of as an impersonal force (*wakana*), which is potentially present everywhere. The circle is a main symbol of holiness.[43] The sacred pipe is used in all of their seven rituals,[44] since it symbolizes the cosmos as a whole. The Sun Dance, a ceremony of penance and self-sacrifice,[45] is perhaps the best known of their rituals.

b. In the evangelism of Native Americans, there are two major areas which present difficulties. One is the antagonism between the Native Americans and white men.[46] The other is the faulty methodology of the missionary, which fail to take the Native American cultures into account.[47] Attempts to contextualize have sometimes ended in syncretism. For instance, the Native American Church is a religion combining traditional spirituality with Christian symbolism, focusing on the sacramental use of the peyote cactus.[48]

6. *Example from Asia: Ancestor Worship*

a. Ancestor veneration is a common animistic practice among the peoples of the Far East. It is based on the assumption that the living and the dead are mutually dependent. The dead depend on the living for sacrifices and remembrance. The living depend on the dead for blessings.[49] Commemorative domestic rites are performed at an altar, either in a hall or room, on which are placed the images of the gods of that household, the ancestor tablets, and often the pictures of the ancestors.[50]

c. In the past it was common to use the term "ancestor worship" and to assume that all ancestral rites were indeed worship. Anthropologist Paul Hiebert prefers to use the term "veneration" until he knows in each case whether the people are "worshiping" their ancestors or showing them respect.[51] However, David Liao considers ancestor worship as a religious practice rather than simply a moral-philosophical filial piety.[52] "The core of ancestor worship is the belief in the continuing existence of the dead and in a close relation between the living and the dead, who continue to influence the affairs of the living."[53]

e. Confucian beliefs of filial respect lead many Chinese, Koreans, and Japanese to emphasize ancestral veneration. Ninety-eight percent of all Chinese in Taiwan zealously venerate ancestors. Ancestor veneration is the great stumbling block hindering the Chinese coming to Christ. Christians are frequently looked upon as those who do not respect elders, since they do not venerate their recently deceased ancestors. Thus the phrase "die without people mourning" has become a derogatory designation of Christians in Taiwan.[54]

h. It is not just the religions of East Asia who practice ancestor worship. Almost all religions of the world have concluded that there is some type of continuity between the living and the dead–including ancient Egyptian and Roman religions, Native American, and African tribal religions. From the standpoint of missiology, the issue of ancestor worship is of major importance among Asian Christians.[55] Missiologist Donald McGavran has said that the two major barriers to effective evangelism in the world are polygamy in Africa and ancestor veneration in Asia.[56]

g. Some Christians make use of the concept of "functional substitutes," culturally appropriate elements which take the place of rituals or practices which are incompatible with scriptural teachings. They are also called "functional equivalents."[57] A positive element of ancestor worship is the gathering of relatives in one place. Christians gather on the anniversary of deceased parents not just to mourn but to praise God for His blessings in giving loving parents, and to pray for the care of the family after the parents passed away.[58]

7. *Christian Witness*

a. Some missionaries deny the validity of folk beliefs and customs, and call those people superstitious. They have to understand the real existence of personal spirits and impersonal spiritual power. Missionaries who deny their existence are ill-prepared to communicate the gospel in non-Western cultures, where this realm is emphasized.

b. People give their allegiance to Christ when they see that His power is superior to magic, witch doctors, malevolent evil spirits, and ancestral influence. Missionaries may notice that new converts may turn to their traditional folk religions if they are given no Christian answers for their everyday problems.

One danger in solving this problem is to make Christianity a new kind of magic in which they seek to use formulas to manipulate God into doing their own will.

c. Folk religionists are often deeply involved in practices such as magic, astrology, witchcraft, and spirit worship.

d. Scripture repeatedly warns us to be on guard in these last days, because Satan will counterfeit the work of God. Many forms of true Christianity are duplicated in other religions. There may be miracles and healings. Missionaries should stress not only the bridges and similarities with other religions, but also the clear differences.

e. Animists tend to follow whatever power works, whether personal or impersonal. Instead of patiently waiting for Creator God to work, animists impatiently seek whatever power might solve their immediate problems. They would never deny God, but would seek other powers in addition to Him. By doing this they expose themselves to Satan's influences.

f. Much of animism is based on manipulation. The animist does not seek a personal relationship with the powers. Rather, he seeks to manipulate spiritual beings and forces to do his will. The animist views impersonal forces as having powers of their own that can be controlled by rituals and religious paraphernalia. While Christianity is relational, animism is largely coercive and manipulative. Animists seek to discover what beings and forces are influencing them in order to determine future action and, if necessary, to manipulate powers that stand in the way of wealth, health, and security.

g. Animists seldom seek to relate personally with Creator God. They consider God to be either distant or unconcerned about human events. They manipulate lower spirits by human rituals and magic. However, the God of the Bible is not distant; He desires an intimate and a personal relationship with His followers. Christians believe that human beings should not manipulate the divine. They must rely on God and pay homage to Him.

h. Christians do not believe in impersonal powers. All such powers, whether benevolent or malevolent, have origin in personal spiritual beings. Behind all the "impersonal" powers stand personalized sources of Satanic origin. Fighting the forces of impersonal spiritual power is battling Satan himself.

8. *Glossary of Common Terms Related to Animism*

a. Ancestral spirits. Soul's spirits that are able to influence the living family, and in many societies are worshiped.

b. Amulet. An object, often decorative, worn to ward off various difficulties and potential dangers. It is believed to automatically radiate supernatural power or good luck. Some amulets were originally small parts of an ancestor's body. In addition to protecting against danger, amulets were also often expected to provide strength, wealth, and good fortune. They are often used as bracelets or necklaces.

c. Animism. The belief and manipulation of supernatural power.

d. Animatism. The belief in impersonal supernatural power. Usually animatism is considered a part of animism. But if animism refers to the belief in spiritual beings, another term was needed for the belief in impersonal powers.

e. Astrology is the belief that the placement of heavenly bodies affects human destinies, and assumes a cause-and-effect relationship between the celestial and terrestrial.

f. *Baraka.* A benevolent impersonal power in the Muslim world–a blessing granted to certain people, places, and things. Folk Muslims consider *baraka* to be a magical force that can be induced by ritual and manipulated for human benefit. Once this power is obtained, it can be transferred to other people, places, and things.

g. Cargo cults. New Guinea cults in which ancestors return by ship, bringing quantities of European and other goods with them, and help to drive the colonizers out.

h. Charm. A small object which can be carried on the person that may include spells and incantations. Charms have been made of all kinds of objects, for a variety of reasons. Color, rarity, shape, and other associations may lead to the selection of a charm.

i. Ghosts. Soul's spirits that hang around for a time. They are either avoided or actively beseeched to go elsewhere. Ghosts are almost always believed to be at least temporarily harmful to their own descendants and often to other persons as well.

j. Magic. The use of rituals and paraphernalia to manipulate supernatural power in order to achieve one's desired goals. White magic is used by a group or society to achieve good goals, such as rain, victory in battle, etc. Black magic is usually used by an individual to harm or destroy.

k. *Mana.* An impersonal and mysterious life force which pervades everything. *Mana* may concentrate on certain things such as stones, plants, trees, animals, and people with varying degrees of intensity.

l. Shaman. A member of certain tribal societies who acts as a medium between the visible world and an invisible spirit world, and who practices magic or sorcery for purposes of healing, divination, and control over natural events.

m. Talisman. A charm which carries good fortune.

n. Witchcraft. An internal psychic act using supernatural power with a malicious intent. Exercising control over another person through individual protective spirits, often to his disadvantage. Witchcraft originally meant the work of a female sorceress. Sometimes the person who exercises witchcraft is a popular figure, while in other situations he may be disliked. In some societies, everyone practices witchcraft; in others, witchcraft may be believed to be a disease.

Notes

1   See John S. Mbiti, *African Religions and Philosophy* (Garden City, NY: Doubleday, 1970), and *Concepts of God in Africa* (New York: Praeger, 1969).

2   Roger Schmidt, Gene C. Sager, Gerald T. Carney, Albert C. Muller, Kenneth J. Zanca, Julius J. Jackson Jr., C. Wayne Mayhall, and Jeffrey C. Burke, *Patterns of Religion*, 2nd ed. (Belmont, CA: Wadsworth, 2005), 71, 72.

3   Donald T. Reagan, "For the Record," *Time* May 16, 1988, 26-40. The astrologer is Joan Quigley. Barrett Seaman, "Astrology in the White House," *Time* May 16, 1988, 24-25.

4   Tite Tienou, "The Invention of the 'Primitive' and Stereotypes in Mission," *Missiology* 3 (July 1991): 295-304.

5   George J. Jennings, "The World View of Ethnoespiritsm," chap. in *All Things, All Men, All Means–To Save Some* (Le Mars, IA: Middle East Missions Research, 1984), 111-15.

6   James V. Hogue and Ebbie C. Smith, "Traditional Folk Religions," chap. in *Christianity Faces a Pluralistic World* (Fort Worth, TX: Christian Literary Publications, 1989), 52-76

7   The latter term is preferred in the documents of the Lausanne Committee for World Evangelization, *Lausanne*, [documents online]; available on April 20, 2006, at http//www.lausanne.org.

8   See Sir Edward B. Tylor, "Animism," in *The Making of Man: An Outline of Anthropology*, ed. V. F. Calverton (New York: Modern Library, 1931).

9   Gailyn Van Rheenen, *Communicating Christ in Animistic Contexts*, foreword by David J. Hesselgrave (Grand Rapids: Baker, 1991), 20.

10   John Kent, "Discovering Animism," *Adventist Frontier Missions*, 2001 [article online]; retrieved on December 1, 2002, from www.afmonline.org/articles/wayahead.

11   William A. Haviland, *Cultural Anthropology* (New York: Holt, Rinehart, & Winston, 1975), 349.

12   Stephen C. Neill, *Christian Faith and Other Faiths* (New York: Oxford, 1970), 125.

13   Timothy Kamps, quoted in Van Rheenen, *Communicating Christ in Animistic Contexts*, 25.

14   Neuza Itioka, "Mission in the 1990's: Two Views," *International Bulletin of Missionary Research* 14 (January 1990): 10.

15   Melford E. Spiro, *Burmese Supernaturalism* (Englewood Cliffs, NJ: Prentice-Hall, 1967).

16   Wayne McClintock, "Demons and Ghosts in Indian Folklore," *Missiology* 28 (January 1990): 37-48.

17   Bess Allen Donaldson, "The Koran as Magic," *Moslem World* 27 (1937): 254-66.

18   Paul R. Turner, "Religious Conversion and Folk Catholicism," *Missiology* 12 (January 1984): 111-21.

19   For a more detailed study on the differences between high and low religions, see Norman E. Allison, "Make Sure You're Getting Through," *Evangelical Missions Quarterly* 20 (April 1984): 165-70; Paul Hiebert, *Anthropological Insights for Missionaries* (Grand Rapids: Baker, 1985), 222-24.

20 Wilhelm Schmidt, "The Nature, Attributes and Worship of the Primitive High God," in *Reader in Comparative Religion: An Anthropological Approach*, 2nd ed., ed. William A. Less and Evon Z. Vogt (New York: Harper & Row, 1965), 21-23.

21 William A. Haviland, *Cultural Anthropology*, 5th ed. (New York: Holt, Rinehart & Winston, 1987), 314.

22 See Robert R. Marett, *The Threshold of Religion* (London: Macmillan, 1914).

23 Van Rheenen, *Communicating Christ in Animistic Contexts*, 209.

24 Paul G. Hiebert, *Cultural Anthropology* (New York: Harper & Row, 1987), 258.

25 Raymond Firth, *Human Types: An Introduction to Social Anthropology* (Chicago: Nelson, 1956), 155-56.

26 Mircea Eliade, *Shamanism: Archaic Techniques of Ecstasy*, trans. Williard R. Trask (New Jersey: Princeton University, 1974), 5, 347, 456.

27 See Michael Harner, *The Way of the Shaman* (New York: Harper & Row, 1980).

28 Lausanne Committee for World Evangelization, "Christian Witness to People of African Traditional Religions," *Lausanne*, Lausanne Occasional Paper 18 [document online]; retrieved on April 20, 2006, from http://www.lausanne.org/ Brix?pageID=14727.

29 Geoffrey Parrinder, *Religion in Africa* (Baltimore, MD: Penguin Books, 1969), 39.

30 Mircea Elliade and Ioan P. Couliano, *The Harper Collins Concise Guide to World Religions* (New York: HarperCollins, 2000), 12.

31 Paul Bohannan, *Africa and Africans* (Garden City, NY: The Natural History Press, 1964), 222.

32 Lausanne, "Christian Witness to People of African Traditional Religions."

33 Jacob K. Olupona, "Introduction," in *African Spirituality: Forms, Meanings, and Expressions*, ed. Jacob K. Olupona (New York: Crossroad, 2000), xvii.

34 Phillip M. Steyne, "The African Zionist Movement," in *Dynamic Religious Movements: Case Studies of Rapidly Growing Religious Movements Around the World*, ed. David J. Hesselgrave (Grand Rapids: Baker, 1978), 20.

35 Tite Tienou, "The Christian Response to African Traditional Religion(s)," in *Christian Witness in Pluralistic Contexts in the Twenty-First Century*, Evangelical Missiological Society Series Number 11, ed. Enoch Wan (Pasadena, CA: William Carey Library, 2004), 212.

36 David Barret, *Schism and Renewal in Africa* (Nairobi: Oxford University Press, 1968), 23-24.

37 Richard Chowning, "Areas in Which the Gospel Meets Spiritual Needs," *Africa Missions* [article online]; retrieved on April 19, 2006, from http://www.africamissions.org/africa/atrneed.htm.

38 William A. Young, *The World's Religions: Worldviews and Contemporary Issues*, 2nd ed. (Upper Saddle River, NJ: Pearson Prentice Hall, 2005), 38.

39 Schmidt et al., *Patterns of Religion*, 90-92.

40 Ibid., 93-95.

41 Young, *The World's Religions: Worldviews and Contemporary Issues*, 40.

42 Raymond J. DeMaillie, *Sioux Indian Religion: Tradition and Innovation* (Norman, OK: University of Oklahoma Press, 1987), 28.

43 Black Elk and John G. Neihardt, *Black Elk Speaks: Being the Life Story of a Holy Man of the Ogala Sioux*, Pocket Books ed. (New York: William Morrow, 1972), 164-65.

44 Young, *The World's Religions*, 44-46.

45 Mary Pat Fisher, *Living Religions*, 5th ed. (Upper Saddle River, NJ: Prentice- Hall, 2002), 60-61.

46 "Conference on Indian Evangelism," MARC Newsletter, May 1975, 2.

47 Bruce Terry, "American Indian Evangelism," *Mission Strategy Bulletin*, Vol. 2, No. 5 (June 1975) [article online]; retrieved on April 20, 2006, from http://bible.acu.edu/missions/page.asp?ID=488.

48 Sam Gill, "Native Americans and Their Religions," in *World Religions in America*, 3rd ed., ed. Jacob Neusner (Louisville, KY: Westminster John Knox Press, 2003), 19-20.

49 Lawrence G. Thompson, *Chinese Religion: An Introduction*, 3rd ed. (Belmont, CA: Wadsworth Press, 1979), 2-3.

50   Maurice Freedman, "Ritual Aspects of Chinese Kinship and Marriage," in *Family and Kinship in Chinese Society*, ed. Maurice Freedman (Stanford, CA: Stanford University Press, 1970), 165.

51   Paul G. Hiebert, *Phenomenology and Institutions of Folk Religions* (Pasadena, CA: Fuller Theological Seminary, 1988), 71.

52   David Liao, "Christian Alternatives to Ancestor Worship in Taiwan," in *Christian Alternatives to Ancestor Practices*, ed. Bong Rin Ro (Taichung, Taiwan: Asia Theological Association, 1985), 209-33.

53   Edward Norbeck, "Ancestor Worship," *NEB* (1974): 1:835.

54   Daniel Hung, "Mission Blockade: Ancestor Worship," *Evangelical Missions Quarterly* (January 1983): 32-40.

55   Lien-Hwa Chow, "Chinese with Cultural Issues," *Asia Theological News* 10 (1984): 2-3. James Hudson Taylor III labels ancestor worship as "one of the most urgent items on the agenda of the church in East Asia" in "Ancestor Practices: The Most Urgent Issue of the 80s," *Chinese Around the World*, September 1984, 6.

56   Donald A. McGavran, "Polygamy and Church Growth," *Church Growth Bulletin* 5 (March 1969): 1.

57   Stephen A. Grunlan and Marvin K. Mayers, *Cultural Anthropology: A Christian Perspective*, 2nd ed. (Grand Rapids: Academic Book, 1988), 279. A chapter on this issue is found in Carlos G. Martin, "Anthropology for Adventist Missions," Class Notes for Missionary Anthropology MSSN 644 (Silang, Cavite: Adventist International Institute of Advanced Studies, 1995), 298-302.

58   Ko Young, "Korean Ancestor Worship in the Light of Biblical Teachings," (Silang, Cavite: Adventist International Institute of Advanced Studies, 1980), 241-42.

CHAPTER 28

Occultism

1. *Introduction*

a. The word "occult" comes from Latin *occultus* (clandestine, hidden, secret), referring to the "knowledge of the secret" or "knowledge of the hidden," and often meaning "knowledge of the supernatural," as opposed to "knowledge of the visible" or "knowledge of the measurable."[1] The occult encompasses several philosophies and religious exercises that include physical and metaphysical energy accessible only to those with the secret wisdom or power. The modern term is often used for "secret knowledge" or "hidden knowledge," meaning "knowledge meant only for certain people" (esoteric) or "knowledge that must be kept hidden."

b. The terms "occult" and "cult" refer to very different concepts. "Cult," as previously discussed, relates to those groups which have grown out of Christianity, but have teachings deviating from orthodox Christian doctrine. The occult, on the other hand, represents a large group of belief-systems which include outright worship of Satan, fortune-telling, contact with spirits, controlling natural forces by means of ritual, and ancient fertility practices.

c. Occultism can deal with subjects ranging from talismans, magic, sorcery, and voodoo, to ESP (Extra-sensory perception), astrology, numerology, lucid dreams, or even certain aspects of world religions, such as Hinduism (Tantrism), Buddhism (Vajrayana), and Judaism (the Cabbala). "It is all encompassing in that most everything that isn't claimed by any of the major religions (and many things that are) is included in the realm of the occult."[2]

2. *Divination*

a. Divination is a way of discovering what supernatural beings and forces will do or what they want us to do. Among animists, questions are specific and worldly: "When do we plant a crop?" "Should we marry our daughter to that man?" "Why am I sick and what should I do about it?" It is widely practiced in oral societies as well as among many traditional religions. "Divination and shamanism are so intimately related that it is not possible to separate one from the other."[3]

b. Uses of divination include forecasting the future,[4] determining what is happening a great distance away, charting a course of action, projecting ways to avoid danger, selecting leaders for office, and knowing the causes of calamities, plague, drought, sickness, and death. Divination in the form of horoscopes, palm readers, and psychics can even be found in every town in America, not just in animistic countries.

c. Selected forms of divination

1) Astrology: Divination from the stars. This is the most common form of the occult. Sometimes, the horoscope is a form of amusement, but at other times and for other people, it is extremely serious business.[5] The belief behind astrology is that the position of the stars and planets have determinative influence on the personality. This influence begins at birth and determines one's entire personality, character, destiny, and events in life.[6] Astrology is a proven occult art. By virtue of its many connections to numerous other forms of occultism (such as witchcraft and spiritism), astrology is a potential introduction to a much wider practice of occult activity.[7]

2) Cartomancy: Divination through the use of tarot cards or regular playing cards. Gypsies traditionally use this technique. Tarot is a deck of 78 cards used for divining in many European countries, and from which our present-day playing cards evolved. The diviner performs by the spreading of the cards and then interpreting their meaning. An underlying philosophy behind tarot is that nothing happens by chance.

3) Geomancy: Divination by random figures formed when a handful of earth is cast on the ground, by dots or lines drawn at random, or by reading the

shapes of cracks in dried mud. The orientation and site of a building have to be considered with reference to the time, day, month, and year of birth of the owner or occupant of the property. Geomancy is very common among the Chinese, where it is called *feng shui*.[8]

4) Necromancy: Foretelling the future, or influencing others, usually by communication with the ghosts of the deceased. The term has been extended to mean almost any kind of magic. The underlying theory of necromancy is that the ghosts of the dead are omniscient, and if they reveal what they know to a mortal, he will have great powers. Necromancy has been widely found in most early societies and has lasted up to fairly recent times.

5) Palmistry: The practice of telling a person's character or fortune by the lines and marks on the palm of his hand. Advocates for palmistry often claim that it provides understanding into a person's character, personality, abilities, and personal relationships. The assertion is frequently made that the palm is the blueprint of one's life.

6) Ouija Boards: William Fuld patented the ouija board in 1892. It is the most popular game rooted in divination in America today. It includes an 18-by 12-inch board on which is printed the alphabet; the numbers 0 through 9; and the words "Yes," "No," and "Goodbye." The players ask questions while their fingers rest on the mobile pointer. The pointer's movement on the board produces the answer. The conscious or subconscious mind may be the origin of much of the information, but a good deal also comes from contact with spirits.[9] Ouija boards are offered to children as a toy, and thus the children are introduced into occultism.

d. How do we respond when people come and want to know how to know the will of God for everyday decisions? Christians must offer a theology of guidance. The following are some principles: God's will is not an option. God wants to know if we are willing to do what He reveals to us. If we are willing, then the responsibility is His to show it to us. We do not need to try to guess that will. God speaks to us through the Scriptures, through inner convictions based on prayer, and our willingness to do His will before we know it. God also speaks through the counsel of mature Christians, through our mind which God has given us to use, and through the opening and closing of doors. When we decide to act, we pray that God's will be done. If the door closes, we must take it as God's intervention at that time.

3. *Magic*

a. By means of magic, people attempt to project human control over spiritual forces. Magic is the use of rituals and paraphernalia to manipulate spiritual powers, and "any act performed in order to cause intentional change in reality in accordance with one's will." It is alternatively spelled as *magick* to differentiate it from other practices, such as stage magic.[10]

b. Means of magic manipulation include curses (verbalizations calling upon spiritual forces to harm a person), oaths (ritualistic declarations based on appeals made to spiritual powers which guarantee that secrets will be kept or that compel one to act in a prescribed way), mantras (powerful sounds and words), amulets (objects with power), and talismans (amulets with inscriptions to obstruct evil and bring about good fortune).

c. Practitioners of magic are basically divided in two groups: There are those who practice white magic, like diviners and shamans, who use helpful magic for productive and protective purposes. Then there are those who practice black magic, like sorcerers, who may use magic for destructive purposes. Black magic "essentially seeks to use Satan as one might use a tool."[11]

4. *New Age*

a. The New Age Movement is large and difficult to define in contemporary America. It consists of numerous adaptations of Eastern religions and philosophy, with traces of traditional religions and sometimes a Christian mask.

Defining the New Age is difficult, because it is not a homogeneous movement, but an amorphous collection of belief systems that at first sight may not have much in common. They range through the alphabet from acupuncture to Zen Buddhism, taking in yoga, mysticism, spiritualism, clairvoyance, biofeedback, reincarnation, tarot cards, ouija boards, astrology, meditation, crystals and many, many more, as well as paganism and witchcraft, the 'old religions.'[12]

b. The term "New Age" itself refers to the "Age of Aquarius." According to astrology, the world is passing from the Age of Pisces to that of Aquarius. During the last two thousand years the world has been under the influence of the constellation Pisces, but soon the constellation Aquarius will be the determining factor. "Its prophets claim that the world is passing from an old age of materialism and secularism into a time of new spirituality, when philosophical, religious and political structures must all be overhauled. Astrologists call it the Age of Aquarius, the age of new beginnings."[13]

c. According to Constance Cumbey, the New Age Movement "is a worldwide coalition of networking organizations. It also includes individuals bound together by common mystical experiences."[14]

d. There are more than ten thousand "New Age" organizations (excluding branches) within the United States and Canada alone.[15] A poll released by CNN in 1990 estimated that roughly 35-40 million people in the U.S. believe in the central tenets of the New Age.[16]

5. *Satanism*

a. Satanism is the worship of Satan. The immediacy of Satan and his concern for man's earthly existence frequently become factors in his worship. Satanists "seem to be striving for communication with some ascending power who is sympathetic to their needs; it is the striving for affection from a cosmic father-figure. God may be too busy to talk with them, but Satan is not."[17]

b. The best-known and probably the largest Satanist group in the U.S. today is the Church of Satan, with headquarters in San Francisco and headed by Anton Zsandor LaVey. His greatest public relations coup to date came when he served as "technical adviser" and had a part in the film "Rosemary's Baby" (he played the role of the devil). The Church started in 1966. LaVey wrote *The Satanic Bible*, which is an occult best seller, in which he also discusses "symbolic" human sacrifices.[18]

c. There are three types of Satanism in contemporary Western society:[19]

1) Religious Satanism. Foremost among them is Anton LaVey. They have meeting places, rituals, and priests. In the Black Mass, the participants try to reverse everything they know about Christianity. The crucifix is hung upside down, the altar is covered in black instead of white, hymns are sung backward, and whenever the Lord or Christ is mentioned, they spit, blaspheme, or perform acts of sacrilege.

2) Satanic cults. Much of their impact is involved in criminal activity. These groups are most likely to be involved in animal sacrifices, as well as in drug trafficking, kidnapping, and pornography. There are persistent reports of

forcing girls to abort their pregnancies at mid-term and sacrificing the fetus to Satan.

3) Self-styled Satanists are usually teenagers who become involved in Satanism through books, movies, and music. Satanic symbols are encountered on album covers, and the lyrics of some music speaks of Satanism. Fantasy role games are often heavily influenced by the occult. "Dungeons and Dragons" is an elaborate fantasy game, played out primarily in one's mind using creative imagination. Gary North said: "I can say with all confidence: these games are the most effective, most magnificently packaged, most profitably marketed, most thoroughly researched introduction to the occult in man's recorded history."[20]

6. *Spiritualism*

1) Spiritualism is a religious movement, prominent from the 1840s to the 1920s, found primarily in English-speaking countries. The movement's distinguishing feature is the belief that the practitioners can contact the spirits of the dead. These spirits are believed to live on a higher spiritual plane than humans, and are therefore capable of providing guidance in both worldly and spiritual matters. "Spiritualism is a system of theories based on whatever information has been supplied by spirit beings who range from the profane and blasphemous to the refined and intellectual."[21]

2) The Fox sisters in popularized contacts with the spirits. In 1848 they claimed that rappings were coming from a murdered peddler who had been buried beneath their home in Hydesville, New York.[22] These events are considered to be the birth of modern spiritualism.

3) Hippolite Leon Denizard Rival (1803-1869), a Frenchman, became convinced that there was an intelligent reason behind the tappings at the séance (Spiritualistic session) table. The spirits answered questions concerning life and the universe. He published his findings in *Le Livre des Espiris* under the pen name of Allan Kardec. The Kardecian group called "Union Espiritista Christiana de Filipinas" had about ten thousand followers by 1980.[23] By 1998 there were about half a million active mediums and shamans of magic spiritism, including Umbanda and Macumba,[24] 15 million professed members, and according to some, a fringe following of up to fifty million, nearly half the population of Brazil.[25]

7. *Wicca*

a. Wicca is a Neopagan religion related to witchcraft, mostly found in English-speaking cultures. The term "Neopaganism" usually refers to the pre-Christian religions of ancient Celtic Europe, the religion of the Norse folk, and the Druids' religion. It may also include a revival of any non-biblical religion. Wicca, Witchcraft, or simply the "Craft," is the largest single segment of American Neopaganism.[26] Wicca claims to be a modern survival of an old witch cult, which had existed in secret for hundreds of years, originating in the pre-Christian Paganism of Europe. Wicca is thus sometimes referred to as the Old Religion. There are Wiccan traditions, each with specific beliefs, rituals, and practices. Most traditions of Wicca remain secretive and require members to be initiated. However, there is a growing movement of Solitary Wiccans who claim to adhere to the religion but do not believe that any doctrine or traditional initiation is necessary.[27] Initiation is a ceremony by which a person is introduced into a society, or other organized body, especially the rite of admission into a secret society or order.

b. Wiccans worship the goddess, a feminine deity often associated with Gaea, or Mother Earth.[28] They also worship the god, her consort (often known as "The Horned God").[29] Wiccans observe the festivals of the eight Sabbats of the year and the full-moon Esbats. They have a code of ethics that they live by: No magic should be performed on any other person without that person's direct permission. Homosexuality is accepted in most traditions of Wicca. Some Wiccans join groups called covens. In typical rites, the Wiccans assemble inside a magic circle, which is marked using various means, in a ritual manner followed by a cleansing and then a blessing of the space. Prayers to the god and goddess are said, and spells are sometimes used.[30]

c. "Witchcraft" refers to the practical arts of casting spells, herbalism, and performing magic. Wiccans see their use of witchcraft as positive and good, and black or evil magic is viewed as antithetical to Wiccan beliefs and activities. In contrast with Wicca, witchcraft does not require any religious element, and may be practiced by people of any religion or by atheists.

8. *Christian Witness*

a. Know what the Bible says about the occult. The Bible recognizes the reality and power of magic. This is evident in many biblical narratives, such as in the account of Moses and the Egyptian plagues (chapters 7-11 of Exodus), of Daniel in Babylon (Dan 1:20; 2:2, 27; 4:7, 9; 5:11), and of Paul in Cyprus and

Ephesus (Acts 13:6-10; 19:19). The Bible also clearly condemns magic and other occult practices. Those who claim to have a special relationship with God are strictly forbidden to play with magic or any occult practice (Exo 22:18; Lev 19:26, 31; 20:6, 27; Deut 4:19; Isa 2:6; 8:19; 47:12, 13; Dan 2:27; Acts 13:10; 19:19; Rev 21:18; 22:15).

b. Deuteronomy 18:9-13 says, "When you enter the land the LORD your God is giving you, do not learn to imitate the detestable ways of the nations there. Let no one be found among you who sacrifices his son or daughter in the fire, who practices divination or sorcery, interprets omens, engages in witchcraft, or casts spells, or who is a medium or spiritist or who consults the dead. Anyone who does these things is detestable to the LORD, and because of these detestable practices the LORD your God will drive out those nations before you. You must be blameless before the LORD your God."

c. You should also know the Bible doctrines—they cannot be compromised. Keep in mind that all use of impersonal power stands in opposition to God, who is a personal being.[31] The Bible testifies that God is in charge of this world. However, when magic is employed, humans are forcing the supernatural to act rather than allowing the divine to act through them. Magic reduces God to a human servant. The true God is one who cannot be manipulated, coerced, or forced, because He is the source of all power. The Bible continuously stands in opposition to the use of impersonal spiritual power. Magical practitioners in the Old Testament were not allowed to live (Exo 22:18). In the New Testament, Paul struck blind a sorcerer who opposed him (Acts 13:6-12), and Peter forcefully taught a converted sorcerer to seek a relationship with God instead of picturing the gifts of God as the source of some power that might be employed by human practitioners (Acts 8:9-25). "Magic is Satan's counterfeit of God's miracles."[32]

d. In the occult there is also the denial of absolute truth and of absolute good or evil. Historically, occult practices are connected to the worship of false gods and to child sacrifice; however, it should be noted that occultists today deny belief in these practices and usually claim to use their abilities and powers for good. Occult practices, whether the intention is good or not, are condemned strongly by God.

e. Remember that, while the occult is sinister and evil, the individuals involved are often average people who are desperately searching (in the wrong direction) for answers to problems, acceptance, and love. While there are celebrated exceptions (the "Son of Sam" and Charles Manson, occultists committed to evil), most occultists are not that different from any other lost person who is apart from the saving knowledge of Christ. Often they are truly seeking supernatural answers for their spiritual needs, unaware that they are playing with fire.

f. Know what you are talking about. People in the occult, just like Christians, hate to be misrepresented. Be sure to perform solid research so that you do not attribute beliefs or actions to the person that do not actually apply to the individual.

g. Because people in the occult reject the Bible, you should also be able to utilize other tools to show the weaknesses in the occultic worldview. Causing people to critically examine their beliefs may be used by the Holy Spirit to make them more accessible to the claims of Christ.

h. Your faith should be made visible in your actions; you should clearly experience and be transformed by the things you share with others.

i. Based on the experience of Acts 19:19, those who have practiced occultism and become converted to Christ should be encouraged to destroy their pagan paraphernalia.

j. Do not approach the occult without proper preparation. Christians should not play with satanic forces. Those who expose themselves to satanic forces come directly under their power. "It is better not to believe in spirits than to dabble with them . . . or to try to use them. Without proper precautions, supervision, and instruction, they are dangerous to humans."[33] Casting demons out is a very delicate work. We dare not enter this lightly or think that the recitation of a few Bible verses will act as a charm to protect us. There must be prayerful preparation, and there should be a team involved.

9. *Glossary of Terms Related to the Occult*

a. Age of Aquarius. Astrologers believe that evolution goes through cycles corresponding to the signs of the zodiac, each lasting from 2,000 to 2,400 years. New Age advocates say we are now moving from the cycle associated with Pisces into the one associated with Aquarius.

b. Aquarius. The Aquarian Age will supposedly be characterized by a heightened degree of spiritual or cosmic consciousness.

c. Astral Body. A spiritual body capable of projection from the physical body. The astral body survives death.

d. Astrology. A pseudoscience claiming to foretell the future by studying the influence of the relative positions of the moon, sun, and stars on human affairs.

e. Black Magick [sic]. Magic performed with the intent to harm people or property, or to force others against their will.

f. Channeling. New Age form of mediumship or spiritism. The channeled yields control of his or her perceptual and cognitive capacities to a spiritual entity, with the intent of receiving paranormal information.

g. Clairaudience. Ability to hear mentally without using the ears.

h. Clairvoyance. Ability to see mentally without using the eyes, beyond ordinary time and space limits; also called "Second Sight."

i. Cosmic Consciousness. A spiritual and mystical perception that all in the universe are "one." To attain cosmic consciousness is to see the universe as God, and God as the universe.

j. Esoteric. A word used to describe knowledge that is possessed or understood only by a few.

k. ESP. Extrasensory perception, encompassing paranormal abilities such as telepathy, precognition, and clairvoyance.

l. Magick. The practice of performing acts with the aid of a spirit.

m. Medium. A psychic whose body is used as a vehicle for communicating with spirits.

n. Neopagan religion. A modern faith which has been recently reconstructed from beliefs, deities, symbols, practices, and other elements of an ancient religion. For example, the Druidic religion is based on the faith and practices of the ancient Celtic professional class; followers of Asatru adhere to the ancient, pre-Christian Norse religion; and Wiccans also trace their roots back to the pre-Celtic era in Europe. Other Neo-pagans follow Roman, Greek, Egyptian, or similar ancient traditions. Sometimes is simply called "Paganism."[34]

o. Ouija Board.   Game board containing all the letters of the alphabet , numbers from 0 to 9, "Yes/No," and "Good bye." A sliding pointer (planchette) spells out words in answer to questions asked by players.

p. Out-of-Body Experience. The perception of leaving the physical body while at rest, asleep, near death, or temporarily dead.

q. Parapsychology. Study of psychic phenomena using scientific methods.

r. Sorcerer. A male who has made a pact with the devil in exchange for magical powers.

s. Spiritualism. Communication, by means of mediumship, with those who live in the spirit world.

t. Spirit Guide. A spiritual entity who provides information of "guidance," often through a medium or channeler. The spirit provides guidance only after the medium relinquishes his perceptual and cognitive capacities into its control.

u. Tarot Cards. Deck of 78 cards that supposedly reveal the personal future, direction, guidance, and secrets of man and the universe.

v. Witchcraft. The craft of magic, utilizing personal power in conjunction with the energies within stones, herbs, colors, and other natural objects.

w. Zodiac. The band of 12 constellations along the plane of the ecliptic, through which the sun, moon, and planets pass across the sky. Each constellation, or sign, is attributed symbolic significance and associations that affect various aspects of life on Earth.

Notes

1   "Occultism," *Wikipedia, the Free Encyclopedia*, 2006 [article online], retrieved on March 18, 2006, from http://en.wikipedia.org/wiki/Occultism.

2   Ibid.

3   Jung Young Lee, *Korean Shamanistic Rituals* (La Hague: Mouton, 1981), 143.

4   When President Ronald Reagan and Premier Michael Gorbachev signed the intermediate-range nuclear forces treaty, the Reagans consulted with Joan Quigley, a 60 year-old astrologer, "who drew up horoscopes to make certain that the planets were in a favorable alignment for the enterprise." Donald T. Reagan, "For the Record," *Time*, May 16, 1988, 26-40.

5   A daily horoscope is found in virtually every newspaper across this country. In the U.S., over two thousand newspapers carry daily horoscopes. Estimates of American believers in astrology range from 32 million up to one-half of the population. "What about Horoscopes?" *True Light Educational Ministry*, 2005 [article online]; retrieved on May 22, 2006, from http://tlem.net/horoscopes.htm.

6   Josh McDowell and Don Stewart, *Understanding the Occult* (San Bernardino, CA: Here's Life Publishers, 1982), 25.

7   John Ankerberg and John Weldon, "Astrology," *Encyclopedia of New Age Beliefs* (Eugene, OR: Harvest House), 53-78.

8   Evelyn Lip, *Chinese Beliefs and Superstitions* (Singapore: Graham Brash, 1985), 22-32.

9   Gary Leazer provides several suggestions as to how the board works, in *The Occult: IWA Manual* (Atlanta: Interfaith Witness Department of the Home Mission Board of the SBC, n.d.), 1.

10   "Magick," *Wikipedia, the Free Encyclopedia*, 2006 [article online]; retrieved on May 21, 2006, from http://en.wikipedia.org/wiki/Magick.

11   Kent Philpott, *A Manual of Demonology and the Occult* (Grand Rapids: Zondervan, 1973), 109.

12   Jean Ritchie, *The Secret World of Cults: Inside the Sects that Take Over Lives* (London: HarperCollins, 1991), 172.

13   Ritchie, *The Secret World of Cults*, 172, 173.

14   Constance Cumbey, *The Hidden Dangers of the Rainbow: The New Age Movement and Our Coming Age of Barbarism* (Shreveport, LA: Huntington House, 1983), 247.

15   According to Partatma Singh Khalsa, ed., *The New Consciousness Sourcebook: Spiritual Community Guide # 5*, Introductions by Daniel Ellsberg and Marylin Ferguson (Berkeley, CA: Spiritual Community/NAM, 1982).

16 William Honsberg and Dean C. Halverson, "The New Age Movement," in *The Compact Guide to World Religions*, ed. Dean C. Halverson (Minneapolis, MN: Bethany, 1996), 160.

17 Arthur Lyons, as quoted by William J. Patersen, *Those Curious New Cults* (New Canaan, CT: Keats Publishing, 1973), 81.

18 See a more extended treatment of the subject in Daniel Cohen, *The New Believers: Young Religion in America* (New York: M. Evans, 1975), 145-57.

19 According to Leazer, *The Occult: IWA Manual*, 36-40.

20 Gary North, *Remnant Review*, December 5, 1980, 5. See a complete treatment of this subject in *Encyclopedia of New Age Beliefs*, 1996, s.v. "Divination Practices and Occult 'Games.'"

21 Bob Larson, *Larson's New Book of Cults* (Wheaton, IL: Tyndale, 1982), 390, 391.

22 A complete treatment of this subject in Ruth Brandon, *The Spiritualists: The Passion for the Occult in the Nineteenth and Twentieth Centuries* (New York: Alfred A. Knopf, 1983), 1-41.

23 Jaime T. Licauco, *The Truth Behind Faith Healing in the Philippines*, rev. ed. (Manila: National Bookstore, 1982), 11-12.

24 Macumba is a form of spiritualism in Brazil. Its basic aim is to find ways and means to persecute enemies or to defend oneself against them. To accomplish this, people lay offerings down at crossroads for the demons, called *exu*, whom they believe often frequent such places.

25 John P. Newport, *The New Age Movement and the Biblical Worldview: Conflict and Dialogue* (Grand Rapids: Eerdmans, 1998), 221-22.

26 Danny L. Jorgensen, "Nature Religions: American Neopaganism and Witchcraft," in *World Religions in America*, ed. Jacob Neusner, 3rd ed. (Louisville, KY: Westminster John Knox Press, 2003), 245.

27 "Wicca," *Wikipedia, the Free Encyclopedia*, 2006 [article online]; retrieved on May 21, 2006, from http://en.wikipedia.org/wiki/Wicca.

28 Chas S. Clifton, *Her Hidden Children: The Rise of Wicca and Paganism in America* (Lanham, MD: Altamira Press, 2007), 29-31.

29 Ronald Hutton, *The Triumph of the Moon: A History of Modern Pagan Witchcraft* (New York: Oxford University Press, 1999), 33-51.

30 "Wicca," *Wikipedia*.

31 Gailyn Van Rheenen, *Communicating Christ in Animistic Contexts*, Foreword by David J. Hesselgrave (Grand Rapids: Baker, 1991), 235-36.

32 Merril Unger, *Demons in the World Today* (Wheaton, IL: Tyndale, 1971), 55.

33 Noel Q. King, *African Cosmos: An Introduction to Religion in Africa* (Belmont, CA: Wadsworth, 1986), 65.

34 Barbara Jane Davy, *Introduction to Pagan Studies* (Lanham, MD: Altamira Press, 2007), 145-62.

Index

Index to
Biblical References

ABOUT THE AUTHOR

CARLOS G. MARTIN holds a Ph.D. in Missions and Evangelism from Southwestern Baptist Theological Seminary, Fort Worth, Texas. He has done research and conducted seminars in over fifty countries in Europe, Africa, Asia, Australia, and the three Americas. His experience of eight years in Asia provided him with an opportunity to meet people of most religions. For 35 years he has served in different forms of ministry, including evangelism, pastoral work, church planting, mission work, administration, and teaching. He is currently the director of the Institute of Missions and Evangelism at Southern Adventist University, Collegedale, Tennessee, and may be contacted by e-mail at martin@southern.edu. Dr. Martin is also the author of *The Science of Soul Winning* and *Turning the World Upside Down*.